"Bernstein has tackled an ambitious project at the intersection of history and geography; of cartography, science, and politics; of colonial expansion and Indian agency."
—G. Rebecca Dobbs, *Historical Geography*

"Well worth reading for historians, cartographers, and cultural geographers, specialists and nonspecialists alike."
—Ellen R. Hansen, *Kansas History*

"A fascinating analysis of the factors that contributed to the creation of maps of the Trans-Mississippi West in the nineteenth century. The focus on tribal contributions to this process makes the subject even more worthy of analysis. This book has the potential to alter significantly the way we view the maps resulting from treaties, exploratory expeditions, and other projects."
—John P. Bowes, professor of history at Eastern Kentucky University and author of *Land Too Good for Indians: Northern Indian Removal*

"Bernstein not only engages the historiography of Native America and cartography, but also joins a growing corpus that reassesses U.S. expansion from the point of view of those on the ground who would subvert and offer contingencies to the path of empire."
—Jimmy L. Bryan Jr., *Western Historical Quarterly*

"The book's well-sourced revisionist examination of history through the eyes of both Euro- and Native Americans, and the influence of indigenous knowledge on cartography, is compelling, and thus it is a worthy addition to any historical examination of the Trans-Mississippi West."
—Brian Croft, *Nebraska History*

"By examining the motives and process of mapmaking, Bernstein restores historical agency to the Pawnee and other tribes."
—R. Dorman, *Choice*

"In this exemplary spatial history Bernstein historicizes the mapping and colonization of what became the American West. . . . The result is a rich, compelling, and detailed history of the 'drawing' of the West, one that simultaneously centers Native actors and exposes the subtle and insidious ways through which dispossession and colonization occurred."
—Raymond Craib, associate professor of history at Cornell University and author of *Cartographic Mexico: A History of State Fixations and Fugitive Landscapes*

"An important reassessment of the cartographic history of the American West, exploring how Plains Indians—specifically, Iowas, Pawnees, and Lakotas participated in the mapping and remapping of the region in the late eighteenth and nineteenth centuries."
—Alessandra Link, *Environmental Histor*

"Bernstein not only makes a convincing argument, but he also corrects some of the problematic ideas scholars have advanced or embraced over the years. . . . [An] excellent selection of 46 map images. Bernstein does an excellent job integrating these maps into his analysis. . . . Anyone interested in space and place in North America would do well to read this book."

—EVAN ROTHERA, *Reviews in History*

"Bernstein's narrative is engaging and meticulously researched, with keen insight into how Native peoples used Euro-American mapping practices as a 'viable geopolitical option' to defend their western interests."

—PATRICK BOTTIGER, assistant professor of history at Kenyon College and author of *Borderland of Fear: Vincennes, Prophetstown, and the Invasion of the Miami Homeland*

How the West Was Drawn

BORDERLANDS AND TRANSCULTURAL STUDIES

Series Editors   Pekka Hämäläinen, Paul Spickard

How the West Was Drawn

Mapping, Indians, and the Construction
of the Trans-Mississippi West

DAVID BERNSTEIN

University of Nebraska Press
Lincoln

Library of Congress Cataloging-in-Publication Data
Names: Bernstein, David, 1973–, author.
Title: How the West was drawn: mapping, Indians, and
the construction of the Trans-Mississippi West / David Bernstein.
Description: Lincoln: University of Nebraska Press, [2018] |
Series: Borderlands and transcultural studies | Includes
bibliographical references and index.
Identifiers: LCCN 2017052576
ISBN 9780803249301 (cloth: alk. paper)
ISBN 9781496224927 (paperback)
ISBN 9781496207999 (epub)
ISBN 9781496208002 (mobi)
ISBN 9781496208019 (web)
Subjects: LCSH: Indians of North America—Great Plains—Maps. |
Cartography—Great Plains—History—19th century. | Great
Plains—Maps. | Names, Indian—Great Plains.
Classification: LCC E98.C17 B47 2018 | DDC 978.004/97—dc23

For Inna
(who really wants to want to read it)

Contents

Illustrations

Acknowledgments

Writing history depends on those who came before. This work is no different. My greatest intellectual debt is to those whose names appear in the notes to this book. From George Bird Grinnell to James Riding In, and from Carl Wheat to Margaret Wickens Pearce, the foundation of this work was built by men and women who knew little of its creation. If any of these people should come across this book, I hope they take some satisfaction in its creation. For while its conclusions are mine, they have only been made possible because of their work. Thank you.

I began my graduate studies at the University of Wisconsin–Madison under the tutelage of Ned Blackhawk. Ned was not only my first intellectual advisor, but he encouraged me to study Native American history at a time when many thought writing about Indians was too politically fraught for a non-Native. His support for my work was echoed by those in the American Indian Studies Program, where I worked for three years under the leadership of Ada Deer and Denise Wiyaka.

As with many who pass through Madison, I have been deeply affected by the earnest guidance of Bill Cronon. There are few people who can claim so vast an intellectual legacy as Bill, and I am honored to count myself among his students. Even more than his direct mentorship, it is the community Bill has built that has had the greatest impact on my development as a scholar. At one of his weekly Monday-morning sessions, early in my stay in Madison, Bill asked us to look around the table. It was these people, he promised, not the professors, who would become the most important intellectual and social connections we would make in graduate school. He was right. One of those sitting around the table that morning was James Feldman. Jim became not only an intellectual advisor and professional mentor but also a great friend. Thank you, Jim. I could not have done this without you. Others from Madison who shaped my intellectual path are Susan Johnson, and Thongchai Winichakul. Michelle Hogue and Adam Laats have remained good friends despite reading various forms of this manuscript multiple times.

I have received funding and inspiration from a number of institutions and workshops. The Newberry Library not only gave me a short-term fellowship, but James Ackerman and Diane Dillon also invited me to participate in a five-week National Endowment for the Humanities summer workshop, "Cartography and Art in the Americas," exposing me to the gem that is the Hermon Dunlap Smith Center for the History of Cartography. Participants in a Summer Institute on Contested Global Landscapes at Cornell University also offered valuable feedback on portions of the manuscript. Gregory Ferguson-Cradler, Bikrum Gill, and Sara Pritchard gave particularly insightful comments.

Countless additional people have contributed to this book in various ways. While I cannot name them all, a few deserve particular mention. Raymond Craib, Susan Schulten, Matthew Edney, Herman Viola, Richard White, and Roger Echo-Hawk have all generously responded to my unsolicited communications. John Bowes has lived with this manuscript as long as I have, and after nearly fifteen years, he became a manuscript reader. David Rumsey's public map collection (davidrumsey.com) is one of the most generous resources on the Internet, and my debt to him is incalculable. Matthew Bokovoy at the University of Nebraska Press has had unwavering faith in this project, even when its author was not sure. Roxanne Willis smoothed out all the rough edges. Piers Turner has been an invaluable cheerleader and sounding board, offering patient and thoughtful advice during my many moments of existential angst.

Finally, I would like to thank my family. My parents, Elizabeth and Richard Bernstein, have supported me in every endeavor I have attempted, and writing history has been no different. Words cannot express my love and affection. Therefore, I have had a special edition of the book created for you with a lanyard inserted in the cover. Now we are even. My other parents, Igor and Elizabeth Simakovsky, have done more child-rearing of my offspring than they have with their own. This book (to say nothing of the marriage) would have not been possible without you. Thank you. And lastly, Inna. It is only because of your strength that I have been able to indulge myself in this project. You have given Simon, Isaac, Avi, and me a wonderful life. You are my best friend, my better half, and this book would mean nothing without you.

How the West Was Drawn

Introduction

In 2012, Aaron Carapella finished a map of North America titled *Map of our Tribal Nations: Our Own Names and Original Locations.* Since boyhood, Carapella had been dismayed by his inability to find a proper map of Indian homelands. "You can get maps of what our reservations look like now," he later explained to a reporter, "and you can get maps that have, like, the 50 main tribes. But I was interested in what our land really looked like circa 1490, before Columbus got here."[1] Unable to locate the map he wanted, the nineteen-year-old activist for Native rights made his own. "It's time to make a REAL map of Native America, as WE see it," he decided.[2] A self-taught mapmaker, Carapella spent fourteen years traveling around the country, scouring libraries, visiting reservations, and communicating with tribal elders—all to determine where the 584 groups he inscribed on his map were located before Columbus and what they would have called themselves in their own language. On Carapella's map, "Comanche" and "Navajo," for example, have been replaced by "Numinu" and "Diné."

By 2014, Carapella's map depicted more than six hundred tribal nations and sold nearly four thousand copies. *Indian Country Today*, the *Navajo Times*, and National Public Radio all did stories on his cartographic creation. A textbook company bought the rights to use two of his maps, and a documentary film company began work on a movie about Carapella's projects, which had expanded to include Mexico, Alaska, Canada, and South America.[3]

Controversy accompanied the notoriety. Commenters on Native social media networks began questioning the map's validity. Some argued that names were incorrect or misspelled. For example, a Southern Cheyenne commented that Carapella used Tsitsistas instead of the more accurate Tsétsêhéstâhese to denote the Cheyenne, while another commenter wrote that Carapella had confused the Howunakut village site with the name of a people. Deeper critiques also appeared. One reader highlighted the problematic nature of condensing thousands of years before Columbus into a single chronological snapshot, and another pointed out the anachronistic use of "nations" as a central organizing principle.[4]

This criticism moved beyond the comments sections. A University of Illinois scholar created a sheet of Carapella's errors regarding the Pueblo Nations. This scholar questioned Carapella's assertion that he gave tribes ownership of their own names. How does he have the "power to give any nation ownership of its own name?" she asked. "Doesn't that sound a bit silly?"[5] A Washington State graduate student's Tumblr feed systematically rebuked Carapella's project on a page titled "Aaron Carapella's 'Tribal Nations' Maps Do Not Do Justice to Indigenous Nations and Here's Why." The author found fault not only in Carapella's execution but in deeper issues as well. "How is a map constrained by colonial borders a map of who we truly are as nations?" she asked. "This is not consistent with ideas of nationhood grounded in specific Native cultures." Drawing maps that included "Western ideas of nationhood or territory," the post claimed, is "wrong and counterproductive to decolonization."[6] Or, as another commenter argued, since mapmaking is "deeply connected to a non-Indigenous set of values," the sheer existence of Carapella's map reinforced colonial power.[7]

Some of the most heated comments arose from the tension between indigenous concepts of territoriality and the American nation-state. "We make our own maps that identify our traditional homeland and territory. We don't really need to fit into a national one," one commenter wrote.[8] When another poster suggested that ignoring the boundaries created by four hundred years of colonial boundaries could reinforce tropes of timeless Indianness, another responded by questioning the author's identity: "Fuck the colonialism! Being native is understanding what your identity is. Are you native?"[9] Intending to make a map to "instill pride in Native people," Carapella's creation had instead thrust him into the morass of Indian identity politics.

The controversy over Carapella's map is—at its heart—a disagreement over how Native people should narrate their past. The conflict centers on how much to privilege culturally specific ways of understanding the world in the Indians' stories about themselves and their relationship to the nation-state.[10] Although this question permeates most investigations into American Indian history—and indigenous history more broadly— maps can distill the debate in ways that narrative histories cannot. Their sheen of objectivity and the immediacy with which they can be consumed give maps a unique semiotic power, pushing questions of history and identity well beyond the academy. As the late geographer Bernard Nietschmann famously declared: "Maps are power. Either you map or you will be mapped."[11]

The relationship between Indians and maps of the American state is the central topic of this book. I argue that Indians were central to the cartographic creation of the trans-Mississippi United States. On its face, there is nothing novel about this interpretation. More than a half century ago, Carl Wheat, the father of American cartographic studies, wrote, "Great is the debt owed to Indians who, with sticks and stones and in the sand, made clear the way ahead."[12] As the conflict over Carapella's map demonstrates, however, the academic and political landscapes in which Wheat wrote those words were very different from the ones I inhabit. Our understanding of both the mapping process and Native history has changed enough that his positivist "way ahead" has become unrecognizable to me: Ahead of what? For whom? Unpacking Indians' role in mapping the western United States involves reassessing both the cartographic process itself and the motivations of the participants.[13]

The Pawnees, Iowas, and Lakotas of the Great Plains are the central Native characters in my story. They had multiple—and often competing—agendas in the nineteenth century; none of which centered on creating cartographic representations of the United States. Yet mapping is a "recursive process which shapes real-world circumstances which in turn shapes its maps."[14] The actions they took left lasting cartographic legacies that shaped the futures of Natives and non-Natives alike. From providing information to signing treaties, Indians' centrality to the mapping process took many forms. Highlighting this centrality is one of my primary goals in this book. By situating the mapping process in particular historical moments and within specific geopolitical landscapes, I explore various ways in which the Siouan and Caddoan Indians living in the trans-Mississippi West shaped both their rapidly changing world and its graphic depiction. Uncovering the central role Indians had in the cartographic creation of the American state, I argue, allows more people to take part in its collective history.[15]

In the first section of this book, "Living in Indian Country," I highlight ethnohistorical factors in the land transfers and boundary-making processes that were central to mapping the trans-Mississippi West. Chapter 1, "Constructing Indian Country," explores the way Caddoan and Siouan peoples of the eastern Plains and Prairies spatially understood the world around them. Focusing on two maps—one by a Pawnee headman and the other by an Iowa Indian—I dispel the notion that Indian concepts, both in cartographic form and on the ground, were incompatible with Euro-American constructs. In so doing, I put the responsibility of colonialism back on the historical actors rather than blaming it on epistemological difference.

Some of those actors are explored in more detail in the following chapter. Chapter 2 is a reconsideration of an 1833 treaty made between the United States and the Pawnees, in which the latter ceded millions of acres of territory below the Platte River. This land became central—both figuratively and literally—to the cartographic creation of the trans-Mississippi West. The chapter reformulates this episode as part of an appropriate geopolitical strategy by the Pawnees that included trading certain rights for the promise of protection and sociopolitical power. While there is no disputing the resultant dispossession of nineteenth-century treaties on the Plains, I contend in this chapter that, at least for the Pawnees, the treaty processes and the maps that were created from them offered a viable geopolitical option in a drastically changing world.

In chapter 3, I argue that the United States' failure to live up to the promises of protection it made to the Pawnees in 1833 forced the Indians to initiate a new aggressive strategy that had dramatic geopolitical effects. The Pawnees' new tactics gave the architects of the 1851 Treaty of Fort Laramie reason to exclude the Pawnees from what they called the "largest Indian meeting ever held," despite the obvious necessity of their inclusion. The resultant 1851 treaty and accompanying map not only decreased the Pawnees' territorial claims compared to those of the Brulé and Oglala Sioux, but it also initiated a binary conflict between a now-unified Sioux Nation and the United States that would reverberate into the twenty-first century. This chapter ties the seemingly localized actions of a few thousand Pawnees to the creation of the trans-Mississippi West, integrating ethnohistorical factors into a contested geopolitical landscape and reminding scholars that discrepancies in cartographic power resulted from more than American colonialism.

My argument that Indians were critical to the cartographic creation of the trans-Mississippi West reflects the use of a historical framework similar to that of the commenter above who claimed that ignoring the historical reality of the American nation-state creates unwanted tropes of its own. However, I also appreciate the anger and alienation her critic displayed toward the U.S. colonial project. Readers of this book hardly need convincing of the failure of the United States to meet its 1787 promise—made as part of the Northwest Ordinance, whose primary purpose was to establish the procedure for politically and geographically incorporating territory into the new nation—that the "utmost good faith shall always be observed towards the Indians."[16] Many Native people understandably view maps of the country—even maps organized around political entities—as continuing the violence and inequality embedded in colonialism.

This belief is built on more than anger or contemporary Native pride; it grew out of the colonial process. Throughout the nineteenth century, Euro-Americans drew rhetorical distinctions between their cartographic systems and those of the Indians on which they relied. Embodied in my story by the explorer John Charles Frémont, Americans measured the success of the scientific topographic surveys in the trans-Mississippi West against the savagery of Indians rather than any universal truths. American expansion into the trans-Mississippi West did not follow a linear trajectory whereby a uniform U.S. state methodically imposed its functions on a resistant Indian populace. Instead, it was a negotiated process, and the agents were often more concerned with mapping the rhetorical distinctions between "savage natives" and "Enlightened scientists" than they were with mapping actual territory.[17]

The second section of this book, "The Rise and Fall of 'Indian Country,'" uncovers these rhetorical strategies and explains how Native and "Western" ways of understanding and depicting space have become—both inside and outside the academy—mutually exclusive. Whereas the Indian Country I explore in the first section was defined by the on-the-ground actions of Native and Euro-American actors, the "Indian Country" that is the topic of the second section was a cultural and political rhetorical device used almost entirely by Euro-Americans. In chapter 4, I explore how a political movement to create a separate Indian state intersected with the cultural desires of an American populace eager to create an authentic past and, in so doing, tied Native Americans to the landscape in unprecedented ways. By inscribing Indians in territory claimed by the United States—but not yet threatened by Euro-American settlement—"Indian Country" became part of the trope of the "vanishing Indian." Americans could safely lament Indians' passing while also appropriating their past.

By 1845, however, it was clear that Indians could not be so easily wished away. In response, John C. Frémont—the most famous American explorer of the nineteenth century—and his supporters turned to scientific instrumentation and the specific forms of knowledge it produced to prepare the American West for Euro-American expansion. Science became part of a nationalist project that both unified the country and sterilized expansion, turning what appeared violent and unseemly into a triumph of Enlightenment thought. In chapter 5, I explain how Frémont deployed the rhetorical devices of scientific Enlightenment and Indian savagery in contradistinction to one another, both to diminish Native participation in the cartographic construction of the trans-Mississippi West and to distinguish his process of acquiring knowledge from that of Indians. In so doing, Frémont turned what was a negotiated process into a clash of cultures, a legacy that—as the debate over Carapella's map demonstrates—reverberates even today.

The third and final section of the book, "Reclaiming Indian Country," offers a way to think about the process of mapping the American West that allows for a more inclusive cartographic history. After examining mapping as an important rhetorical tool in the process of state building, this chapter delineates how the northern and central Great Plains, as inscribed by the most important map of its time, were truly a fusion of American Indian and Euro-American naming traditions. Examining both naming practices and names themselves, this chapter demonstrates that Gouverneur Kemble Warren's 1857 *Map of the Territory of the United States from the Mississippi to the Pacific Ocean ordered by the Hon. Jeff'n Davis* neither ripped this indigenous knowledge from its epistemological moorings nor covered over "authentic" Indian geographies with spurious American places. Instead, Gouverneur Warren's map exemplified the syncretic nature of how the West was drawn.

The story of Gouverneur Warren's map epitomizes the problem of how to narrate the territorial expansion of the United States. How do we include meaningful stories of colonized or otherwise marginalized peoples' participation in the creation of the American state without minimizing the violence its creation perpetuated? Or, put another way, "How can we combine ideas of empire and nation, tribe and people to capture the fullness of the indigenous past in North America?"[18] For an answer, this project looks to the words of anthropologist David Scott. Instead of an attitude of "anti-colonial longing," Scott writes, scholars must "think of different historical conjunctions as constituting different conceptual-ideological problem spaces, and to think of the[m] less as generators of new propositions than as generators of new questions."[19] The mapping of America offers such a problem space. Rather than accepting the process of top-down colonialism, we can unpack this seemingly monolithic enterprise to reveal a complex web of negotiations and contestations, broadening our understanding of mapping's Native and Euro-American participants.

Since the 1970s, historians of cartography have utilized the ideas of Michel Foucault, Michel de Certeau, Edward Said, and Anthony Giddens to resituate the map as a form of discourse that contains power, rhetoric, and value, rather than as an objective representation of reality. Tying map creation into other imperial processes—such as military expansion and exacting taxation—geographer Brian Harley famously declared that cartography was a "teleological discourse, reifying power, reinforcing the status quo, and freezing social interactions within charted lines." And unlike music, art, or other expressions of resistance employed by those without formal power, maps have been used almost exclusively as tools of oppression. Thus, Harley argued, mappings' "ideological arrows" flew in only one direction.[20]

Although some scholars criticized Harley's approach for designating maps as texts (disregarding the process of map creation), scholars began to follow Harley's lead by exploring maps' hegemonic functions—the ways in which colonizing powers gain and maintain control—in specific historical circumstances.[21] In 1992, Gregory Nobles published an article on mapping as spatial control in colonial America. Examining the political order of the "Anglo-American Frontier," Nobles proposed that Euro-Americans established political and social boundaries before settlement patterns. By creating what appeared to be a priori plans of what the North American interior looked like, Anglo-American mapmakers envisioned future dominance. "By drawing lines across the continent and imposing themselves in print," Nobles states, "they literally mapped out a New World order." Nobles's article was accompanied by explorations into maps' hegemonic functions in a variety of colonial settings.[22]

These investigations not only unveiled the destructive power inherent in the seemingly neutral activity of mapping and depicting geopolitical borders, but they also defined mapmaking as *essential* to the process of state building. In the most practical sense, maps were necessary tools of the state. In his exploration of Thai nation building, Thongchai Winichakul explains: "A map was now necessary for the new administrative mechanisms and for the troops to back up their claims. . . . The discourse of mapping was the paradigm which both administrative and military operations worked within and served."[23]

While scholars were beginning to examine maps as tools for colonial and imperial powers, there was also a resurgence in the study of maps made by Native North Americans. Led by G. Malcolm Lewis and followed by scholars like Richard Ruggles, Barbara Belyea, and Margaret Pearce, this group used poststructuralist models to investigate indigenous maps on their own terms. Rather than treating Native maps as immature versions of the mathematical representations of European scientific cartography, these scholars have shaped both the popular and scholarly understanding of Native maps as sophisticated cultural documents. According to these scholars, Natives have a different understanding of the world than contemporary Euro-Americans.[24] Belyea goes so far as to say that not only are Indian and Euro-American constructions of space and place different, but "we must acknowledge a gap between these conventions is essentially unbridgeable." While there has been considerable—and sometimes heated—debate about how to characterize Indian mapping, this divisive rhetoric has masked the common assumption that Native constructions and representations of space are inherently different from Euro-American constructs.

This argument certainly has some validity. Many of the famous examples of Native cartography are best understood through religious or cultural research that highlights the differences between Indian and Euro-American worldviews. For example, the Pawnee Skidi Star Chart is not a scientific representation of the night sky at a particular moment, according to scholar Douglas Parks, but rather a conduit through which the tribe interacted with "heavenly forces." For Parks, the chart is "best appreciated as a complex mnemonic device that is referenced as much to Pawnee mythology as to their astronomy."[25] Such interpretations have added much to our understanding of Indian cultures. Yet they have also had the unintended effect of essentializing Indian spatial understanding to either a knowable or unknowable "other" that lies outside of history.[26] Combined with the growing understanding of maps only as documents used to administer the nation-state, scholars have all but removed Indian spatial and cartographic constructions from the history of how the West was drawn.

"The story of the mapping of America," scholar Joanne van der Woude writes, "plots the history of colonization, westward expansion, and hemispheric hegemony."[27] Similarly, in the prescriptively titled resource *Why You Can't Teach United States History without American*

Indians, Adam Jortner argues that "maps have played a particularly insidious role in Native American history." Including another scholar's version of the standard narrative of the relationship between Indians and maps of North America, Jortner writes, "Postcontact Europeans 'dispossessed the Indians by engulfing them with blank space,' suggesting an empty continent that could therefore be (unproblematically) occupied by Europeans."[28]

It has become a scholarly truism that Indian understandings and depictions of place were incompatible with maps of the expanding U.S. state.[29] Unlike Native geographies based on lived experiences, where "mythical beings, ancestral spirits, daily life, and geopolitical concerns interplayed," Euro-American maps of the eighteenth and early nineteenth centuries were simply "statements of territorial appropriation."[30] These imperial maps "sought to legitimize territorial claims (and delegitimize those of Indians) by superimposing their lines across the North American landscape."[31] By the mid-nineteenth century, those territorial claims came not from competing empires but from an increasingly divided one, and this quickened the pace by which Americans "erased Native Americans from both mental and actual maps."[32] Indians' lived experiences were thus drawn out of the growing American state. In this interpretation, the creation and circulation of maps of the United States meant the erasure of indigenous ways of understanding their place—literally—in the geographic creation of the republic. As one historian of the U.S. West has written, "Inescapably, the making of the National Map brought about the unmaking of indigenous geographies."[33] The cartographic elimination of Native peoples' geographies was concomitant with their dispossession.

Like all peoples, Indians have had multiple ways of spatially understanding their world, some of which have been culturally specific.[34] Unfortunately, these historical constructions have frequently been reduced to one phenomenological category of "indigenous geographies," which were inescapably at odds with Euro-American constructions.[35] Yet, evidence abounds of Native mapmaking outside of any indigenous cultural construct. Throughout the 1840s, for example, the most widely circulated map of the central and southern Great Plains was in Josiah Gregg's *Commerce of the Prairies*, an account of the trader's time on the Santa Fe Trail. Because his caravan traveled through a country that Gregg described as "wholly untrod by civilized man, and of which *we*, at least, knew nothing," Gregg was "extremely anxious to acquire any information" from those who did know something. This information came in the form of Comanche chief Tabba-quenna (Big Eagle). After unsuccessfully trying to communicate in Spanish and then in signs, Gregg found a compatible language in cartography: "Finally we handed him a sheet of paper and a pencil, signifying at the same time a desire that he would draw us a map of the Prairies. This he very promptly executed; and although the draft was somewhat rough, it bore, much to our astonishment, quite a map-like appearance, with a far more accurate delineation of all the principal rivers of the plains—the road from Missouri to Santa Fe, and the different Mexican settlements, than is to be found in many of the engraved maps of those regions."[36]

In the first half of the nineteenth century, Indians were fundamental to drawing the trans-Mississippi West. Although Native motivation was different from that of the Euro-Americans, we should not assume that Indians were duped into participating in a process they could not understand. As with any historical actors, Indians had complicated political, social, economic, and personal reasons for their actions. We cannot discount Native participation in the cartographic construction of the region because of the eventual displacement it brought about.

Juliana Barr astutely argues that historians "cannot seek to recognize and read Native borders by simply redrawing a North American map with a different set of lines; we must still seek the ideas, attitudes, and practices that gave meaning to diverse territorial claims."[37] At the same time, we should not assume that these ideas, attitudes, and practices were inherently incompatible with the creation of the United States. If so, mapping the United States would become a zero-sum process, in which only the failure of the nation-state could change Indians' relationship to it. This model not only excludes Native people from one of the fundamental aspects of nation building, but it also removes culpability from colonial actors.

Not all scholars agree that we can only understand Indian cartography as a representation of indigenous culture. A number of works have astutely examined the political context of Indian mapping. Yet, these pieces have reified a dichotomy between Native and white concepts of space by exploring how Indians—consciously or not—used their constructs to maintain "Indianness" in the face of colonial hegemony. When Indian concepts were used, they were too often removed from their epistemological moorings and added to a European spatial construction, creating a space that was either foreign to Indians or illegible to all parties.[38] This book, on the other hand, explores the mapping of America as processes of geopolitical negotiation rather than simply as clashes of cultures.[39]

Unlike cartographic historians, practitioners of the so-called "new Indian history" have moved beyond binary models to explore the complicated and diverse roles Indians played in the creation of the American state.[40] Focusing on the colonial and early national periods, these scholars have, in the words of historian Ned Blackhawk, "recast the spatial, temporal, and thematic parameters of the field, locating America's indigenous peoples at the centers of national inquiry."[41] Yet, due to the sheer weight of contemporary colonial processes, the nineteenth century has largely been ignored as a time in which to find Native participation in national narratives. When Indians do appear in stories of state formation, they are generally victims in the reifying tales of forced migration of southeastern Indians along the "Trail of Tears" or the restriction of nomadic Plains Indians to reservations. Because of this, it is easy to draw a connection—both thematically and spatially—from the removal of the eastern tribes in the early 1800s to the high Plains "Indian Wars" of the late 1860s and 1870s. This leaves seemingly little reason to explore how Indians living in the trans-Mississippi influenced national narratives.

By demonstrating the importance of Native actors in mapping the trans-Mississippi West in the mid-nineteenth century, this project puts Indians living on the plains and prairies squarely into stories of American state building. In so doing, it continues the work of scholars who have chipped away at the dominant historiographical model. Kathleen DuVal, for example, has written convincingly of the geopolitical importance of the Osages on the lower Missouri until well into the 1820s. John Bowes has advanced the conversation into both the nineteenth century and the eastern Plains in his examination of property-owning Shawnee and Delaware Indians in the new state of Kansas. These emigrant Indians were not simply exiles from their homelands east of the Mississippi; they were pioneers for both their tribes and the entire nation. Pekka Hämäläinen and Brian DeLay have also written award-winning books on the importance of the Comanches and their imperial struggle to control the southern Plains in the nineteenth century, which changes our understanding of both these people and international geopolitics.[42]

Unlike the Lakotas, Comanches, or Cheyenne, whose strength made an alliance with the United States irrelevant, or the emigrant Indians who had dealt with the ramifications of Euro-American expansion for nearly one hundred years, the nonimmigrant Indians of the trans-Mississippi West at the heart of this project were in a more ambivalent geopolitical situation throughout much of the nineteenth century. Having neither the military force to counter the western Sioux alliance nor the direct

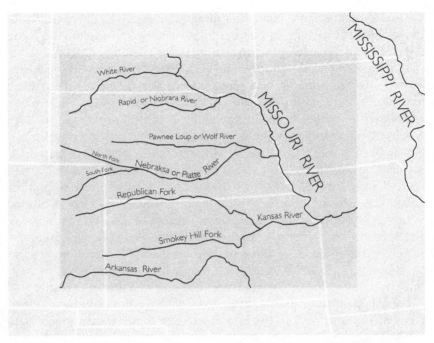

MAP 1. Primary study area with major rivers overlaid on contemporary boundaries of Great Plains states. Map created by author.

American support received by the emigrant tribes, the Indians who lived on the eastern Plains and prairies in the first half of the nineteenth century were caught between various expanding spheres of influence. This unique geopolitical situation gave them the unlikely authority to help determine how the West was drawn. By focusing on these nonemigrant Indian groups, this book pushes our understanding of meaningful Indian participation in the creation of the American state further into both the nineteenth century and the trans-Mississippi West.

In addition to examining Indians' role in the cartographic creation of the American state, this book brings greater complexity to our understanding of Natives living in the trans-Mississippi West by situating American expansion within a wider set of lived circumstances. Because of the size of their land and population losses, the Pawnees offer a salient population to examine. Whereas most histories of the Pawnees start with the second half of the nineteenth century and look backward for patterns that created their dispossession and dependency, the following

chapters periodize Pawnee geopolitics without bowing to the inevitability of U.S. colonialism. The Pawnees demonstrate the contingent aspects
of historical change, and they disrupt the linear trajectory of declension
that dominates nineteenth-century Native American history. Keeping
Pawnee cultural norms in mind, this book examines Pawnee politics in
the first half of the nineteenth century as more than a prelude to the
mass dispossession and economic dependency of the second half of the
century but rather in the terms that were most important to the Pawnees
themselves: inter- and intratribal relationships.

The geographic region with which I am concerned falls within the
current states of Kansas and Nebraska. Most of the historical action I
describe occurs between the Niobrara or Rapid River on the north and
the Arkansas River on the south and the Rocky Mountains on the west,
with either the Mississippi or Missouri River on the east. I refer to this
region as either the trans-Mississippi West or the trans-Missouri West,
depending on the context. I also use more specific delineations—such as
eastern prairies or northern Great Plains—when applicable.

In the chapters that follow, I tell the story of a map, or a set of maps,
that offers a new perspective on the relationship between Indians and the
growing American state. Some maps were chosen because of the place
they hold in national narratives; others were chosen precisely because
they do not.

PART 1

Living in Indian Country

1 /   Constructing Indian Country

In the late summer of 1844, Lt. Henry Carleton sat on the floor of a Pawnee lodge, watching an Indian draw a map in the dirt. Sharitarish, a chief of the village, was illustrating the region's geopolitical and topographical landscape to Carleton; his commander, Maj. Clifton Wharton; and a complement of American dragoons.[1] As Carleton described in his journal:

> [Sharitarish] drew a mark with his finger upon the ground introducing the Missouri, Kansas, and Nebraska Rivers. Then he placed a mark for Fort Leavenworth, and then in a manner surprising accurate, located the different tribes in their proper places—cutting them off by names as he went along, at the same time touching the exact spot each one occupied, thus "Shawnee," "Delaware," "Kickapoo," " Ioways," "Otoes," "Omahas," "Pawnees." All this was done in half the time it has taken me to describe it.[2]

The Pawnee chief was elaborating on an exchange of hand signals, during which he had inquired what route the Americans traveled to his village, in what is now southern Nebraska. "It was curious," Carleton wrote of the Indian's response, "to see how readily he understood our explanations." Perhaps wanting a more complex representation of the region than hand signals allowed, Sharitarish drew his map.[3]

For Carleton, Sharitarish's simple but elegant communication in a geographic language compatible with his own was both "curious" and "surprising." Geographic knowledge was, after all, one of the defining characteristics of Enlightenment thought, a worldview that—to men like Carleton and Wharton—separated civilization from savagery. This Indian was not only able to relay geographic information in a way Carleton understood, but he did so with a talent that was exceptional even among Americans.[4]

Many twenty-first-century scholars would understand Carleton's surprise. Like the American dragoon, many researchers have held that indigenous territorial constructs were incompatible with Euro-American cartographic conventions. Such arguments posit that, unlike the measured mathematical space of traverse surveys and Ptolemaic maps, Indians understood and represented their spatial existence in very different ways than Euro-Americans. Barbara Belyea, a leading scholar of Native maps, has written that "the Native sense of space and ground is the complete antithesis of European map construction. . . . There is no 'common ground.'"[5] Similarly, Martin Brückner explains that Meriwether Lewis and William Clark got lost on their famous Louisiana expedition not in spite of their Mandan informants but because of them: "Reading Native American maps with the goal of translating them into the code of European scientific geography inevitably became an exercise in misreading."[6] In this interpretation, the creation of any map of the United States would mean the erasure of indigenous ways of understanding their place— literally—in the geographic creation of the American republic.

What, then, should we make of the interaction between the Pawnee and American diplomats on the banks of the Platte in 1844? Cartographic scholars agree that one defining characteristic of Native maps is a lack of internal scale; the distance between two points on a map is irrelevant. In Native maps, the argument goes, there is no spatial connection between a map's design and the ground it represents.[7] Yet, Sharitarish seemed to be literate in the Euro-American convention of establishing a direct correlation between actual distances on the ground and those represented on the map. There was what was called spatial equivalence, when the surface of the map represents a portion of the earth's surface. Sharitarish's map was "surprising accurate," according to Carleton, and even blank spaces had geographical meaning.

Further confounding the distinction between Euro-American and Indian mapmaking conventions, the Pawnee depicted Indian groups as having distinct territorial claims. We do not know if Sharitarish drew explicit lines, but Carleton's description that the Indian touched "the exact spot each one occupied," and "cut them off by names," implies an understanding of linear boundaries. Such an acknowledgment contradicts the standard characterizations of Native maps, which are partially defined by their "absence or weakness of linear boundary concept."[8]

The Pawnee's delineation of discrete geopolitical spaces is particularly interesting because three of the seven groups that Sharitarish named had been living in the region for less than a decade. The Shawnees, Delawares, and Kickapoos had all moved from their lands east of the Mississippi River to new, bounded territories west of the Missouri, under the auspices of an American program to create a permanent Indian territory west of the Missouri.[9] Sharitarish's map thus contradicts standard interpretations of Indian territorial claims—which have been understood to be free of distinct borders—and how these territories have been cartographically represented.

If we assume that there is no "common ground" between Native and non-Native cartographic practices, we must conclude that Sharitarish's map was an aberration: a unique appropriation of a foreign system that would displace and ultimately erase Native spaces. But what if Sharitarish's drawing in the dirt represented an accepted spatial understanding of the plains and prairies by the Siouan and Caddoan peoples living there? Suddenly, the story of the mapping of the trans-Mississippi West in the nineteenth century becomes more than just another tale of colonialism. There is room for stories of negotiation and cooperation, in addition to the instances of coercion and contestation that have been so well documented.

The primary purpose of this chapter, therefore, is to examine some of the ways in which the Caddoans and Siouans living in the trans-Mississippi West understood the world around them, both as they lived it on the ground and how they chose to represent it (in Sharitarish's map, this was also literally on the ground). This examination will consider how these representations were compatible with Euro-American cartographic practices. In this way we can create the narrative space into which new stories of American mapping can emerge.

Unfortunately, as was the case with Sharitarish's construction, few Native maps exist beyond Euro-Americans' interpretations of them, limiting our "astonishment." Such an ephemeral existence, however, was normal for Indian cartography. If not performed through song or dance, Native maps of the Plains usually took the form of Sharitarish's creation: lines in the dirt. As such, descriptions of these maps reach us via the interpretations of a secondary or tertiary party, making their analysis more difficult. Yet a few Indian maps from the nineteenth-century trans-Mississippi West have survived in physical form.[10] Such extant maps

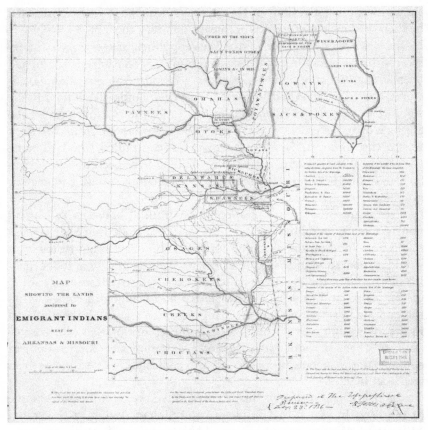

MAP 2. *Map Showing the Lands Assigned to Emigrant Indians West of Arkansas and Missouri.* 24th Cong., 1st sess., 1835–36, serial 289, H. Doc. 181. Courtesy of Library of Congress.

allow us the opportunity for a closer textual reading of the document itself than cartographic descriptions provide and give us the opportunity to understand the role Indians played in the spatial, cartographic, and geopolitical creation of the trans-Mississippi West.

One such map was created by an Iowa Indian named Notchininga. Unlike Sharitarish's map, which was drawn in the context of a specific meeting, the Iowas' map was created beyond the purview of Euro-Americans. Though the Iowas had American treaty commissioners in mind, the map's creation was apparently completely unsolicited. As such, Notchininga's map is a valuable document with which to examine how these Siouan people expressed their spatial imaginings and territorial constructs. In the second half of this chapter, I examine this map and assess the Iowas' territorial constructs as they related to other political and cultural concerns. The ultimate goal of this chapter is to show that the way Native and Euro-Americans spatially imagined their lived environment left room for the same negotiation in the mapping process that historians have elucidated in other cultural, social, economic, and political settings in the trans-Mississippi West.

"These Boundaries Here Named Are Not Imaginary"

In his work on Indian land tenure in Nebraska, geographer David Wishart has written that "it is wise to forget about the concept of hard boundaries and to consider Indian territories as grading out through a village core, through a hunting range, to a far-flung trading and raiding periphery."[11] The same can be said about the territorial claims of all non-emigrant groups living in the trans-Mississippi West, whose overlapping hunting and raiding lands became areas of bloody conflict in the eighteenth and nineteenth centuries. Still, this definition of land use does not mean that the Siouan and Caddoan people did not understand the concept of boundaries. Simply because territorial claims overlapped did not mean that these claims were amorphous; they were simply contested. In fact, there is considerable evidence that Indian groups living on the eastern Plains recognized distinct boundaries.[12]

John Dunbar—the son of a missionary by the same name who spent much of the 1830s and 1840s living with the Pawnees—described "Pawnee territory" as extending from the Niobrara River in present-day Nebraska south to the Arkansas, while "in the east they claimed to the Missouri." In the west, "their grounds were marked by no natural boundary, but may be described by a line drawn from the mouth of the Snake River on the Niobrara southwest to the North Platte, thence south to the Arkansas." Dunbar emphasized that these were not generalized claims made after the fact but were, rather, the territorial boundaries the Pawnees actively defended. "These boundaries here named are not imaginary," he wrote. Instead, they were the limits of a territory where the "Pawnee remained proud masters of the land."[13]

A map created in 1816, titled *A Map Exhibiting the Territorial Limits of Several Nations and Tribes of Indians*, reinforces Dunbar's description. Drawn using the notes of fur trader Auguste Chouteau, the word

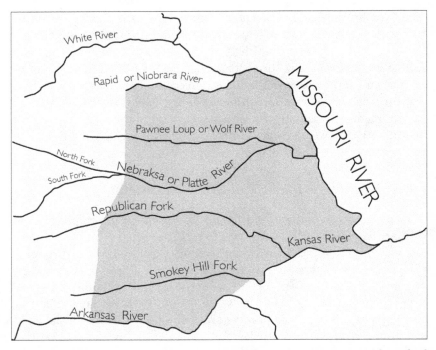

MAP 3. Boundaries of the Pawnees' nineteenth-century territory, as described by John Dunbar in the late nineteenth century. Map created by author.

"Pawnees" is the only label within a territory bounded by the Kanzas (Arkansas) River, the Missouri River, and a now renamed river labeled "Potato Fork," which lies between the Platte and Missouri in the approximate location of the Niobrara.[14] Thus, with the exception of the Omahas' and Otoes' inclusion within this territory (most likely due to their proximity to the Missouri, the fur traders' main thoroughfare), the two descriptions are remarkably similar.

Further demonstrating the concept of distinct territorial ownership, the Pawnees complained throughout the 1820s that other groups were "killing buffalo on their lands." This was not simply a linguistic misinterpretation by Euro-Americans but the declaration of specific territorial claims of the Pawnees.[15] Evidence for this comes from the fact that these claims were frequently recognized by other groups, who either asked permission to hunt on Pawnee lands or, as in the case of Kansa chief White Plume, asked for protection from American soldiers when they hunted in "Pawnee Country."[16]

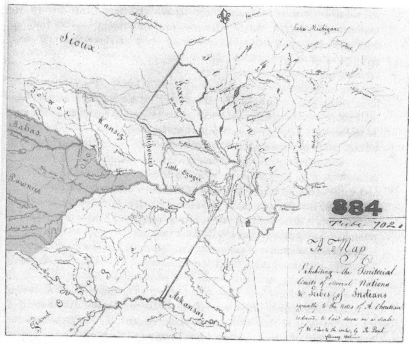

MAP 4. Chouteau's *Map of Indian Territories* (1816), with the same boundaries highlighted. Courtesy of National Archives, Central Map Files, RG 75, no. 884.

The Pawnees were also aware of the boundaries established by Euro-American powers. In 1826, twenty Pawnees angered the regional Indian agent when they robbed an American trading party returning from Santa Fe. The Pawnees moderated any potential American reprisal by making it clear that they were acting "more for the sake of plunder than blood," in the words of the Indian agent. Further, the Pawnees picked the spot of their offense—"just beyond the line of the United States"—quite deliberately. "The great bulk of these robberies [are] committed upon the Simeron, a branch of the Arkansas, and beyond the jurisdiction of the United States. Why this particular spot should be selected for their depredations I am unable to say unless it should proceed from a belief in them that they can cannot be punished for an outrage committed beyond our borders."[17] The Pawnees quickly learned to use Euro-American borders to their benefit by altering their raiding patterns.

It was intertribal contexts, however, in which these boundaries were most relevant. In 1823, Auguste Chouteau reported that, when Pawnees wanted to hunt below the Arkansas, they held a council with an Osage chief "to obtain permission to hunt on their land." The chief consented, under the condition that they "must leave hunting as they went."[18] More evidence of territorial ownership can be found in a letter from Indian agent John Dougherty to Superintendent William Clark in 1830. In it, Dougherty created what amounted to a territorial map when he relayed the following delineations:

> I understand their [Omaha, Otoes, Ioway, Sacs of Missouri and Sacs of Mississippi] languages and have heard them converse repeatedly on the subject of their several limits and claims. . . . The following statement of claims is as correct a one as you will be able to procure from the Indians themselves or anyone else. The Ioway tribes claim all of the land lying north and west of the state of Missouri and east of the Missouri River and as high up the same river as the entrance of the Nodoway and back east following the Nodoway to the Desmoines river. The Otoes claim from the entrance of the Nodoway to that of the Bonjeau below Council Bluff and back to the sources of the Bonjeau and Nodoway to the divide between their waters and the waters of the Desmoines. The Omahas claim from the entrance of the Bonjeau to that of the Big Sioux or Calumet River opposite their old Black Bird village on the Missouri and back following the Bonjeau and Big Sioux rivers to their sources.[19]

As alluded to in this description, such claims could and often did overlap, fostering decades of violence. The fact that the claims overlapped did not mean that boundaries were not fixed, only that they were not agreed upon. The following example of just such contestation demonstrates the compatibility of Native and Euro-American constructions of space in the trans-Mississippi West.

One of the most intriguing stories of Indian geopolitics in the nineteenth century was the near creation of a massive territory on the eastern Plains to be set aside for "fixed permanent homes" where Indians would live as they acculturated to Euro-American society. Though never passed by both the House and the Senate, between 1824 and the middle of the 1840s, the creation of a permanent Indian territory west of the Missouri River was the de facto government policy. Its premise was that Indians east of the Missouri could exchange their lands for "equal" holdings in the west, where they could remain "as long as the sun shall set."[20]

Exactly where in this vast territory a "suitable" place for Indians could be found, however, was limited by the current state of American geographic knowledge.

Between 1826 and 1846, the responsibility of locating such a place fell largely to Reverend Isaac McCoy.[21] Though none of his maps were printed for commercial uses, they became the standard interpretation of the region for Euro-Americans, turning the vague space of the eastern Plains into bounded place.[22] Unlike Henry Carleton—who was surprised by his ability to understand Sharitarish's map—McCoy seemed unfazed by the common cartographic language that many Euro-Americans and Natives shared. On one of his tours to bring emigrant Indians west to find their permanent homes, the group met an Osage Indian who was "wholly ignorant of English, and I knew nothing of his language." Yet, through signals, McCoy was able to discern the distance from the Indian's village and the names and locations of three surrounding streams. McCoy then explained to him where they had camped the previous night and where they were going to camp that night, and he asked the Osage to join them. When they reached camp a few hours later, the Osage was waiting. According to McCoy, "the extent to which ideas may be communicated by signs . . . would appear almost incredible to one who has no experience in this mode of intercommunication."[23] Cartography required little translation. Yet conceptual compatibility did not necessarily mean practical success when it came to establishing boundaries.

Before Indians could be removed to their new homes, the office of the U.S. secretary of war had to obtain clear title to the land to which they were going to be moved. So, in 1823, William Clark recommended to Secretary of War Calhoun that it would be "good policy to purchase at once, from the Osage & Kansas tribes, a tract of country . . . extending from the Missouri river to the head of the Canadian Fork of the Arkansas."[24] In June 1825, a treaty was signed: the tribes would cede to the United States all of their land west of the Missouri, with the exception of swaths of fifty and thirty miles wide (their distance west was not determined), which would become their permanent territory.[25]

On May 14, 1827, Maj. Angus L. Langham and his assistant R. P. Beauchamp established the northeast corner of the Osage reservation, as agreed to in 1825. According to the treaty, the corner, "five miles east and ten miles north" of Osage chief White Hair's village, was about twenty-five miles west of the Missouri state line. From that corner, Langham headed due south to demarcate the entire eastern side of the fifty-mile

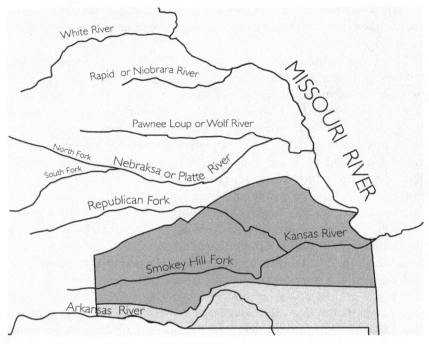

MAP 5. Study area with Kansas (*dark gray*) and Osage (*lighter gray*) cessions in 1825. The placement of the boundaries was unknown to Euro-Americans at the time of the treaty. Charles Royce determined his boundaries at the beginning of the twentieth century by taking future cessions into account. Based on Charles C. Royce, "Indian Land Cessions in the United States, 1784–1894," *Eighteenth Annual Report of the Bureau of American Ethnology to the Secretary of the Smithsonian Institution, 1896-1897.* Map created by author.

reservation border. A few days into the survey, "a large party of naked, painted, yelling Osages" came riding through camp "in a solid phalanx," trampling tents and equipment. The Indians "wound up demonstrating with an impromptu war dance, and an emphatic demand for the surveyor and his party to vamoose," which, according to John C. McCoy—the son of Isaac and the surveyor assigned to complete the task the following year—the Americans "did with alacrity."

This anecdote may appear to illustrate the clash of spatial systems this chapter brings into question. Yet, if we dig deeper, it is apparent that the Osages' war dance was initiated by more specific complaints. John McCoy claimed that the Osages initiated their attack on Langham only

after they "saw the lines of demarcation being drawn so near them."
When McCoy attempted to finish the abridged survey in 1836, he noted
that Langham's northeastern point was "only about three miles above
the chief town of the Osages," as opposed to the ten miles agreed upon in
the treaty. In fact, Langham wrote that the crew "had a view" of White
Hair's village from this point, something difficult to imagine if had he
actually been ten miles from the village.

McCoy surmised that the establishment of the northern boundary
seven miles below where the Osages had expected it to be "curtained
their tribal limits much more than they had anticipated." The Osage
chief articulated something similar the following year, telling McCoy
that "their line was away up north" and that he should not run the line
where he was.[26] Whether deceitful or not, Langham's placement of the
northern boundary of the Osage reservation did not correspond with the
Osages' expectations. Rather than objecting to the spatial system Langham was trying to establish, the Osage were simply disagreeing with the
boundary's placement.[27]

Beyond the cartographic representation of boundaries, there is
limited but enticing historical evidence that some Indian groups constructed boundaries where natural markers could not be found. When
Col. Stephen Kearny led his dragoons past the so-called "Pawnee Forts"
on the Arkansas River, Lt. William Franklin surmised that heaps of
stone on a sandstone bluff were "thrown up for the purpose of defense."[28]
Yet such a conclusion makes little sense, because the Pawnees' occupation of the region was transient. What would they be protecting? Their
military conflicts were usually raids and counter-raids by small, mobile
war parties, and victories were measured in captives, horses, or goods.
Why would the Pawnees protect an arbitrary bluff?

While not conclusive, there is some evidence that the rocks might have
been boundary markers. In the 1844 map that Josiah Gregg included in
his best-selling *Commerce on the Prairies,* there is a graphic depiction
of small hills, captioned "boundary mounds," not far from Franklin's
description of the Pawnee Forts, raising the possibility that these were
the same mounds.

Similarly, on Isaac McCoy's 1828 exploration of the eastern Plains
for the planned creation of a permanent Indian territory, McCoy found
inexplicable "heaps of stone" that were "situated as to attract the notice of
the traveler." Though McCoy acknowledged that stones were often used
to mark the bodies of deceased tribal members, he concluded that these
piles were fundamentally different. He decided that these stones were

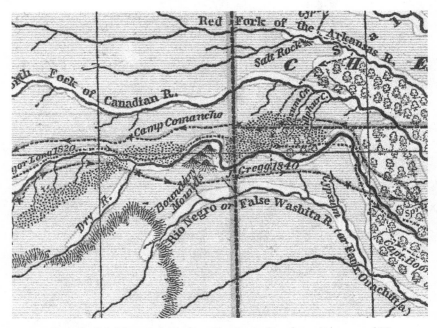

MAP 6. Detail of *A Map of the Indian Territory, Northern Texas, and New Mexico Showing the Great Western Prairies* by Josiah Gregg. Published in Gregg, *Commerce of the Prairies*. Courtesy of David Rumsey Historical Map Collection.

left by Indians in moments of "gaity or grandeur."[29] Indian whimsy is certainly a plausible explanation for the rocks' placement. However, considering the assertion of specific territorial claims by Indians to treaty commissioners, it is also possible that these markers were used in the absence of natural boundaries to demark territory.

Joseph Nicollet noted a similar phenomenon during his reconnaissance of the Upper Mississippi River. There he found that, wherever the wind had exposed loose granite, "the Sioux take advantage of these loose materials to erect signals on the most elevated spots, or to designate the place by some conical structure." "They give names to these localities," Nicollet continued, "which thus serve as landmarks in a country where there are no other geographical beacons." These monuments may have been simply for way-finding, but considering the innumerable claims of territorial control, it is easy to see how these structures could have been used to mark edges of specific claims.[30] In Nicollet's description of tuyan-watchashta-karapi (the place where has been built up a man of stone) and Butte-aux-Os (bone hillock, a large heap of animal bones the Indians had gathered up), he does not offer any religious or cultural rationale for their construction, characteristics to which—as we will see in later chapters—he was particularly attuned.

Indian monuments were not limited to the eastern Plains; they were also found on both the northern and southern Plains. In 1853, Isaac Stevens reported sighting a set of buttes: "Assiniboins, Crows, and Blackfeet all know them well in their geography and their summits are marked with their monumental stone heaps." Similarly, while on a reconnaissance in the Southwest, William Emory found "a sand-stone black on end and topped by another shorter block [which] a mountain man, versed in these signs, said was in commemoration of a talk and friendly smoke between some two or three tribes of Indians." While we cannot know the precise reason why Indians erected such markers, there does seem to be a correlation between the geographic placement of these piles and historical accounts of territorial control.[31] Regardless of why they were demarcated, for Indians and non-Indians alike, by the beginning of the nineteenth century the concept of boundaries was an accepted part of life in the trans-Mississippi West.

"Looking Like a White Man"

One of the strongest pieces of evidence supporting the idea of compatible Native and Euro-American spaces on the eastern Plains comes from a map made by an Iowa Indian by the name of Notchininga. The remainder of this chapter examines this map in the cultural and political context in which it was created. Importantly, these strategies did not save the Iowas from massive land loss. They did, however, secure some of the Iowas' homeland in a period of massive encroachment from Indians and Euro-Americans alike. Just as significantly, highlighting the compatibility of Iowa and Euro-American constructs disproves the model of inevitable Indian dispossession due to incompatible knowledge systems. Instead, it places the resultant history where it belongs: in the hands of human actors.

Throughout the eighteenth century, the Iowas lived in semi-permanent villages in present-day Iowa and Kansas, controlling much of the region.[32] They subsisted by hunting, farming maize, beans, and pumpkins—and to a lesser degree, trading deer, beaver, otter, and raccoon skins with the English and the French. Bands established camps

from fall to early spring, in what is now southern Wisconsin and northern Iowa, to hunt and make maple sugar. They returned to their villages
in the early summer to tend garden patches, then moving to the plains
west of the Missouri for the summer buffalo hunt. The Iowas returned
once again to their villages in late summer and early fall for harvesting.[33]
Recalling the Iowas' strength in the eighteenth century, future commissioner of Indian Affairs Thomas McKenney declared, "Of all the tribes
that hunt between the Mississippi and Missouri Rivers . . . next to the
Sioux . . . the Ioway were once the most numerous and powerful."[34]

At the turn of the eighteenth century, French explorer Pierre Charles
Le Sueur reported that the Mississippi was under control of the Scioux
(Sioux), the Ayavois (Iowas), and the Otoctatas (Otoes). Le Sueur claimed
that, for the Indians, "it was not their custom to hunt on ground belonging to other, unless invited to do so by the owners." To travel the river
without following this protocol, the Frenchman continued, put one "in
danger of being killed."[35] Along with the Teton and Yanktonai Sioux, the
Iowas controlled the land between the Mississippi and Missouri Rivers.

Le Sueur's comments not only illustrate the authority of the Iowas, but
they also demonstrate a system of land use in which groups controlled
fairly defined territories, and villages or bands had to obtain permission to hunt on others' lands. The recognition of such territoriality—and
arguably sovereignty—supports my argument that a syncretic process
guided the mapping of the trans-Mississippi West. This does not mean
that tribal boundaries were static. Anthropological investigations into
Indian land claims have emphasized the fluidity of property ownership
throughout the Upper Mississippi, affirming that violent conquest was
a viable form of land acquisition.[36] For smaller groups to compete with
larger bands, they had to attach themselves to larger populations and
create what anthropologist Patricia Albers calls a "merger."[37]

The need for mergers and alliances accelerated throughout the eighteenth century. As France, Spain, and England vied for colonial control
of the Mississippi, the diseases their traders and explorers carried reca-
librated the elaborate system of alliances among various Indian groups
and imperial powers.[38] By the mid-1760s, the first of two smallpox epidemics struck the Iowas, halving their population.[39] Although population estimates for the period vary, French trader Auguste Chouteau's
observation that the Iowas were "afraid to hunt on their own lands lest
they might be attacked by the Sioux" illustrates both the decline of Iowa
power and the expansion of the Western Sioux.[40]

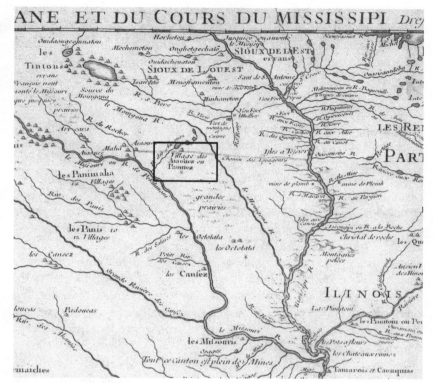

MAP 7. Detail of Guillaume Delisle's *Carte de La Louisiane et du Cours du Mississippi* (1702), showing the location of the Iowas' village. Delisle's placement of the village corresponds with LeSueur's assessment of their strength. Courtesy of Library of Congress.

Drawn to the region by the fur trade, the Teton and Yanktonai Sioux quickly became dominant trappers and traders, acquiring European guns and forcing the poorly armed and less populous Omahas, Otoes, Missouris, and Iowas to the south.[41] Finding a safe haven from growing Sioux aggression became increasingly imperative for the Iowas' survival. When a second wave of smallpox struck at the turn of the nineteenth century, the Iowas' numbers were once again halved, leaving just eight hundred people.[42]

On December 16, 1815, just months after a particularly devastating Lakota attack, the Iowa Indians made their first treaty with the United States, at a meeting also attended by Kickapoos, Big and Little Osages, and both groups of Sacs. In letters to Secretary of War Henry Calhoun, Treaty Commissioner William Clark explained that his treaty proposals were met with "a considerable backwardness, if not positive reluctance," by several of the tribes, most notably the Mississippi Sacs. However, despite confining the parameters of the treaties to the "sole object of peace," as directed, Clark reported that unlike the other participants of the meeting, the Iowa Indians were "extremely solicitous that they embrace other subjects."

According to Clark, the Iowas proposed a "spontaneous offer" to come more closely under the protection of the United States, in exchange for annuities and the loss of a small portion of their lands.[43] The Iowas' "spontaneous offer" to Treaty Commissioner Clark to cede the rights to some of their lands for promises of protection must be understood within the context of a dwindling population forced to find security in a region of growing violence. It was, therefore, neither a "spontaneous" nor an unqualified "offer." By signing the 1815 treaty, the Iowas agreed to share some lands with the Americans in exchange for an alliance in warfare. The treaty between the Iowas and Americans was similar to the same "merger" process that the Iowas had been relying on since the first smallpox epidemic had decimated their population sixty years earlier. On September 16, 1815, Clark and fifteen Iowa representatives signed a treaty of "peace and friendship."[44]

Although the Iowas allied with the United States to gain territorial security, this agreement did little to stop the violence between rival Indian groups. One traveler noted that the Iowas were in a state of "perpetual warfare," as they engaged in conflicts with their neighbors on all sides.[45] The Kansa and Big and Little Osages threatened from the south; the Yanktonai and Teton Sioux came from the north; the Pawnees pushed from the West; and the Mississippi Sac continued pressing their claims from the east.[46] Ceaseless bloodshed prompted Iowa chief Hard Heart to approach Indian agent George Sibley in 1819. He reiterated the tribe's desire for protection and assistance. In a letter to Governor William Clark, Sibley forwarded an explanation of Hard Heart's request: "They are surrounded [Hard Heart] says on every side by enemies, who are continually making war upon them; which compels them to be always on the watch, sleeping with one eye open, and one hand on their guns; so that they have but little time to hunt for the subsistence of their families."[47] Hard Heart's words were more prescient than he knew; early next year, he was killed by a band of Yankton Sioux.[48]

After five years of piecemeal attempts to end the growing violence, Governor Clark called a council of all the regional Indian groups, during which he hoped to establish "permanent" boundaries among the tribes. This treaty session—called to clarify boundaries—inspired a seemingly innocuous agreement between the Sacs and Foxes and the Iowas; however, the agreement would ultimately result in massive land loss for the Iowas, and it would initiate more than a century of diplomatic and legal wrangling.[49] Rather than a clash of territorial systems, however, this struggle was over the specifics of boundary making. Ironically, it is in these conflicts that we find evidence of the compatibility of Native and Euro-American spatial imaginings.

Familiar with the politics of treaty making over the last twenty years, the Iowas, Sacs, and Foxes knew of the American tendency to recognize territorial claims of larger groups over those of smaller ones. Overlooking previous disagreements, the three tribes knew they must speak with one voice to counter the Sioux's strength. The leaders saw this council as an opportunity to exclude the Sioux from the region. To do so, the Iowas would have to align their fortunes with the Sacs and the Foxes. When Clark arrived at Prairie du Chien on July 30, 1825, nearly one thousand Chippewa, Sioux, Winnebago, Menominee, Pottawatomie, and Ottawa Indians had already established themselves on the grounds, but the Sac, Fox, and Iowa delegations had not arrived. Then, on August 4, a flotilla of seventy canoes came rushing down the Mississippi carrying the missing participants, who were armed with spears, clubs, guns, knives, and the loud notes of war songs. According to one report: "No tribes attracted so intense a degree of interest as the Iowas and the Sac and Foxes, tribes of radically diverse languages, yet united in league against the Sioux.... They beat drums. They uttered yells at definite points. They landed in compact ranks. They looked the very spirit of defiance."[50] For a moment, at least, the battle lines were drawn, as the Sacs, Foxes, and Iowas joined in concert against the Sioux.

Fortunately for the Iowas, this strategy worked. The Sioux boundary line was established at the upper fork of the Des Moines River, north of the Iowas' primary hunting ground. To achieve this demarcation, however, the Iowas agreed to respect the boundary between themselves and the Sacs and Foxes, and they would "peaceably occupy the same, until some satisfactory arrangement can be made between them for a division of their respective claims to country."[51] Therefore, while the 1825 Treaty of Prairie du Chien secured the southern portion of the land between the rivers from Sioux warriors, it did nothing to augment the Iowas' shrinking supply of game. Iowas now had to share hunting grounds with both the Missouri Sacs—who had remained in the region after the divisive

1804 Sac treaty—and the Rock River Sacs—who now agreed to move to the land between the rivers. The search for a "satisfactory arrangement" brought the tribes into conflict, and it determined the Iowas' political tactics for the next twelve years.

Despite their promises, neither the Iowas nor the Sacs were actually willing to give up their control of the shared region. Just five years after they agreed to "peaceably occupy the same," both groups petitioned the governor to clarify the boundaries between the groups. This led to the second Treaty of Prairie du Chien in 1830. Soon into the treaty session, the Iowas' new political strategy emerged: they would emulate some aspects of American society, and by doing this, they hoped to elevate themselves above the Sac and the Sioux in the eyes of the American representatives.

The Iowas' tactic became apparent as soon as the treaty session began. While other leaders claimed large portions of the territory as necessary hunting grounds, insisting that all available lands were needed for securing game, Iowa representatives highlighted their communities' agricultural activities. Iowa chief White Cloud contrasted his tribe's success at farming with other Indian groups by declaring: "Look upon me and you look upon almost a white man. . . . I have learned to plough and I now eat my own bread and it makes me large and strong. These people (pointing to delegates of the Sacs and the Foxes) eat everything, and yet are lean. They can't get fat even by eating their own words."

White Cloud hoped that by illustrating the Iowas' recent transition to an economy based on agriculture rather than hunting, the treaty commissioner would accept the Iowas' land claims over others. White Cloud knew that American recognition of a larger territorial base would give him more bargaining power in future treaty negotiations. Another chief, The Crane, extended the Iowas' claim by explaining that "our Great Father has been trying, and we have been trying for several years to make us like the white people. We wish you to continue it a little longer, and you will perhaps see some of our young men profit by it."[52]

The words of White Cloud and The Crane reveal a complex set of motivations that defy absolute categorization.[53] By "learning to plow" and becoming metaphorically "like white people," the chiefs consciously described their tribe's political policies and the cultural changes they believed the Iowa should employ to meet social and environmental pressures. White Cloud's metaphorical assertion of being "almost a white man" did not signify his desire to assimilate. Instead, for the Iowas, being "like white people" involved a set of activities, some of which could be "continued a little longer" or stopped at will. In fact, just moments after making his pledge to continue these "white people" activities, The Crane also declared to the assembly, "You know we are not like white people to lay up money."[54]

So while the chiefs claimed to act "as white people" in some circumstances, they distanced themselves from such comparisons when necessary. For these representatives of the Iowas, being "like a white man" referred to a specific set of actions such as farming with a plough, not to cultural assimilation. Rather than a dichotomous vision of Indian-white relations, Iowa leaders understood that their communities had potentially much to gain from aspects of white expansion, particularly security from the rapidly expanding Western Sioux. As we shall see with the Indians' cartographic representation of their land claims, the Iowas used the tools at their disposal to gain economic and political advantages.

Like the first meeting at Prairie du Chien, Americans delayed the delineation of separate Iowa and Sac lands. No doubt hindered by problems that Americans had exacerbated by incorrectly surveying the Delaware Outlet, Clark proposed a common hunting ground, encompassing the modern state of Iowa, with intertribal boundaries to be "marked as soon as the President of the United States may deem it expedient." In an inversion of stereotypical land-use portrayals, Iowa and Sac Indians demanded private corporate ownership, while the U.S. government was—at least for the time being—interested in a communal hunting ground. In April 1834, the Iowas—understanding the tenuous nature of this agreement—asked agent Andrew Hughes for a meeting to discuss the possibility of selling all of their land that was not part of the common hunting ground. According to Hughes, the Iowas wanted to sell because "they were tired of the chase and wish to become like whitemen." In return, the tribe asked for domestic animals, an educational fund for their children, and farming equipment. They also wanted to maintain a small portion of their territory for agricultural purposes.[55]

For the second time in four years, the Iowas expressed their desire to make agriculture their primary mode of living. Hughes granted that request, and on September 17, 1836, the Iowas ceded all of their land lying between the Missouri River and the northern boundary of the state of Missouri. They also agreed to move to a strip of land on the west side of the Missouri River, abutting the Wolf River. They would receive $7,500 cash, rations for a year, a farmer, a blacksmith, a schoolmaster, an interpreter, a ferryboat, a mill, and five "comfortable houses." In addition, two hundred acres of ground were to be broken for farming, and the tribe would receive one hundred cows and calves, five bulls, and one hundred stock hogs.[56] According to a letter from Agent Hughes, the Iowas quickly moved to their new land, where they seemed "highly pleased with their situation." On the land, they erected forty-one bark houses, each one with a small patch of corn.[57]

At the same time the Iowas were participating in treaty negotiations with the United States, the Mississippi Sacs were also working to solidify their land claims. Keokuk—who had gained control of the band after the failed "Blackhawk Wars"—attempted to cede the land jointly controlled by the Sacs and Iowas to the United States, a maneuver that greatly disturbed the Iowas.[58] While the Iowas agreed that the 1825 treaty allowed the Sacs to hunt on lands west of the Mississippi, the Iowas had not intended to give up any ownership of the land. Further, the Iowas held that the Mississippi Sacs never took the land by conquest, the most important factor of land claims by Indians in the region.

As support for their claim, the Iowas asked William Clark—now the superintendent of the St. Louis Bureau of Indian Affairs—to write a letter on their behalf. Clark wrote that, when he first arrived in the area, the Iowas possessed "an immense tract of land" between the Mississippi and the Missouri, an area in which they still held an undivided interest. Clark's letter persuaded the commissioner of Indian Affairs to invite the Iowas and the Sacs to Washington.[59] The Iowas needed to convince the commissioner that they had historic control of the land between the rivers, thereby producing an exclusive Iowa claim that made negotiations with the Americans potentially more beneficial. For their part, the Sacs hoped to prove that they had taken the area by force, justifying their ability to bargain with Americans for the region. The success of the Iowas' claim was now contingent upon their political maneuvering and their ability to clarify their competing territorial claims with the Sacs. To do this, they used a tool they knew would be understood by the Americans: a parchment map.

On October 7, 1837, representatives of the Iowa and Sac Indians arrived at a rented Presbyterian church to meet with U.S. Secretary of War Joel Poinsett and Commissioner of Indian Affairs Carey A. Harris to discuss the extent of each groups' land claims. Notchininga, the second chief under White Cloud, and several other Iowa chiefs had come to Washington to dispute the terms of both the 1825 Treaty of Prairie du Chien and the subsequent treaty of 1830. The Iowas argued that the Sacs had ceded lands to the U.S. government that could not be traded away without the Iowas' consent.

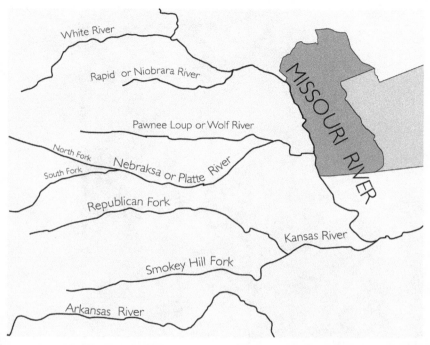

MAP 8. Study area with 1837 Iowa cession (*dark gray*) and part of the contested Sac and Fox cession (*light gray*). Cession areas taken from Charles C. Royce, *Indian Land Cessions in the United States*, 56th Cong., 1st sess., 1899, serial 4015, H. Doc. 736. Map created by author.

Notchininga presented a map to the Americans that showed the extent of the lands claimed by the Iowas. The map depicted an area extending from what is now northeastern Wisconsin on Lake Michigan, to western Nebraska on the Missouri River, and from southern Minnesota on the Mississippi River to an area just south of St. Louis, Missouri. The map represented the migrations of the Iowa people and the villages they had occupied since the fifteenth century. "This is the route of my forefathers," Notchininga stated, pointing to a series of dotted lines; "it is the land we have always claimed from old times—we have always owned this land—it is ours—it bears our name." Finding settlements that could only have belonged to the Iowas, twentieth-century archaeologists have upheld Notchininga's depiction of the Iowas' migration.[60] *Notchininga's Map*, or *No Heart's Map*, as it has come to be known, does not share

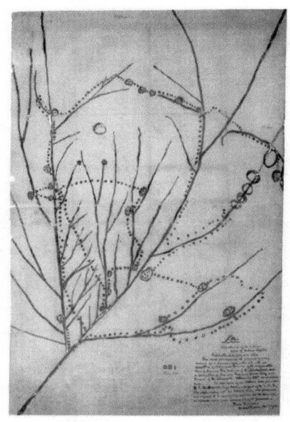

MAP 9. *Notchininga's Map* is an untitled manuscript map on parchment (1837). Photo courtesy
of the Cartographic Branch, National Archives,
College Park, Maryland (RG75, map 821, tube 520).

many of the characteristics of other extant Amerindian maps.[61] These
differences include the lack of frame or other indicators of spatial existence beyond of the map's limits and a constantly shifting scale derived
from a principle of "linear coherence."[62] In maps with "linear coherence,"
objects closer to a point of origin appear bigger than those farther away,
but the objects are still depicted in the order that they would be found if
one were to travel in a straight line. *Notchininga's Map* contradicts both
of these conventions of Amerindian cartography. While there is neither

a formal frame nor lines of longitude or latitude that might represent the knowledge of the map as a section of a larger spatial construction, the lines depicting rivers bleed directly off the page—this map uses the edges of the parchment to create a frame. This convention indicates an understanding of a world beyond the boundaries of the document.

In addition, once the map is flipped on a vertical axis, we can see that the spatial representation does not follow the model of linear coherence, but rather it follows a European convention of spatial equivalence. In other words, rather than a representation in which the scale is dependent upon one's point of view, *Notchininga's Map* uses a constant scale with the familiar perspective "from above."[63] In fact, *Notchininga's Map* is so spatially accurate, it differs from a modern hydrography map of the region only in details.[64] The question one must ask, therefore, is why does this map lack the most important characteristics of other "Indian" maps? The answer does not lie in abstract claims about indigenous cultures but rather in the specific shifting geopolitical concerns of the Iowas.

It is impossible to know why the Iowas created the map that they did. However, based on the Iowas' political maneuvering at other meetings, we can see how the creation of this map fits into a larger strategy. By highlighting conventions that were compatible with European spatial representations, the Iowas were continuing the tactic they had used seven years earlier at the second Treaty of Prairie du Chien. At the earlier meeting, White Cloud and The Crane tried to separate themselves from the Sacs by claiming they were like "white men," while the Sacs were untrustworthy. With the creation of the map, the Iowas emulated another aspect of Euro-American culture. By creating a document similar to the ones with which Americans created territorial boundaries in 1825 and again in 1830, the Iowas demonstrated their understanding of Euro-American territoriality. Notchininga's demarcation of all the previous Iowa villages, dating back hundreds of years, but not the villages in the area ceded in 1830, offers more evidence of this.[65] This indicates that, despite his claim against the Sacs, Notchininga respected the Iowas' land cession to the Americans under their concept of land ownership.

Cartographic strategies aside, Notchininga was more direct in his verbal claim to the area. While he did not dispute the Sacs' current military dominance over the Iowas, Notchininga rested his argument on his tribe's historic control of the region. He also cited an arrangement that the Iowas and Sacs had initially reached in 1825, when they agreed to use the territory as a shared hunting ground. Sac leader Keokuk, citing the importance of territorial conquest, rebutted that regardless of the Iowas'

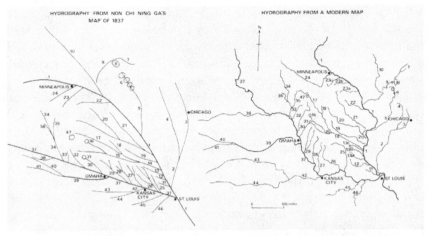

HYDROGRAPHY FROM NON CHI NING GA'S MAP OF 1837

HYDROGRAPHY FROM A MODERN MAP

MAP 10. Interpretation of hydrography of *Notchininga's Map*. By David Turnbull in *Maps Are Territories: Science Is an Atlas* (Chicago: University of Chicago Press, 1993), 23. Photo used by permission of University of Chicago Press.

past claims, the Sacs had forcefully taken the Iowas' land, thereby gaining control of the region.

Perhaps legitimizing their own methods of conquest, the Americans decided that Keokuk's claim was strong enough to give the Sacs control of the remaining land between the rivers. Thus, the meeting called by both the Iowas and the Sacs in order to clarify each tribe's territory ended with the Sacs' gaining control of land that they had occupied with the Iowas for less than two decades. This allowed the Sacs to dictate the terms of cessions to the Americans. Disgusted, the Iowas withdrew from the treaty council, turned down numerous cession proposals, and refused to participate in further meetings in Washington.[66]

While the Iowas now "owned" a fraction of the land that they had controlled just twenty-five years earlier, their attempts to adapt to the social pressures around them reveals a perseverance that counters the tragedy of land loss. Despite their anger, the Iowas knew that American support was still necessary to aid their transition to an agrarian economy. Otherwise, as the Iowas confessed to one of the Indian agents, they would be forced to move back to the Des Moines River, where they would be unable to compete with the Sioux and Sacs for resources.[67] So, rather than suffer complete dispossession and diaspora, the Iowas secured a small portion of their former lands. A few months after the

1837 Sac treaty in Washington, the Iowas agreed to move south of the Missouri River, to the Great Nemaha, where Isaac McCoy sent his son John to survey their new home in what he hoped would be the permanent Indian territory.[68] In exchange, the Iowas were to receive $157,000 in investments, with at least 5 percent interest paid annually to the tribe in perpetuity. Also, the Americans were to provide funds for education, agriculture, blacksmith facilities, and "the construction of ten houses with good floors, one door and two windows."[69]

For many Iowas, life on the Great Nemaha was very different than the one they had envisioned just twenty-three years earlier at their first treaty with the Americans. In the first years of the century, they hunted across hundreds of thousands of acres; by 1840, they lived primarily as farmers on a few hundred acres. However, framing the story of the Iowas in the first half of the nineteenth century as just a narrative of dispossession disregards their social adaptation and political maneuverings. Such a framework not only ignores the creativity of Iowa leadership, but it also simplifies the social landscape into an Indian-white binary. The Iowas repeatedly allied themselves with the United States to gain political leverage. They made conscious decisions about which political and social strategies to employ in the face of a dwindling supply of game and serious encroachment onto their lands.

Notchininga's Map demonstrates creative geopolitical tactics that defy easy categorization in a historical period that is frequently depicted in black-and-white—or, in this case, red-and-white—terms. Along with farming with a plow and metaphorically becoming "like whitemen," the Iowas' creation of a parchment-based, spatially equivalent map should be understood as a distinct political tactic that cannot be described as either "resisting" or "acculturating to" American expansion.

I have explicitly refrained from arguing that the map's creation demonstrated the Iowas' replacement of an epistemologically "Indian" way of representing the eastern prairies with a uniquely "Euro-American" one. As with any people, the Siouan and Caddoan peoples living in the trans-Mississippi West had multiple ways of understanding and representing the world around them. Some of these constructions were no doubt culturally unique. Yet Indian groups used many of the same spatial practices as the Euro-American explorers, traders, and Indian agents with whom they came in contact, making the process of determining the origins of uniquely Iowan or Siouan or Caddoan spatial constructions not only futile but irrelevant. Whether by hybridization, syncretism, or simply compatible ways of understanding their place in the landscape,

Native and Euro-American people on the eastern Plains were able to communicate through maps. Acknowledging this fact removes the veneer of inevitability that still dominates nineteenth-century American Indian history and places the burden of the subsequent Indian dispossession squarely on the shoulders of human actors. There is no better way to describe this process than to expand upon the story of the Pawnees with which I began this chapter.

2 /   Sharitarish and the Possibility of Treaties

On October 9, 1833, Sharitarish—probably the same chief who would draw the dirt map for American dragoons eleven years later—and fifteen other Pawnee leaders signed a treaty with American representatives Edward Ellsworth and John Dougherty. The Indians believed that this treaty would provide them with military protection, diplomatic assistance, and material goods. In exchange, the chiefs agreed to "cede and relinquish to the United States all their right, interest, and title in and to all the land lying south of the Platte River," an area that twentieth-century Pawnees argued was at least 23 million acres.[1] Such was the start of more than a century of broken promises and legal wrangling that came to typify American territorial appropriation in the trans-Mississippi West.

This treaty, and dozens like it, represented the most essential process in the mapping of the trans-Missouri West. As the editors of a seminal collection of essays on the American West argue, "Land that belongs to me, lands that belong to you; the history of the West is the story of how the American map came to have the boundaries it shows today."[2] Along with treaties with the Osage and the Kansa in 1825, the 1833 treaty with the Pawnees marked the beginning of land transfer in the trans-Missouri West. This transfer gave the United States the ability to determine where western boundaries would be drawn. And because of the financial inequity of the treaty—the Pawnees received $148,200 for slightly more than half of the 23 million acres they claimed as theirs— the standard historical interpretation posits that American representatives either forced or tricked the Pawnees into signing the agreement.

Historians have used words like "scheme" and "persuade" to describe the American government's participation in the negotiations.[3] During the 1950s Indian Claims Commission hearings, Pawnee lawyers argued that it was only through "duress, misrepresentation, undue influence, mistake of the Pawnees, [and] breach of trust by the [United States]," that the treaty was procured at all.[4] In this interpretation, the drawing of Indian territorial boundaries appears to consist entirely of what cartographer J. B. Harley calls "ideological arrows."[5]

An alternative narrative of American land appropriation in the trans-Missouri West demonstrates how the Pawnees played a central role in the creation of geopolitical boundaries of the region. Whereas most histories of the Pawnees start with their land dispossession and government dependency in the second half of the nineteenth century and look for the historical patterns that created this structure, this chapter periodizes Pawnee geopolitics without bowing to any presupposition of the inevitability of U.S. colonialism. For nineteenth-century Pawnee leaders, the United States was not their future colonizer but just one of many players in an increasingly violent landscape. The Pawnees saw both problems and opportunities as Americans expanded their presence in the region. Rather than being forced to sign the 1833 treaty, Pawnee leaders saw an opportunity to maintain their sociopolitical standing and to provide security for their people.

By the 1820s, violent conflicts with both the central-Siouans to the east and nomadic groups to the west had made life harrowing for the four Pawnee tribes. As Osage-, Comanche-, and Lakota-led alliances pushed into the Great Plains from all directions, the Pawnees looked for new geopolitical alliances to maintain control of their primary hunting grounds, located between the Niobrara and Arkansas Rivers.[6] It was at the very moment that the Pawnees were looking for diplomatic and military assistance that the United States' presence in the region—one previously limited to the remnants of a failed factory system and the skeleton of an Indian Bureau whose agents rarely crossed the Missouri—began to expand. Pawnee leaders saw the potential—and the problems—in the establishment of the Santa Fe Trail, the coming of scientific and military expeditions, and the expansion of the Indian bureau.[7] They looked to U.S. representatives not as harbingers of a colonial order but rather as tools for them to maintain power within their group, to feed and clothe their people, and to secure themselves against the threats from other Indian groups. Seen in this light, the 1833 treaty exemplifies the ways in

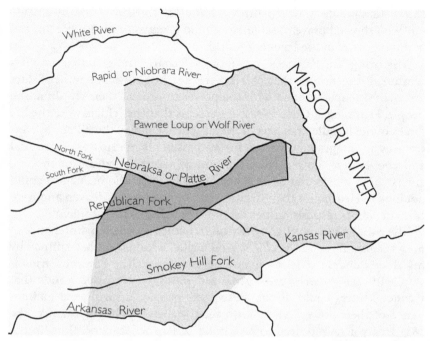

MAP 11. Study area showing the extent of Pawnee territorial claims in the nineteenth century and the much smaller region that the Pawnees were credited with ceding during the 1833 Indian Claims Commission Hearings. Map created by author.

which Indian groups—in this case the Pawnees—played an active role in the creation of the geopolitical landscape of the trans-Missouri West.

Pawnee leaders saw an alliance with the United States as a means to secure their geopolitical claims. Still, there was a more immediate reason why Pawnee headmen wanted to participate in a treaty: to control a consistent supply of Euro-American goods. For the Pawnees, chiefly status was determined by birthright and social worth, and the most important gauge of social worth was a leader's ability to provide goods for his people. Such action resulted in more than individual acclaim; it was also an integral part of the Pawnees' social and cultural fabric. Through the chiefs, the celestial being Tirawahut and the sacred bundles—the foundation of the Pawnees' world—showed the people the right way to live. This knowledge could be passed on only by the chiefs or priests, who could manipulate and explain the bundles. Thus, a powerful chief—one who showed bravery, selflessness, and generosity—was necessary to maintain order in the Pawnees' world.

Mirroring the Pawnees' astronomical charts, religious ceremonies reinforced the notion that chiefs were not just men but rather "stars on earth," people imbued with the power to protect their children, the people. Ethnologist Gene Weltfish explains that the "chiefs were the life forces of the bundle-transferred power which enabled the village to continue as an integrated unit. . . . The success of all enterprises, individual and cooperative, flowed from the bundle via the medium of the . . . chiefs.[8] This interpretation is echoed by a Pawnee idiom: "Chiefs could not look to Heaven for their decisions as *they* were now Heaven and were carrying all its responsibilities for the well-being of the people."[9]

The entire Pawnee religio-political structure relied on maintenance of both the bundles and the chiefs. And a chief's status was determined by his chiefly characteristics—including generosity. The Pawnees' friendship with the Americans—formalized in 1833—promised goods that Pawnee leaders could distribute to their people, ensuring the maintenance of their power. Along with securing a geopolitical alliance, the 1833 treaty also appeared to be a boon to Pawnee leaders. Thus, in the story of American land appropriation in the trans-Mississippi West—the heart of the American colonial project—we find tales of cooperation and negotiation alongside those of contestation and violence.

Stars on Earth

Since the middle of the nineteenth century, the term "Pawnee" has been used to describe four divisions of Caddoan-speakers who lived in semi-permanent villages in what would become southern Nebraska and northern Kansas. This confederation consisted of four semi-autonomous tribes: the Chaui (Grand), the Pitahawirat (Tappage), the Kitkahahki (Republican), and the Skidi (Wolf), with the first three groups known collectively as the South Bands.[10] Originally a single people known as Karawakis, the South Bands as well as the independent Skidi descended from central Plains horticulturalists, who were called the people of the Loup Focus. According to their South Band descendants, the Karawakis either migrated to—or were created in—the eastern Great Plains where they conquered the Otoes, Poncas, Omahas, and Skidi, who themselves had traveled north a century earlier. Members of the South Bands have claimed that the Siouan Otoes, Poncas, and Omahas lived relatively harmoniously as subjugated wards of the Kawarahkis, while the Skidis repeatedly asserted their independence but were systematically subdued. The Skidis have refuted this interpretation, claiming that they were the dominant group and only much later became part of the South Bands' political confederation.[11]

Regardless of who held primacy, the addition of the horse to the eastern Plains ecosystem increased interaction between the Kawarahkis and the Skidi. Sometime in the seventeenth century—partially because the 1680 Pueblo Revolt put more of these animals in Indian hands—horses became an important commodity for southern Plains Indians. Allowing hunters to travel farther and to carry more by tapping the Plains' most abundant energy source—grasses—horses prompted the Apaches and Jumanos to combine seasonal bison hunting with their agricultural system to create the first horse cultures on the Plains. When the Comanches and their Ute allies swept down from the southern Rocky Mountains in the eighteenth century, they quickly mastered nomadic hunting and warfare to become a fully equestrian people. By the middle of the eighteenth century, they had used their new skills to conquer the Apaches in the region.[12] Maintaining their herds by raiding Spanish ranches, Comanches and their Comancherías—massive trading centers—supplied horses for three distinct regions: the northern Plains, where environmental conditions quickly diminished horse populations; the southern Plains, where most tribes did not have access to Spanish horses; and New Mexico, where Comanche raiding created a deficit in the region.[13]

Not long after the Comanches arrived on the southern Plains, the Kawarkhis and the Skidi began trading with—and raiding from—the Comanches, and by 1714, they had acquired enough horses for the Europeans to refer to the Pawnees as good horsemen. By the end of the eighteenth century, these groups had integrated horses deeply into their culture. Whereas a Pawnee on foot might kill a single buffalo during one of the four charges that made up a typical hunt, a well-mounted hunter could kill three or four. Horses turned what had been a secondary aspect of Pawnee life—the buffalo hunt—into one of its defining characteristics, as the hunt became more institutionalized.[14]

The addition of the horse to Pawnee lifeways altered both ceremonial and quotidian aspects of Pawnee life.[15] New rituals were created that incorporated buffalo into existing religious structures now that the animals' meat composed as much of the Pawnee diet as Mother Corn. Scholar James Riding In speculates that this change must have stirred debate among Pawnee spiritual leaders who feared celestial retribution for deviating from the traditional focus on agriculture.[16] The buffalo hunt was ultimately absorbed into Pawnee society, and by the middle of the nineteenth century, Chaui chief Pita Resaru explained: "We want the buffalo as long as there is buffalo. We are afraid that the Great Spirit [Tirawahut] will punish us if we give him no meat."[17]

Horses also positioned Pawnees as important players in a vast Great Plains trade network. Pawnees supplied Spanish horses to the Otoes, Omahas, and other Siouan people to the east and transported guns and other manufactured goods to the nomadic tribes in the Southwest.[18] It was the Pawnees' role as middlemen that dictated the importance of trade in their sociopolitical system. Though they did not accumulate as much wealth as their Upper Missouri neighbors, the continental trade network was no less important for Pawnee leaders, as trade (and the control of it) became their primary means of solidifying political power. Like his celestial forebearer, the chief was the protector of the village, and his decisions were made according to the needs of his people. Though he held considerable authority, his control was based on generations of precedent, and his decisions had to be mindful of his people's interests.

If a chief lacked the necessary qualifications to hold office—generosity among them—he could be stripped of his power.[19] Both trade goods and trade-related gifts were only briefly kept at the top of the hierarchy. As Edwin James—the chronicler of Stephen Long's 1819 expedition— explained, this arrangement often resulted in an inverse relationship between material goods and authority: "The chiefs are amongst the poorest of the Indians, having parted with their horses, clothes, trinkets, &c. to ensure the farther patronage of their adherents."[20] Vertical gift giving was an integral part of the Pawnees' regimented sociopolitical structure. Not coincidentally, gift giving also became important to the treaty process, and thus it was an essential component of how the West was drawn.

While generosity was an important way to maintain power, it was also a route to usurp it. Although authority was traditionally passed to the eldest son of a recently deceased chief, an ambitious member of an important family sometimes attempted to wrest power from an ill-suited patrilineal heir. James wrote that this kind of ascendancy depended "upon the resources of his own mind, aided by his reputation for generosity and valour."[21] Horse raiding offered just this type of opportunity. Young warriors looked to raiding as an important means of attaining prestige and leadership positions. In addition to the bravery displayed in raiding, young men could offer horses as a dowry for marriage, or they could give horses to priests and chiefs in exchange for their ceremonial knowledge and services. Because status was partially determined by the number of horses one could give away, the chiefs were required to return some of the horses they received back to the group. Those who received horses were then expected to repay the leader with political allegiance.[22]

Once he proved himself to be a worthy provider, a Pawnee chief held more power than most chiefs of other American Indian groups. Chiefs had the authority to whip and even to kill anyone who threatened the common good. One traveler noted that a Pawnee chief could "whip one of the young men with impunity," but if a Lakota chief were to perform the same act, "he is sure to have some of his horses killed."[23] Unlike the Lakota, whose nomadic traditions favored a loose organizational structure, the Pawnees were highly subordinate to those in power. Chiefs arbitrated personal disputes, controlled intratribal contact, and decided diplomatic matters. When asked why they were not moving to a new village site, a group of Chaui chiefs responded that their head chief "was like [your] president." Since he was absent, they would have to wait for his return, because "they could do nothing without him." John Dunbar wrote that, when a well-suited chief gained power, "the will of these men was law." Maintaining order within the villages and deciding on tribal alliances both depended on the will of the chief.

Similarly, the chief and his village police controlled all aspects of the trading process. A Pawnee who failed to adhere to the protocol that regulated trade with other Indian groups or with Euro-American traders might have been beaten or killed at the hands of *raripakusus* (the village police, literally meaning "fighting for order").[24] The traveler John Treat Irving, who was present during the 1833 treaty, recalled that Wild Horse, head of the Chaui village police, was so ferocious in his discipline that he was as much "an object of jealousy to [the Pawnees] as dread to their enemies."[25] This control of trade activities and goods was the reason that, according to Irving, the young men who were excluded from the council were so defiant.[26]

Inversely, when an agent refused to stop trade at the lodges of less important Pawnees, the chiefs refused to receive their annuities and claimed that "they were displeased and felt they had been lowered in the estimation of their people and others were enjoying privileges which belonged exclusively to them."[27] It was the control of trade, rather than the volume of it, which ensured political power. For Pawnee leaders, an unregulated flow of goods would have been difficult to control and might have diluted their power, threatening the sociopolitical system. At the same time, the strict regulation of trade goods and processes—from which Pawnee leaders banned alcohol, ensuring greater control—had the unforeseen benefit of insulating the Pawnees from the material dependency that undermined the sovereignty of many other Native groups in the region.

Pawnee leaders had to balance the need to ensure a steady supply of goods to provide for their people with their ability to control these transactions so that they alone would be responsible for their dispersal. Despite Pawnee leaders' reluctance to trade as much as their Upper Missouri neighbors did, they often requested that Euro-American traders visit their villages during the first decades of the nineteenth century.[28] While the small volume of this trade made these trips only slightly profitable for the traders, these interactions had legacies beyond their sociopolitical benefit to Pawnee leaders. As Indians incorporated horses and European trade goods into their lifeways, Euro-Americans adopted Native trading patterns of gift giving, along with other rituals.

The rituals attached to the trading process established patterns for future negotiations when the Pawnees were looking to create new geopolitical alliances in the 1810s and 1820s.[29] For the Pawnees, the Hako ceremony—perhaps the first calumet ceremony on the Plains—established fictive kinship ties between the trading parties, as a "father" presented a calumet pipe to a receiving "son," which ensured peaceful relations.[30] Gifts of medals and flags took the place of robes and arrows as American representatives tried to solidify their favored-nation status with Pawnee leaders. In 1833, when the time came to negotiate a more explicit diplomatic alliance between Pawnee and American representatives, many of the rituals that would bind these groups together were already in place.[31] The foundation for the United States' appropriation of land in the trans-Missouri West—the process that separated the "land that belongs to me" from the "land that belongs to you"—had been laid long before any land transfers actually took place.

From Two Fathers to One

Proposing that the Pawnees' sociopolitical structure was compatible with the treaty process that resulted in the American appropriation of huge amounts of land in the trans-Missouri West is one thing. Demonstrating that the Pawnees' active participation in this process was a conscious geopolitical strategy is quite another. The remainder of this chapter describes the Pawnees' geopolitical situation between 1800 and

1830 and argues that Pawnee leaders saw the United States as a potential ally in an increasingly violent world. In exchange for security, the Pawnees ceded ownership of their land below the Platte River. In this exchange, they also helped determine how the West was drawn.

Decades before the Pawnees and the Americans signed the 1833 treaty, the question of which imperial power would claim ownership of the trans-Mississippi West was still largely unanswered. Like the Americans, Spanish officials used a combination of military bravado and gift giving to gain Pawnee friendship and a potential ally in future regional conflicts. After the purchase of Louisiana Territory transferred millions of acres from French to American title, officials in both Washington and Mexico City tried to secure an upper hand in the region. Both looked to Indians on the southern and eastern Plains to provide a buffer between themselves and their imperial rival. Thus, for the first two decades of the nineteenth century, Pawnee leaders held considerable authority in their dealings with Euro-American powers, establishing a pattern of diplomacy that was an important factor in their decision to sign the 1833 treaty. In the early nineteenth century, Pawnee leaders viewed their relationship with the United States as one of mutual benefit rather than one between colonizer and colonized.

In a letter written to Joaquin del Real Alencaster in September 1805, commandant general of the interior Spanish provinces Nemesio Salcedo informed the New Mexican governor of the U.S. government's new geopolitical machinations.[32] According to Salcedo, the United States was instituting a "well-coordinated system [of] defense and security" by providing firearms and ammunition to the innumerable Indians living between the established territories of New Spain and the United States. It was "absolutely necessary to oppose these indicated plans," the commandant wrote, and he ordered the governor "to practice the most urgent diligence to strengthen [our friendship] with the Pani nation." Salcedo dispatched Spanish troops to the Pawnees, to lavish them with gifts and "inspire [such] horror towards the English and Americans" that the Pawnees would agree to intercept Meriwether Lewis and William Clark on their expedition to the Pacific Northwest.[33] Salcedo's letter to Alencaster was written just one day after James Wilkinson, the governor of the Louisiana Territory, wrote a similar correspondence to Secretary of War Henry Dearborn, confirming the need to secure a Comanche alliance. For both the nascent United States and the deteriorating Spanish empire, the vast numbers of Indians living throughout the Louisiana Territory were valuable geopolitical allies.[34]

In addition to the Comanches, Wilkinson wanted to gain the friendship of—or at least deter a Spanish alliance with—the Pawnees, Osages, Kansas, and other Plains Indian groups, and he organized a small contingent of U.S. troops under the command of Lt. Zebulon Pike to further this goal.[35] On September 25, 1806, after a painful march under an oppressive sun, Lieutenant Pike's detachment reached a lofty chain of ridges outside of a Kitkahahki village along the Republican River. The group had met a contingent of Pawnee scouts the day before, and they were undoubtedly prepared when a delegation of warriors stopped them on the ridge and asked them to wait for their chief. The Americans were seemingly less prepared for the Pawnee leader's dramatic arrival. From a half mile away, Sharitarish—probably the grandfather of the Sharitarish who signed the 1833 treaty—and three hundred horsemen, painted white, yellow, and blue, came charging at the American soldiers: "At the word of the chief, the warriors divided and pushing at full speed, flanked us on the right and left, yelling in the most diabolical manner. [Sharitarish] advanced in front, accompanied by Iskatappe . . . and his two sons, who were clothed in scarlet cloth. They approached slowly, and when within a hundred yards, the latter halted, and [Sharitarish] advanced in great state and when within a few paces of us, stretched out his hand and cried 'Bon jour.'"[36] Combining Euro-American and Indian protocol, the Pawnee chief successfully demonstrated his nation's military prowess and his understanding of foreign diplomacy, both of which would be important assets for the Pawnees in the coming years. Sharitarish's actions also reinforce this chapter's argument that Pawnee leaders used the tools at their disposal to secure a viable future for their people.

The first few days of Pike's visit went well. The Americans were feted, as were the Osage and Kansas diplomats traveling with Pike, despite their antagonistic relationship with the Pawnees. The mood changed, however, when Pike explained the political situation in the recently purchased Louisiana Territory. According to Pike, the United States now controlled a vast unmapped region far to the west of the Pawnee villages, and he was obligated to continue his exploration.[37] Consequently, Pike "demanded to purchase a few horses" so the Americans could continue on their way. Showing even more disrespect in the Pawnees' eyes, Pike reproached the chief for flying a Spanish flag and told Sharitarish to replace it with the American colors. In response, the chief grabbed a flag in each hand to demonstrate that there was room for two fathers.[38] Unmoved, Pike again demanded the exchange of flags, to which Sharitarish angrily responded that the Pawnees had known the Spanish a long time. They loved the Spanish for providing them with horses, especially since the Americans only gave them flimsy trinkets.[39] Further, in the case of war, Sharitarish continued, the Spaniards could reduce their village to rubble simply by running their army of horses through it, a feat far beyond the American military's abilities.

Pike was shocked that the Pawnees had a Spanish flag at all. After his arrival, Pike learned that a full infantry of one thousand Spanish troops had visited the Pawnees only a few weeks before. In addition to the flag, Spanish lieutenant Don Facundo Melgares supplied Sharitarish with a large medal featuring the bust of King Carlos VI, a smaller medal for his son, two mules, a commission of friendship from the governor of Santa Fe, and a promise to build a military outpost close to the Kitkahahki when he returned. Although a Spanish fort would have had its share of problems for the Pawnees, Sharitarish looked at this possibility the same way his son and grandson would later view U.S. military establishments over the next forty years: as an increasingly necessary geopolitical alliance as well as an opportunity for personal gain.

Like the Americans, the Spanish were on a mission of exploration and diplomacy, and they wanted to pass through the Kitkahahki village to explore the farthest extent of their claims. As historian Donald Jackson has summarized, the Spanish interpreted the Louisiana Purchase much more narrowly than did the Americans. They believed they had perfect right to trade with any Indian tribes along the Missouri, "west of the confluence of the Platte." Unlike the Americans, however, the Spanish infantry honored Sharitarish's request not to go farther than the Kitkahahki village. Understanding the importance of a Pawnee alliance in the event of a war with the United States, the Spanish commandant decided to return to Santa Fe rather than risking a military conflict with the Indians. Sharitarish explained the Spanish commander's obedience to Pike in the hope that the American would be equally submissive. Pike would not be swayed, however, and at the meeting's conclusion, the Pawnees had neither sold the Americans horses nor given them permission to continue west, although Sharitarish did agree to replace the Spanish flag with an American one, at least for the duration of Pike's visit.

The tense days following this meeting concluded with a dramatic standoff between Sharitarish and a few hundred of his warriors on one side and Pike's contingent of twenty soldiers on the other. Impressed with Pike's resolve and not wanting to start an unnecessary conflict, Sharitarish allowed the Americans to continue on their journey to Santa Fe, where they were promptly detained by Spanish officials for the remainder of 1806. Sharitarish's posturing with Pike illustrates the fine diplomatic line Pawnee leaders had to walk. This continued until the mid-1840s, when it became clear that the United States was not going to live up to its promises from earlier treaty meetings. Acting neither too submissive nor overtly hostile, Sharitarish had managed to demonstrate the South Bands' military strength. Yet by conceding to raise the American flag and allowing Pike to continue west, the Pawnee chief left open the possibility of a political alliance.[40]

As the geopolitical landscape changed, the likelihood of such an exclusive alliance grew. Just five years after giving Pike an ambivalent reception, Sharitarish told Indian agent George Sibley that he had a strong desire for friendship. Since 1793, when Pedro Vial mediated a truce between the Comanches and the Kitkahahki, the Spanish had been playing the role of Great Father to the Pawnees. However, as the Spanish hold on the Southwest deteriorated in the face of Comanche expansion, allegiance to Santa Fe became less attractive to the Pawnees.[41] Understanding the weakening Spanish position in the region, Sharitarish now "expressed a strong desire to know more of the Americans," and he offered to "throw away" all his Spanish medals and replace them with those of the United States in exchange for regular supplies of merchandise. Sharitarish understood that geopolitical circumstances had changed enough in the five years since Pike's visit that an alliance with the United States could be more beneficial than one with the Spanish. To this end, the Pawnee chief gave Sibley a gift of thirty "good looking" horses. In turn, Sibley provided the four Pawnee nations with large flags, and he gave Sharitarish the largest of the medals he distributed to the chiefs.[42]

For their part, the Spanish representatives continued to try to solidify a friendship with the Pawnees. According to Sibley, Sharitarish was "much courted by the Governor of St. a Fe," and the chief showed him "no small quantity" of medals, papers, and flags. The governors of both Santa Fe and Baton Rouge wrote a letter two years after Pike's visit that was "expressive of their satisfaction of his loyalty and adherence to the Spanish government."[43] Still, Sharitarish's statements of friendship to Sibley—combined with his promises to avoid contact with Spanish officials and not to visit the governor in Santa Fe—marked an important shift in Pawnee foreign policy. In contrast to the high regard shown by the Chaui leader for the Spanish during his meeting with Pike in 1806, Spanish traders and settlers in New Mexico were now subjected to frequent raids by Pawnee war parties. The Spaniards' situation became so

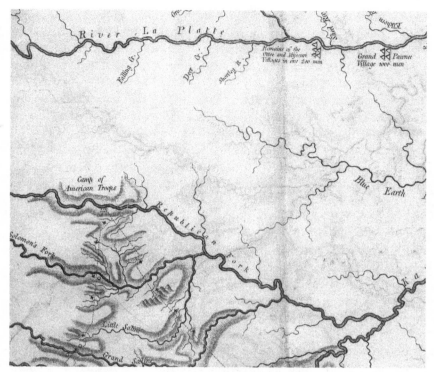

MAP 12. Detail of Pike's *First Part of Captn. Pike's Chart of the Internal Part of Louisiana* (1810), which was published in the account of his tours. Interestingly, though Pike inscribes the "Grand Pawnee Village" on the Platte, he does not indicate the village on the Republican Fork from which the river gets its name and the place where he met Sharitarish. The inscription simply reads, "Camp of American Troops." Courtesy of David Rumsey Historical Map Collection.

dire that Joseph Anthony Vizcarra implored Alexander McNair, the new governor of Missouri, to put an end to the Pawnees' "perfidious hostilities." If the hostilities did not end, Vizcarra declared, he would be "compelled to declare war against them and should require the consent of your government."[44]

Perhaps, as Sibley reported, the Pawnees' interactions with Indian agents Bob McClelland and John Dougherty had impressed the Indians with the power and bravery of the United States.[45] Or perhaps the Pawnees decided that raiding Spanish ranches for horses took precedence over a formal alliance with Santa Fe. Or even more likely, Pawnee leaders determined that the annual gifts from agent Benjamin O'Fallon that had begun in 1819—gifts that were worth as much as twenty thousand dollars per year—helped them maintain political power.[46] Whatever the reason, the Pawnees' relationship with Spanish officials and Spanish traders continued to deteriorate. By 1823, an unidentified Pawnee would tell a traveler that "the bearded people toward the west [Spaniards] . . . hate the red men, and since the time of our fathers have driven us out and have killed our people. For this reason we drink their blood and hate them."[47] While perhaps embellished, the Pawnee's statement reflected a definite shift away from the government in Santa Fe. The Pawnees would no longer look to two fathers, as they had in 1806. Instead, Pawnee leaders recognized who would become the dominant Euro-American power in the region. Sibley's visit in 1811 set the stage for Pawnee-U.S. relations for the next half century. Until the mid-1840s, when the United States would prove unworthy of their trust, the most powerful Pawnee leaders would look to the Americans as a geopolitical ally.[48]

This is not to suggest that the Pawnees simply acceded to U.S. demands or that the chiefs could completely end the Pawnee raiding of American traders. During a meeting with agent O'Fallon in the fall of 1824—a meeting called so the Pawnees would surrender an Indian accused of robbing an American trader—twenty-nine chiefs and warriors left Fort Atkinson after refusing to deliver the offender. The Pawnees insisted that, if they returned to their nation without settling this matter, they could not restrain their young men from starting a war with the Americans.[49] In order to maintain the flow of goods that reinforced his position, the head Chaui chief took matters into his own hands. Two months later, O'Fallon wrote that the conflict between the Americans and the Chauis had been "happily adjusted by the severe punishment of the offender by the hands of the principal chiefs of that tribe himself."[50] While the specifics of his diplomatic wrangling are unknown, once again a Chaui chief deftly placated American demands without sacrificing his personal authority. The name of this Chaui chief was Sharitarish, the son of the chief who met Pike in 1806.

Just a few years earlier, Sharitarish's other son, Tarecawawaho, had also looked to the presence of American representatives as a precursor to a favorable diplomatic alliance. "You are a chief, and I am a chief," the Indian told Maj. Stephen Long in 1820; "I am happy to hear what you say about peace that we particularly desire, especially with the whites." Like his father, Tarecawawaho wore an American medal to demonstrate his allegiance to the burgeoning friendship. He explained: "This medal which you see on my neck, is my father's image. It is dear to me." The

Chaui chief made it clear that he welcomed white traders on the eastern Plains, and he was also responsible for their protection: "Those whites, and all those people around me, I consider as my children, and am glad to see them."[51] As his father before him (hereafter Sharitarish I) and his brother after (hereafter Sharitarish II), Tarecawawaho was hoping to solidify his own prestige by strengthening diplomatic ties with the Americans without losing any of his own political authority.[52]

It was not just the Chaui chiefs who saw the United States as a potential ally. In just a few years, some Skidi chiefs had already shown their willingness to alter their cultural landscape in exchange for the sociopolitical gains of a U.S. alliance. Most importantly, they claimed to quash the Morning Star ceremony that centered on human sacrifice. Performed each spring, this ceremony was believed to ensure the harvest of maize, beans, and pumpkins on which the Pawnees relied for food. A few months after Major Sibley's visit in 1811, Ritsiresaru (Knife Chief) of the Pumpkin Vine village of the Skidi met with Superintendent of Indian Affairs William Clark to discuss the growing American presence in the region.

Impressed with Clark's argument that the practice of human sacrifice would jeopardize diplomatic ties with the United States, Ritsiresaru tried to convince the priests and warriors that they needed to alter the Morning Star ceremony to gain the Americans' friendship. At least twice in the next eight years, Ritsiresaru and his son Pita-risaru (Man Chief) would physically remove captives from the sacrificial altar, angering the members of the tribe who were unwilling to stop the practice.[53] When Long's expedition reached the Skidis in 1819, the chronicler reported—incorrectly, it turns out—that Knife Chief and his "gallant son" had succeeded in ending human sacrifices. We do not know whether their attempts to change the Morning Star ceremony were genuine or simply political theater, but the chiefs' "civilizing" attempts nonetheless impressed Indian agent Benjamin O'Fallon, who "applauded [the Skidi] for their uniformly good deportment."[54] Just like the Chaui leader, select Skidi leaders and their followers looked to American representatives as potential allies and trading partners.

Just like some Skidi chiefs, the most important Chaui leaders, Sharitarish I and his two sons, Tarecawawaho and Sharitarish II, hoped to use positive relations with the United States—and its concomitant gift-giving obligations—to maintain political power within their tribe.[55] These leaders foresaw that the United States was emerging as the most important Euro-American power in the region, and they treated American representatives with diplomatic deference to avoid direct confrontation in their villages. Despite these amicable diplomatic councils, however, Pawnees had diverse responses to the growing presence of the United States between 1800 and 1820. Interactions between Pawnee raiding parties and American traders along the Arkansas River strained diplomatic attempts to secure a peaceful coexistence. This realization forces us to look at other factors in the Pawnees' participation in the 1833 treaty.

In 1828, citing growing attacks on the new Santa Fe trail, agent John Dougherty reported that "the Pawnees conduct is becoming daily more and more outrageous." At a meeting with Dougherty, some Chaui and Skidi "publicly declared they would rob and murder every white man who should have the misfortune to fall into their power," and if the Americans would meet them in battle, the Pawnees would "run them down like buffalo on the prairie." Dougherty explained that these Pawnees had such faith in their own strength that "one of their distinguished War Chiefs proclaimed that the Santa Fe road should henceforth become a home to himself and his band for the purpose of plunder." According to Reverend John Dunbar, some Pawnees did exactly that, taking up residence with the Wichitas on the Red River for more than twenty years.[56]

What accounts for this seemingly inconsistent attitude of deference to the United States on one hand and blatant antagonism on the other? One answer is that, as with any political body, the Pawnees' political strategy was not monolithic. In addition to tribal divisions, various members of the sociopolitical hierarchy saw different opportunities from a growing American presence. While established leaders saw a way to maintain authority through gift giving, younger warriors saw an opportunity to display bravery and raise their sociopolitical status through raiding. This dualistic approach reinforced itself: American representatives offered Indian leaders gifts in exchange for "peaceful relations," which led to more traders passing through the region, who then became targets for warriors' raids, which would initiate another round of gift giving. So, while Chaui and Skidi leaders benefited from peaceful relations with Euro-Americans, they still did not necessarily want their warriors to end all depredations against American traders—even if it had been within the leaders' power to stop them.

This explanation, while accurate, implies a conscious, coherent strategy toward Americans that exaggerates the importance of U.S. representatives in Pawnee politics. While traders and diplomats brought opportunities for both gift giving and raiding, these opportunities were not exclusively provided by Euro-Americans. In fact, the most important trade good was not provided by the Americans but rather by the Comanches, who controlled the entire equestrian population of the Great Plains. Virtually every horse passed through Comanchería, giving the Comanches unprecedented control of the technological, economic, and military evolution of the North American interior.[57]

Pawnee leaders were careful not to create any unnecessary antagonism with the United States, and they readily accepted opportunities to solidify their hierarchical status. Still, during the first three decades of the nineteenth century, the United States was not the Pawnees' biggest concern. Instead, Pawnee geopolitics was determined by the growing reach of the nomadic tribes to the west and the increasingly destructive attacks from central-Siouans to the east. Along with a steady supply of goods, Pawnee leaders looked to the Americans for security from these growing threats in exchange for signing the 1833 treaty, a treaty that would be foundational to how the West was drawn.

"A Most Discordant Portion of the Continent"

In 1809, a doctor traveling with the St. Louis Missouri Fur Company described the chaotic nature of the eastern prairies and Plains in the first years of the nineteenth century. "[Fort Osage] appears to be the general rendezvous of all the Missouri Indians, whose continual jars kept the commandant on the alert. Osages, Ottas, Mahas, Ponnis, Cansas, Missouri, Souex, Sac, Fox, and Ioway, all mingle here, and serve to render this quarter a most discordant portion of the continent." The doctor described an attack by the Kansa in which forty Kitkahahki were "cut to pieces," forcing the rest of the tribe to find security in the larger Chaui village.[58] These violent battles were not the result of some a priori animosity between distinct tribes, as many travelers suggested, but rather they were indicative of larger territorial realignments in process throughout the eastern Great Plains and prairies. We can characterize these shifts as central-Siouan and central-Algonquian responses to colonial pressures, but the specifics of both the pressures and responses differed significantly between groups.[59]

On the Pawnees' northeastern flank, the last years of the eighteenth century were violent ones, as the French, Spanish, English, and American colonial powers provoked rival Indian bands to fight for land, furs, and trade. As European colonial forces jockeyed for positions in the middle of the continent, fur-bearing animals were quickly decimated, and groups like the Winnebago, Potawatomies, Iowas, Omahas, Otoes,

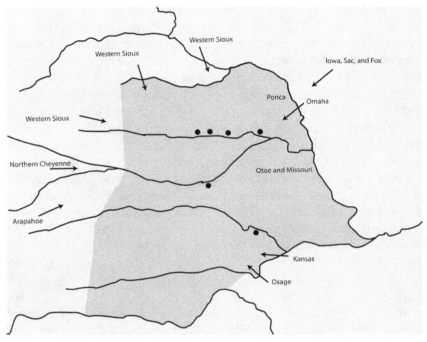

MAP 13. Threats to Pawnee territorial control in the early nineteenth century. Some of the groups—such as the Ponca and the Otoe—had claimed parts of the region for many decades, while others were new to the area. Dots signify the location of Skidi and South Band villages. Locations taken from David Wishart, *An Unspeakable Sadness*. Map created by author.

Missouris, Sauks, Meskwaki, and various bands of Lakota fought for control of what remained. On paper, the 1814 Treaty of Ghent simplified the imperial contest, theoretically reducing the colonial contests over furs and the alliances they brought. On the ground, however, violence only increased following the War of 1812. New epidemics decimated Indians, encouraging groups to replace their populations through raiding; American trading houses continued to facilitate the destruction of animal populations; and most auspiciously for the Pawnees, bands of Lakota joined together to wrest control from smaller regional groups.[60] This violence quickly spread west to include the Pawnees. After suffering multiple military defeats at the hands of the Yankton Sioux, an unknown traveler reported in 1819 that the Otoes had moved to their current position on the Platte River, "which is near the Pawnees, with whom they are now in strict alliance and friendship." As the violence continued to spill west, the Pawnees engaged the Sauks, Iowas, Omahas, and Lakotas in warfare. Alliances shifted quickly during this time, and it was barely a decade after the Otoes and Pawnees were in "strict friendship" that an Otoe war party set fire to a Pawnee encampment, killing five of their protectors and dozens of their horses.[61]

To the southeast, another powerful group of Indians was dealing with more direct colonial pressure. The Osages had long held sway on the lower Mississippi, as Thomas Jefferson acknowledged in the early 1800s. "The truth is," wrote Jefferson, "they are the great nation South of the Missouri, their possessions extending from thence to the Red River, as the Sioux are the great North of that river. With these two powerful nations we must stand well, because in their quarter we are miserably weak."[62] Beginning in the 1790s, however, immigrants crossed the Mississippi to build ranches and farms along the Arkansas River. By 1820, about five thousand migrants had settled on lands traditionally claimed by Osages. These settlers not only competed with the Osages for deer, bear, and buffalo, but they also tried to claim ownership by stating that the land was previously uninhabited wilderness, peopled only by Osage "savages." While such a story may seem familiar, in this case, the settlers were not Anglo-Americans but rather Cherokees. During the initial half of the nineteenth century, the first challenges to Indian land tenure in the trans-Mississippi West were frequently not from Euro-American settlers; instead, they were from displaced eastern Indians.[63]

Pushed by competition for game and warfare with the Cherokees, the Osages turned their attention to the northwest, the heart of the Pawnees' hunting ground.[64] While Pawnee-Osage warfare had been ongoing since the late seventeenth century—when the acquisition of horses created overlapping hunting ranges along the Arkansas River—the violence escalated as the Osages lost agricultural land to Cherokee settlers. In 1818, for example, the *Missouri Gazette* and the *Illinois Advisor* both reported that four hundred Pawnees killed nearly fifty Osages in an ambush near the Arkansas River. Describing the animosity between the Pawnees and their Siouan rivals, one Osage Harmony mission visitor wrote: "To cut off the head of a Pawnee, or even strike him after he has fallen is a source of greater distinction than the knowledge of letters or the arts of civilized life."

Similarly, missionary William Vail wrote that the Osages would "no sooner shoot a bear than a Pawnee and so vice versa in toto." In 1829, the Osages even volunteered to assist the U.S. Army if the Americans decided to use force to combat the Pawnees' alleged raiding on the Santa Fe Trail.[65] Although the government declined their offer, the Osages continued their own aggressive tactics. During the next year, an Osage war party drove ninety Pawnees into a lake near the Upper Arkansas, killing them all as they stood helpless in the water. Returning to their village with eighty-four horses and five captives, the Osages boasted that they had never shed so much Pawnee blood.[66]

Osage leaders also pursued military alliances with neighboring tribes to defeat the Pawnees. When Lt. Zebulon Pike left the Republican village in 1806, he failed to achieve either of his diplomatic goals: to impress the Pawnees with the strength of the U.S. military and to foster a relationship of peace between the Pawnees and their Siouan rivals. Unfortunately for the Pawnees, Pike was more successful in reconciling the Kansas and Osages, making them an even stronger threat to Pawnee territorial claims on the Upper Arkansas. Brief alliances between the two Siouan groups had occurred since the 1760s, which reflected the larger process of ethnogenesis—establishment of new ethnic identities—occurring throughout the Great Plains and eastern prairies. But Pike's visit was specifically influential, as evidenced by the drastic change in Kansa-Osage relations after his visit.[67]

On his visit to the Republican Valley, Pike's Osage guides steered him on a one-hundred-mile detour because they were "more afraid of the Kaws than could possibly have [been] imagined." Similarly, during the spring before Pike's visit, the governor of the Louisiana Territory wrote that the Kansa and Osages were "at war."[68] Immediately following Pike's diplomatic junket of the Kansas and Osages to the Pawnees, however, the Siouan groups spent the winter together, hunting and trapping on the tributaries of the Arkansas and Lower Smokey Rivers.[69] George Sibley reported in 1811 that, since Pike's visit, "[the Kansas] have formed such extensive connections with the Osage by intermarriages that it is scarcely probable that any serious difference will ever occur again between them." Edwin James validated Sibley's claim, writing that the Kansas had produced so many children of mixed heritage that "their features more and more approached those of the Osage."[70] Thus, while Pike's visit with the Pawnees did not improve the Indians' opinion of the Americans, it had great influence on other geopolitics in the region.

This renewed alliance had immediate effects for the Pawnees. It is no coincidence that the Kansas' attack on the Kitkahahki village that forced the Republicans to seek security under the larger Chaui tribe occurred just months after Pike's visit. In another conflict, eighty Pawnees were killed after the Kansas surrounded them in a shallow ravine.[71] Not having to worry about protecting themselves from Osage attacks, the Kansas could now concentrate their energies on pushing the Kitkahahki north, away from *their* primary hunting ground between the Republican and Smokey Hill Rivers. Even when a severe winter prevented any successful hunts and killed most of their horses, the Kansas continued their attacks against the Pawnees. In an 1831 report, Kansa agent Marston Clark wrote: "The Kanzas Indians are at this time as Retched as human beings can. . . . They are roving about on foot begging and stealing . . . driven on by distress they have renewed the war with the Pawoneys [and] have lately taken scalps and horses." This violence included one "bloody and unprovoked" attack on the Kitkahahki village in which nine Pawnee women and children were scalped.[72] The death of Osage chief White Hair in 1832 and a call for an "expedition against the Pawnees in honor of their chief" ensured that attacks on the Pawnees by the Kansas-Osage alliance would continue.[73]

In addition to the central-Siouans, who traditionally hunted and farmed land adjacent to the Pawnees, the 1830s saw a new threat to Pawnee territorial claims emerge from the east. In 1829, the Delaware Indians signed a treaty with the United States, exchanging their lands in southwest Missouri for a permanent home west of the Mississippi. These lands just north of the Kansas River included an area called the "Delaware Outlet," a tract of land ten miles wide and two hundred miles long acquired from the Kansas in 1825. This land would theoretically give the Delawares unfettered access to the western bison range.[74] Unfortunately, mistakes made by American surveyors undermined this agreement and ensured Indian warfare would continue.

On August 16, 1830, Isaac McCoy, his sons Rice and John, and second Delaware chief John Quick proceeded from Cantonment Leavenworth to mark out the boundaries of the newly created Delaware territory, including the "outlet" that would give the Delawares a path to the buffalo range in central Kansas. McCoy knew that this outlet would run close to existing Pawnee towns and would undoubtedly cause conflicts between the groups. Still, he had to get the Pawnees' permission if his plan of emigrant and nonemigrant Indians living close together would have any chance of succeeding. So, as he did when he met with the Kansas to "give them some explanation of our designs," McCoy requested a meeting with the Pawnees to explain his intentions. Though McCoy wrote to the secretary that the Pawnees "stated no objection to the prosecution of our work," he would later admit that he was less than forthcoming about the location of the survey.[75]

FIGURE 1. *Indian Record of a Battle between the Pawnees and the Konzas, Being a Facsimile of a Delineation upon a Bison Robe.* Drawn by the artist S. Seymour during the expedition from Pittsburgh to the Rocky Mountains under the command of Major Stephen A. Long, 1819–1820. Courtesy of Yale Collection of Western Americana, Beinecke Rare Book and Manuscript Library.

> I went into Fort Leavenworth on the 24th of September 1830, to meet in council one hundred Pawnees, who had come in agreeably to the message sent by express a few weeks before. They were informed that I was surveying the lands of the Delawares, but not that I should pass near their village, because their knowledge of the latter have exposed us to danger. We ascertained at what time they would be absent on their autumnal buffalo hunt, and that time we embraced to pass through the part of the country that was near their towns.[76]

Rather than engage the Pawnees in a messy debate over territorial limits, McCoy simply snuck around them.

Once McCoy finished the survey, he realized that this outlet impeded on the Pawnees' land more than he first realized. According to the 1825 treaty with the Kansas, the northern line of the acquired land—and thus the northern line of the Delaware Outlet—was to run in a straight line from the source of the Great Nemaha River to the source of the Arkansas River. But Angus Langham's faulty placement of the northeast corner of Osage territory combined with the Osage attack that prematurely ended his survey of the Kansas (described in chapter 1) left McCoy with "a want of correct knowledge of the geography of the country, by which I felt myself not a little embarrassed."[77] McCoy soon realized that the Delaware Outlet that he ran "near" the Pawnee village was actually in the middle of Pawnee territory. Even worse, there seemed no way to remedy the situation: "Should the line, according to the late treaty, incline southwardly somewhat, as has been heretofore supposed, then the termination of our late survey must have been within Pawnee lands; and, if another outlet should be set off north of our late survey, it would run still further on to Pawnee lands."[78]

In March 1832, citing McCoy's placement of "this slip of land . . . leading into the heart . . . of Pawnee hunting ground," Indian agent John Dougherty wrote to Superintendent Clark about the escalating tensions between the Delawares and Pawnees. The following month, the Pawnees attacked a Delaware hunting party, killing three, including a chief named Ponshees.[79] A new chief responded by burning a Chaui village to the ground while the Pawnees were out hunting. "I found [the village] full of lodges," the Delaware later boasted; "I left it in a heap of ashes." By the summer of 1832, due in no small part to mistakes by American surveyors, the Pawnee bands were facing a newly energized force of Osages, Kansas, and Delawares. As an Indian agent wrote to the commissioner of Indian Affairs in 1834: "The failure to extinguish the rights of the Pawnees and Ottoes [sic] to land between the Kanzas and Platte rivers, before assignments were made to emigrating Indians, caused a bloody war among the claimants, fighting on one side to defend what had never been relinquished, and, on the other, to maintain what was guaranteed by the government."[80]

Surrounded by Violence

In addition to the growing violence from eastern rivals, intrusions from nomadic groups to the west and north of the Pawnees increased as well. In 1822, after Maj. Stephen Long explained his party's desire to travel west via the Platte then south to the Arkansas, Tarecawawaho warned the Americans that the area was filled with bands of powerful

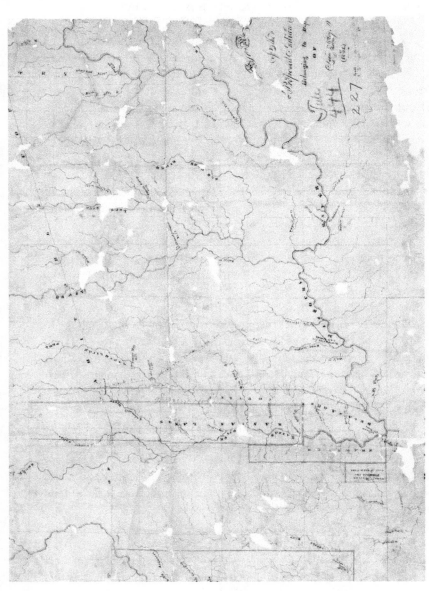

MAP 14. Detail of McCoy's manuscript map. The map has been oriented here with north at the top. The western limit of Indian country is marked by "line of habitable country." Notice also the Delaware "Outlet." Courtesy of National Archives.

Cheyenne, Arapahoe, Comanche, and Lakota. "You must have long hearts, to undertake such a journey with so weak a force," the Chaui chief cautioned.[81] Documents justifying the Pawnee's anxiety appeared a few years later when agent Dougherty reported that a war party of Cheyennes and Arapahoes had surrounded a large party of Kitkahahkis on a hill on the Arkansas, killing all seventy Pawnees, while a party of Skidi were similarly beaten by a Comanche war party the following year.[82] Neither of these attacks, however, was as ominous as the 1832 offensive mounted by party of Sioux. In a scene that would become far too familiar to the Pawnees in coming years, a band of Miniconjou raided a hunting village, killing at least nineteen. This battle marked the first mounted Sioux attack on a Pawnee village, and the battle foreshadowed nearly a half century of violence between the two nations.[83]

The Miniconjou were one of seven subdivisions of Teton or Lakota Sioux, who—along with the Yankton (Ihanktowan) and Yanktonai (Ihanktowana)—made up the Western or Plains Sioux.[84] Though never united under a central government, these groups shared cultural and political ties. Often several tribes would unite against a common enemy. Between 1685 and 1876, these Western Sioux collectively conquered an area from what is now central Minnesota, west to the headwaters of the Yellowstone, and south to the Upper Arkansas River. As historian Richard White has explained, Sioux expansion occurred in three distinct phases. The first was subduing groups on the prairies east of the Missouri—such as the Iowas and Sauks; the second was the subjugation of the horticultural villagers on the Upper Missouri; and the third was a sweep west and south to control the bison range in the central plains. It was this final stage that was so devastating to the Pawnees.

During the mid-1700s, the Western Sioux dominated beaver trapping on the northern prairies, and they used profits from the fur trade to acquire guns, with which they pushed the Otoes, Omahas, Missouris, and Iowas to the south and west. These weapons also helped to defend against Cree and Assiniboine raiders, who also participated heavily in the beaver trade. By the end of the eighteenth century, however, beavers had become scarce east of the Missouri, as did the buffalo on which the Western Sioux relied for food. Thus, a new phase of Sioux military expansion began at the end of the eighteenth century, which focused on buffalo on the eastern Plains west of the Missouri.

The Western Sioux's ability to defeat the horticultural villagers of the Upper Missouri was a function of biology as much as warfare. While smallpox decimated the Mandans, Hidatsas, and Arikaras, the nomadic lifeways of the Western Sioux protected them from the most devastating effects of a disease that spread quickly through the populous agricultural villages. Thus, while almost every other group on the Plains lost huge numbers to epidemic diseases around the turn of the nineteenth century, the Western Sioux had an estimated increase from about five thousand in 1804 to around twenty-five thousand in 1850. This population increase—coupled with a high demand for both buffalo and horses—made the third phase of Western Sioux expansion an important factor in the lives in the Pawnee.[85] In fact, this expansion was the most important factor in the Pawnees' decision to trade ownership of their land below the Platte River in exchange for the promises of security.

Until the 1820s, the region between the White River and the northern fork of the Platte River was a hotly contested area, as Arapahoes, Crows, Kiowas, and Cheyennes all fought for territorial superiority. Because only war parties would travel in these volatile regions, de facto buffer zones were established in which buffalo could find relative safety. Attracted by the dense animal populations, Oglala and Brulé Sioux bands began moving up the White River basin, driving the Crows west and forming alliances with the Cheyennes to gain control of the region. The Western Sioux occupation was initially not much different than the previous years had been for the Pawnee tribes, with occasional Lakota horse-raiding parties replacing the previous Cheyenne and Crow raids.

In order to supply their growing population in an ecosystem that could not provide their horses with enough nutrients, however, the Western Sioux soon stepped up their attacks to the south. In addition, the American Fur Company—the largest Euro-American trading company—decided that traders should set up trading posts among the Indians as they hunted rather than requiring Indians to travel to trading houses hundreds of miles away. This change effectively removed any logistical constraints to buffalo hunting that may have hindered the Lakotas' expansion to the south.

The need for better foraging range and more access to traders brought the Western Sioux to the Pawnees' doorstep. Further complicating Pawnee geopolitics, an 1831 smallpox epidemic killed so many Pawnees that they "ceased to bury their dead." The now-depleted Pawnees needed a new ally against the growing Western Sioux alliance. Although the Pawnees were still equal to the Western Sioux as one of "two master tribes in the Upper Indian Country . . . who govern nearly all the smaller ones," according to agent John Dougherty, increased attacks from nomadic groups to the west and Siouan groups to the east coupled with a damaging smallpox epidemic left Pawnee tribes in an untenable geopolitical situation: one that led to the transfer of nearly 23 million acres of land between the Platte and Arkansas Rivers from the Pawnees to the Americans and to the eventual creation of the boundaries of Kansas and Nebraska.[86]

"Our Friends the Whites"

A dramatic upsurge in violence and the sudden loss of population to disease left the Pawnees in a vulnerable state. Thus, when treaty commissioner Edward Ellsworth came marching up the Platte River in October 1833 to reiterate American friendship and—as the Pawnees understood it—to provide military protection, his offers were met with enthusiasm. During the ensuing treaty session, the head chief of the Chaui band—the most important diplomat in the nation—declared: "I now speak for all those young men you see bounding the door. They desire peace, and will eat out of the same bowl with all nations. . . . You cannot want peace more than we do." That chief, described as a "tall, powerful Indian" wearing a "large mantle of white wolf-skin," was the third Chaui chief since 1800 to answer to the name Sharitarish. He was almost certainly the son of Sharitarish II, who had died shortly after his trip to Washington in 1822.[87]

Like his father and grandfather, Sharitarish III recognized the potential advantages of an alliance with the Americans. When Ellsworth explained that he could "remove the difficulties" between the Pawnees and the surrounding tribes, the Chaui chief responded that the Americans "desire of us exactly what we wish ourselves." Chiefs of other bands followed Sharitarish III's lead, and they welcomed their Great Father's assistance to quell the escalating violence.[88] On October 6, 1833, leaders of each band—along with agent John Dougherty and Edward Ellsworth—signed a treaty that promised the Pawnees annuities, agricultural implements, blacksmiths, and other material goods, as well as diplomatic mediation. The Pawnees understood the Americans also to be offering military assistance against aggressive tribes in exchange for the "interest and title" to all lands lying south of the Platte River.[89]

In 1833, the Pawnees had little reason to believe that the United States would not live up to its promises. In addition to the meetings with Lieutenant Pike, Major Sibley, and Major Long, the Pawnees' trip to Washington, D.C., and their intermittent contact with Indian agents—from whom they received annual gifts worth as much as twenty thousand dollars—the Pawnees signed treaties of friendship with the United States in 1818 and 1825.[90] In all of these cases, the United States seemed to be living up to its responsibilities as Great Father by mediating intratribal disputes and providing ceremonial and tradable goods. [91]

The Pawnees' faith in the Americans was rewarded just one month after the 1833 treaty was signed when Ellsworth negotiated another treaty in which "the different chiefs and warriors of the small tribes of the vicinity of the Pawnees all agree[d] to bury their hostility and regard them as friends. These offers were thankfully received by the Pawnee." While the Americans' attempts at establishing peace were sometimes ineffectual—as they ultimately were with the Delawares—U.S. agents were nonetheless fulfilling their promise of diplomatic intervention in a world of increasing violence. As we saw with the Kansas and the Osages—whose alliance following Lieutenant Pike's visit lasted for decades—these diplomatic negotiations could bring about real geopolitical change, and the Pawnees regularly asked to see their Great Father in Washington to help them secure peace.[92]

Even more important than diplomatic assistance, Pawnee leaders were thrilled with the Americans' promise of military intervention. While the treaty never explicitly guaranteed U.S. military participation should the Pawnees need protection—only a supply of guns and ammunition in the case of attack—the Indians did not make this distinction. John Dunbar recollected this costly misunderstanding a few decades later. In his four-part series on the Pawnee Indians in the *Magazine of American History*, Dunbar wrote:

> The treaty of 1833 contains no direct provision that the United States should protect the Pawnees from the Dakotas on the north, and the Comanches and other tribes on the south. But unfortunately, the Pawnees distinctly understood that this was the case, i.e. that so long as they did not molest other tribes, such tribes should not be allowed to trouble them. Accordingly for several years they scrupulously refrained from any aggressive hostilities, though meantime suffering severely from their various enemies. It was only after a final declaration from the Government in 1848 that it had no intention to protect them that they at last attempted to reassert their prestige. Thus, during this period, while they stood in need of the utmost vigilance, the general influence of the Government was to lull them into fancied security and center upon them the intensified efforts of their hereditary foes.[93]

Dunbar's analysis cannot be underestimated. Until it became clear that the United States would not live up to its promises of protection, the

Pawnees limited both their raiding of Euro-American traders and their acts of retribution toward other nations, in an attempt to placate U.S. officials. Many leaders also took American protection for granted when they moved to a new village that put them closer to Oglala, Brulé, and Miniconjou raiders. This mistake led to huge material, cultural, and sociopolitical losses for the Pawnees. In essence, Dunbar recognized the same critical moment in the cartographic construction of the trans-Missouri West that is the focus of this chapter, a moment that the Pawnees hoped would result in military protection.

In June 1835, when Col. Henry Dodge led an expedition of forty men and three pieces of field artillery onto the plains to take an inventory of Indian tribes, the Pawnees were nothing but supportive. This American display of strength reinforced the Pawnees' diplomatic and military power by increasing their geopolitical authority with other groups in the region. Sharitarish III emphasized the importance of the Americans' presence during the council with his American ally: "It is the words of our great father that has caused us to throw our weapons behind us and make peace. Here are our brothers around us, they go where they choose without the fear of being killed. It is our friends the whites that have produced all this change. I am desirous to have as many red friends as possible wherever I go. Here is our father who is traveling all over this country. What is it for? It is for good; to make peace with all the different tribes and see his friends."[94] Skidi chief Big Axe concurred, stating that he now no longer wanted to die on a faraway battlefield, and he hoped an American-led peace agreement would allow him to die in his own village. The Pawnees believed that peace would be attainable if the United States fulfilled its obligations of protection.

To this end, a number of Pawnees accompanied Dodge on his expedition, hoping to make peace with the Cheyennes and Arapahoes, to whom the Pawnees had made previous overtures but had always been rebuffed. The Indians hoped that the dragoons' presence would encourage the High Plains tribes to return the symbolic gestures of peace that the Pawnees had offered them three times before. Appropriately moved, the Cheyennes gave the Pawnees twelve horses and promised peace. Later, the parties exchanged even more goods, with the Pawnees receiving more than one hundred horses and the Cheyennes getting half as many guns. It is impossible to know if either side intended to fulfill their promises, but these diplomatic gestures were more than the Pawnees could elicit by themselves.[95] The Pawnees placed great geopolitical value on their new American alliance, and the following summer, when

Colonel Dodge asked a Comanche leader how he obtained his village's American flag, the Comanche man responded that the Pawnees had sent it to them. The Pawnees understood the expansionist history of the Comanches, and they wanted to quell any notions the Comanches might have had of incorporating the Pawnees into their empire.[96]

Pawnee leaders also hoped that their Great Father could help them make peace with their most feared rival, the Western Sioux. When the Pawnees learned that a party of Lakotas were going to Washington, D.C., they implored agent John Dougherty to take them, so that a "permanent peace could be affected between them." Though we do not have records of their meetings, the Pawnees were reportedly "delighted" with the outcome.[97] After 150 Pawnees traveled to Fort Leavenworth to participate in a Fourth of July celebration the week following Dodge's visit, diplomatic relations between the Pawnees and the United States seemed to be at an all-time high.[98]

Beyond promises of security, the 1833 treaty included both ceremonial gift giving and a consistent supply of goods through annuities, which—as described at the beginning of this chapter—were necessary for a chief to maintain power. Pawnee leaders did not need many goods to maintain their status, but they did require a consistent supply. The promise of agricultural implements, guns, and other merchandise at regular intervals was very attractive to the Pawnee leadership.[99] In 1835, Sharitarish III stated: "I love you, my father, and so do most of these young men; and why should they not? They know that when you come amongst them they always receive presents." Little Chief of the Pitahawirat echoed this sentiment: "You pay our annuities and I distribute them among my people. They listen to me, but you are the cause of it all."[100]

In addition to the regular annuities, the promise of a blacksmith shop, replete with tools and iron, could meet the need for more immediate items. Thus, in the eyes of the Pawnee leaders, Edward Ellsworth and other American representatives could maintain social stability during a time when violence and environmental conditions were shifting village locations and tribal populations. Sharitarish III understood this when he told the American contingent in 1833: "I am in hopes things will now be changed; that the whites while not do as they have done. They go *around* us to get to the mountains and Mexico because they fear us; but now I hope they will come to us, as to a *home*. . . . It is a great distance to go to Missouri for little things. I am glad, of course to have a shop anywhere, but would like it nearer."[101] Like his father and grandfather, the Chaui chief recognized the sociopolitical benefits inherent in American expansion.

Even before the 1833 treaty, Pawnee chiefs wanted more regular visits from traders and asked that the Indian agent live with them to guarantee that their young men did not rob the traders who made the journey.[102] Whether this request for the agent to live with the Pawnees was simply to secure more visits from the traders or a tactic to defer any blame for the transgressions of young warriors away from Indians, the result was the same—the maintenance of status for Pawnee leadership.[103]

With the prospect of geopolitical and social stability, alliances between Pawnee leadership and American representatives grew, the most conspicuous example being the arrival of two Presbyterian missionaries in 1834. When Pawnee leaders traveled to Omaha to receive the first installments of the annuities that had been promised to them the previous year, the Indians met Reverend John Dunbar and Samuel Allis, who had come from Ithaca, New York, to start a mission. Although the two had planned on living together among the Chaui, leaders of the Skidi and Chaui tribes each laid claim to the men, hoping to benefit from the prestige and goods they brought. Consequently, Allis went to live with Big Axe of the Skidi, and Dunbar resided with the Chaui. For the next eleven years, Dunbar and Allis would live among the Pawnees.[104]

Although the letters of Dunbar and Allis reveal their ethnocentric attitudes toward Pawnee religious practices, the men respected the Indians as "kind-hearted, liberal people." Lack of support from the church meant that Dunbar and Allis were too busy with basic survival to impose any worldview on the Indians. The missionaries' tenuous situation no doubt encouraged a more positive relationship with the Pawnees. The Pawnees' seasonal rounds—including a bountiful bison hunt—required certain rituals, as prescribed by Tirawahut. When the buffalo appeared closer to the Chaui village than they had in twenty years—most likely due to the Oglala and Brulé's control of what had until recently been a buffer zone above the northern Platte—the Indians attributed their renewal to Dunbar. "A man has come to live with them who loves [Tirawahut]," an unidentified Pawnee declared, "and he has sent back the buffalo." Both the Chaui and the Skidi repeatedly proclaimed their respect for the missionaries. Big Axe declared that if any person should attempt to hurt Allis, they first "must step over [his] dead body."[105]

The missionaries were not the only ones who followed the correct celestial path. Returning home from Washington, D.C., members of the Indian delegation declared that the "white man does many things like Te-rah-wah [Tirawahut]." Perhaps clouded by his own optimism, Allis nevertheless had ample evidence that "a better state of feeling among this people toward our government and its subjects never existed."[106] Thus, during the 1830s, the United States seemed to be fulfilling its role as peacekeeper, and U.S. representatives living among the Pawnees were viewed as instruments for maintaining status, and if properly taught, they were honoring Tirawahut, not agents of a destructive colonial empire.[107]

Had the United States continued to fulfill its promises of protection in the coming decades, perhaps these positive feelings among the Pawnees could have been maintained. Instead of the drastic increase in Pawnee raids on travelers passing through their territory in the 1840s, we might have seen a more overt synthesis of American and Caddoan forms of territorial ownership. Perhaps the Pawnees would have given up ownership of the vast region between the Platte and the Arkansas Rivers, asking only to be permitted to hunt on this land, as Article Two of the 1833 Treaty explicitly stated.[108] And maybe the confusion over the exact boundaries of the cession could have been worked out diplomatically.[109] As we shall see in chapter 3, however, none of these possibilities came to pass.

With the benefit of hindsight, the 1833 treaty appears to be little more than a land grab by the United States. The meager compensation promised for more than 20 million acres of Pawnee heartland was—in the word of the claimants of the Indian Claims Commission hearing with which this chapter began—"unconscionable." A century after the treaty, there was much truth to the claimants' argument. In a court of law, where the oppositional nature of the dialogue eliminates the possibility of multiple narratives, the twentieth-century Pawnees' claim was more right than wrong.[110]

As historians, however, we have more latitude in our constructions of the past. We are not limited to the binary options that constrain a legal decision. In spite of later Pawnee claims, we must not assume because of the ultimate inequity of the terms that the nineteenth-century Pawnees were tricked into signing the treaty. If we consider the fulfillment of previous treaties, the prestige chiefs gained during these treaty meetings, and most importantly, the promises of protection from the growing violence in the region, Pawnee participation in this seemingly lopsided treaty makes more sense. In fact, the years immediately following the treaty seemed to validate Pawnee participation as an astute political tactic. In exchange for goods, mediation, and the promises of protection, Pawnee leaders gave up the rather ineffable claim of "ownership" to land on which they could still hunt. They stopped raiding the

American traders who now provided goods directly to their village, and they refrained from only the most blatant retributive attacks on rival Indian groups. During the 1830s, if one were to claim inequity in the terms of the 1833 treaty, Pawnee leadership would probably have argued that the Americans proposed the terms, and they simply agreed to them.

It is difficult to overestimate the damage done to Native peoples living in the trans-Missouri West by the nineteenth-century treaty process. Still, we must not conflate the oppression that the cartographic creation of the region has come to represent to many Native peoples with the opportunities that these agreements offered contemporary Indians. Territorial appropriation by the United States did not inherently mean the destruction of Native lifeways. The Pawnees ceded ownership of the land that ultimately became the states of Kansas, Nebraska, and Colorado with no more or less knowledge of the future than their American counterparts had. The boundaries inscribed in a contemporary map of the region were predicated on the United States' appropriation of land from Native groups. This process, at least for the Pawnees in 1833, seemed to offer as much opportunity as tragedy.

3 /   Nonparticipatory Mapping

Deputy Surveyor Charles A. Manners was accustomed to having Pawnees around his camps. For weeks the Indians had allowed the surveyor's crew to proceed "unmolested" as they established a guide meridian from the third to fourth standard parallels in Nebraska Territory. The crew was laying the groundwork for the rectangular survey that would eventually blanket the trans-Mississippi West.[1] Therefore, the surveyor was surprised when a group of "fifteen old men, accompanied by a young Indian who spoke very good English," ordered them to leave, "in the most peremptory manner . . . or they would be shot." Demonstrating the veracity of their threat, the Indians then "pulled up all the posts set on the north side of the [Platte] river, told us they would destroy all the landmarks made in that vicinity, and that we must and should leave." On October 6, 1855, Manners wrote John Calhoun, surveyor general of the Territories of Kansas and Nebraska, "The progress of the surveys under my charge has been suspended since the third of this month, on account of the positive refusal of the Pawnee Indians to allow us to proceed."[2]

At first blush, this historical snapshot resonates with the same ambiguous "clash of visions" that historian Elliot West has argued produced the violence that engulfed the Great Plains in the second half of the nineteenth century.[3] In this interpretation, the Pawnees' actions could be understood as a rejection of an incomprehensible territorial system. Yet as I have demonstrated in the first two chapters, the Pawnees and other Indians on the eastern Plains played active roles in the boundary making that would become the basis for the rectangular survey. If it was not the process of surveying that the Pawnees were responding to, what then was responsible for their anger?

Just two weeks after his first letter, Deputy Surveyor Manners again wrote the surveyor general after a similar interaction with the Pawnees. This time, however, the Indians articulated more specific complaints. "Their excuse for their conduct . . . [was] that *they* owned the land," wrote Manners. The Pawnees let him continue his survey only after he told them—perhaps disingenuously—"that we were only sent to survey [the land], and that we did not wish to occupy it, and also that if it *was* theirs, the running and marking of lines and erection of corners did not invalidate their title thereto."[4] The Pawnees did not lash out at the American survey party as a rejection of their territorial system but rather because they were left out of it.[5]

In this chapter, I argue that the failure of the United States to live up to their 1833 promises to protect the Pawnees initiated new strategic warfare, which gave the architects of the 1851 Treaty of Fort Laramie reason to exclude the Pawnees from the "largest Indian meeting ever held." This chapter ties the localized actions of a few thousand Pawnees to the creation of the trans-Missouri West as a whole, integrating ethnohistorical factors into a contested landscape and reminding us of the myriad of ways Indians helped draw the American West.

The exclusion of the Pawnees from the treaty session—and the map that accompanied it—both diminished their territorial claims relative to the Brulé and Oglala Sioux and allowed the United States to dictate the terms of an 1857 treaty held under very different circumstances than those at Fort Laramie. The ensuing six years of aggressive warfare had diminished the Pawnees' population, and the few dozen Pawnees who met the American commissioner in 1857 paled in comparison to the twelve thousand to fifteen thousand Indians who met their counterparts in 1851. Thus, although the participatory mapping of the Lakotas at Fort Laramie allowed them to maintain vast territorial claims throughout the nineteenth century and beyond, by 1872 the Pawnees had been forced to relinquish the last remnants of the land they had occupied for centuries.[6]

To understand how this happened, we must return to the 1830s and the Pawnees' burgeoning friendship with the United States. During the first third of the nineteenth century, the Pawnees controlled the region between the Loup fork of the Platte and the Arkansas River and from the Missouri to the 100th meridian, where the Great Plains transitioned from tall to short grass. They frequently traveled as far north as the Niobrara and as far south as the Canadian, through regions in which no

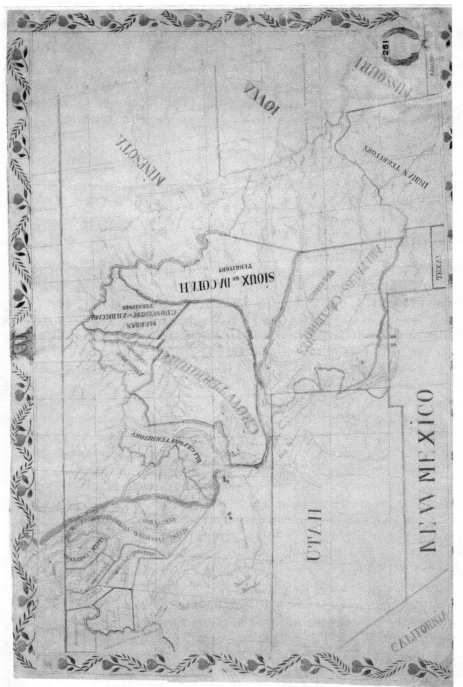

MAP 15. Father Pierre-Jean De Smet's untitled map from the Fort Laramie Treaty sessions (1851). Courtesy of Library of Congress.

single group maintained control. Indian agent John Dougherty wrote that the Pawnees "have great confidence in their own strength, believing themselves to be more numerous, warlike, and brave than any other nation on earth." They were, he continued, "without doubt the most powerful and most important tribes that inhabit our frontier." Scholars have estimated the four tribes to include approximately fifteen thousand people at the end of the 1820s, but a more useful estimate of the Pawnees' sense of their strength comes from Kitkahahki chief Schak-ru-leschar, who told a visiting German dignitary that his nation "numbered as many heads as stars in the sky."[7]

The 1830s, however, brought new problems to the Pawnees. Increasing violence and an 1831 smallpox epidemic greatly reduced their numbers, taking a toll on Pawnee lifeways. In turn, Pawnee leaders looked to a new presence in the region—the United States—to help stabilize internal politics and, more importantly, to ensure military and diplomatic assistance in fending off the aggressive Western Sioux. In exchange, the Pawnees gave up "ownership" of their territory below the Platte, although as the treaty stated, they could continue to hunt on these lands.

When the Oglala and Brulé Sioux brutally attacked the amalgamated Pawnee mission village in June 1843, therefore, the effects were dramatic. The Americans' failure to keep their promises of protection destroyed the political hierarchy of the mission Pawnees, who advocated a closer alliance with the United States. This leadership vacuum—along with the devastating failure of American representatives to live up to their promises—initiated a new level of aggression toward the United States. This led to the Pawnees' exclusion from the treaty that would lay the foundations of how the northern Great Plains were drawn. The ensuing map would also inscribe a new geopolitical entity onto the region: "The Sioux."

A Fateful Decision

For most of the 1830s, little was asked of the Pawnees in exchange for diplomatic assistance, military protection, and regular annuities. The Pawnees had stopped raiding American traders on the Santa Fe Trail, but the annuities more than made up for merchandise not acquired by raiding. The Skidis had essentially abandoned the Morning Star ceremony, but this was a political maneuver rather than one made at the demand of U.S. officials. And while the Delawares and other emigrant Indians impinged upon Pawnee sovereignty, the Pawnees blamed this on Indian malfeasance rather than American negligence.

It was during this period of good feelings that John Dunbar and Samuel Allis received the funds—and authority from the government—to continue their civilization program by creating a mission village. Many of the Pawnees were, according to Dunbar, "desirous that we should go out to their settlement, build houses, and live with them."[8] For their part, the missionaries were happy to abide by the terms of the 1833 treaty, but they wanted to do so at a single Pawnee village. In order for the Pawnees to receive their promised goods, they would have to relocate to a central amalgamated village.

A combination of environmental, cultural, political, and military factors determined the location of Pawnee villages. Large horse herds and a scarcity of wood encouraged smaller, more distant villages, while enemy raids and dynamic leaders made larger, denser villages more attractive. Similarly, while one oral history tells us that young warriors were encouraged to start their own bands, another reminds us that Tirawahut determined the sociopolitical structure, which had to be followed precisely. This tension between fissure and fusion had always been a part of Pawnee village life, but the 1830s' population loss, increased enemy raids, and internal political instability exacerbated this contradictory dynamic, making the missionaries' request even more difficult for the Pawnees to fulfill.[9]

By this point, however, tribal leaders saw the United States as a proven ally, and they welcomed the protection and agricultural assistance that a mission village would provide. Many aspiring chiefs also saw an opportunity for sociopolitical gain by abiding by American demands. Thus, when Reverend Dunbar was first given the authority to help the Pawnees establish their new village, he reported that leaders of all of the tribes—including the Skidis—were in favor of moving to a centralized location on the south side of the Platte, near the Chaui village. This place was "chosen by them on account of it being fine corn country," and while there was not much wood, there was more on the islands of the Platte than elsewhere in the region. What Dunbar did not mention was that, by locating this new village south of the Platte, the Pawnees would have a natural barrier between themselves and Western Sioux raiding parties. The Skidis had borne the brunt of these attacks for nearly a decade, and consequently they welcomed the assistance to relocate to a safer location. In fact, Capot Blue and a few thousand Kitkahahki had recently relocated to a new village south of the river for that very reason.[10]

Unfortunately, a few months after Dunbar tried to find a new village site in collaboration with the Pawnees, the reverend was told that the new village must be north of the Platte River, per the 1833 treaty. This left Pawnee chiefs with a difficult decision: abide by U.S. demands and relocate to a more vulnerable position or jeopardize a beneficial alliance.

Despite their people's increased vulnerability, some Pawnee leaders still believed that the United States would protect them. If—as Dunbar wrote of the Pawnees' wishes—they were "not permitted to settle on the south side of the Platte," they would move near the existing Skidi village. Big Axe of the Skidi, a consistent proponent of an American alliance, was the first chief to choose a spot for his lodge, followed by a Pitahawirat chief. While Capot Blue was "loath to leave" the village he had just built on the south side, he eventually relocated to the North Loup site. By May 1842, the head chief of the Kitkahahki, two prominent Skidi chiefs, and the third and fourth chiefs of the Pitahawirat had all moved to the new mission village, with the head Pitahawirat chief only prevented from doing so by sickness. Dunbar also reported that "the Grand Pawnee Chief Us-a-ru-ra-kue-el, the man of greatest influence in the nation," had moved to the new site. The missionary was encouraged that "so many of the most influential men have come at the outset."[11]

By the winter of 1843, the leaders of the Kitkahahki, Pitahawirat, and Skidi had put their faith in U.S. military protection and relocated north of the Loup. Joining them were all of the Skidi, most of the Pitahawirat, and a spattering of Kitkahahki. Nearly all of the Chaui and the bulk of the Kitkahahki ignored Us-a-ru-ra-kue-el's lead, however, and stayed at the village on the south side of the Platte with a charismatic leader named Sharitarish. This same Sharitarish would, in the following year, surprise Lt. Henry Carleton with his map drawn in the dirt.

Just before dawn on June 27, 1843, a Pawnee from the mission villages drove his horses a few hundred yards from their pens to graze. The Pawnees had seen traces of a Lakota raiding party for days—matted grass, pieces of feathers—and were on watch for an attack. Perhaps due to a protracted guard shift earlier in the night, the Pawnee fell asleep as his horses grazed nearby. A contingent of Brulé—seeing the horses and their defenseless caretaker—drove the animals away and killed the sleeping Indian. A Pawnee who witnessed the event hurried back to the village to sound the alarm. As dawn broke, a group of Pawnees set out on foot to retake the horses and exact revenge. The small war party traveled a little over a mile before they met five hundred Lakota warriors, led by chiefs Bull Tail and Iron Shell. After a brief skirmish, the overmatched Pawnees retreated to their village to protect their families. The Pawnees were no match for the mounted warriors, however. Oglala and Brulé men formed a line more than a mile long on a nearby bluff and took turns attacking the village for hours. A party would rush down the hill, gather horses, torch lodges, and retreat back to the bluff, while another party would take their place. Pawnees who fled burning lodges were shot as they looked for safety.

Around eleven o'clock—five hours after the first attack—a party of Chaui warriors from the south side of the Platte arrived after an eighteen-mile sprint, and the group created a barricade inside Middle Chief's lodge. Unable to protect the horses, the Pawnees did manage to hold off the Sioux for three hours until the attackers withdrew, taking all two hundred Pawnee horses with them. The Pawnees hastily buried the dead and returned with the Chaui to their village that same afternoon.[12]

The losses from this attack were tremendous. Surveying the damage the next day, Samuel Allis described Pawnees filled with arrows, scalped, and even some with their hands and feet cut off. One victim had a gun barrel thrust several feet into his body. More than seventy Pawnees— thirty-five Pitahawirat, twenty-eight Kitkahahki, and six Chaui—were killed, including the Kitkahahki chiefs Capot Blue and Mole in the Face and the head chief of the Pitahawirat.

On a strictly material level, the damage from the attack was devastating. In addition to the horses, the Pawnee lost twenty of their forty-one earth lodges in the mission villages. Unlike the Kansa or Osage who could construct a dwelling in a few days, the Pawnees' lodges took up to four months to build, and they remained intact even when the village was on the plains hunting. These huge conical structures measured between forty and fifty feet in diameter and twenty to twenty-five feet in height, and they held up to fifty people. The Pawnees typically had to plan at least two years in advance to locate, process, and season the willow saplings, timbers, grass, and other materials it took to construct the lodge. Their destruction put a huge strain on the villages.[13]

The Sioux's demolition of the Pawnees' lodges was also a cultural loss. According to Chaui oral tradition, Tirawahut told the first people how to construct a lodge: four poles to represent the sacred directions; willow branches to represent gods' ribs; and a conical shape to celebrate the life-giving powers of womanhood. Thus, the mud-lodge was an altar to Tirawahut and the center of worship. As such, one of its most important functions was to house the sacred bundle. "I will give you a sacred bundle to hang on the wall above your altar," Tirawahut commands in one oral

tradition. All the information flowed to the chiefs through these bundles, which instructed them on the proper ways to act. If these bundles
were destroyed, so too would the Pawnee people. According to James
Murie, "the loss of the bundle would mean the end of the religio-political
ordering which maintained the chief and held the people together under
him." While it is impossible to know how many bundles were ruined in
the attack, some of these sacred objects were surely destroyed.[14]

Equally devastating was the death of many caretakers of the bundles,
who were women. Perhaps as a function of stability, Tirawahut declared,
"woman will have command of the bundle."[15] While able to absorb losses
of the men who went to battle, the violence against women disrupted
both the Pawnee social system and the villages' productive capacity. This
was not by accident. The Lakotas no doubt understood the importance
of women to the livelihood of the village. While chiefs and priests dominated intertribal relations, women controlled the Pawnees' social and
production networks, responsible for everything from cleaning hides to
properly raising a hereditary chief. Women worked and controlled the
land, supplied foodstuffs and clothing, and had important ceremonial
functions. Women were also the heart of the Pawnees' kin network.
While the bundles descended through the male line—chiefs passed on
their status to their sons—the Pawnees were otherwise matrilineal. The
relationship between a mother and her child was the foundation of the
Pawnees' kinship system. As historian Richard White writes: "The kinship and status relations both created the political organization of a village and controlled the distribution of goods that the Pawnees obtained
from agriculture, the hunt, raiding, and outside exchanges. . . . The fates
of Pawnee chiefs and the buffalo, of Pawnee priests and women and the
cornfields were intertwined."[16]

Throughout their expansion, the Western Sioux attacked Pawnee
women as they traveled in search of wood, hoping to entice the Pawnees
to leave a contested area. Yet, none of the ambushes to this point had
reached this level of sustained slaughter. The attack on June 27 was a
direct strike at Pawnee social stability. A Pitahawirat chief described the
Lakota strategy many years later: "I am afraid not because [the Sioux]
would fight us like a man but because he will kill our women as [he has
done]."[17]

Material and cultural losses were great; still, it was in the geopolitical
realm that this attack truly initiated a new phase for the Pawnees. Most
immediately, it was the largest attack by the Western Sioux on a Pawnee
village at that time, marking a new phase of Lakota aggression. The 1840

peace between the high plains Cheyenne, Arapahoe, and Western Sioux allowed the Tetons, Yankton, and Yanktonai to expand eastward, as they no longer had to worry about their western borders. Superintendent of Indian Affairs D. D. Mitchell acknowledged this in a letter to Commissioner Hartley Crawford. He wrote that the Pawnee could always defend themselves from the Sioux, with tolerable success, "but this last attack . . . will greatly retard if not entirely breakup" the new agricultural village.[18]

The attack also worsened the tenuous relationship between the Skidis and a large portion of the other three bands. Despite the fact that the Skidis' village was closer to the mission villages than the Chauis', it was the latter who helped the battered mission villages on Plum Creek. The Skidis remained in their village on Wolf Creek, just a few miles away. Forty years later, Samuel Allis could not recollect the year of the attack, but he remembered that the Skidis remained spectators, while the Chauis came to the aid of the mission villages.[19]

The attack brought Americans promises of protection under great scrutiny and showed the Pawnees the dangers of a sedentary agricultural lifestyle. In his 1843 annual report, Superintendent David Mitchell summarized the consequences of the Americans' failure to protect the mission villages:

> I recommended the establishment of military posts for their protection. I regretted to find that the Genl. in chief did not concur. . . . Still I am inclined to believe that justice and humanity require it. . . . The destructive attack by the Sioux last summer fell upon that portion of the nation who assembled round the government farms for the purpose of becoming tillers of the soil. It is believed that a fear of a similar misfortune will retard all farming operations until such time as they can feel themselves secure against the Sioux.[20]

While Mitchell oversimplified the position of those Pawnees who had moved closer to the government farms, he correctly pinpointed the responsibility of the U.S. government and the ramifications of its failure to keep its promises. In a subsequent letter, Mitchell made this point more clearly, citing a provision of the October 1833 treaty.

In the 1833 treaty, the United States agreed to provide guns and ammunition in the event of attack. If they did not, Mitchell warned, "the Pawnees will say [that] if our Great Father had done as he promised by giving us the guns and ammunition we would have been able to have protected our wives and children from slaughter and our property from waste and plunder."[21] Mitchell even suggested placing a large field artillery at the villages to deter future Sioux attacks.[22] If this was not done, Mitchell continued, the Pawnees would surely face a "ruinous defeat." This proposition of defeat ultimately forced the Pawnees to adopt a more aggressive stance toward the Americans, thereby giving officials the rationale they needed to attempt to draw the Pawnees out of the cartographic construction of the trans-Missouri West.

"I Have Lost Much by Coming"

Immediately after the attack on June 27, the Kitkahahki, Pitahawirat, and Chaui Indians living at the mission villages retreated to a Chaui village on the south side of the Platte. Since it was only a few days until the summer buffalo hunt, the Pawnees quickly regrouped and left for the plains between the Platte and Smokey Hill Rivers.[23] While there had obviously been conflicts over the location of the villages and how much faith to put in the American allies, the schisms were not so great that the main body of Chaui did not welcome the now homeless mission villagers. It is easy to imagine, however, the heated debates that must have occurred between those who had stayed on the Platte and those who had not.

This division became more evident the following spring, when the mission villagers had to decide whether to return to the Loup and cast their lot once more with the Americans. Since most of the leaders who had initially supported the move were dead, those who returned would have to establish a new political hierarchy. This would prove difficult in a society that demanded leaders prove themselves worthy before being given authority—a fact not lost on the South Band members who opposed moving to the mission villages. Samuel Allis wrote to his superior in Boston: "Those that were killed in the last battle were those that had fulfilled the treaty by moving, consequently [the rest] are in a bad situation from the fact that those that are opposed to moving make use of everything like the present calamity to induce others not to move."[24]

Yet some South Band members who had lived at the mission before the attack did choose to return. Many factors went into this decision, including familial and clan alliances, the perceived ability of the Americans to offer protection, and opportunism by those who saw a leadership vacuum. Thus, in the spring of 1844, most of the Pitahawirat and a few hundred of the four or five thousand Chaui and Kitkahahki decided that, despite promises of violence by the Lakota—their agent reported the Sioux hoped to "exterminate the Pawnees"—they were better off returning to the north side of the Loup. At the suggestion of their agent, this amalgam of South Band Pawnees combined forces with the Skidis—who had also lost a dozen warriors and hundreds of horses since the June attack—to build a single fortified village, surrounded by ditches and a turf wall. They also requested two hundred guns and ammunition.[25]

Although the United States probably never provided the guns, the fortifications were enough to discourage attacks for the remainder of the spring. These barriers, however, did nothing to ease the alarms that made it virtually impossible for women to attend to the fields or to gather wood. Every time the alarm sounded, the women had to make a five- or six-mile trek back from the low-lying fields near the river to the village high on the bluff for protection. Then, once it was determined safe to do so, they had to turn around and head back again.[26]

Equally problematic, the Americans continued to alienate the Pawnees who had returned to the mission villages. If the United States was not going to protect the Pawnees, the Indians believed that they would at least receive the agricultural assistance that the government owed them per the 1833 treaty. Unfortunately, the Americans also failed in these obligations. These failed promises would be important factors in the Pawnees' decision to initiate an aggressive campaign against American travelers. This, in turn, gave the treaty commissioners reason to exclude the Pawnees from the 1851 Fort Laramie treaty.

In the spring of 1844, the mission Pawnees left their single fortified village, and once again they established villages along band lines. Though located close enough that the Kitkahahki leader described the Skidi as "among us," the bands maintained distinct agricultural fields.[27] When it was time for the Americans to plough the fields as promised, James Mathers, the head government farmer, declared that he would not plough the Kitkahahkis' ground until he had finished with the Skidis'. By the time he finished, it was too late, and the Kitkahahkis were left without government assistance.[28]

Some of the problems between the Pawnees and the government farmer resulted from a misunderstanding about the farmer's role in village life. As with most civilization projects, the government's goal was to teach the Indians to become self-sufficient. Thus, American representatives expected to help the Pawnees get started and then quickly turn the responsibility over to the Indians. The Pawnees had a much different interpretation. They believed that the Americans would provide a farmer to do the work for them. "My father told me he would give me a man to plough for me," a Kitkahahki chief declared in council, "[but] he does not plough for me." For the Pawnees, a farmer who would plough their fields was an essential part of their agreement with the Americans. The Skidi chief explained: "The reason I came [back to the mission villages] was I thought these men were going to work for me. But [the farmer] has no ears; he does not listen to us. . . . These men plough more for themselves than for us."[29] For the Pawnees, the farmer was not supposed to help a destitute tribe become civilized, but rather, he was to fulfill an agreement made between two nations. Despite their hope for protection, neither the South Band nor the Skidi leaders considered themselves to be submissive to the Americans, and they expected them to meet their obligations, both military and agricultural.

Unfortunately, neither farmer Mathers nor agent Miller shared the Pawnees' view. Unlike either John Dougherty or Joseph Hamilton—the previous agents who had a moderate understanding and respect for Pawnee traditions and political culture—agent Miller completely ignored internal Pawnee dynamics. Greatly overestimating his authority, Miller saw himself as a regulator, working to ensure the Pawnees were following American demands. It was Miller, after all, who had instigated the return of the South Bands to live in a single village with the Skidis, the same Indians who had refused to help the Pawnees the previous summer. Miller continued to show his contempt for Pawnee traditions when he called a meeting in the fall of 1844. Rather than holding the council in a chief's lodge—with the headmen of the various tribes, as was custom— Miller disrespected political traditions by demanding that the meeting be held "in the public square" and requiring all men, women, and children to attend.[30]

Even before this meeting, the Pawnees complained about Mathers's disrespectful and often violent treatment. Mathers repeatedly whipped and beat Pawnees "like dogs, without distinction to age or sex," for trifling offenses. Mathers repeatedly threatened to kill Pawnees, and on one occasion, he had encouraged his son to shoot a hungry Indian who had taken a few ears of corn from his field, leaving dozens of shot holes in the Pawnee's left hip and shoulder. The farmer also nearly killed a Pawnee when he found a missing ax in the Indian's lodge. While this punishment was not foreign to the Pawnees, it was unacceptable that a white man would deliver it. "The Chiefs and Braves tell us that if we will be still they will whip their bad members," Allis reported, "but it is bad for us to whip."[31]

Following this incident, the Skidi chief, exasperated by Mathers's disrespect for his authority, declared that he would no longer restrain his young men from committing depredations. Armed with bows and guns, the young men immediately began digging potatoes out of Mathers's personal plot, challenging the farmer to defend his property, which he wisely declined to do. Soon after, a combined delegation from the four bands living near the mission visited Daniel Miller in Council Bluff, demanding Mathers's removal. Rather than removing the embattled farmer, however, the agent promoted Mathers to superintendent of farms, blatantly disregarding the Pawnees' belief that they would control who worked at the mission. Thus, in addition to failing to provide military assistance, the Pawnees living at the mission now had to deal with American insolence and ineptitude.[32] It is easy to imagine how the mission Indians might have been wondering about the prudence of again trusting their American allies.

Miller's bungling attempts at maintaining positive relations with the villagers led the mission Pawnees to meet with agent Miller, Mathers, Dunbar, and Allis in the fall of 1844. The Indians were all in agreement. They wanted to keep Dunbar and Allis at the mission and remove Mathers and another farmer. After recalling the Skidi whom Mather's son had filled with buckshot for taking a few ears of corn, one Skidi summarized the sentiments of the rest of his people quite simply: "It would be good for him to go off." Unconvinced, Miller asked what this Indian was doing in the field to begin with. The Pawnee's response—that he was hungry and getting something to eat—was not what the agent wanted to hear. "How dare you go into the field!" the agent screamed hysterically.

Miller proceeded to proclaim the Pawnees a nation of thieves and to say he was ashamed of all of them and their chiefs. He supported the whipping of any Indian caught stealing. If anyone complained to his chiefs, the chiefs should then give that person another sound flogging. And if any Indian should mistreat a white man, their grandfather would "send his war chief with soldiers plenty as the grass of the prairies, and with his big guns beat down and destroy their village." This outburst was enough for the Skidi chief, who left immediately with many members of his band in tow, followed quickly by the Pitahawirat.[33]

Before the agent left the village, the head chief approached Miller to reiterate his concerns about the poor treatment of the Indians, and he warned the agent about possible ramifications.[34] "It would be easy," the chief declared, "for my young men to do bad if I permit them." Again, the agent promised troops and big guns if the Indians got out of line. The Indian responded that, if his great father sent troops, it would be good for him to die with honor. His father, brother, and son-in-law were killed at the village to which his grandfather had asked them to move. The chief reminded the agent, "And it would be good for me to lie with them when the soldiers come." The Pawnee shared his feelings about moving to the north side of the Loup with the Americans by stating, simply, "I have lost much by coming."[35] Whether the chief was referring to family members, authority, wealth, security, or political alliances, this sentiment was becoming clear to the Pawnee chiefs who had continued to trust their American allies.

For over a quarter century, the Pawnees' relationship with the Americans had brought status to individual Pawnees and a new material culture to the community. The Americans had promised protection and mediation that, though leaving much to be desired, required only that they give up some amorphous claim to land on which they could still hunt. After the Sioux attack of 1843—and the Americans' lackluster response to it—that equation was quickly changing. Punctuated by a drastic change in the tone of their dialogue, the last three years had proven that the Pawnees' alliance with the Americans was fatally flawed. The Americans wanted to dictate the shape of the geopolitical landscape rather than find common ground. Yet determining how the West was drawn was not so easily done. Regardless of American designs, Indians would continue to shape the cartographic construction of the American West.

"Worse Than Murder"

It is difficult to exaggerate the importance of this failed meeting in the fall of 1844. A government official who witnessed the talks wrote that, when the Skidi and Pitahawirat left the council, it was "nothing less than a declaration of war."[36] Dunbar reported that this meeting was the "most dissatisfactory to the Pawnees" of any council in which he had participated. "It will be a long time before [the Pawnees] forget this treatment," Dunbar reported prophetically.[37] For decades, Skidi leadership had been steadfast in their allegiance to Americans, even in the face of outright threats from other bands and dissention within the Skidis. To disrespect Pawnee leadership and to undermine a political system based on the ability of a leader to command authority was too much. While many of the mission Pawnees continued to live north of the Loup—if only for a few years, until another Lakota attack would drive them south—the opportunity for a meaningful Pawnee-American political alliance was now closed. The majority of Skidi and South Band leaders who had emphatically stood by the Americans now understood that their Great

Father did not see the same reciprocal relationship that the Indians saw. Instead, the Americans wanted submission, something that the Pawnees were unwilling to give.

In May 1847, after another devastating Brulé attack killed twenty-three mission village residents, virtually all of the remaining Pawnees moved south to join the South Band members who had refused to move north. While this attack also closed the mission, Secretary of War William Marcy still did not see this as a good reason to let the Pawnees remain south of the Platte. Marcy suggested that their army "destroy their villages south of the Platte; drive them north of that river, compel them to give up the plundered property they have in their possession, and take and hold some of their principal men as hostages."[38] On its face, Marcy's suggestion was uninformed and mean-spirited. In light of what the War Department knew about the situation on the ground, it was reprehensible.

Just days before the June 1843 attack, agent Miller moved his family from Council Bluffs to St. Joseph. He feared the Sioux, who were not only attacking traders and trappers but also "gathering to come down and attack the [Pawnees]."[39] Yet, even after learning of the vicious attack, the War Department continued to ignore calls for intervention. The agent for the Western Sioux informed his superintendent in St. Louis that the Oglala and Brulé pledged to come "in great numbers" to once again invade the Pawnees. Unfortunately, the warnings fell upon deaf ears, and the Pawnees were again undermanned and short of weapons when the Lakotas launched their promised attack the following spring.[40]

Repeatedly, Indian agents and missionaries stated that, if the Pawnees were to survive, they needed U.S. protection. In October 1844, Thomas Harvey, the secretary of Indian Affairs in St. Louis, echoed Superintendent Mitchell's 1843 call for the establishment of military posts to protect the Pawnees. Writing to Secretary of War Hartley Crawford, Harvey suggested that a strong garrison on the Missouri would provide "ample protection" for the border tribes and common hunting grounds by cutting off the "ingress of the Sioux."[41] In 1846, Harvey wrote to William Medill: "Not much can be done for the Pawnees in the ways of improving their condition, until they are protected at home from their relentless foes, the Sioux. It is greatly hoped that the line of posts contemplated to establish from Missouri to the mountains will preserve peace between the different tribes."[42]

Those who lived in what was still Indian Territory repeatedly recommended protection for the Pawnees, Otoes, Omahas, Kansas, and other groups vulnerable to Western Sioux expansion, only to be ignored by the War Department. Whereas the Iowas, for instance, successfully transformed into a fully agricultural society on some of the ground they occupied for centuries, the Pawnees could not even sustain the agricultural development they had achieved before the demise of the buffalo made agricultural adaptations more urgent. Just when the Pawnees needed to expand their horticultural activities, the failure of the Americans to protect them made that impossible.

By 1848, even agent Miller—who just a few years before was threatening to send "big guns . . . and destroy their village"—acknowledged the Americans' responsibility to prevent the outright slaughter of the Pawnees. He wrote to Marcy that a "war of extermination" by the twenty-five thousand Sioux who lived north of the Pawnees made it impossible to live north of the Platte. Reminding the secretary of previous attacks on the mission villages, the agent reiterated that a line of posts should be established in the vicinity of the mission villages, so the Pawnees had a chance at transitioning to an agricultural economy. Citing one chief's forecast that the Sioux would destroy the tribe, Miller wrote that if the Pawnees were killed, "it will be [the secretary's] fault." Refusing to give the Indians adequate protection, the agent added, would be "worse than murder."[43] Nevertheless, Marcy and the War Department continued to ignore their responsibilities.

The Pawnees continued to demand that they be given the protection they were promised. In May 1844, leaders from each tribe found common ground in their disgust with the Americans' attempts to help. Pointing to a mélange of combs, forks, spoons, pins, and tin plates that comprised their last annuity payment, the Indians scoffed, "See what our Great Father sends us to fight the Sioux with." And while the blankets they received were suitable for Indians at peace, the Pawnees quipped that they made very poor shields. When asked what they wanted, Indians responded with one voice, "GIVE US PLENTY OF GUNS."[44] Clearly, the most pressing concern for the Pawnees was finding protection from the Western Sioux alliance, but Washington officials continued to ignore the pleas of the Indians and those of officials closest to the them. Instead, their administrative time was spent hearing claims against the Pawnees—some as old as twenty years old—for alleged depredations.[45]

In 1846, the U.S. military was sent to the region. Unfortunately for the Pawnees, the flying artillery, blockhouses, howitzers, guns, carriages, and other accouterments that were "lavished upon" the forts of the eastern Plains were not intended for the Pawnees' protection from the

Lakotas. Instead, the Americans were preparing for a British attack. In fact, according to the *Daily Missouri Republican*, the "shirtless Pawnee warriors" could easily be kept off, even without big guns. Besides, they were too busy taking Sioux scalps, stealing horses, and participating in other "amusements incidental to Indian life."[46]

Rather than being viewed as a result of the United States' failure to fulfill its promises of protection, the incessant attacks and counterattacks by the Western Sioux alliance were seen—at least by one newspaper editor—as simply the high-risk games that were part of Indian life. The inability of American officials to grasp their culpability in the Pawnees' dire circumstances only furthered this misinformed view. Ultimately, it was the Pawnees—not the Americans—who dramatically changed their geopolitical stance.

South of the Platte

Unlike the mission villages plagued by internal dissention, the South Platte village remained steadily led by a Chaui named Sharitarish.[47] In the fall of 1844, Maj. Clifton Wharton and a detachment of the first dragoons marched up the Platte with the naïve instructions to "urge . . . the policy of peace among [the Pawnees] and their neighbors."[48] As the dragoons made their way to the Chaui village, the increased violence in the region was immediately evident. Posted at regular intervals for miles along the bluff, the river sentinels stood ready to warn of approaching enemies.

The village was situated on a high bluff that could be seen for miles in every direction, and two thousand Indians lived in fifty-eight lodges there. As the detachment approached the village, Pawnees on horseback met the Americans with displays of horsemanship and salutes to every member of the column. After an appropriate period of greeting, the Americans were ushered into Sharitarish's lodge, where they enjoyed a corn feast and agreed to a council the next day. It was during this initial meeting that Sharitarish drew his map in the dirt. Considering the Chauis' message at the subsequent meeting, Sharitarish's map's compatibility with Carleton's spatial understanding is even more noteworthy.[49]

A small group of Indians had been sent to the mission villages to join the council, but only a handful of Pawnees from the Loup arrived the following morning. They believed their invitation was from the Chauis, not "the White War chief."[50] Thus, when the council convened, the Indians who formed a circle at the center of the council lodge were Chauis and Kitkahahkis, with Sharitarish and Colonel Wharton at the center. Although he brought an impressive army, the officer stated that his objective was one of peace. As long as the Indians behaved themselves, Wharton explained, he would protect the Pawnee and punish any aggressive Indians. He then reminded the Pawnee of their obligation to move north of the Loup, as they had agreed to do in 1833, and he cited all the "advantages of instruction" that those who had already moved were now enjoying.[51]

While Wharton may have not grasped the absurdity of his claim—considering the Lakotas' attack the previous June—Sharitarish certainly did. After first thanking the Americans for improving the material condition of the Pawnees, he pointed out the flaws in the colonel's demands. "Our father promised us many things which we have not received," the chief began. The most notable failure was security. The Americans had never provided adequate guns and ammunition to deter the Sioux; instead, they had allowed traders to bring more guns to their enemy.

Rather than fearing American retribution, Sharitarish declared, the Sioux felt free to "come amongst us and burn our villages, and murder our women and children." In the South Band Pawnees' view, if the Americans were to follow through on their promises, they would at the very least make the Sioux return any prisoners they had taken. Or, as a Kitkahahki warrior would later say, they should at least pay retribution for all the Pawnees they killed. The Pawnees loved their Great Father, the Chaui chief explained, as he displayed the American medal he had received in Washington, but he saw no reason to believe their promises would be fulfilled. Sharitarish closed his speech with a veiled warning for the Americans, intimating that he was not sure how long he could keep his young men at bay.[52]

As if on cue, a Kitkahahki—adorned in Lakota scalps by the name of Tic-ta-cha-rico (Wild Warrior)—took the floor. Though he wanted to live in peace as his Great Father wanted, the "Sioux came down upon us and murdered our fathers, our mothers, our wives and our little ones; and the lodges in which they dwelt were burned to the ground. What could we do?" the warrior asked rhetorically. Though some of his chiefs wanted peace, he could not agree while his "people's bones lay unburned and unrevenged." In front of Wharton, he spread a buffalo robe that depicted of all the Sioux Tic-ta-cha-rico had killed since the attack. He then offered the robe to the Americans and resumed his position on the floor.[53] Whether the Americans understood it or not, the Pawnees were making a clear statement: if the Americans were not going to protect them, the Pawnees were going to take matters into their own hands.

The reception that Wharton received in Sharitarish's village in August 1844 was very different from the one he received a few days later at the mission village. This demonstrates the degree to which Indian agent Daniel Miller's disastrous meeting affected the Skidis' attitudes. At this meeting with Wharton—two months before agent Miller called the Pawnees thieves and threatened to bring "big guns" to destroy the village—many Skidi leaders still saw the possibility of a meaningful alliance. The leaders at the mission villages distanced themselves from both Sharitarish and talk of violence, emphasizing their peaceful nature. "I am a woman and know nothing of War," Petalesharo declared. Is-ke-to-pa said that he did not seek fights like a crazy dog but only spilled blood in defense of white men. Sta-ro-ta-ca-ro explained that he did not know what bravery was and had never distinguished himself as a warrior. Che-yene (the American chief) stated that, while he used to be a great warrior, his trip to Washington convinced him that he no longer wanted war.[54]

The Skidi leaders were not just telling Wharton what they thought he wanted to hear. Before Miller's outburst ended any hope of a meaningful Skidi-American alliance, Indian leaders living at the mission villages demonstrated their allegiance to the United States in a noteworthy exchange. Returning from California and his much-ballyhooed second expedition, Lt. John Charles Frémont encountered a group of Pawnees who displayed "unfriendly rudeness" and "insolence."[55] This demeanor was quite different from that displayed by the Pawnees at the mission village in 1842, during which the expedition "obtained a welcome supply of vegetables." Frémont was troubled by these attitudes, since he was "confidently expecting good treatment from a people who receive regularly an annuity from the Government."[56]

Between the time that Lieutenant Frémont received a "welcome supply of vegetables" and his meeting with the "insolent" Pawnees, the Lakota attack had forced most of the South Band Pawnees to adopt an anti-American stance for failing to keep their promises of protection. Meanwhile, the Skidis, who were not the victims of the brutal attack, continued to look to the Americans for material assistance. When Frémont met a mixed group of Chauis and Skidis on his return from California, his fate rested with the persuasive powers of the Skidis. According to Henry Carleton—the chronicler of Wharton's expedition—the Indians "passed part of a day seriously discussing the proposed measure . . . of murdering [them]." Ultimately the "firmness of the Loups (Skidis)," prevented the Chaui from harming the group. The Skidi escorted Frémont to his camp that night to ensure his safety.[57] Considering Dunbar's declaration that Miller's incompetence during the October meeting had initiated a "declaration of war" by the Skidis, it is very likely that had Frémont met with this group in late October rather than early June 1844, the cartographic creation of the trans-Missouri West would have evolved much differently.

More importantly, the willingness of the South Band Pawnees to kill Frémont indicated a change in geopolitical strategy. Led by Sharitarish—who would draw a map in the dirt for Carleton and Wharton just one month later—Pawnees living below the Platte now saw violence as their only option. The United States' failure to live up to its promises of protection narrowed possible Pawnee geopolitical strategies from an alliance with the Americans to one that called for violence against all intruders on their land. After the Americans alienated the Skidi and the remaining Pawnees living at the mission village, they were also left with violence as their only option.

Rise of Pawnee Militancy

In November 1845, the new Indian agent for the Oregon Territory and his three companions met "abusive, pillaging Pawnees" who relieved them of their goods and all their clothing. After what was certainly a chilly night, the four Americans were given "a few scant garments," supplied with "poor lame ponies," and sent on their way. The Chaui ensured their guests understood their request to leave by setting fire to the prairie behind them.[58] The following summer, newspapers reported that between four and five hundred Pawnees left some teamsters dead while they made off with 160 mules.[59] When agent Miller asked Sharitarish to return the mules, the Chaui made his position clear: if his Great Father wanted his mules, he had better come and bring plenty of soldiers with him. If not, Sharitarish warned, "they would *whip* him and keep the *mules* too."[60]

The Chaui chief was expressing a geopolitical tactic that he had alluded to in his 1843 meeting with Lieutenant Wharton but was now fully realized. No longer interested in an alliance, the Chaui leader saw violence as the only possible stance toward the Americans. After the 1843 Sioux attack—when the United States' inability to protect the Pawnees became clear—Pawnee attacks on emigrants throughout Indian Country drastically increased. Partly, this was caused by busier traffic on the Platte River roads, as emigrants made their way to Oregon and California, and the explosion of newspapers that could now print the stories of such attacks.[61] Yet, the increased volume of traffic does not explain why there were virtually no Pawnee attacks in the years between 1825 and 1843, when traffic on the Santa Fe Trail was at its peak. One of the few complaints against Pawnees during these years was discovered to have been set up by a group of white traders to look like an Indian attack.[62]

The dramatic increase in confrontations between Pawnees and emigrants traveling through their country was a result of the United States' inability to protect the Pawnees and the Americans' bungling attempts to placate the few Pawnee allies they had left. This change in political strategy resonated with many Pawnees. "[A] party of Pawnees," John Dunbar wrote his superiors in Boston, "composed of the ill disposed and unmanageable part of the tribe, have been on the emigrants route the whole time of their passing, stealing, pilfering, and robbing. These thieves and robbers live on the south side of the Platte." As Sharitarish's tactics gained influence, more Pawnees moved south of the Platte, calling into question the legitimacy of those who stayed north.[63]

From a nonissue the previous decade, reports of Chaui-led depredations suddenly became a regular occurrence in agents' records and newspaper accounts. The *St. Louis Daily Union* reported that the Pawnees on the Platte robbed fur traders of 140 packs of robes in September 1846. The next month, "400 to 500" Pawnees attacked a Santa Fe–bound government supply train, killing one man and injuring two others.[64] In October of that year, the Pawnees took arms, horses, and clothing from the wagon train, and they also found a unique way to express their attitudes toward their Great Father. After destroying the remainder of the wagons' contents, the Pawnees cut open three hundred sacks of flour so that the "prairie for miles around the spot was . . . as white as if covered by snow." The Pawnees then "frolicked in the flour," powdered themselves, and threw flour-balls at each other. They then turned the empty sacks into breechcloths, so that the letters "U.S." were displayed over their genitals.[65] On this day, at least, the Pawnees living on the Platte had the Americans right where they wanted them.

For Indians frustrated with the previous decade's geopolitical losses and raiding restrictions—limiting ambitious warriors' ability to gain prestige—Sharitarish's new strategy was a welcome change. By 1848, Pawnee war parties had gone beyond attacking emigrants and traders. Sharitarish's son was one of thirty who decided to "do some mischief" at Mann's Fort on the Arkansas River, resulting in a firefight and the chief's son's death. Dripping with symbolism as overt as that of a Hollywood western, he was wearing the same medal his father had shown Colonel Wharton four years earlier when he died.[66]

A year later, "60 hostile Pawnees" attacked three mail carriers traveling to Fort Leavenworth, despite the presence of a twenty-dragoon escort. The Pawnees successfully turned the mail carriers back to Fort Kearney and wounded seven of the dragoons.[67] That same year, another mail carrier—this one coming from Fort Hall—was "murdered" by "twelve Pawnee Indians" in Ash Hollow on the Platte. Members of the War Department were so concerned with Sharitarish's escalating tactics that they advocated an assault on his village. "I have no doubt but the Pawnees on the south of the Platte must be chastised before they will quit depredations on the whites," a Major Richardson wrote his superior: "Their village should be destroyed . . . the leader of their marauding party should be sentenced and executed . . . and some twenty of their principal men [sent to] prison for some months."[68]

Sharitarish's militaristic strategy benefited both individual Pawnees and the broader sociopolitical system. Younger Pawnees received new opportunities, and the strategy also solidified the South Band's political hierarchy. Unlike the villages north of the Loup—which had no clear leadership—the southern villages could again put their faith in the chiefs, the conduit through which Tirawahut instructed. This structure was the foundation of the Pawnee world. Without a proper chief, the knowledge transferred through the bundles would be lost. Without this instruction, the Pawnees would die. Sharitarish reaffirmed the proper flow of knowledge through a worthy leader.

Henry Carleton, the chronicler of Wharton's expedition, noted Sharitarish's command of the 1843 meeting: "There was no foolish clap-trap, or ridiculous intonation of voice, or unnecessary ranting about it. It was spoken in a deliberate and dignified manner; and with an ease and self-possession. . . . All was simple and strait forward."[69] This description mirrors what Preston Holder has called a "proper chiefly personality." Generalizing the characteristics of Pawnee leaders throughout the early nineteenth century, Holder writes that they were "quiet and secure in the knowledge of their power. Their voices were never raised in anger. . . . The image was one of large knowledge, infinite patience, and thorough understanding. . . . These were secure, calm, well-bred, gracious men whose largess was noted and who had no need to shout of their strength."[70] Conversely, if one failed to display these traits, even a hereditary chief would not have any real authority.[71] Certainly this depiction echoes the stereotype of a noble Indian leader, but it is meaningful, especially when compared to meetings at the mission villages, where the chiefs' demands for authority undermined their very claims.

Unlike Sharitarish's "proper chiefly personality," there was no clear hierarchy at the mission villages. Us-sa-ru-ra-kur-ek was unable to gain support from the South Band members still living north of the Platte, and the Skidi were also having leadership problems. At an 1845 meeting, for example, internal dissension is evident throughout the speeches. After the "First Loup Chief" declared his disgust with the mission farmer, a Skidi by the name of Spotted Horse said while he was also unhappy with the farmer, he was more concerned with his political standing. Spotted Horse wanted the commissioner to know that he was among the first to move to the mission village, and he wondered why he was not considered a chief. "I would like to know the difference between me and the chiefs today," Spotted Horse declared. Taking this claim even further, he asked the commissioner to "speak it that all may hear that I am first chief of my band." Yet another Skidi, Big Chief, also claimed to be the first chief of the nation: "The Spirit gives me power to be chief. . . . My father you see all the chiefs belong to me."[72] Unlike the Sharitarish's village, the members of which were unified in their decision to escalate violence, those Pawnees—mostly Skidi, who still wanted to stand by the Americans— were having a leadership crisis.

In the spring of 1847, a government farmer reported that the Indians living near the abandoned mission were "very much disheartened by so many staying on the other side of the river," and that these Indians were "more of a danger than the Sioux." While certainly an exaggeration, the Indians north of the Platte seemed to be in more dire circumstances than Sharitarish's band, thus reinforcing the viability of militancy as the most effective strategy. Major Richardson warned Harvey in the summer of 1847 that "[Sharitarish] is growing in strength and influence daily," while those who still supported the Americans had "lost their influence." Unless the government wanted "their citizens robbed and murdered," Richardson warned, immediate steps had to be taken to quell Sharitar-ish's expanding power.[73]

We have already determined two important factors in the rise of Pawnee aggression: anger at the failure of the United States to provide promised protection, and bungled diplomacy by agents on the ground. Still, part of the reason for the Indians' new militaristic strategy lies in the specifics of Pawnee culture.

When the most important chief at the mission villages told agent Miller that "it would be good" for the chief to follow his relatives who had died in battle, he was not making an empty threat.[74] Rather, he was articulating an accepted Pawnee cultural strategy; if death was inevitable, than there was no better way to achieve it than in battle. This tradition stemmed from both secular and spiritual factors. For one, the elderly and infirm were not given any assistance for travel in this society that moved at least every four months. So while tolerably cared for at their villages, the elderly and the sick faced extreme hardship during hunts, leaving hours before the rest of the group to begin their travel. If they were simply unable to travel, the infirm were left with food and the responsibility to protect themselves against Oglala or Brulé war parties. Thus, death due to illness or old age was not particularly pleasant.[75]

Perhaps more importantly, for the Pawnees—as with many cultures—death was not to be feared but rather understood as a gateway to another existence. At the end of the nineteenth century, ethnologist George Bird Grinnell spent much of his time among the Pawnee in Oklahoma, gathering ethnographic information. One of the stories Grinnell called "folktales" illustrates this belief about death. According to the story, a woman who had died in childbirth came back to visit her grieving husband and child. She asked them to follow her to a place where "no evil will come to you." The man, however, wanted the woman to come back to the living. After a long discussion, she agreed. All was well until the man took another wife who was very jealous of the first woman:

At length, one day the last married became angry with the other, and called her bad names, and finally said to her, "You ought not to be here. You are nothing but a ghost, anyway." That night when the man went to bed, he lay down, as was his custom, by the side of his first wife. During the night he awake, and found that his wife had disappeared. She was seen no more. The next night after this happened, the man and the child both died in sleep. The wife had called them to her. They had gone to that place where there is a living. This convinced everybody that there is a hereafter.[76]

Referred to as *ti-he-it-aruk-cu-ri-wa* (when we are all together again), the next life was partly based on the bravery of the deceased. One story explains that, after death, the spirit crosses a plain of thickly falling arrows. If brave, the spirit passes quickly through into a new country of leisure and ease. If not, the spirit is forced down a safe path, but it was strewn with axes, hoes, and other implements of manual labor.[77] In this example, collected in the late nineteenth century, the timid soul is not only unable to find the peace of the brave soul but also is forced into the intensive agricultural labor that the Pawnee rejected during the 1840s. Perhaps, had the Americans been able to protect these sedentary agricultural villages, a different story about the afterlife would have emerged. As it was, according to John Dunbar, son of the missionary of the same name, bravery was a "genuine Indian theology."[78]

This theology was articulated in another Kitkahahki story, in which a mother imparts the importance of bravery to her fatherless son: "I would not cry to hear that you have been killed in battle. That is what makes a man: to fight and be brave. I should be sorry to hear you die from sickness. . . . Love your friend and never desert him. If you see him surrounded by the enemy do not run away. Go to him, and if you cannot save him, be killed together, and let your bones lie side by side."[79]

This is not to suggest that the Pawnees relished death or wanted to die. Many years later, this same boy was captured by some Wichitas and intended to die at their hands. The chief of the Wichitas was so impressed with his determination, however, that he gave him his freedom. "By your bravery you have saved yourself," the head chief declared. This warrior not only saved his life, but he also renewed an important alliance between distant bands of Wichitas and Pawnees. The chief declared: "Let there be no more war between us. We are brothers. Let us always be brothers."[80] Death was not a goal, but if there were no other options, a brave death would bring more rewards than a cowardly one.[81] In 1852, an unnamed Pawnee chief said that he intended to stop traveling through their country, "for they were starving . . . and they preferred a more honorable death defending their homes and families."[82]

This strategy, however, did not come without consequences. The most immediate was the drastic loss of adult men. Between 1840 and 1860, the Pawnees lost approximately one-third of their entire population. As geographer David Wishart points out, many tragedies could show the depth of the Pawnees distress: a severe drought in 1850, two different cholera epidemics, and rapidly diminishing bison populations. All of these contributed to the Pawnees' population decline from six thousand in 1840 to four thousand in 1860. Yet, there are indications that warfare accounted for the largest percentage of deaths among the Pawnees. In 1848, Reverend Dunbar listed almost 30 percent more women than men over the age of ten. By 1859, that difference had risen to almost 50 percent, and it would stay there until 1872, when the Pawnees moved to what is now Oklahoma.[83]

In addition to their population decline, the Pawnees' aggressive strategy greatly influenced the public's perception of the Indians. In 1849, a soldier from the Oregon Battalion wrote to *Daily Missouri Republican* to allay a public "terribly scared" of an imminent war with the Pawnees. "Wars and rumors of war have been all the rage in this part of the world for the last week," the correspondent wrote. Though this spike in "public anxiety" was the result of a miscommunication, it nevertheless demonstrates the impact that Sharitarish's strategy had on public perception. According to the correspondent, two officers met a Pawnee near Fort Kearney who "commenced telling by signs and Pawnee language, neither of which they understood, some story, in which the name, 'Si-re-cherish,' frequently figured—together with the sign of cutting throats, &c &c. They at once thought, and very naturally too, that this chief, whom Col. Powell had reprimanded a few days previous, for his general conduct towards the whites, had taken the war path against us, and considered it their duty to send the Colonel the information, particularly as several of our train were still below the Indian village."[84] It was only after the battalion had put "the Pawnee village under the muzzles of two of our long twelve-pounders," that the Americans understood that the sign language was an indication of a "domestic tragedy" involving Sharitarish's daughter and her husband.

These two factors—a public "terribly scared" of the Pawnees and a steep population decline, both a direct result of the new militant strategy—gave American policy makers a reason to exclude the Pawnees from the most important War Department treaty session on the Great Plains. Adding to these dynamics, there was a treaty organizer with a particular animosity toward the Pawnees. Now, a clearer picture of the reasons for the Pawnees' exclusion from the 1851 Treaty of Fort Laramie emerges. While this exclusion was never articulated, correspondence and reports before the 1851 treaty clearly indicate that the United States had no intention of including the Pawnees in the "largest Indian meeting ever held."

"Displaced in One or Other of the Ways Mentioned"

By 1848, the idea of a single Indian territory west of the Mississippi (see chapter 4) had been replaced—at least temporarily—with a plan that called for two discrete colonies: one below the Kansas River and one in what would become Dacotah Territory. Although scholars debate the level of American malfeasance driving this policy change, there was no doubt that removing Indians from the Platte and Kansas valleys would—in the words of Commissioner of Indian Affairs William Medill—leave "six geographical degrees," in which the United States could provide "a wide and safe passage for our Oregon emigrants; and for those to California as may prefer to take that route." In order to implement this plan, however, the Indians previously promised homes in what would become Kansas and Nebraska would have to be moved.

According to Commissioner Medill's 1848 report, the Delawares, Potawatomies, and Kickapoos could probably stay in some portion of their recently created reservations, but the same could not be said for the Iowas, Otoes, Missourias, Omahas, Poncas, and Pawnees. Although the former tribes could be moved to the proposed southern colony, Medill articulated the special circumstances surrounding the Pawnees: "The last mentioned tribe are back some distance from the frontier, on the Platte river, directly on the route to Oregon, and have been the most troublesome Indians to the emigrants to that territory." Since the Pawnees were "so obnoxious to the tribes to the south that they could not . . . be colonized with them," Medill continued, "they must eventually be driven west or exterminated by the Sioux."

Since there would soon be a military force in that region that could "afford them protection from the Sioux," the commissioner allowed that the Indians could be "properly compelled" to abide by the 1833 treaty and moved north of the Platte. As Medill himself stated, however, "no amount of military force," had the Americans even desired, could "prevent the[m] being killed off in detail by the Sioux."[85] Thus, while the new de facto policy assumed the "border" tribes could be enticed to move to the southern colony, there was no plan for the Pawnees. Instead, according to Medill, they were going to be "displaced in one or other of the ways mentioned."[86]

While the U.S. representatives living closest to the Pawnees continued to plead for their protection, those in Washington had no intention of encouraging further Indian settlement in Kansas and Nebraska. The Pawnees were unique. Not classified as one of "our colonized Indians," as the new commissioner of Indian Affairs, Orlando Brown, wrote in his 1849 annual report, the Pawnees were in a particularly tenuous situation. Echoing William Medill's statement, Brown wrote:

> The smaller tribes scattered along the frontier, above the Delawares
> and Kickapoos, embracing the Sacs and Foxes of the Missouri, the
> Iowas, the Omahas, the Ottoes and Missourias, the Poncas, and,
> *if possible*, the Pawnees, should be moved down among the tribes
> of our southern colony, where suitable situations may be found for

them, in connection with other Indians of kindred stock. Such an arrangement, in connection with the change which must inevitably take place in the position of the Sioux, would, as remarked by my predecessor, open a wide-sweep-of country between our northern and southern Indian colonies, for the expansion and egress of our white population westward, and thus save our colonized tribes from being injuriously pressed upon, if not eventually overrun and exterminated before they are sufficiently advanced in civilization, and in the attainment of its resources and advantages, to be able to maintain themselves in dose proximity with, or in the midst of, a white-population.[87]

Due in no small part to the dramatic rise in Pawnee violence, as Brown had written the year before, moving the Pawnees was not, in fact, possible. And rather than address this inconsistency, government officials were content to let the Western Sioux displace these Indians who lay "directly on the route to Oregon," "in one or other of the ways mentioned."

As Brown suggested, however, simply allowing the Western Sioux to displace the Pawnees would not guarantee "unmolested passage." This would require a "change which must inevitably take place in the position of the Sioux," and the "other Indians who have so long roamed free and uncontrolled over the immense prairies." While the United States could coerce the smaller border tribes into recognizing the government's territorial ownership under the auspices of previous treaties, they had no such sway with the more powerful tribes to the west. Therefore, similar to the treaty sessions of 1825 and 1830 at Prairie du Chien, U.S. officials initiated a process to create legibility among their more powerful adversaries by creating discrete Indian boundaries. As the superintendent of Indian Affairs in St. Louis explained in 1849, "Each tribe could be held responsible for any depredations that might be committed within their respective territories."[88] Again, scholars may disagree about the veracity of claims made by various politicians and policy makers, who said that Indian well-being was the major impetus for the 1851 Treaty of Fort Laramie. There was no debate, however, that government officials wanted to create Indian national boundaries to clear the way for American transcontinental travel.[89]

But who, along with the Western Sioux, should be included in this group of "other Indians" that would establish each tribe's national domain? Historian John K. Killoren recently discovered a circular in the Jesuit Missouri Province Archives that describes the scope and intent of the proposed meeting. Addressed to "the Indian Traders and others, on the Upper Missouri Arkansas and Platte Rivers," the circular asks these men to gather "all of the Prairie Tribes of Indians residing South of the Missouri River and North of Texas" to a treaty session at Fort Laramie on September 1, 1851. Though all the "objects" of the session were "too numerous to be stated or commented on this brief Circular," the primary goal was clear: "It is hoped among other beneficial arrangements (intended for the permanent good of the Indians) that we will be enabled to divide and subdivide the country into various geographical districts, in a manner entirely satisfactory to the parties concerned."[90]

If—as Commissioners Brown and Medill both indicated—the Pawnees were not classified as border tribes who could be removed to the southern Indian territory, would they be classified as "other Indians" and asked to participate in the treaty? By the government agents' own reports, the Pawnees defined the circular's call for Indians who "infest the two routes to our possessions west of the Rocky Mountains" and face "great suffering" as their resources were being depleted, thus leaving them on a path to "bloody collisions and exterminating wars."[91]

Perhaps more importantly, the United States acknowledged the Pawnees' ownership of a large portion of one of the "two routes" across the continent. Just three years earlier, Lt. Col. Ludwell E. Powell had contracted a treaty with the confederated band of Pawnees. The treaty ceded Grand Island and a sixty-mile strip of land on the north side of the Platte River. While not large enough to ensure the unmolested passage of immigrants, it was enough land on which to build a U.S. fort. The Pawnees and the United States had differing opinions as to whom Fort Childs (later Fort Kearny) was intended to protect. The Pawnees hoped the United States was finally fulfilling its promises to protect them from the Western Sioux, while the War Department was solely interested in protecting emigrants from Indian depredations, primarily those committed by the Pawnees. Still, both implicitly understood that this land was the Pawnees' to trade. In 1857, under very different circumstances, the United States held a treaty session with the Pawnees, in which the Indians ceded almost 10 million acres of northern Nebraska. This cleared the way for the Union Pacific Railroad to meet the Central Pacific Railroad on Promontory Summit in Utah Territory in 1869. It would seem, then, that including the Pawnees in the 1851 treaty session was a forgone conclusion.[92]

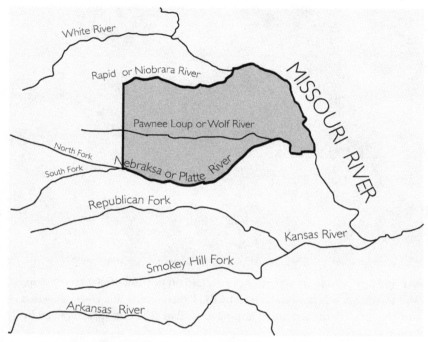

MAP 16. Study area, with the land ceded by the Pawnees in 1857 (Royce cession 408). Map created by author.

Yet this was not the case. In the fall of 1851, Superintendent of Indian Affairs D. D. Mitchell and agent Fitzpatrick concluded a treaty with more than twelve thousand "Sioux or Dakotahs, Assinaboins, Arickras, Gros Ventres Crows, Cheyennes, and Arrapaoes." The Pawnees, however, were not mentioned. Why would "the largest Indian meeting ever held," one that would establish future bargaining power by parsing the country into "geographical or rather National domains," exclude the most immediate barrier to a permanent overland route?[93]

As previously noted, the Pawnees' aggressive stance toward any intruders had a drastic effect on their population, which, by 1851, comprised no more than 4,500 souls. While those close to the Pawnees commented on the Indians' effort to combat population loss—in 1850, agent John Barrow reported an "almost astonishing number" of Pawnee children, and two visitors were "struck by the large proportion of children" at the village in 1851—many in the government agreed with Agent

MAP 17. Pawnee cession area in 1857, overlaid on portion of 1851 treaty map. Even by the boundaries established by the United States at a treaty six years later, the 1851 "Sioux Territory" impinged on Pawnee lands. Map created by author.

Fitzpatrick that the Pawnees were a "doomed race who must fulfill their destiny." A horrific cholera epidemic in 1849, which killed more than 1,200 members of the nation, only added to this sentiment.[94]

With a population that appeared to be in a precipitous decline and a public "terribly scared" of their repeated attacks on overland travelers, it is no surprise that the Office of Indian Affairs' plan for the Pawnees was simply to have the Sioux displace them "in one or other of the ways mentioned."[95] Yet, as demonstrated by the 1848 treaty, the War Department understood that the Pawnees must be treated with to ensure access along the Platte River. At the same time, travelers were depleting resources in the Platte valley so that it was "fast becoming uninhabitable." This condition—combined with the ongoing attacks by the Brulé and Oglala—left the Pawnees, as Jesuit missionary Pierre-Jean De Smet claimed, "in a state of nearly absolute destitution."[96] But with little public sympathy for the Pawnees, American officials seemed content to let the Western Sioux solve at least one of their Indian problems.

As with most federal Indian policy in the nineteenth century, some of the government's failure to include the Pawnees in the 1851 treaty was the result of a bureaucracy unequipped to deal with the large numbers of Indians under its charge. Yet, along with the evidence already given, there are indications that the exclusion of the Pawnees was more insidious.

The Treaty of Fort Laramie was the brainchild of two men, Superintendent of the Indian Affairs D. D. Mitchell and Indian agent Thomas Fitzpatrick. After returning from the session, Mitchell made his annual report, in which he explained that if the United States hoped to civilize the trans-Missouri West, there should be an "intermixture with the Anglo-Saxon race" and the Indians living there. "In order to carry out this plan," Mitchell continued, the department should establish "Nebraska Territory" with the following boundaries: "Commencing on the Missouri, at the mouth of the Kansas river, and running up the Missouri to the mouth of the L'eau qui court, or Running Water river; following up the Running Water river to its source, about thirty-five miles above Fort Laramie, where this stream issues from the base of the southern range of mountains, known as the Black-hill; from thence due south to the Arkansas river; thence along our established boundaries to the western line of the State of Missouri, to the place of beginning."[97] Mitchell described the treaty, at which a map was created that "shows the different sections of country claimed and occupied by the different tribes."[98] Aligning his proposal for Nebraska Territory with this map, it easy to understand why Mitchell was content to let the Pawnees meet their fate fighting the Brulé and Oglala.

The map covers the entire trans-Mississippi West, and it is dominated by territorial boundaries drawn at the treaty session. Along with the newly established territories of New Mexico and Utah, the lands claimed by the tribes present at the Treaty of Fort Laramie are inscribed in thick colorful lines. Similarly, the capitalized titles "SIOUX or DACOTAH TERRITORY" and "ARAPAHOES & CHEYENNES TERRITORY," for example, leave little doubt as to the landowners. While the territories of the Sioux, the Arapahoe, and the Cheyenne do overlap in the western third of Mitchell's proposed Nebraska Territory, most of the Indians' territory lay outside of it. The only potential territorial conflict lies in the almost invisible titles of "Pawnees," "Ponkas," "Omahas," "Otoes," and "Iowas," which float in the territory of the western Indians and "IOWA" and "MISSOURI." While both Commissioners Brown and Medill had planned to move the latter four tribes—whose inscriptions hug the Missouri River—to the new Indian Territory to the south, the Pawnees were—according to this map—alone in a no-man's land. Mitchell might not have wanted the

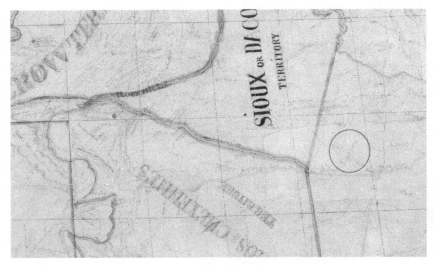

MAP 18. Detail of 1851 map. Map created by author.

Western Sioux to exterminate the Pawnees, but he was not going to do anything to stop it.

Thomas Fitzpatrick, on the other hand, endorsed the active removal of the group he saw as the biggest hindrance to overland travel. Fitzpatrick's own history is deeply entwined with that of the Oregon Trail. After working for decades as a trapper with the likes of Jim Bridger and Jedidiah Morse, Fitzpatrick helped to popularize the trail when he worked as guide for John Frémont in 1843 and 1844. By 1851, he was, as historian Robert Trennert writes, "a living legend." When it was announced that he would oversee the treaty session, one St. Louis paper declared that Fitzpatrick "had more ability to control the Indians than the Army."[99]

It was Fitzpatrick, after all, who wrote the oft-quoted report that demanded "free and unmolested passage" to California and Oregon, "cost what it may." Less often quoted is from whom he sought unmolested passage. In the previous paragraph, Fitzpatrick cited "considerable expense," thus far wasted on trying to protect "immigrants to Oregon and California . . . from the Pawnee Indians, who were the main and principal depredators . . . and have kept far ahead of the white man in the perpetration of rascality." The previous year, Fitzpatrick wrote to Superintendent Harvey with his plan for the Pawnees who refused to move north of the Platte: "I question very much whether the Panies will ever allow the government to benefit them much until they give them a severe chastisement, which must be done sooner or later. . . . You may rest assured it is the only means by which to reform, and bring them to a sense of their duty not only to themselves but to the government."[100] Fitzpatrick clearly saw the Pawnees as the primary impediment to overland migration. Including them in the treaty session would further impede passage to Oregon and California. Although one man's ego may not have been enough to keep the Pawnees from the treaty session, his personal animosity for them probably played a part in their absence from Fort Laramie.

In fact, according to an agent's report a few months after the session, the Pawnees claimed American malfeasance: "[One chief said] they never had fought the whites but he did not comprehend why his Father to not invite them to his great feast at Fort Laramie when he gave all the other nations of Indians the pleasure of their invitation, especially those who robbed and killed the whites . . . but he who submits to be robbed and murdered gets no favors shown us."[101] Although it is possible that the Pawnees were never informed of the treaty, a more likely reason for the Pawnees' absence came from Colonel Wharton. According to a letter he wrote in the summer of 1852, the Pawnees were "anxious to be present" at the treaty, but they were wary of traveling so far into Teton Sioux territory without a military escort. As the circular distributed by Superintendent Mitchell promised a "large military force" for the "perfect safety" of the Indians, the Pawnees "stationed themselves on the Little Blue River . . . and waited several weeks for Colonel Mitchell whom it was their intention to accompany." Unfortunately, the escort never materialized, which ended any possibility of Pawnee participation. Wharton never explicitly connected the Pawnees' exclusion to their "utterly abject" and "hopelessly destitute state." Still, his acknowledgment that this condition was "not a result of their own actions" and his explanation of the Pawnees' absence from Fort Laramie imply that their attendance might have alleviated some of these conditions.[102]

The War Department's failure to escort the Pawnees stood in stark contrast to the treatment the Shoshones received on their journey to Fort Laramie. After a war party of Cheyenne attacked the tribe—killing two—the Snakes (as they were called) demanded an escort, or they would not continue. Though it would have been a "ten to twelve day trip," Captain Duncan was ordered to take a portion of his command from Fort Laramie and "escort them in." This episode is particularly telling because as Indians attached to the new Utah superintendency, Mitchell considered them outside the treaty's parameters. Governor Brigham Young, however, acting as ex officio superintendent of Indian Affairs for Utah, saw a chance to wrest some territory from the troublesome Indians and ordered his agents to lead the Shoshones to Fort Laramie, where they participated in the treaty. With no such advocate for the Pawnees, they were left with no representation at the seminal treaty of the Great Plains.[103]

Creating National Domains

Until 1851, the only attempts to define tribally specific land ownership in the trans-Missouri West had been related to the idea of a permanent Indian territory. The 1825 treaties with the Kansa and Osage and the 1833 treaty with the Pawnees were only as precise as they needed to be, given the government's objective to create discrete spaces for emigrant Indians—such as the Delawares, Shawnees, and Potawatomies—on the far eastern side of the cessions. By 1851, however, political pressure led both the War Department and the Indian Office to see the division of lands among the western Indians as the only way to protect Euro-American emigrants on the overland trail. As Commissioner Mitchell concluded at the end of the treaty:

> The laying off of the country into geographical or rather national domains, I regard as a very important measure, inasmuch as it will take away a great cause of quarrel among themselves, and at the same time enable the Government to ascertain who are the depredators, should depredations hereafter be committed. The accompanying map, upon which these national boundaries are clearly marked and defined, was made in the presence of the Indians, and fully approved and sanctioned by all. As a map of reference, it will be of great service to the Department.[104]

The Treaty of Fort Laramie established the basis for all further land claims on the northern Great Plains. Article 5 established the "territory of the Sioux or Dahcotah Nation" as:

> Commencing the mouth of the White Earth River, on the Missouri River; thence in a southwesterly direction to the forks of the Platte River; thence up the north fork of the Platte River to a point known as the Red Buts, or where the road leaves the river; thence along the range of mountains known as the Black Hills, to the head-waters

of Heart River; thence down Heart River to its mouth; and thence down the Missouri River to the place of beginning.

To understand the importance of this treaty to the Brulé, we must address two aspects of this article. The first is the placement of the boundaries that inscribed a huge parcel of land—some if it claimed by other tribes—for the Sioux. The second is the very existence of a "Sioux or Dahcotah Nation."[105]

Despite the definite description, much of the territory claimed by the Sioux was still contested. While the 1840 Great Peace among the High Plains tribes may have garnered some territorial compensation for the Kiowa and Cheyenne—who had been forced west by the expanding Western Sioux—it gave no relief to the tribes pushed east, such as the Pawnee, Omaha, and Ponca, leaving them no choice but to fight the Lakota militarily. In 1855, Gouverneur Kemble Warren explored the region lying between the Black Hills and the Missouri River, and he described the tenuous geopolitical situation: "This is the common war ground for the Dacotas, Crows, Omahas, Poncas, and Pawnees. The character of the country is well calculated to cover a stealthy approach or retreat, and if one keeps as much as possible in the hollows he may even fire his rifle within a quarter of a mile of an enemy's camp without the faintest sound reaching it. Two parties may pass close without it being aware of each other's presence, and I consider it hopeless to attempt to capture any who had sought refuge in the Sand Hills."[106] Reinforcing the Pawnees' claim to the region, a Chaui named Tom Morgan declared during the Indian Claims Commission hearings that "his uncle used to tell him that they also used to go hunting north of the Platte River, clear up to the Niobrara, and by that, he believed this land belonged to the Pawnees too."[107]

Ponca chiefs, too, reinforced the contested nature of this area at a treaty meeting in 1858. At this meeting, the Ponca delineated their land as running "from the Ioway fields to the Black Hills, from thence to the head of waters of White (Earth) River and from thence down to the mouth of the same. This is what we have heard from our forefathers."[108] Countering this claim, the American treaty commissioner showed the Ponca chiefs the map created at the Fort Laramie Treaty.

> I want you all to look at this map [Father De Smet's] and delineate thereon, with the aid of your friends now present, what you consider your boundaries. . . . Do you not know that a portion of the Sioux claim and occupy some of the land embraced within the

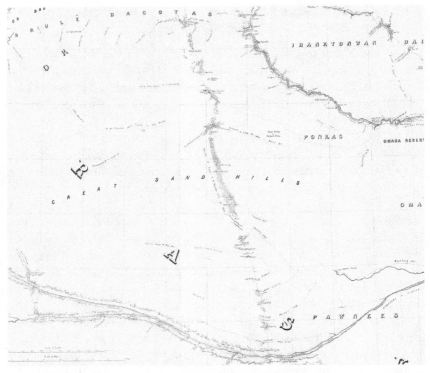

MAP 19. Detail of Warren's *Reconnoissances in the Dacota Country*, printed in "Explorations in the Dacota Country in the 1855," by Lieut. G. K. Warren, 34 Cong., 1st sess., S. Ex. Doc. 76. The control of the Great Sand Hills was still ambiguous in 1855 (as hinted at in Warren's cartographic labeling), bringing further into question the 1851 Fort Laramie boundaries that gave "The Sioux" territorial ownership of them.

boundary which you have described? I presume you have heard of a Military post, called "Fort Laramie." At the treaty of 1851 at that fort, it will be seen that a large portion of the country now claimed by you was awarded to the Dacotah Sioux.

The Ponca chief Whip replied: "It makes me feel bad—it makes me fairly sweat that when I hear that others have been claiming our land. I am so distressed at it, that I am hardly fit to look at my great father."[109] Thus, the creation of the "Sioux Territory" during the 1851 treaty session inscribed Lakota control onto what was still a highly contested area.

The scope of the Sioux claim delineated at Fort Laramie was supported by the aggregate capabilities of the Western Sioux warriors. As Black Hawk, an Oglala chief, explained during the session, "these lands once belonged to the Kiowas and Crows, but we whipped these nations out of them, and in this we did what the white men do when they want the lands of the Indians."[110] Yet, there is no reason to assume that Black Hawk was speaking of the Lakota as a whole. As historians such as Richard White and Jeffrey Ostler have shown, the Western Sioux were linked by common culture and language, but almost no evidence suggests that geopolitical decisions were coordinated beyond the *tiyospaye* (sometimes glossed as "band," but literally it means a group of people living together). Black Hawk demonstrated this when he explained that the land was taken by a combined force of "Cheyenne, Arrapahoes, and Ogallalahs." Thus, it wasn't "the Sioux," or even "the Teton" or "the Lakota" for whom Black Hawk spoke, but as he specified, it was the "Ogallalahs" who "claim their share of the country."[111]

In fact, the greatest obstacles for the American commissioners during the treaty session was not *where* each group's boundaries would lie, but of *whom* each group would consist. After a few days of preliminary protocol, Colonel Mitchell explained that the gathering should "divide into geographical districts—that the country and its boundaries shall be designated by such rivers, mountains and lines as will show what country each nation claims." However, Mitchell continued, your Great Father will not recognize "bands or small tribes" and will only deal with "the tribe or nation as a whole." As they had for decades, the United States wanted to treat with the most powerful political unit to create administrative legibility.[112]

The Lakotas had no qualms about dividing the country into geographical units, but they refused to appoint a chief to speak for the entire population. Terre Blue, a Brulé chief, agreed that "some things you propose are very well," but "we have decided differently from you . . . about this Chief for the nation. We want a Chief for one's band." A correspondent from the *Daily Missouri Republican* reported that this sentiment was shared by almost all the Lakota: "A number of speeches were made by the chiefs from the various bands of Sioux, giving reasons why could not select a principal chief for the whole nation."[113] Later, the paper stated emphatically that the "only difficulty that presented itself was the selection of a *Chief* for the Sioux nation."

Ultimately, Colonel Mitchell cajoled a young Brulé named Mahtoe-wah-ye-whey (Scattering Bear) to accept the position, despite his protesting that he was "not a powerful chief, and [his] opponents would be on [his] trail all the time."[114] Thus on September 12—an "entire day given up to an attempt to designate on the map the territory of each of the nations, and to mark it, by metes and bounds"—it was the "Sioux or Dacotah Nation" whose collective territory would be inscribed on the map rather than any existing geopolitical units of the Lakota.

This is another notable legacy of the 1851 Treaty of Fort Laramie. For the United States, the location of "national domains" was much less important than to whom these territories were assigned. As Mitchell told the Indian representatives bickering over boundary lines, "fixing a boundary to their country, had no purpose of limiting them to that boundary in hunting or to prohibit them from going into the territory of another Nation, so long as they remained at peace."[115] Instead, as Mitchell reported at the end of the session, "the laying off of the country into geographical or rather National domains will . . . enable the Government to ascertain who are the depredators."[116]

Since neither the Pawnees nor the Poncas had been included in the treaty session, the United States would have encouraged the Brulé to claim as much land as possible in the contested area from the Niobrara to the Platte River—an area of several hundred square miles—making both administrative and future land claims more legible. The government would no longer have to manage the claims of Pawnee, Ponca, Brulé, and other Sioux depredations. In 1855, Warren wrote that "many of the depredations along the Platte are committed by the Unkpapas and Sihasaps [Blackfeet], whose homes are further from it than any of the other Titonwans and the Isanties or Dacotas of the St. Peter's also carry their ravages into Nebraska." From now on, the War Department could simply hold "the Sioux" accountable.

The man who created the cartographic companion to the text of the treaty was Pierre-Jean De Smet, a Catholic missionary who had spent almost a decade attempting to establish himself among the tribes of the Upper Missouri.[117] Along with Fitzpatrick, De Smet had—at least according to the *Daily Missouri Republican*—"a more perfect knowledge of the topography of the country, than anyone now living." Thus, when Commissioner Mitchell discovered that he was planning to establish a mission on the Upper Missouri, "chiefly among the Yancton Sioux, Crows and Blackfeet," he asked for De Smet's help in determining each tribe's national domain. The "Sioux," "Crow," and "Blackfoot" *might* have had undisputed control of the massive territories depicted on the map. It is also true, however, that inscribing each tribe with such a large domain could only underscore the importance of De Smet's establishing missions among these three tribes.[118]

It is impossible to know what the northern Great Plains would have looked like if the Pawnees been included in the 1851 Fort Laramie Treaty. It is difficult to believe that their exclusion—and the coalescing of a geopolitical unit known as the Sioux—did not have an impact on their respective futures. The Pawnees continued their dramatic population loss until 1872, when fewer than 2,500 gave up their last remaining land in Nebraska and moved to Indian Territory.

The Western Sioux, on the other hand, continued to expand until the 1870s. At the same time, the boundaries established at the 1851 treaty became the foundation of the 1868 Fort Laramie Treaty session, which became the heart of a land claims case that continues to reverberate into the twenty-first century.[119]

PART 2

The Rise and Fall of "Indian Country"

4 / The Cultural Construction of "Indian Country"

During the first half of the nineteenth century, Indians dictated the geopolitics of the trans-Missouri West. Although Indians and Americans both debated the possibility of a permanent Indian territory, and Euro-Americans settled past the Mississippi River, Native people were the final arbiters of the geopolitics of the Plains. As a result, Indians were inscribed in cartographic depictions of the western half of the continent. Many commercially printed maps, for example, took *Lewis and Clark's Track, across the Western Portion of North America from the Mississippi to the Pacific Ocean* (1814) as their starting point.[1] Exemplifying Indians' cartographic presence, it placed "4,000 souls" of the "Great Pawnee and Republican Vill[age]" on the south side of the Platte River.

As the century wore on, the maelstrom of Indian villages drawn on maps such as Lewis and Clark's were simplified to depict larger (and often more imposing) tribally controlled areas. As the United States made treaties with Indian groups, Americans helped consolidate and circumscribe tribal identities and their concomitant territorial claims.[2] Yet, this fact does not fully explain why the Indian cartographic presence in the trans-Missouri West increased in the second quarter of the nineteenth century. This shift is demonstrated by the growth of depictions of "Indian Territory" in the land immediately west of the Missouri River.[3] Even as the possibility of an organized political territory faded, the cartographic presence of Indians continued to increase. In 1844, the *Democratic Review*—the same publication in which John L. O'Sullivan would

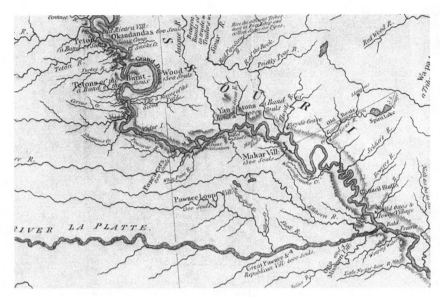

MAP 20. Detail of *Map of Lewis and Clark's Track, Across the Western Portion of North America.* Courtesy of David Rumsey Historical Map Collection.

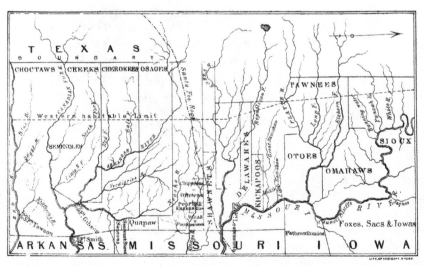

MAP 21. Map accompanying an article in the 1844 *Democratic Review* defining the trans-Missouri West as "Indian Territory." As with Isaac McCoy's original on which this map is based, the compass rose points to the right side of the page to indicate north.

MAP 22. Map from William C. Woodbridge, *Modern School Geography* (Hartford CT: Belknap and Hamersley, 1844).

coin the term "Manifest Destiny" the following year—printed a map that *defined* the trans-Missouri West as Indian Territory.[4] Why would this ardently expansionist newspaper print a map that firmly inscribed Indians as an obstacle to the opening of the West to Euro-American settlement?

The same question could be asked of William Woodbridge's popular 1844 textbook, *Modern School Geography*. In this book, "Indian Territory" dominates the center of map, filling the space from the Missouri River in the north to the Red River in the south, and from the western boundary of Missouri in the east to the Rocky Mountains in the west. This strong assertion of Indian presence is curious, especially considering another Woodbridge map that appeared in his 1826 school atlas and was reprinted in new editions for more than a decade. In his *Moral and Political Chart of the Inhabited World*, Woodbridge color-coded parts of the globe to show their level of civilization. The lightest shades indicated areas that were "civilized," and the darkest hatching showed the "savage" areas. The "unsubdued" region of North America was larger than that of any other continent.[5] Considering his implicit endorsement of enlightened expansion, why would Woodbridge give credence to a geopolitical construction that was not even formally recognized? Why not simply ignore Indians?

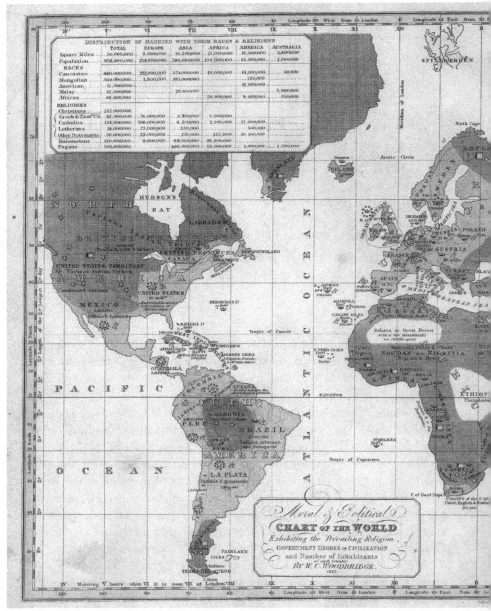

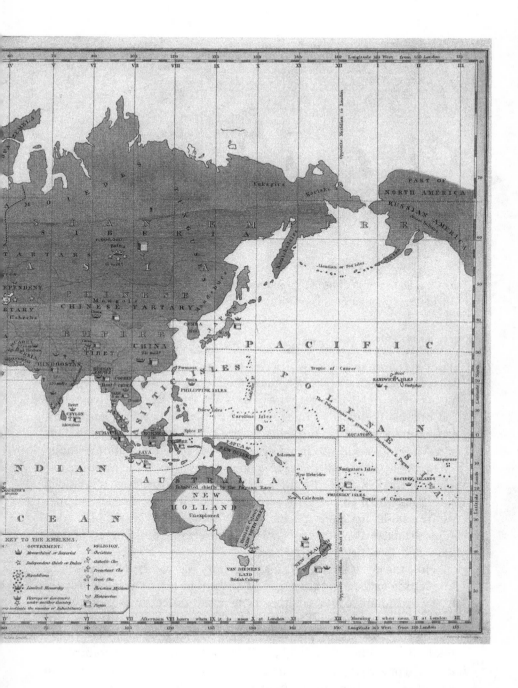

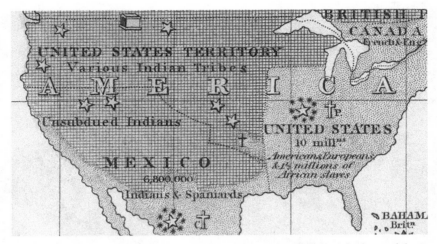

MAP 24. Detail of William C. Woodbridge, *Moral and Political Chart of the World* (1828). Courtesy of David Rumsey Historical Map Collection.

One answer is that for American politicians unsure about the United States' standing in the world, solving the "Indian Problem" would prove its credentials as a truly enlightened country. By the middle of the 1820s, the American idea of a permanent area set aside for all Native people had become the most popular solution to the "Indian Problem." Most Americans considered the existing policy of incorporating Indians into American society to be a failure.[6] Rather than integration through "civilizing," policy makers began to view separation as the most feasible solution. In 1817, the Committee on Public Lands suggested a bounded space into which all Indians could be placed.[7] In 1824, President James Monroe called for more specificity and "some well digested plan" that would establish a territory for Indians "between the limits of our present States and Territories, and the Rocky Mountain and Mexico."

While the location of this Indian Territory was vague, its purpose was not. Setting aside a territory for Indians would not only create a space in which Indians could safely become acculturated, but it would also demonstrate America's understanding of universal rights and its worthiness as a nation. Such a plan—according to President Monroe—would link Indians' rights "to the rights of humanity, and to the honour of this nation." For a young country that viewed its standing among European powers as the "object of the highest importance," the treatment of its Natives became a litmus test for its legitimacy as a nation.[8]

Unfortunately, John Quincy Adams had no better idea of where to place Indians than Monroe had. In 1826, Adams's secretary of war, James Barbour, offered that a large—but geographically unspecified—piece of land west of the Mississippi should be set apart for the "exclusive abode" of Native people.[9] Three years later, President Andrew Jackson echoed the previous administration's desire to remove Indians to "an ample district west of the Mississippi," where tribes would be free "to pursue happiness in their own way and under their own rude institutions." As presidents before him, however, Jackson had no idea what the geographic parameters of this ample district should be. Also like his predecessors, he emphasized that such a plan was "deeply interesting to our national character."[10]

Ironically, it was the debate over national character that pushed northern politicians to return to Indian Territory as the measuring stick against which the strength of the nation could be measured. More than European powers, however, it was the growing call for "states' rights" that worried these politicians. Embarrassed by their president's disregard for two Supreme Court rulings, Whigs in Congress used the call for an Indian territory to retaliate against Andrew Jackson's decision to ignore Justice John Marshall's famous 1830 and 1832 rulings that gave the federal government and the Cherokees control of their lands in western Georgia.[11] The Indian Territory proposal gave these politicians an opportunity to reassert congressional power.[12] When the Committee on Indian Affairs endorsed the creation of a permanent Indian territory in 1834, Vermont representative Horace Everett explained how important this plan was to the health of the young nation: "This territory is to be dedicated to the use of the Indian tribes forever, by a guaranty the most sacred known among civilized communities—*the faith of the nation.*"

Everett argued that creating an Indian territory not only demonstrated the federal government's honor but also the extent of its power. Previously, "conflicts between the rights of the States and of the United States" had made it impossible to honor Indian cessions, but now "by the constitution . . . and charters," Congress has an "unqualified power to dispose of the territory belonging to the United States."[13] Creating a permanent Indian territory—and inscribing it on maps of the trans-Mississippi West—became a moral imperative for the federal government.

Political grandstanding was certainly one reason for the cartographic creation of a land dominated by Indians. Yet, to fully understand why even ardent expansionists would include depictions of a permanent Indian territory in maps of the trans-Mississippi West, it is important to remember that the cartographic creation of the United States was as much cultural as it was political. Since 1773, when angry shippers dressed as Indians "overpowered" sympathetic guards to dump tea in Boston Harbor, "Indian" and "American" identities have been inexorably linked. As many scholars have described, Indians have long embodied American anxieties about industrialization, technology, capitalism, and history.[14] As historian Brian Dippie argues, Americans were insecure about their claims to a sufficiently rich past and "lacked a moral grandeur." Indians offered the new citizens a way to root themselves in a New World antiquity and to find "a lost heritage distinctly American."[15] This sentiment was demonstrated by Henry Schoolcraft, who wrote in 1846, "[The Indians] are relatively to us what the ancient Pict and Celt were to Britain or the Teuton, Goth and Magyar to continental Europe."[16] By drawing this comparison, the Indians *were* the American past.[17]

By imbuing the Indians with the nation's history, however, Americans created a new problem: how to justify forcing eastern Indians out of their homelands. Historian Philip Deloria explains that "Americans wanted to feel a natural affinity with the continent, and it was Indians who could teach them such aboriginal closeness. Yet in order to control the landscape they had to destroy the original inhabitants."[18] From this moral quandary, the narrative of the "vanishing Indian" was born. From James Fenimore Cooper's *Leatherstocking Tales* to George Catlin's paintings, which he hoped would "snatch from oblivion" the "memory of a truly lofty and noble race," American culture highlighted Natives' demise.[19] Poets, scholars, and politicians all declared that the Indian was disappearing: "like the morning dew"; as the "snow melts before the sunbeam"; as a "promontory of sand, exposed to ceaseless encroachments of the ocean"; and like leaves "swept away by the autumn."[20] While some blamed American policies for the Indians' disappearance, others claimed it was simply progress. All agreed that Indians would undoubtedly fade before the march of civilization.

The increased cartographic presence of Indians in the trans-Missouri West in the 1820s, 1830s, and 1840s was due, in part, to this same cultural phenomenon. By inscribing Indians in territory claimed by the United States—but not yet threatened by Euro-American settlement—Americans could safely lament Indians' passing while also appropriating their past. After the editor of the *North American Review* read a proposal for removing Indians to lands west of the Mississippi, he agreed that setting aside a territory for Native Americans was the proper course. He wrote, however, that this project would only "defer the fate of the Indian.

In half a century, their condition beyond the Mississippi will be just what it now is on this side. Their extinction is inevitable."[21] Creating "Indian Country"—culturally, if not politically—allowed Americans to embrace the history of freedom and simplicity that Indians signified, while also waiting for their future demise.

"Aboriginal Eloquence"

In the fall of 1821, Secretary of War John C. Calhoun invited members of the Pawnees, Kansas, Otoes, Missourias, and Omahas to Washington. Calhoun hoped to facilitate better relations with the Indians and to awe them with the "wealth and strength" of the United States.[22] Tarecawawaho, the Chaui Pawnee chief, declined the invitation, explaining that the Pawnees were the "greatest people on the planet" and that his traveling to Washington would be "too great a condescension."[23] Tarecawawaho did allow his brother, Sharitarish—the son of Sharitarish who met Zebulon Pike in 1806 and probably the father of Sharitarish who signed the 1833 treaty—to go in his stead. No official reports of the meeting between President James Monroe and the O'Fallon Delegation (named for the Indian agent who brought them east) remain. On February 16, however, the *Daily National Intelligencer* ran a story entitled "Aboriginal Eloquence," largely comprised of an oratory purportedly given by Sharitarish during the Indians' meeting with the president on February 4, 1822. "My Great Father," his speech began, "I have traveled a great distance to see you—I have seen you and my heart rejoices. . . . [I] have seen your people, your houses, your vessels on the big lake and a great many wonderful things beyond my comprehensions, which appears to have been made by the Great Spirit."[24]

The Pawnee's tone quickly changed, however, from deferent to defiant. Sharitarish explained that Indians were not like white people and that they led a different life. "The Great Spirit made us all . . . and intended that we should live differently from each other. He made the whites to cultivate the earth, and feed on domestic animals, but he made us, red skins, to rove though the uncultivated woods and plains." Unlike the whites' sedentary, market-oriented lifestyle, the Indians had no permanent home and traveled the country, taking only what they needed to survive. Before they knew the whites, Sharitarish declared, everything was under the Indians' control; they could go to sleep and find buffalo feeding around their camp.

Now, however, the whites "caused the destruction of our game," by forcing the Indians to kill animals just for their skins, leaving their

FIGURE 2. Portrait of Sharitarish, painted by Charles
Bird King during the Chaui's 1822 visit. McKenney and
Hall, *Biographical Sketches and Anecdotes of Ninety-
Five of 120 Principal Chiefs from the Indian Tribes of
North America*. Philadelphia, 1838.

"children [to] cry over their bones." Although Sharitarish claimed to
love white people, he nonetheless wanted to maintain his people's way of
life. While the Pawnee acknowledged that "wild animals [will] become
extinct," he hoped that the president would let his people "exhaust their
present resources" before making them toil in the ground. Sharitarish
reached the climax of his speech with a declaration that the "red skins"
had "plenty of land" as long as "you will keep your people off of it."[25]

The massive dispossession, population decline, and cultural devas-
tation faced by the Pawnees in the second half of the century make it
tempting to view this speech as part of Pawnee strategy of geopolitical
resistance to U.S. expansion. Both scholarly studies and popular Indian
histories highlight this speech as an example of the Pawnees' stoicism in

the face of massive population and land loss.[26] Despite its seductive tones of resistance and political independence, there are problems with using "Sharitarish's Speech"—as I will designate these words—to represent the Pawnees' attitudes toward American expansion in the first half of the century. As demonstrated in the previous section, before it became clear that the Americans would not fulfill their promises of protection, the Pawnees neither feared American encroachment nor wanted to bar them from their country.

This speech is unique among the dozens of recorded interactions with Pawnee leaders in its demanding American exclusion. Also, the internal inconsistencies in this speech make its Pawnee provenance doubtful. Still, "Sharitarish's Speech" is an important historical document. It provides a window into American attitudes toward the Pawnees, and it helps to explain why inscribing Indians in the trans-Missouri West became such a potent cartographic creation. Like James Fenimore Cooper's novels and George Catlin's paintings, cartographic depictions of Indian Territory allowed Americans to commemorate vanishing Indians, even as they also appropriated their history.[27]

Sharitarish's Speech rightly claimed that the Pawnees saw differences between their lifeways and those of the Americans. The relative importance of agriculture to each, however, was not one of them. Although the speech claimed that the Great Spirit made "whites to cultivate the earth" whereas "red skins" were created to "rove the through uncultivated woods and plains" in search of game, the Pawnees were actually expert horticulturists. In addition to collecting and cultivating crops—including beans, squash, watermelon, Indian potatoes (*Glycine apios*), water chinquapin (*Nelumbo lutea*), onions (*Allium*), cucumbers (*Micramepelis Labota*), and wild plums (*Pruns americana*)—the Pawnees cultivated around one thousand acres of corn per year during the nineteenth century. After visiting a Pawnee village in 1811, George Sibley reported: "The adjacent hills produce an abundance of dwarf plum bushes which yield a great quantity of delicious fruit. This shrubbery and the few scattering forest tress appear to be very carefully husbanded and preserved from injury by the Pawnees."[28] Pawnee oral history recalls a time when buffalo were used primarily for clothing and sinew, and corn provided the Pawnees with most of their food.[29] Corn was the most important agricultural foodstuff for the Pawnee, and along with the buffalo, it occupied the center of the Pawnees' religious world. Pawnees held numerous ceremonies each year that reaffirmed corn as the Mother to all people.[30]

Perhaps the most glaring incongruities in Sharitarish's Speech concern hunting and the buffalo—especially the claim that Pawnees were killing "just [to trade] their skin." As discussed in chapter 1, trade goods were important to Pawnee political life and tightly regulated by those in power.[31] A Pawnee who failed to adhere to the strict protocol that regulated trade with Euro-American traders and other Indian groups might have been beaten or killed at the hands of *raripakusus* (literally "fighting-for-order"), or village police.[32] Chiefs held similar authority when it came to the hunt itself. Pawnee ethnographer Gene Weltfish described one such situation: "A group of [Chaui] once tried to anticipate the tribal attack on the herd and were severely whipped. The leader of the party was beaten over the head with the club until he lay unconscious and his head was bleeding. When he appealed to [the chief], he was told it was 'the law' and that he had to submit to his punishment."[33] Sharitarish's complaint that his people were killing buffalo simply for trade was implausible, since this could have only occurred with the consent of the Pawnee chief.[34] Also, as Richard White has shown, the Pawnees' buffalo trade was insignificant compared to other trade in the trans-Missouri West, such as the Upper Missouri trade or the Rocky Mountain network. Thus, it was the consistency and control of trade—rather than the volume—that interested the Pawnee chiefs. This undermines the claim that the Pawnees were hunting simply for material gain.

In fact, the buffalo population on the Pawnees' hunting ground may have actually increased during the 1820s, as constant warfare between the Pawnees and both the Osage-Kansa alliance and the high plains tribes of Comanche, Cheyenne, Arapahoe, and Western Sioux created a buffer zone in present-day western Kansas, in which the animals found relative security.[35] Even if the buffalo population were decreasing in number, the Pawnees would not have viewed this as a problem of "exhausted resources," as Sharitarish's Speech claimed. In the Pawnees' world, animals could not "become extinct" through overhunting, since they were controlled by the Pawnees themselves.

Ceremony and ritual ordered Pawnee life. Through contact with Tirawahut and other celestial beings—such as the Corn Mother—the Pawnees received instructions on the proper ways to live and act. These deities gave the first people sacred bundles that symbolized the covenant between the Pawnees and their gods. Proper conduct was mediated through these bundles, and the Pawnees' actions could bring either good fortune or disaster. As Pawnee scholar James Riding In writes: "In Pawnee eyes, worship in the manner pr[e]scribed would ensure their collective survival. Economic prosperity and good fortune would come as long as they worshipped faithfully with the bundles."[36]

This interaction was so powerful that it dominated all aspects of Pawnee life, from defining the roles of the chiefs to providing buffalo for food and shelter. In 1823, when a traveler asked if the bundle ceremonies truly dictated his existence, an unidentified Pawnee replied that if the ceremonies were not followed, "old men would starve to death and the priests would perish."[37] In other words, buffalo were not a "resource" that could become "extinct," but instead, they were part of the world of plenty and balance that would continue if the proper rituals were followed.[38]

Sharitarish was part of a delegation of Indians that met with American representatives in Washington, D.C., in the winter of 1822. Yet, the singular nature of his plea for American exclusion from his country and the internal contradictions in the words attributed to him make it doubtful that the speech printed under the heading "Aboriginal Eloquence" was spoken by a Pawnee. The speech *does,* however, fit a cultural pattern of celebrating Indian oratory—systematically referred to as "eloquence" by nineteenth-century Americans—that scholar Thomas Guthrie argues fulfilled a collective purpose: "The way Euroamericans interpreted and celebrated Indian speech and produced and circulated texts of Indian oratory precisely positioned Indian subjects in this predetermined framework. Indian eloquence, inextricably tied to primitiveness, confirmed that Indians as a race were doomed and dying; the more eloquently they spoke, often uttering their own elegies, the more certain was their passing."[39]

In a separate *National Intelligencer* article—offered as a letter by an unnamed "subscriber" who supposedly attended the meeting between the Indian delegation and the president of the United States—the author described the exchange and offered the following analysis:

> It is impossible to see these people, and believe as I do, that they are destined, in no very long lapse of time, to disappear from the face of the earth, without feeling for them great interest. With some vices, and much grossness, they possess many fine traits of character; and we never can forget that they were the native lords of that soil which they are gradually yielding to their invaders. . . . It is certain that all the tribes which have remained among us have gradually dwindled to insignificance or become entirely extinct.[40]

Admiring "Indian Eloquence"—as the second article was titled—allowed Americans to pay homage to Indians, while simultaneously allowing for a linear narrative of progress that dominated nineteenth-century historical thinking.[41]

"The General Burial-Ground of Their Race"

It was one thing for Americans to fill discursive space with narratives of progress. It was quite another to fill cartographic space with images of the same. Regardless of how quickly Americans believed Indians were dying, even virulent Indian haters had to acknowledge the two to three hundred thousand Indians living between the Mississippi River and the Rocky Mountains. This fact created a new problem for a populace whose identity was grounded in a geographic understanding of their domain. As Martin Brückner explains, Americans' geographical knowledge helped form their Revolutionary identity. Once that knowledge was established, however, it could not easily be undone: "To a literate population that had been educated in a geographic vein, the incompleteness of the North American geography on maps and in textbook entries was construed as an eyesore and a source of national embarrassment. The map-logo that had once worked to provide a shorthand for national unity and identity was now viewed as truncated and thwarted. The geographically literate eye desired to see the map extending neatly across the entire continent, achieving not only a political imperative but an aesthetic one."[42] How could Americans complete this aesthetic imperative, acknowledge the real Indian presence in the trans-Mississippi West, and still remove them from the dominant narrative of progress? Indian Territory offered an answer.

Supreme Court Justice Joseph Story articulated this sentiment in 1828 during a commemoration of the settlement of Salem, Massachusetts: "What can be more melancholy than [Indians'] history? By a law of nature, they seem destined to a slow, but sure extinction. Everywhere, at the approach of the white man, they fade away. We hear the rustling of their footsteps, like that of the withered leaves of autumn, and they are gone forever. They pass mournfully by us, and they return no more." For Story, the Indians' march to oblivion was not just metaphorical but physical as well. Story claims to have watched them leave their homes to travel "beyond the Mississippi," from where they will go "one remove further . . . to the general burial-ground of their race."[43]

It is no coincidence that the version of Sharitarish's Speech that was ultimately more accessible to the public than that which appeared in the *National Intelligencer* was one printed by Reverend Jedidiah Morse, the so-called "Father of American Geography." Morse was a Congregational clergyman, whose textbook, *American Universal Geography*, became the standard reference work in American schoolrooms across the country.[44] By the end of his life, Morse had established an interest in Native people, and in 1820, he was sent by Secretary of War John Calhoun to report on the condition of Native Americans living in American territory "to render a more accurate knowledge of their state and how to advance their civilization and happiness."[45] Morse's ninety-page report was followed by a two-hundred-page appendix of assorted charts and documents related to Indians, which included Sharitarish's Speech.

The subtitle of Morse's report describes two of its telling inclusions. The first is that the book was "ornamented by a correct portrait of a Pawnee Indian." The portrait, the frontispiece of the report, depicts "A Pawnee Brave, Son of Old Knife" or Pita-risaru—called Petalesharo here—the Skidi who earned American praise for "ending" the Morning Star ceremony (figs. 3 and 4), which included human sacrifice.[46] The choice to use Charles Bird King's portrait of Petalesharo to represent the Indians, despite the fact that Morse did not visit the Pawnees, highlights just how popular the Skidi had become. The romanticized story of Petalesharo's saving victims from the sacrificial altar, also included in the report, first appeared in newspapers in the fall of 1821.[47] By the time the Indian delegation reached Washington in the winter of 1822, Petalesharo had become a hero in parlor rooms on the East Coast. He was the embodiment of the redeemed savage and even received a medal from "the young ladies of Miss White's Seminary . . . as a token of their sincere commendations of the noble act of rescuing one of their sex, an innocent victim, from a cruel death."[48]

Petalesharo became so representative of the civilized Indian that Samuel F. B. Morse—Jedidiah's son and future inventor of the telegraph—included him in his 1823 painting *The House of Representatives*. In this painting, the Indian—along with the elder Morse and one of his mentors—gaze down on members of Congress, the Supreme Court justices, and President Monroe, in the harmonious glow of an oil-burning chandelier. (Although, as in Indian Territory, the Indian is isolated from both the politicians and the other observers; see fig. 4.)[49] Using Petalesharo as the frontispiece of Morse's report encouraged readers to associate the Indians it describes with the possibility of salvation through civilization.

The subtitle of the report also described the work as "illustrated by a map of the United States." This foldout map delineated each state's

FIGURE 3. Charles Bird King's portrait of Petalesharo and the frontispiece to Morse's *Report.*

boundaries, highlighting them in color. It also emphasized a region whose eastern border would, over the next two decades, become Indian Territory for the American public. Although Morse labeled this country as "Missouri Territory," he explained what the best use of the region would be: "Should the plan be popular with the Indians, and the prospect is that it will be, and the prospect is, that it will be, a large colony, enough perhaps to form a *Territory* or even a *State,* may be ultimately collected here, educated together, and received into the Union, and to the enjoyment of the privileges of its citizens."[50] Within this territory, a reader could easily find Petalesharo's "Pawnee Loup Vill" on the eastern Plains.

The connection of these two tropes—the geographic depiction of Indian Territory and the Indians' transition to civilization—was not arbitrary. By highlighting Native presence within the boundaries of the United States, Americans could fulfill their need to complete that nation while safely removing Indians—at least cartographically—to its far reaches. Advertisements for the commercial version of Morse's report highlighted both the portrait of the "Pawnee half-chief, who bravely rescued [a captive] from death" and the Indians' geographic relationship

FIGURE 4. Samuel Finley Breese Morse. *The House of Representatives* (1822), probably reworked 1823. Oil on canvas. Corcoran Collection (Museum Purchase, Gallery Fund). 2014.79.27.

to the United States. After mentioning the portrait for a second time, an advertisement lists the first topic covered by the report to be "the great accession of Indians to the United States, made by the recent extension of our territory to the Pacific Ocean, and consequent condition of these Indians."[51] The advertisement ends its description of the report with three topics expressly related to Indian Territory: "On geography . . . and the parts of our territories possessed by the Indians; On the plan of colonizing . . . and experiments for civilizing and evangelizing the Indians; On the objections made to attempting the civilization of the Indians, and answers to these objections."[52] Taken together, the "correct portrait of a Pawnee Indian" and the foldout map allowed Americans to imagine Indians at a safe distance while they waited for them to be civilized. Even before President Monroe's proposal for an Indian territory in 1825, American culture was binding Indians to the physical landscape of the trans-Missouri West.

The 1821 meetings between Indian and American representatives were geographically and politically forgettable. Culturally, however, the O'Fallon Delegation left a legacy for the American public. Five years after the delegation's visit, James Fenimore Cooper re-created Petalesharo's

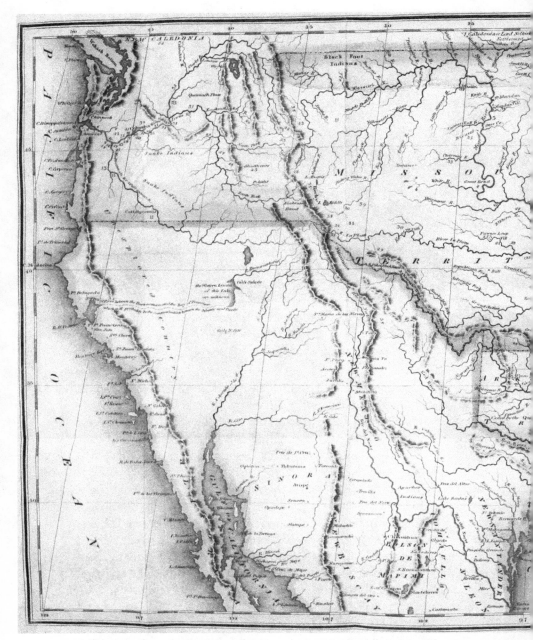

MAP 25. Map accompanying Jedidiah Morse, *Report to the Secretary of War* (1822), which includes a bounded territory for Indians.

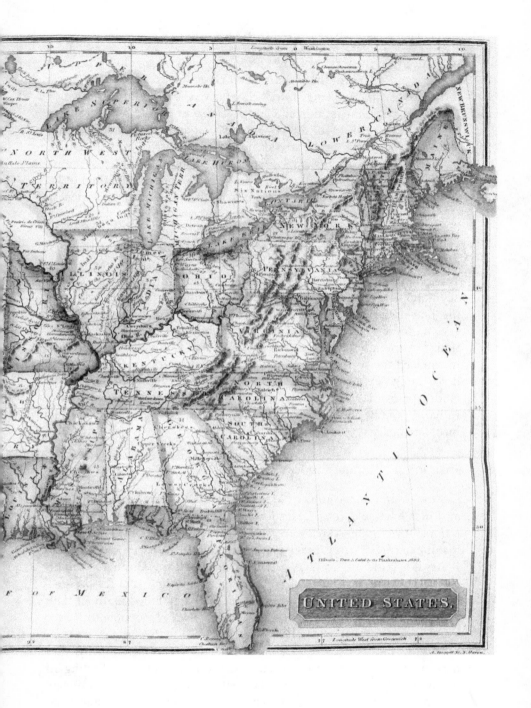

UNITED STATES,

noble deeds in the form of Hard-Heart, a Pawnee protagonist who saves a Comanche girl from the Morning Star ceremony in *The Prairie* (1827), the third *Leatherstocking Tale*.[53] Similarly, the O'Fallon Delegation inspired a young artist named George Catlin to devote his life to portraying these "lords of the forest." Whereas other artists painted Indians in their eastern studios, he would memorialize Natives in their natural habitat. Before they vanished, he aspired to create a "fair and just monument" to how Indians lived "in the uncivilized and regions of their uninvaded country."[54] For Cooper and Catlin alike, the Indians' placement in the unspoiled land west of the Missouri was critical to their depictions.

Petalesharo's tale first came to the public's attention through the *Daily National Intelligencer.* Information about this incident was first gathered, however, by Maj. Stephen Long's expedition two years earlier. This group included painter Titian Ramsay Peale, draughtsman Samuel Seymore, naturalist Thomas Say, and physician Edwin James, who kept the journal of the expedition. Long created a graphic record of the scenery and Indian life that would serve as a model for many future expeditions.[55] Although the explorations of Lewis and Clark and Zebulon Pike introduced the American public to Natives of the trans-Missouri West, it was Long's expedition that began the process of fixing Indians to the landscape of the Great Plains, which initiated the cultural creation of Indian Country. Not coincidentally, the information that established its most lasting legacy came from Indians.

Inscribing "Roving Bands of Indians"

Edwin James's accounts of Maj. Stephen Long's explorations in 1819 and 1820 have been roundly criticized for their lack of cartographic precision. "It would be scarcely possible to find in any narrative of Western history so careless an itinerary, and in a scientific report like that of Dr. James it is quite inexcusable," wrote historian Hiram Chittenden in his classic *The American Fur Trade.*[56] From a twenty-first-century perspective, Chittenden's critique makes sense. The party failed many of their assigned cartographic tasks. They were, for example, unable to fix the sources of the Platte or the Red Rivers. This was due in part to their mistaking the Red for the Canadian, but more problematically, they descended the river eastward, eliminating any chance of finding its headwaters in the west. On their descent of the Arkansas, a contingent commanded by Captain Bell traveled two hundred miles without making any notes about the country through which they traveled. And the first mention of any astronomical reading does not appear until almost the two-hundredth page of the second volume.[57] Although Long's reputation has improved since Chittenden first made his claim, he is still predominately known as the man who incorrectly solidified the idea of the "Great American Desert" in the minds of the American public.[58]

Still, Long has another cartographic legacy that has been overlooked. Many scholars have highlighted James's declaration that his group had "little apprehension of giving too unfavourable account of this portion of the country." But the second part of that same paragraph has an equally illustrative declaration: "This region may for ever remain the unmolested haunt of the native hunter, the bison, and the jackal." The *Account* equated the Indians living on the central and eastern Plains with the territory itself, tying Natives to the landscape in the cultural creation of the region.

Secretary of War John Calhoun's stated "objective of the expedition" was to gather "thorough and accurate knowledge" of the region, which required that Long enter into his journal "everything interesting in relation to soil, face of the country, water courses, and productions, whether animal, vegetable or mineral."[59] Long, however, viewed his purpose differently. In the second paragraph of the introduction to the *Account*—before any mention of cartography, geography, or maps—Long explains what the reader should expect: "In the following pages we hope to have contributed something towards a more thorough acquaintance with the Aborigines of our country. In other parts of our narrative where this interesting topic could not be introduced, we have turned our attention towards the phenomenon of nature."[60] Long's descriptions of the "Aborigines," particularly the Pawnees, Kansas, and Omahas, represent the *Account*'s greatest legacy. No other traveler gathered as much information on the lifeways of these groups in the first half of the nineteenth century.[61]

Part of this focus was borne out of necessity. Before their travels began, Long wrote to his subordinates that "the prime object of the expedition . . . [is] a topographical description of the country to be explored."[62] A number of setbacks, however, curtailed this goal. A budget reduction forced Long to limit his surveying equipment to one small sextant, one mercury horizon, one watch, three small compasses, and two thermometers. Even in the best circumstances, such equipment could only chart general latitudes and was virtually worthless for measuring longitudes. These were not the best circumstances. Bad weather often made observations impossible, and the rough terrain was hard on the fragile instruments. In addition, part of the team deserted halfway through the expedition, taking one book of topographical observations with them.[63] Little wonder that Long decided to focus on ethnographic information.

Still, there are other clues that hint at the party's conscious prioritization of ethnography over topography. On their way to the Pawnee villages on the Platte River, the Americans covered the same ground they would pass over the following spring. When he was editing the published journals, Edwin James had to choose when to describe the landscape. James decided to prioritize his "transactions and interviews with the natives," as it would have been "superfluous to note the appearance of the country over which we passed." In addition to numerous catalogues of "Indian sign language," Indian speeches, and the vocabularies of various groups, the three-volume work makes some reference to Natives on almost every page.

Throughout the journals, members of the expedition, particularly Thomas Say, record indigenous life, combining ethnographic interviews with excellent observational skill. Upon his arrival at a Kanza village, Say included the following description of the political order:

> Ca-ega-wa-tan-ninga, or the Fool Chief is the hereditary principal chief, but he possesses nothing like monarchical authority, maintaining his distinction only by his bravery and good conduct. There are ten or twelve inferior chieftains . . . but they do not appear to command any great respect from the people. Civil as well as military distinction arise from bravery or generosity. Controversies are decided amongst themselves; they do not appeal to their chief, except for council.[64]

As with any historical source, these descriptions must be evaluated within the context in which they were written. Without them, however, our understanding of many Indian groups in the early nineteenth century would be greatly decreased.

Long's prioritization of ethnographic information encouraged readers to identify geographic regions with their Indian occupants rather than their topographical features. There were actually very few identifiable topographical features to which a lay reader could relate. As Long remarked, "We feel the want of ascertained or fixed points of reference."[65] A reader of the *Account* would have a difficult time placing the major river systems of the trans-Missouri West, but he would be able to identify which groups lived along them. Long's report explained *who* made up a region rather than *where* its topographical features lay. Nearly twenty years after the expedition, the president of the new National Institute for the Promotion of Science emphasized this characteristic of expedition.

It was the "accomplished observer Long" who—along with the "brave and gallant Pike" and the "indefatigable and scientific traveller [Joseph] Nicollet"—first mapped the country beyond the Mississippi.[66]

Long also visually tied Indians to the landscape. Long and Lt. William Swift created a map that one scholar argues "impressed itself on the public's mind more than all of the text it accompanied." Historian Richard Dillon was primarily referring to the words "Great American Desert" that are inscribed in large letters across the Great Plains. Dillon cites Henry Tanner's 1822 *Map of North America* and Henry C. Carey's 1833 *Map of Arkansas and Other Territories of the United States*, both of which include Long's inscription as examples of its impact. William Woodbridge also added "Great American Desert" to his map *North America and the West Indies* in 1824. Although scholars continue to debate the effects of Long's topographic characterization on settlement patterns, the concept became well established in the public's geographic imagination. As geographer John Baltzly Garver writes, "The image of a Great American Desert entered geography, cartography, history, literature, and legend and it would take a generation to erase it."[67] Long's description of the Great Plains did more than describe the soil, however; it also tied this "desert" to the people who lived there.

On the printed—rather than manuscript—version of the *Country Drained by the Mississippi Western Section*, an important element was added. Above the word "Great," a smaller but more legible description reads "Great Desert . . . frequented by roving bands of Indians who have no fixed place of residence but roam from place to place in quest of game." Not only does this desert run the width of the Great Plains, but that entire swath of land—from the Missouri to the Rocky Mountains and between the Platte and the Arkansas—is comprised of "roving bands of Indians."[68] As much as it implied about the quality of the soil, Long's references to the Great American Desert inscribed its inhabitants into the trans-Missouri West.[69]

Like the Great American Desert, the concept of a region populated by "roving bands of Indians" permeated into American culture. Washington Irving, for example, referred to the region between the Missouri and the Rockies as a "lawless interval" filled with "new and mongrel races" and "maurading bands of savages."[70] Similarly, an 1824 textbook declared: "From longitude, or the meridian of Council Bluffs, to the Chippewan [Rocky] Mountains, is a desert region of 400 miles in length and breadth. It is at present, and for a length of time must be, only a range for tribes of savages, and herds of buffaloes." Commercial mapmakers also applied

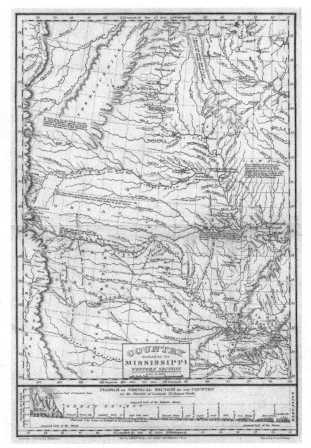

MAP 26. Stephen Long's *Country Drained by the Mississippi Western Section* (1823). The inscription of the "Great American Desert" is marked by the red square. Courtesy of Library of Congress.

Long's descriptions of the region. Eleazer Huntington and Henry Phelps each labeled the immediate trans-Missouri West with various forms of "desert," populated by "roving bands of Indians."[71] Long's expedition began the process of creating a distinct Indian territory in American culture. Ironically, Long did not encounter any Indians—roving or otherwise—in the region most obviously connected with this label. Instead, he gleaned this information from Pawnee informants.

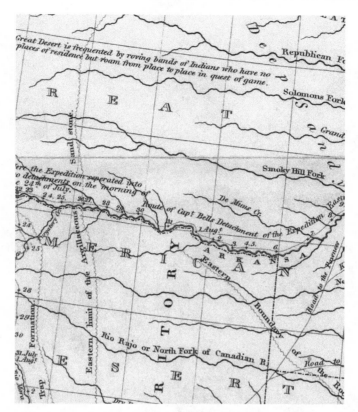

MAP 27. Detail of Stephen Long's *Country Drained by the Mississippi* (1823). The inscription "Great American Desert" is frequently cited as the Long's greatest legacy, yet it is the more legible inscription above it that had the more lasting impact: "Great Desert . . . frequented by roving bands of Indians who have no fixed place of residence but roam from place to place in quest of game." Courtesy of Library of Congress.

Encountering "Roving Bands of Indians"

Of course, the trans-Missouri West *was* home to various Indian groups. Semi-nomadic Caddoan and Siouan peoples—such as the Pawnees and Kansas—did inhabit the lands between the headwaters of the Arkansas and Platte Rivers when they were looking for buffalo. (They also lived in more permanent villages farther east.) And both of these groups left their marks on Long's expedition and its cartographic

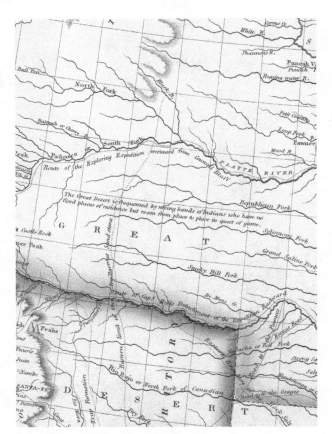

MAP 28. Long's depiction of "roving bands of Indians" had a significant influence on contemporary maps, including Henry C. Carey's *Map of Arkansas and Other Territories of the United States* (1822). Courtesy of David Rumsey Historical Map Collection.

contributions to the construction of the American West. Sometimes by providing physical assistance and other times by providing information, Indians shaped Long's legacy.

The most immediate impact Indians had on Long's expedition was by providing aid. Although they had their own reasons for offering goods and services, Indians still determined the group's success. After observing enough Kansa political dynamics to record the earlier ethnographic entry regarding Fool Chief, the detachment acquired needed supplies of "jerked bison meat, pounded maize, bison fat put up like sausages, moccasins, leggings, spoons made of the horn of bison, two large wooden dishes, &c." In addition, Fool Chief dispatched a group of Kansas to protect the Americans on their first night away from the Kansas village. His apprehensions proved correct when a large group of South Band Pawnee, who were "decorated and painted for battle," approached the detachment later that night. One of the Kansas quickly "seized his gun and ran towards the advancing multitude . . . whilst his companions disappeared in the bushes in an instant." The Americans meanwhile "drew up in a line and all prepared themselves for defense in case of extremity." In the ensuing confusion, the Pawnees made off with goods and a few horses. Although the horses could not be retrieved, the Kansas limited the losses, pursuing "the trail of the Pawnees . . . and restored to [the Americans] some bacon and other articles which had been carried off by the fugitives."[72]

In his summary report to Secretary of War John C. Calhoun, Long did not mention the help he received from the Kansas. He did claim that the robbery by the Pawnees "rendered it necessary for [the party] to change their route, and shape their course for the Missouri," thus exemplifying another way Indian groups affected expeditionary parties. Although silences in the sources make it difficult to identify Indian motives—as in this case of the Pawnees—the impacts of these interactions on the cartographic construction of the trans-Missouri West are easier to determine.

When Long's party reached the Arkansas, in what is now western Kansas, they asked for assistance from a "Kaskaia [Kiowa-Apache] and his squaw" to help them find a place to ford the river. The Indians led the detachment back along the trail they had come until they reached a spot the party had missed a few hours earlier. Long then inquired if the Indian knew how to reach the Red River, and the Kaskia gave them "information and advice on that subject," including a "map traced in the sand, giv[ing] us a minute account of the situation of the spring and of the surrounding company." The Calf, as James called him, also told the group where they could find rock salt at the river and sold Captain Bell a much-needed horse. The Calf stayed with the group for two more days, providing a vocabulary of the Kaskia language and presumably, acting as guide, although James never explicitly stated such. After the Indian left, the American division split, with Captain Bell leading a detachment down the Arkansas to Fort Smith and Major Long continuing south to find the source of the Red River.

By July 28, Long determined that since he had "not found a single feature of the country to correspond . . . to [The Calf's] descriptions . . .

it was probably his intention to deceive." This is a possibility, although one that does not coincide with the more positive aspects of the Indian's interaction with the group. More likely, Long simply did not know where he was. In fact, in his report to Calhoun, Long acknowledged that he did not have a good grasp of the region's geography, and the group's only "dependence" was on Zebulon Pike's faulty map.[73]

Long concluded the same about Indian informants when a group of "Kaskaias or Bad-hearts" told him "without hesitation" that they were currently riding along the Red River. The Indians also gave him very specific distances from their location to the permanent villages of the Pawnee Piques (Wichitas), so Long felt secure in the Kiowa-Apaches' declaration that the river they were following was the Red as he hoped. When Long realized a few hundred miles later that they were following the Canadian and not the Red, he placed the blame on the deceitful declarations of the Kaskaia.[74]

Again, this is a possibility. We can only guess at the intentions of the Kiowa-Apaches. Yet, there are other clues that indicate that the Indians had not intended to deceive the American. As Long himself was aware, there was a "degree of ambiguity and confusion in the nomenclature of the rivers," and many—most notably the Canadian—were given the name Rio Colorado (Blood Red River) because of the red sediment they contained. It is not difficult to see how this confusion could have led to a miscommunication between the two groups. After all, Long's party came across both the recently abandoned Comanche village, and the blue hills "whose sides were covered with forests," as the Kiowa-Apaches said they would.[75] Finally, as Long himself notes, why would the Indians want to deceive the party "in an affair of such indifference to them"?[76]

Whether deceitful or not, the Kiowa-Apaches' assurances led to Long's trip down the Canadian. And it was in his description of this landscape that James famously wrote that "they had the little apprehension of giving too unfavourable an account of this portion of the country . . . [which] may forever remain the unmolested haunt of the native hunter, the bison, and the Jackall."[77] James might not have written this sentence had they been traveling down the Red, a hundred miles to the south, rather than down the Canadian. Regardless, the Native inhabitants of the region had a major effect on the outcome of Long's expedition and the cartographic creation of the American West.

Perhaps none helped more than two "French Pawnees"—traders of French ancestry—who lived permanently among the Pawnees. Hired at the Skidi village after the previous guide quit, Bijeau and Ledoux were

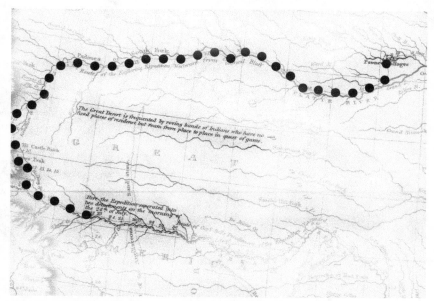

MAP 29. Detail of Long's *Country Drained by the Mississippi* (1823). Between the Pawnee village and their meeting with a Kiowa-Apache, Long's expedition (*dotted line*) did not meet "a single savage," raising the question of where they got their information regarding "roving bands of Indians." Courtesy of Library of Congress.

to guide the detachment to the Red River. When they left after several months of work, Long could not acknowledge their departure "without expressing our entire approbation of their conduct and deportment, during our arduous journey; Bijeau in particular was faithful, active, industrious, and communicative. Besides the duties of guide and interpreter, he occasionally and frequently volunteered his services as hunter, butcher, cook, veterinarian &c."[78] Long's sentiments no doubt inspired the inscription of "Bijeux Creek" on his map.

The lavish praise given to two men living among the Pawnees is ironic, considering both the robbery and the Americans' previous refusal to accept Pawnee advice. Earlier in the journey—after Major Long explained his party's desire to travel west on the Platte, then south to the Red—Skidi leader Petalesharo advised against that route. There would be no water and little game on large sections of the journey, the Skidi advised, and the area contained bands of powerful Cheyenne,

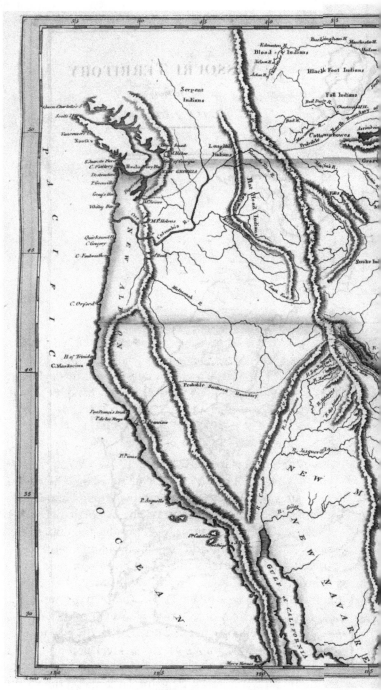

MAP 30. Matthew Carey's *Missouri Territory Formerly Louisiana* (1814). Courtesy of Library of Congress.

MISSOURI TERRITORY

formerly

LOUISIANA.

SCALE.

GULF OF MEXICO

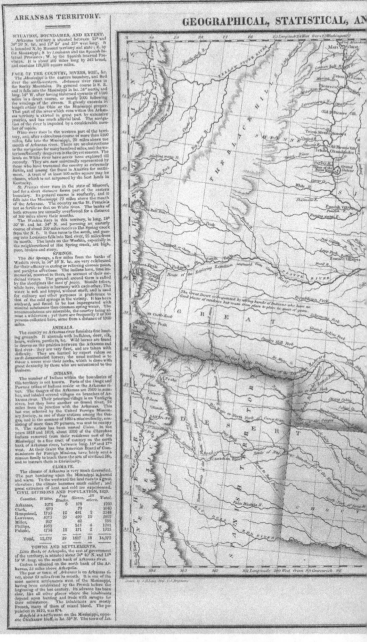

ARKANSAS TERRITORY.

SITUATION, BOUNDARIES, AND EXTENT.

Arkansas territory is situated between 33° and 36° 30′ N. lat. and 12° 2′ and 23° west long. It is bounded N. by Missouri territory and state; E. by the Mississippi; S. by Louisiana and the Spanish Internal Provinces; W. by the Spanish Internal Provinces. It is about 500 miles long by 242 broad, and contains 121,000 square miles.

FACE OF THE COUNTRY, RIVERS, SOIL, &c.

The Mississippi is the eastern boundary, and Red river the south-western. Arkansas river rises in the Rocky Mountains. Its general course is S. E. and it falls into the Mississippi in lat. 34° north, and long. 14° W. after having traversed upwards of 1500 miles in a direct course, or nearly 2000 following the windings of the stream. It greatly exceeds in length either the Ohio or the Mississippi proper. That part of the river which runs within the Arkansas territory is skirted in great part by extensive prairie, and has much alluvial land. The navigation of the river is impeded by a considerable number of rapids.

White river rises in the western part of the territory, and, after a circuitous course of more than 1200 miles, falls into the Mississippi, 20 miles above the mouth of Arkansas river. There are no obstructions to the navigation for many hundred miles, and the water is sufficiently deep even in the dryest season. The lands on White river have never been explored till recently. They are now universally represented by those who have traversed the country as extremely fertile, and among the finest in America for settlement. A tract of at least 100 miles square may be chosen, which is not surpassed by the best lands in Kentucky.

St. Francis river rises in the state of Missouri, and for a short distance forms part of the eastern boundary. Its general course is southerly, and it falls into the Mississippi 72 miles above the mouth of the Arkansas. The country on the St. Francis is not so fertile as that on White river. The banks of both streams are annually overflowed for a distance of 100 miles above their mouths.

The Washita rises in this territory, in long. 18° 30′ W. and lat. 34° N. and pursuing an easterly course of about 200 miles receives Hot Spring creek from the N. E. It then turns to the south, and passing into Louisiana falls into Red river, 25 miles from its mouth. The lands on the Washita, especially in the neighbourhood of Hot Spring creek, are high, poor, broken and stony.

SPRINGS.

The Hot Springs, a few miles from the banks of Washita river, in 34° 16′ N. lat. are very celebrated for their efficacy in curing or relieving chronic pains, and paralytic affections. The Indians have, time immemorial, resorted to them, on account of their medicinal virtues. The ground around them is called by the aborigines the land of peace. Hostile tribes, while here, remain in harmony with each other. The water is soft and limpid, without smell, and is used for culinary and other purposes in preference to that of the cold springs in the vicinity. It has been analysed, and found to be less impregnated with mineral substances than common spring water. The accommodations are miserable, the country being almost a wilderness; yet there are frequently 2 or 300 persons collected here, some from a distance of 1000 miles.

ANIMALS.

The country on Arkansas river furnishes fine hunting grounds. It abounds with buffaloes, deer, elk, bears, wolves, panthers, &c. Wild horses are found in droves on the prairies between the Arkansas and Red river; they are very fleet, and are taken with difficulty. They are hunted by expert riders on swift domesticated horses; the usual method is to throw a noose over their necks, which is done with great dexterity by those who are accustomed to the business.

INDIANS.

The number of Indians within the boundaries of this territory is not known. Parts of the Osage and Pawnee tribes of Indians reside on the Arkansas river. The Osages of the Arkansas are 2500 in number, and inhabit several villages on branches of Arkansas river. Their principal village is on Verdigris river, but they have another on Grand river, 25 miles from its junction with the Arkansas. This last was selected by the United Foreign Missionary Society, as one of their stations among the Osages, and in the summer of 1820 a mission family, consisting of more than 20 persons, was sent to occupy it. The station has been named Union. In the years 1818 and 1819, about 5000 of the Cherokee Indians removed from their residence east of the Mississippi to a fine tract of country on the north bank of Arkansas river, between long. 16° and 17° west. At their desire the American Board of Commissioners for Foreign Missions, have lately sent a mission family to teach them the arts of civilized life, and to instruct them in Christianity.

CLIMATE.

The climate of Arkansas is very much diversified. The part bordering upon the Mississippi is humid and warm. To the westward the land rises to a great elevation; the climate becomes much colder, and great extremes of heat and cold are experienced.

CIVIL DIVISIONS AND POPULATION, 1820.

Counties.	Whites.	Slaves.	Free Blacks.	Total.
Arkansas,	1075	178	6	1260
Clark,	970	70		1040
Hempstead,	1743	481	12 3	2248
Lawrence,	6073	499	29 10	3602
Miller,	917	82		999
Phillips,	1052	143	4	1201
Pulaski,	1738	171	12 2	1923
Total,	12,579	1617	39 18	14,273

TOWNS AND SETTLEMENTS.

Little Rock, or Arkopolis, the seat of government of the territory, is situated about 34° 40′ N. and 13° 15′ W. long. on the south bank of Arkansas river.

Cadron is situated on the north bank of the Arkansas, 35 miles above Arkopolis.

The post or town of Arkansas is on Arkansas river, about 53 miles from its mouth. It is one of the most ancient settlements west of the Mississippi, having been established by the French before the beginning of the last century. Its advance has been slow, like all other places where the inhabitants depend upon hunting and trade with savages for their subsistence. The inhabitants are mostly French, many of them of mixed blood. The population in 1810, was 874.

Mouchfield is a settlement on the Mississippi, opposite Chickasaw bluff, in lat. 35° N. The town of Lit-

---

MAP 31. H. C. Carey's *Map of Arkansas and Other Territories of the United States* (1822). In this atlas by H. C. Carey, the boundary of the region remains the same, but the "Missouri Territory" label has been replaced by individual Indian tribes' names. Courtesy of David Rumsey Historical Map Collection.

MAP
OF
ARKANSA
AND OTHER
TERRITORIES
of the
UNITED STATES
Respectfully inscribed to the
HON. J. C. CALHOUN
SECRETARY OF WAR
By S.H. Long Major T. Engineers.

SCALE OF MILES.

CHIEF TOWNS, *(continued.)*
du Prairie is on the Mississippi, in about lat. 36° 30′ N. The settlements on St. Francis river are as yet very inconsiderable.

GOVERNMENT.

The executive power is vested in a governor, who holds his office for three years, unless sooner removed by the president of the United States. He is ex officio superintendent of Indian affairs. The secretary holds his office for four years. The legislative power, until the organization of the general assembly, is vested in the governor and the judges of the superior court. The judicial power is vested in a superior court, and in such inferior courts as the legislature shall from time to time establish. The governor, secretary, and judges of the superior court, are appointed by the president of the United States.

HISTORICAL SKETCH.

Of a district, the separation of which from another territory took place only two years since, the history must necessarily be brief. Much that concerns the settlement of Arkansas, together with that of the remaining portions of Louisiana as it was originally conveyed to the United States, has been related in the historical sketches of the states of Louisiana and Missouri.

The earliest settlement within the limits of the territory of Arkansas was made by the chevalier de Tonti, in 1685. Proceeding from a fort then recently established at the Illinois, to assist the enterprising but unfortunate La Salle, he penetrated to the mouth of the Mississippi. His search having been fruitless, he ascended the river in order to return to his post. On his way he entered the Arkansas river, and sailed up to the village of the Indians of that name, with whom he formed an alliance. Here he built a fort, and, at the desire of the natives, left two of his own to settle among them. At that period the Arkansas Indians were deemed one of the most powerful tribes in the country; and the French, to preserve peace with them, and to secure their trade, intermarried among them, and adopted most of their habits and manners. The new settlers found their numbers gradually augmented by the arrival of emigrants from Canada, who descended the Mississippi. The progress of settlement was, however, extremely slow, and whatever events may have happened in this territory between the commencement of the eighteenth century and the period of its transfer to the United States, history has not recorded them.

When the cession of Louisiana to the United States took place, the ceded territory was at first divided into two parts. The district on the west bank of the Mississippi, lying south of latitude 33°, was called the territory of Orleans; and the remaining portion, comprising the vast extent of country between the Mississippi and the Pacific ocean, was, at the same time, constituted the district of Louisiana, and placed under the superintendence of the governor and judges of the Indiana territory. In March, 1805, it was denominated the territory of Louisiana. The executive power was vested in a governor appointed by the president of the United States for three years, and in a secretary appointed in the same manner for four years; who, in case of a vacancy in the office of governor, was to discharge his duties. The legislative power was vested in the governor and three judges, and the judicial in the three judges, who retained their offices for four years, and held two courts annually in the district. In 1805 a settlement was commenced near the Hot Springs, on the head waters of the Ouachita or Washita river. Emigration to this distant spot has been attracted by the salubrious qualities of the springs, and continues to the period. In 1808 a treaty was concluded at Fort Clark with the Great and Little Osage Indians, by which these tribes agreed for certain stipulated advantages, that the boundary line between them and the United States should be as follows, viz. "beginning at Fort Clark on the Missouri, five miles above Fire Prairie, and running thence a due southerly course to the river Arkansas, and down the same to the Mississippi, ceding and relinquishing for ever to the United States all the lands which lie east of the said line, and north of the southern bank of the said river Arkansas, and all lands situated to the northward of the river Missouri. They further ceded at the same time, a tract of two leagues square, to embrace Fort Clark.

In 1812 the district of Louisiana, under the same boundaries, was constituted a territorial government, under the name of the territory of Missouri. The form of government was nearly similar to that of other territories. The executive power was exercised by a governor, who was appointed by the president and senate for a term of three years. The legislative power was vested in a general assembly, consisting of the governor, a legislative council and house of representatives. The legislative council was composed of persons chosen one for each county, to serve two years. The representatives were also elected every two years. The assembly met only once in two years. The territory of Missouri remained in these boundaries and under this government until the year 1819, when the inhabitants of the southern part were formed into a distinct district. The southern boundary of this territory was fixed by an act of congress passed in March, 1819, as follows, viz. "a line beginning at the Mississippi river at lat. 36° north, running thence west to the river St. Francis; thence up the same, north, to lat. 36° 30′ thence west to the western territorial line." In February, 1819, a bill having been brought into congress to establish a separate territory in the southern part of the then Missouri territory, a motion to amend the bill by providing that the further introduction of slavery, except for the punishment of crimes, should be prohibited, was lost by a close vote, the numbers in the affirmative being 70, and in the negative 71. A subsequent part of the same resolution, providing that all children born of slaves should thereafter be free, was carried by a majority of two votes, the number in the affirmative being 75, and those in the negative being 73. On the succeeding day, however, a motion to recommit the bill prevailed; and the committee having struck out the amendment, their report was concurred in, the ayes being 89 and the noes 87. The bill then passed without restriction as to slavery.

Soon after the act establishing the territory was passed, colonel James Miller, a brigadier-general by brevet, who had distinguished himself in the late war with England, was appointed governor. An election for a delegate to congress for the first time was held in December, 1819. The territory is rapidly increasing in population, and will probably in a short period take a station among the members of the union.

GOVERNOR.

1819 James Miller to 1823.

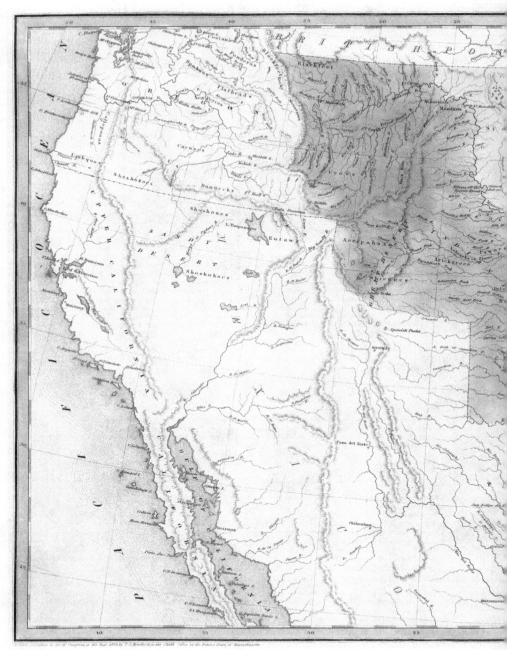

MAP 32. "Indian Territory," as labeled in Thomas Bradford's 1838 atlas. In the original color version, the Missouri River separates the green-tinted "Indian Territory" from the red of "Wisconsin" and the yellow of Missouri, clearly defining their boundaries. Courtesy of David Rumsey Historical Map Collection.

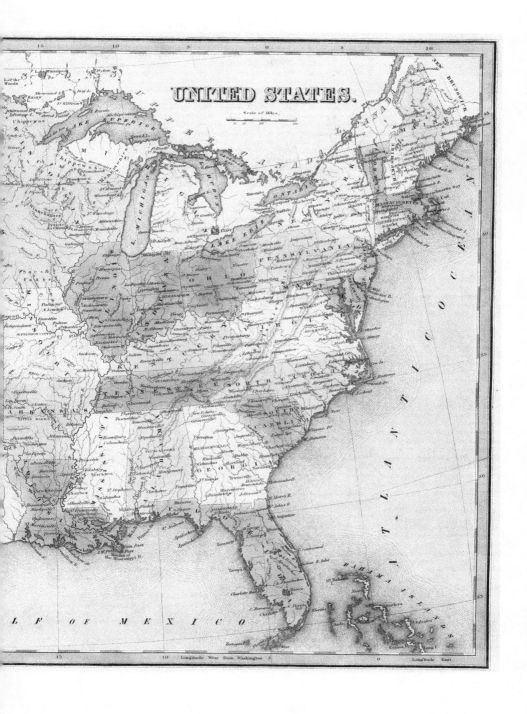

MAP 33. *A Map of the Indian Territory Northern Texas and New Mexico Showing the Great Western Prairies by Josiah Gregg.* Published in Gregg, *Commerce of the Prairies* (1844).

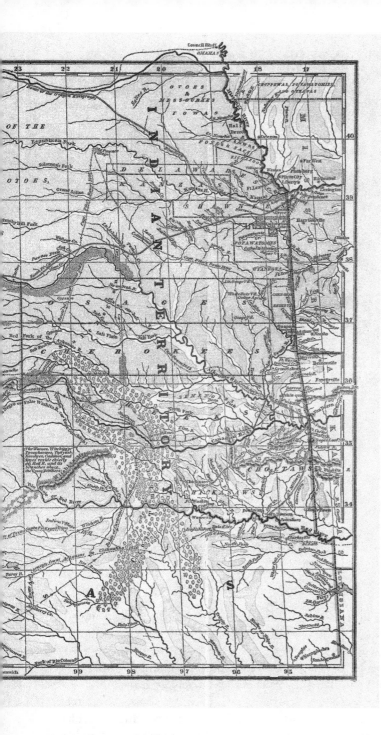

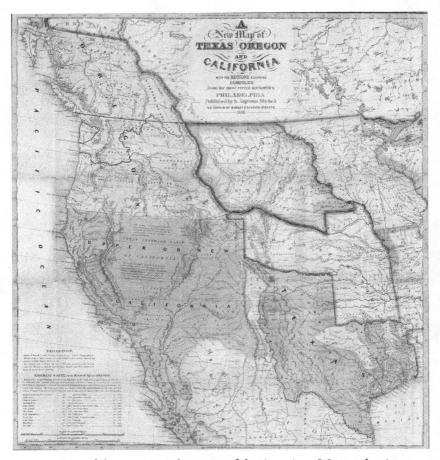

MAP 34. One of the most popular maps of the American West at the time, Augustus Mitchell's *A New Map of Texas Oregon and California* (1846) clearly inscribed "Indian Territory."

Arapahoe, Comanche, and Lakota. "Your heart must be strong to go upon so hazardous a journey," said the Skidi, "may the Master of Life be your protector."

James, however, believed these warnings were simply a ploy. Even after acknowledging that the "Pawnees are at war with the Arrapahoes, [Comanches], and other erratic bands, who wander about the sources of the Platte and Arkansa," James concluded that it was "highly probable their unwillingness to have us pass through their hunting grounds was the most productive cause of all the anxiety."[79] It was precisely the lack of water and the bands of Cheyenne, Arapahoe, Comanche, and Lakota that would later inspire Long to affix the description "Great Desert . . . frequented by roving bands of Indians" directly between the Platte and the Arkansas Rivers. This is particularly noteworthy since James wrote in his journal that, from the Pawnees' village on the Platte, past the Arkansas to the Canadian, they had not met "a single savage."[80] Clearly, the Americans' information concerning the "roving bands of Indians" was not firsthand knowledge. Therefore, Long's most lasting cartographic legacy was based on information he received from the Pawnees.

To a contemporary eye, Long's maps did little to help American's understand the landscape of the trans-Missouri West. Yet, in the first half of the nineteenth century, as Americans searched for ways to deal with the contradiction between real and imagined Indians, Long's map and report tied Native people to the landscape and helped to usher in the cultural creation of Indian Territory. Washington Irving; James Fenimore Cooper; George Catlin; and scores of artists, poets, and writers would build on Long's legacy, and although the desert would be gradually pushed west, the Missouri River remained the demarcation between savagery and civilization for decades.

In 1839, Thomas Farnham described the scene as his group crossed a tributary of the Missouri: "[We] approached the border of the Indian domains. . . . Before us were the treeless plains of green, as they had been since the flood. . . . A lovely landscape for this, for an Indian's meditations!"[81] Amelia Hadley had a similar reaction after crossing the Missouri a few years later; she declared that she was "now in Indian Territory and more wild and barren place I never saw." She mentioned this, despite being just a few miles from her crossing at St. Joseph, a landscape that looked much like the previous hundred miles in the state of Missouri.[82]

As late as 1855, many travelers maintained the fantasy of crossing into a different world once they reached the western side of the river. Butler Chapman recalled that as one particular group of "ladies of intelligence from the east" crossed the Missouri, "every heart beat with the consciousness of having launched into the Great Wilderness Prairie—from under the protection of the municipal laws or society." Despite the reference to law, the ladies were not making a geopolitical distinction but a cultural one. As Chapman noted, the group had indeed crossed the Missouri River, but they had done so while still in the thirty-year-old state of Missouri. Although Chapman explained that the towns they were passing had existed for decades as meeting places between Indians and

MAP 35. Mitchell also produced a wall map, which, along with the *New Map of Texas Oregon and California*, displayed "Indian Territory" in relation to the rectangular surveys in the adjacent states. Courtesy of David Rumsey Historical Map Collection.

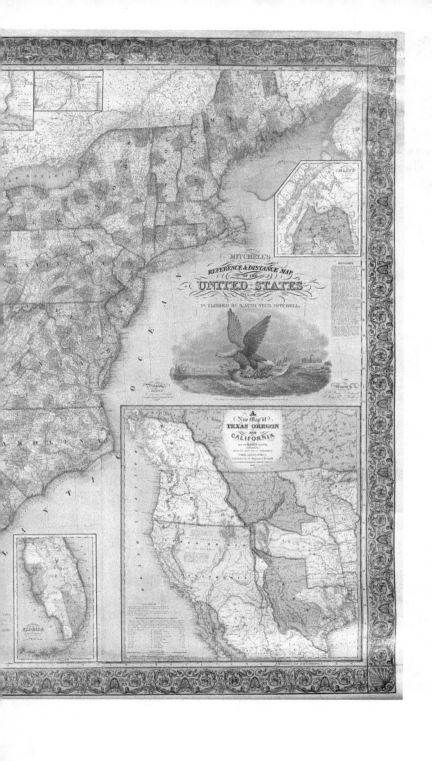

MITCHELL'S
REFERENCE & DISTANCE MAP
OF THE
UNITED STATES
PUBLISHED BY S. AUGUSTUS MITCHELL.

A
New Map of
TEXAS OREGON
AND
CALIFORNIA

whites, the group "had it fixed in their minds that they were in *Indian country* and they looked for everything as nature fixed it."[83]

Even though it was never a political reality, contemporary maps often depicted "Indian Territory" as a bounded space. Such a delineation not only represented the geopolitical reality of the Jacksonian West, but it also allowed the American public to construct a commemorative Indian past while they waited for Indians to become extinct.

5 / Science and the Destruction of "Indian Country"

The cultural and cartographic creation of "Indian Country" in the first half of the nineteenth century allowed Americans to appropriate Native history while still keeping Indians at a safe distance as they waited for them to be civilized. Yet as Euro-Americans began crossing Missouri in unprecedented numbers, this rhetorical balancing act became harder to maintain. As it became clear that Indians were not vanishing nearly as quickly as many desired, the question became how to draw new distinctions between "Indian" and "American" spaces. Otherwise, what separated American expansion from previous, unenlightened imperial conquests? For John Charles Frémont and his supporters, the answer was science.

One of the most telling episodes about the creation of space and mapping in the trans-Mississippi West involved the literary use of a bumblebee. In his journal, published in 1843, John Charles Frémont described ascending to what he believed to be the highest point in the Rocky Mountains. After unfurling an American flag at the summit, "a solitary bee (*bromus, the bumble bee*) . . . lit on the knee of one of the men." According to Frémont, this small creature was "a solitary pioneer to foretell the advance of civilization." The explorer ended his description of his summit by incorporating the bee into his scientific readings: "The barometer stood at 18.293, the attached thermometer at 44°, giving for the elevation of this summit 13,570 feet above the Gulf of Mexico, which may be called the highest flight of the bee."[1]

FIGURE 5. *Planting the American Flag upon the Summit of the Rocky Mountains* (1856). Woodcut from Samuel M. Smucker, *The Life of Col. John Charles Fremont*. Notice the bee flying above the seated figure on the left.

It was incidental that the peak Frémont and the other members of the Corps of Topographical Engineers climbed in 1842 was actually three hundred feet shorter than the peak just north of his vantage point and seven hundred feet shorter than the highest peak in the Rockies.[2] It was also not important that the entire encounter with the bee was most likely fabricated by either Frémont or his wife, Jessie, who actually penned much of the journal. What was important to the American public and what Frémont readily understood was that sounding exacting was more important than being exacting, and nothing was more important than a good story.[3]

The story of Frémont's explorations across the Great Plains—through the Rocky Mountains to Oregon and California in 1842, 1843, and 1844—captured the public's attention. After ten thousand copies of the reports were printed, the Senate contracted with the *Congressional Globe* and *Daily National Intelligencer* to publish a commercial version of the story, which quickly became a best seller.[4] Frémont's technical language proved to be an important factor in the book's success. A writer for the *U.S. Magazine and Democratic Review*, seemingly unaware that the book

FIGURE 6. *Col. Fremont Planting the American Standard on the Rocky Mountains* (1856). Wood engraving used to create banners during Frémont's 1856 presidential run. Notice the bee has been replaced with a more visible bird. Courtesy of Library of Congress.

was an extrapolation of Frémont's journal, declared that its scientific tone was evidence that it was "transcripts of notes made in the field." As such, the author continued, the Pathfinder's greatness surpassed even Lewis and Clark's, who "lack[ed] the science which Capt. Frémont carried into his expeditions."[5] This science—taken together with the sublime Romantic imagery so prevalent in nineteenth-century travel writing—caught the public's attention.[6] Reminiscing on the impact of reading Frémont's mise-en-scène with the bee during his childhood, poet Joaquin Miller wrote: "I fancied I could see Fremont's men, hauling the cannon up the savage battlements of the Rocky Mountains, flags in the air, Fremont at the head, waving his sword, his horse neighing wildly in the mountain wind, with unknown and unnamed empires at every hand. It touched my heart when he told how a weary little brown bee tried to make its way from a valley of flowers far below across a spur of snow, where he sat resting for a moment with his men."[7]

Frémont's use of a bee was very deliberate. By 1843, the "bee as advanced scout" had become a familiar trope in American literature.[8] Frémont's biography, printed during his 1856 presidential bid, even included the text of William Cullen Bryant's *The Prairies*—which describes the bee as "a more adventurous colonist than man"—emphasizing that the explorer's interaction with the bee was a "curious commentary" along "familiar lines."[9] Yet acknowledging the bee-as-civilization metaphor may still not fully recognize Frémont's linguistic acumen. Bees were not only a symbol of the Romantic sublime or a metaphor for western expansion, but they were also a harbinger of environmental change and sociopolitical upheaval. Since honeybees arrived in Jamestown in the early seventeenth century, Native groups viewed the bee as a portent of the growth of Euro-American settlements. The honeybee was so intertwined with the drastic changes Euro-Americans brought that French American writer Jean de Crèvecoeur wrote in 1782 that the first sight of one in a new territory "spreads sadness and consternation in all [Indian] minds."[10] In 1811, John Bradbury made a similar observation: "Bees have spread over this continent in a degree and with a celerity so nearly corresponding with that of the Anglo-Americans, that it has given rise to a belief, both amongst the Indians and the whites, that bees are their precursors, and that to whatever part they go the white people will follow. I am of the opinion that they are right, as I think it is impossible to stop the progress of one as of the other."[11] Just seven years before the *Report* was first printed, Washington Irving wrote that "Indians consider [bees] the harbinger of the white man . . . and say that, in proportion as the bee advances, the Indian and Buffalo retire."[12]

Thus, Frémont's use of the bee was particularly powerful. His precise record of the bee's flight represented not just the coming of civilization but the end of savage chaos. As Frémont well understood, the landscape of trans-Mississippi West was not a virgin land, but rather it had been shaped by humans for centuries. In the scene Frémont described, he brought scientific order not to an empty land but to something even more daunting: an undefined and uncontrolled Indian country.

For Americans in the 1840s, the land north of Iowa territory and west of the Missouri River was Indian country. Despite the geopolitical failure of the permanent Indian territory, the prospect of erasing Indians—even metaphorically—would have seemed ludicrous. Not only did their physical control of the lands between the Missouri and the Rocky Mountains make such a claim geopolitically impossible, the cartographic impact of Long, McCoy, Gregg, and Woodbridge—along with the literary and visual popularity of Cooper, King, and Catlin—made the western prairies and the Great Plains "Indian Country" in the eyes of the American public.

For territorial expansionists, Indians posed both a physical and representational problem. This chapter argues that Frémont and his supporters turned to scientific instrumentation and the specific forms of knowledge it produced to prepare the American West for Euro-American expansion. Science became part of a nationalist project that both unified the country and sterilized expansion, turning what appeared violent and unseemly to many Americans into a triumph of Enlightenment thought. Frémont deployed the rhetorical devices of scientific Enlightenment and Indian savagery in contradistinction to one another, as he did with his bee, both to diminish Native participation in the cartographic construction of the trans-Mississippi West and to distinguish his process of acquiring knowledge from that of Indians. In so doing, he turned what was in actuality a negotiated process into a clash of cultures, a legacy that reverberates even today.

"A Certain Degree of Relative Truth"

No figure in nineteenth-century American history—with the possible exception of George Armstrong Custer—has a legacy as elusive as John Charles Frémont's. Pathfinder, hollow man, scientist, blowhard: all these descriptions have been leveled at the intrepid explorer. Part of the reason for this lies in the ebbs and flows of historiography and the very meanings of American history. What historians once viewed as exceptional expansion is later understood to be violent imperialism. Yet Frémont's reputation is even more confounding than these sorts of generational shifts. Much of the confusion arises from the difficulty of separating Frémont's actions from his own descriptions of them. Much of what we know about Frémont comes from his own writings, partisan excerpts of his reports in newspapers that extoll his expansionist zeal, and his own memoirs. These sources have encouraged a conflation of Frémont's rhetoric and his actions that confounds scholars. Particularly confusing is the role of science in his expeditions and the maps that his excursions produced.

Carl Wheat, the patriarch of American cartographic studies, wrote that Frémont "changed the entire picture of the West and made a lasting contribution to cartography." However, while Wheat stated that Frémont's maps were "carefully drawn" with "locations adequately checked by astronomical observations," he never used the word "scientific" to describe Frémont's maps.[13] Bernard DeVoto was more critical of the maps' cartographic importance, writing in his landmark study *The Year of Decision* that "Frémont did little of importance beyond determining the latitude and longitude of many sites which the mountain men knew only by experience and habit. . . . They were adventure books, they were charters of Manifest Destiny."[14] Yet, even those scholars who criticized his cartographic contributions have been unable to completely displace Frémont from his scientific perch. Although he agreed that Frémont's reports "made few original contributions to geographical science," William Goetzmann hedged his bets by claiming that they "created a matchless cartographical picture of the West which was all the more valuable because it was largely based on fact."[15] Similarly, Robert Utley claims that while "science did not benefit" from Frémont's expeditions, he "explored it with the eye of a scientists, eager to . . . place the whole firmly within a framework of longitude and latitude."[16]

More recently, the ambiguity surrounding his scientific contributions seems to have disappeared. A catalogue for a 2007 exhibition at the Newberry Library claims that Frémont and his cartographer Charles Preuss created the "first scientific view" of the American West.[17] Similarly, biographer Tom Chaffin writes that it was Frémont's "scientific maps and measurements" that allowed Americans to reimagine western landscape. Even more succinctly, Chaffin claims that Frémont "placed mapmaking of the American West on a scientific foundation."[18] Later in his book, however, Chaffin admits that the scientific importance of the maps created from the first two expeditions lies in their omission of information rather than what knowledge they contained or the methods of their construction. Frémont had, unlike some other contemporary cartographers, correctly excluded the fabled "Dividing Waters" of the Rocky Mountains (these falsely illustrated the headwaters of the Rio Grande, the Arkansas, and Buenaventura as existing in the northern Rockies). According to Chaffin, "Frémont's greatest achievement as a mapmaker may lie in the things that do not appear on the map."[19] That not including information would be offered as evidence of a "scientific foundation" describes the difficulty of characterizing what was scientific about Frémont's maps.

Along with the mantle of science, scholars have associated Frémont with a cartographic project that erased Native people from the expanding American state.[20] Andrew Menard explains that, whereas the journals of Lewis and Clark included Native people as either objects of study or geopolitical actors, Frémont, on the other hand, "deliberately pushed them to the background—and then out of the picture altogether." This "arc of invisibility" did not reach its apex until later in the nineteenth century, but according to Menard, its "origins can be traced directly

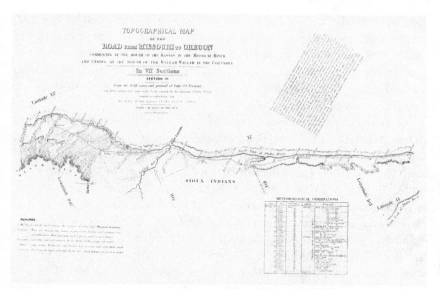

MAP 36. Section 3 of 7: *Topographical Map of the Road from Missouri to Oregon*. In addition to the label "Sioux Indians," the text excerpted from the *Report* focuses on the presence of Indians in the region. Courtesy of National Archives.

to Frémont's report."[21] This is an odd claim, especially considering the prominent place that Indians have in both his maps and reports. Indians' geopolitical presence is inscribed on both the small-scale maps of the West included in Frémont's *Report,* and the famous seven-part map of the Oregon Trail, which one scholar calls the "equivalent of a modern road atlas."[22]

This map of the Oregon Trail—printed on large sheets and also in rolls, so travelers could use it on their own journeys across the Plains— not only labeled Indian tribes' locations but also included paragraphs from the *Report,* describing various Indians activities. In the "Remarks" section, readers are warned that "good guards ought to be kept all the way. Sioux Indians are not to be trusted." Considering the maps' content and how this region was understood to be Indian country, it is difficult to see how someone looking at these maps could classify Indians as invisible.

Rather than erasure, a more accurate depiction of Frémont's treatment of Indians would be as foil: he placed Native knowledge and activity in deliberate juxtaposition to scientific language. By distinguishing applied scientific knowledge from the information provided by Indians, Frémont sanitized expansion for a country facing the harsh realities of Indian removal. Scientific language transformed the violent processes of territorial acquisition into one of Enlightenment progress, while it also masked Native contributions to the cartographic construction of the trans-Mississippi West.

As will be discussed below, much of that scientific rhetoric was proven either incorrect or useless. For example, the meteorological chart that acted as a visual counterweight to the narrative text about Indians might seem to give critical scientific information to a traveler on the Platte River route. However, as cartographer Gouverneur Kemble Warren wrote of the descriptions ten years later, "Nothing could give more incorrect view of . . . the portions of Nebraska we have explored than would be obtained by merely looking over our meteorological register for the past two years." Similarly, the grid of longitude and latitude appeared to help a user locate his position within a larger system. In fact, however, this would require someone already on the Oregon Trail either to carry his own instruments or to have a much smaller map that included an equally precise graticule (a graphic representation of latitude and longitude). Warren declared that, although these maps were excellent for travelers, they were not, "however, accurately constructed."[23] Frémont's inclusion of the readings was meant to distinguish his knowledge from that of the "Sioux Indians" rather than provide usable information.

As with his meteorological observations, Frémont's vision of a single enlightened figure bringing order to a savage landscape does not hold up under the scrutiny of historical analysis. During his journeys, Indians acted as guides, interpreters, scouts, hunters, and protectors. Belying his later claim that Indians should not be trusted, a group of Brulé and Oglala chiefs assigned a security detail to watch after the expedition after some young warriors declared they would attack the Corps if it continued.[24] With their Sioux protectors, the party continued unmolested. As described in chapter 3, Frémont's legacy would have been much different had a group of Skidi Pawnee not helped him on his return from his second trip. Only after the Skidi spent an afternoon talking the Chaui Pawnee among them out of "murdering" the entire expedition was the Corps allowed to go on its way.[25]

Frémont could not have survived—let alone have brought back any information—without Native assistance.[26] Less dramatic, but more frequent, was the Indians' role in the daily success of the expedition. In a letter to botanist John Torrey, Frémont explained that he "ascertained from the Indians the medicinal qualities" of many new plant and tree samples, as well as which plants could be used for food.[27] Even more directly, two Shawnees, James Rogers and his son Thomas Jefferson Rodgers, traveled with the Corps for the majority of the first expedition, working as interpreters, hunters, and guides.[28]

For cartographic purposes, the information that Frémont received from Native people proved to be extremely important. A few weeks before Frémont climbed what he believed to be the highest point in the Rockies, he had a telling interaction. After crossing the Kansas River, the Corps met with three Cheyennes returning from a failed horse-stealing expedition. Learning that the Indians had just traveled some three hundred miles northeast to raid a Pawnee village, the Americans asked about their route: "I placed a sheet of paper between us, on which they traced rudely, but with a certain degree of relative truth, the watercourses of the country which lay between us and their villages, and of which I desired to have some information."[29] While he was no doubt thrilled to obtain the information that allowed the Corps to reach the Wind River Range, the Cheyennes' map presented Frémont with a dilemma. If the Indians could depict the region in two-dimensional cartographic form, why were Frémont's expeditions necessary? What could Frémont offer that Indian knowledge could not?

This problem was not unique to Frémont's group. All expeditions relied on Native support and information. At the same time, explorers were expected to gather information that would legitimize the expansion of the growing nation-state. As historians of science have demonstrated, the perceived authority of science has played an essential role in state-making and colonial projects. The belief that universal truths could be explained through rational problem solving and then used for human benefit became the framework of a bureaucratized state.[30] According to one scholar, this formula was "inextricably woven into the whole fabric of colonialism."[31] Although Frémont had never traveled in the country that the Cheyenne described, he nevertheless recognized the symbols that the Indians drew as comprising a topographical map. While he relied on their information, Frémont needed to distinguish the Indians' intimate knowledge of places from his own scientific understanding of the world. Trying to accomplish both tasks, he thus declared that the Cheyennes' map contained "a certain degree of relative truth."[32]

As historian David Turnbull has demonstrated, all knowledge systems are "messy and complex, replete with unbridged gaps and over-lapping spatialities." They are "assemblages" that rely on webs of local knowledge. Enlightenment science—despite its veneer of universality—was no more based on abstract principles than either the knotted string instruments that Incan census takers used to create administrative systems or a particular brand of dead reckoning, known as *Etak,* which Pacific Islanders used to navigate.[33] Only through the creation of "social strategies and technical devices" was local knowledge that was classified as science moved from its site of production to bureaucratic "centers of calculation"—such as Washington DC or London—where it was transformed into abstract representations.[34] Although he relied on Native information to construct his maps, it was Frémont's translation of that information that made it useful to his readers.[35] Yet demonstrating superior knowledge over Native people was more than just a cultural framework for Frémont; it was also part of a geopolitical strategy.

"Not Merely a Survey"

On December 25, 1824, Thomas Hart Benton, a young senator from the even younger state of Missouri, visited Thomas Jefferson at his home in Monticello. During this conversation, Benton's views of America's westward expansion took shape.[36] It was Jefferson, after all, who had first sent the Corps of Engineers to explore the newly acquired Louisiana Territory in 1804, looking for the easiest route to the Pacific. "Mr. Jefferson," Benton recalled in his memoirs, "was the first to propose the North American road to India." Everything the senator wrote or said about the subject was, according to Benton, "nothing but the fruit of the seed planted in my mind by the philosophic hand of Mr. Jefferson."[37] Their conversation was premised on the belief that commerce with Asia was the key to creating an American empire and that, therefore, the United States required a new Pacific trade route. Not long after his visit to Monticello, Benton showed a map in Congress that he had procured from Jefferson, and he made his first demands for a national road through the North American West.[38] By 1841, Benton had decided that Oregon was the key to wresting control of Asiatic trade from England. In order to do this, however, he needed to encourage American settlement.

Throughout the previous decade, Congress had refused to abrogate the Treaty of 1818, which declared a joint occupation of Oregon with Britain. This frustrated Benton and his western colleagues. With President John Tyler and Secretary of War John Spencer worried that any provocation could bring another war between the empire and its former colony, the options for government support for Americans to immigrate were small indeed. To circumvent political obstruction, the senators planned to use the newly organized Corps of Topographical Engineers to promote expansion.[39] For Benton, the use of the Corps—whose operating funds were controlled by the Senate—was the perfect solution to executive interference with the Oregon question. Benton believed he could encourage western migration by "fixing" the route through which people would pass over the Plains and through Rocky Mountains on their way to Oregon. In so doing, he would deliver "encouragement from the apparent interest which the government took in their enterprise." He would later boast that the Corps' objectives were "conceived without [the president's] knowledge, and executed upon solicited orders, of which the design was unknown."[40] For Benton and his colleagues, the Topographical Engineers could further the geopolitical ends they could not pursue through traditional political means. After another holiday dinner, this one eighteen years after his Christmas meeting with Jefferson, Benton announced to Senator Lewis Linn and other western congressmen that it would be his son-in-law, John Charles Frémont, who would follow those secret orders.[41]

What, precisely, those orders entailed has been the subject of scholarly debate.[42] As with Frémont, it is difficult to separate Benton's actions from his own reports of them. On April 25, 1842, Lt. Col. John James Abert, the head of the new Corps, instructed Frémont to survey the Platte River to the head of the longest tributary of its northern branch.[43] This would have ended the survey at the base of the Rocky Mountains, in what is now central Wyoming. According to Benton's memoir, however, this assignment did not meet Frémont's expectations. He quickly returned to Abert to get his instructions altered. He wanted "the Rocky Mountains inserted as an object of his explorations, and he thought the South Pass in those mountains should be examined and its position ultimately fixed by him."[44] Despite Benton's declaration that Frémont was the one who felt the instructions "did not come up to his views," recently discovered letters confirm that it was the senator who pressed the expedition to continue into the mountains: "I think it would be well for you to name, in the instructions for Mr. Frémont, the great pass through the Rocky Mountains, called the South West Pass. It will be a thoroughfare for nations to the end of time. In the mean time we only know it from the reports of hunters & traders, its lau. & lat. unknown, its distance & bearings equally unknown."[45] Hinting at Benton's role in setting the goals for the expedition, Frémont wrote in his memoirs that, during his frequent meetings with the western senators, he felt he was "being drawn into the current of important political events; the object of this expedition was not merely a survey."[46]

Abert initially rejected Benton's suggestion, believing that such an exploration would require several seasons to complete. As a man of science, Abert knew how difficult it would be to complete a precise instrumental survey. After all, Frémont had not even finished the map of the region between the Mississippi and the Missouri Rivers that he and Joseph Nicollet had explored during the previous two years. Not only was that "highly scientific reconnaissance" through more accessible country, but Nicollet also was a seasoned astronomer, in whose science Abert had "utmost confidence." Frémont, on the other hand, had only a few years of surveying experience, and only the previous two under Nicollet had used astronomical observations and scientific equipment to fix points. After considering the matter further, however, the commander of the Corps gave Frémont permission to "do what [Benton] desires," although he would not include the South Pass in his formal instructions.[47]

Historians have pointed to this alteration of plans as a decisive moment in the narrative of Manifest Destiny. While the place where Frémont should end his exploration may seem insignificant, this change encapsulated the imperialist moment of the 1840s. Whether highlighting the expansionist nature of Benton's designs or arguing that this was the moment that genuine scientific inquiry gave way to geopolitical concerns, scholars have rightfully underscored the importance of this exchange. Yet, this emphasis on Benton's geopolitical aims has overlooked the faith that those who oversaw the surveys had in the power of science. This project combining science and nationalism was embodied by Frémont's first mentor, Joel Roberts Poinsett.

"The Application of Science to Useful Purposes"

As a young South Carolinian, Joel Poinsett was passionate about travel. In his twenties, he financed his own exploration through Russia, Ukraine, and the Caucasus. Later, he was appointed the United States commercial agent in Chile, a position that allowed him to travel to Argentina and other parts of South America. Poinsett's travels would develop his interest in scientific exploration, modeled after the German explorer and naturalist Alexander von Humboldt. While scholars have debated exactly what defines this particular form of inquiry—now classified as "Humboldtian Science"—its primary characteristics include using scientific instruments to measure universal laws of nature and encountering these laws in the field rather than in the laboratory.[48]

In 1830, Poinsett returned home after serving as the first U.S. minister to the Republic of Mexico.[49] In South Carolina, the peripatetic fifty-one-year-old College of Charleston trustee met an eager John Charles Frémont, who had graduated from the same institution the year before. Poinsett absorbed Frémont into his intellectual and political circle, leaving a lasting impression on the latter's worldview—a view built on the pillars of unionism, exploration, and science.[50]

Poinsett was an ardent nationalist who came home from Mexico to a state beset by economic stagnation. Many Americans—including fellow South Carolinian John C. Calhoun—blamed the state's problems on protective tariffs, which were designed to encourage northern manufacturing. Calhoun argued that the state had a constitutional right to "nullify" the tariff, and in 1832, he helped the state to adopt the Ordinance of Nullification, which declared the 1828 and 1832 tariffs unenforceable within the state. Although Poinsett opposed the tariffs, he saw South Carolinians' declaration of states' rights as a "strange and pernicious" threat to the Union. President Andrew Jackson agreed, and in the winter of 1832, he sent the sloop-of-war *Natchez* to the Charleston harbor, threatening to unleash fifteen thousand troops to enforce the tariff. For four months, Frémont watched as Poinsett helped the president manage the so-called Nullification Crisis. The Compromise Tariff, which passed both houses of Congress, averted the threat of military confrontation between South Carolina and the federal government. A toast was offered to Poinsett at a Charleston society house: "To the honorable Joel R. Poinsett, his exertions in the holy cause of Union and Liberty, has obtained for him the love and confidence of every true Carolinian."[51] While Frémont would later conflate his time teaching navigational mathematics aboard the *Natchez*—beginning two months *after* the Compromise Tariff was signed—with his informal assistance to Poinsett during the Nullification Crisis, his time with Poinsett instilled in him a faith in the importance of a strong American state.[52]

Just as important as his faith in the union were the lessons that Frémont would learn from Poinsett about how best to encourage its fruition. Influenced by his early Humboldtian explorations, Poinsett came to believe in the rhetorical and practical powers of science. In the 1820s and 1830s, Poinsett was a member of the Columbian Institute for the Promotion of Arts and Sciences, which grew out of the surge in nationalism following the War of 1812. After the collapse of the Columbian Institute,

Poinsett was elected the first president of the National Institute for the Promotion of Science, formed in 1840 to compete for the $500,000 that Englishman James Smithson had bequeathed to the United States to create "an establishment for the increase and diffusion of knowledge among men." The goal of this new organization was to create a scientific body with a direct relationship to the national government.[53] Although it was the Smithsonian—a new organization created in Smithson's name—that ultimately received the bequest, the creation of the National Institute and its competitors underscored the importance of science to the nationalist project of the 1840s.

In a speech he gave during the National Institute's first anniversary celebration, Poinsett declared that the improvements in manufacturing and commerce that the world had experienced during the previous fifty years were "due altogether to the application of science to useful purposes." For the United States to keep "pace with the most enlightened nations of the world," science must be funded directly through the state. Although individuals might acquire scientific knowledge or possess the best instruments, they must receive a "stamp of authenticity, which a Government alone can give them."[54] For Poinsett, science needed to work closely with the state for the nation to thrive.

Part of the reason science was readily appropriated by nation-states was because the term could be applied to a wide range of activities. Exemplifying the elasticity of the term, Poinsett declared that the National Institute would include eight separate areas of scientific investigation: astronomy, geography, and natural philosophy; natural history; geology and mineralogy; chemistry; the application of science to the useful arts; agriculture; American history and antiquities; and literature and the fine arts.[55] Science became a hollow term with which the state could classify any number of enterprises. The meaning of science depended on the context in which it was deployed.[56] Nothing epitomized this elasticity better than cartography.

As the secretary of war, Poinsett had authorized J. J. Abert to send Joseph Nicollet; John Frémont and his assistant; and two other members of the Corps of Topographical Engineers to travel into the Indian Country between the Mississippi and Missouri Rivers. Over two years and two separate expeditions, the explorers—along with the "zealous cooperation of men of science" stationed semi-permanently in the region—made "not less than two hundred and forty five" astronomical readings and completed "a very extensive series of barometric observations." From these calculations, Poinsett promised Congress, an accurate map would be constructed, one that would be "useful to both the Government and the people." This map would be a model by which other regions could be cartographically incorporated into the Union. Stressing the scientific nature of this process, Poinsett said that no survey should be contemplated without being accompanied by astronomical and barometrical observations.[57]

In addition to their scientific rigor, Poinsett was confident that these maps would achieve geopolitical ends. Using virtually the same language in his speech to the National Institute as he did to Congress, Poinsett pointed out that little was known "scientifically and accurately" about the interior of the country. To rectify this problem, Poinsett declared that a "map of the United States ought to be constructed upon a uniform plan, and under the immediate direction of the scientific officers of the United States." This map would have immediate social and geopolitical uses, and it would aid in the "rapid settlement and improvement of our country." Every European empire had either completed or was working on mathematical surveys of their territories. These maps—originally created to plan military strategy—were now so accurate that armies and sentinels were dispatched with no more knowledge than what was inscribed on the map.[58] Whatever secret plans Thomas Hart Benton might have had in mind when he conspired to send Frémont across the Great Plains and into the Rocky Mountains, Joel Poinsett was happy to provide a scientific rationale to help accomplish these goals.

"Due Immediately to the Perfection of the Instruments"

During the first half of the nineteenth century, the most potent form of science accomplished two tasks. Although the United States joined other enlightened nations in their use of science to legitimize the state, its particular brand of science also distanced the young republic from its European precedents. Americans considered themselves a practical people, and they required a particular kind of science—applied science—to fit their challenges and goals (Alexis de Tocqueville devoted an entire to chapter of *Democracy in America* to the question of "Why Americans Are More Addicted to Practical Rather Than Theoretical Science"). Rather than competing with European science, which was based on theories established in the laboratory, American science created its own corpus of knowledge built on experience in the field.[59] Practical fieldwork—particularly scientific exploration—had a strong resonance with Americans.

In his memoirs, published four decades after his first expedition, John Frémont highlighted the practical nature of his scientific endeavors. As Frémont recalled, "strict engineering had lost its inspiration." Instead, it was the "thought of penetrating into the recesses of that wilderness region," that filled him with enthusiasm. He would "study without books, learning from nature herself . . . where in all her features there was still aboriginal freshness."[60] Frémont believed that freeing himself from established tropes would ultimately prove more valuable to science. In the introduction to his *Report*, Frémont explained that the map accompanying it "may have a meager and skeleton appearance," but it was "more valuable to science on that account, being wholly founded upon positive data and actual data in the field." The *Democratic Review* endorsed Frémont's strategy, explaining, "Capt. Frémont does not indulge in theories and speculations." As such, the maps were created "by a scientific and practical man, who has travelled the whole distance,—compass in hand taking courses; barometer in hand measuring elevations; telescope in hand, determining longitudes and latitudes; pencil in hand sketching the country."[61] Such experiential science would be, according to an 1845 advertisement for a commercial edition of the *Report*, important for all U.S. citizens, since it would improve "American enterprise and skill."[62]

The *Democratic Review*'s assessment of Frémont's journeys offers another clue to decipher the peculiarities of the Humboldtian science that had catapulted the Pathfinder into the national spotlight. Because science still had such indefinite characteristics, those who hoped to assert its authority—along with that of the American state—needed tools to separate their scientific work from other knowledge acquired in the field. Charts, graphs, maps, and statistical tables—all measured by precise instrumentation—separated scientific exploration from what an English reviewer of the *Report* called the "voluminous emptiness and conceited rodomontade so often brought forth by [England's] costly expeditions."

Frémont's narrative of his first journey was contained in a lively 76 pages, and the reviewer declared its scientific worth came in the narrative's 130 pages of addenda, which contained astronomical and meteorological observations.[63] It did not matter that this information was largely inaccurate and not even included in the majority of the *Report*'s printings. The charts were important in that they demonstrated to the public how scientific instruments were deployed. These instruments—including barometers, thermometers, telescopes, sextants, and chronometers— became the talismans of Frémont's expeditions. They allowed for what Bruno Latour calls the "immutable and combinable mobiles"—the translation of local phenomena into a seemingly universal system of knowledge. As with his meteorological observations, however, the rhetoric of precision was more important than the reality.[64]

"Traveling 'Scientifically' with Instruments"

In his speech to the National Institute, Joel Poinsett explained that the reciprocal relationships among technical instruments and the science they illustrated had allowed for the extraordinary scientific improvements over the first half of the nineteenth century: "The progress made in astronomy, navigation, geography, and the kindred science are due immediately to the perfection of the instruments prepared by the mechanician[s] . . . whose minds are deeply imbued with the principles of the science for the advancement of which those instruments were to be employed."[65] These instruments—and the readings, graphs, charts, and maps they provided—defined American progress. Yet, as was clear to his contemporaries, Frémont did not know how to use them properly.

The year before Frémont set out to lead his own expedition, Joseph Nicollet refused to let him carry a barometer on the relatively tame journey from Baltimore to St. Louis, since Nicollet believed that Frémont was not "used to carrying this sort of instrument."[66] Charles Preuss—the cartographer for both the 1842 expedition to the Rocky Mountains and the 1843–44 expedition to Oregon and California—was also unimpressed with both the Corps' scientific equipment and Frémont's ability to use it properly. "Our big chronometer has gone to sleep," the German wrote. "So far I can't say that I have formed a very high opinion of Frémont's astronomical manipulations."[67] In fact, Frémont himself wrote to Colonel Abert that he had "but little confidence" in many of the longitudes he recorded.[68] As such, many of the readings were changed in subsequent editions of the *Report*.[69] It is no wonder that Preuss challenged the methods of the expedition by sarcastically highlighting the differences between a trading caravan—loaded with hides—and the Corps, who "travel[ed] 'scientifically' with instruments."[70]

The most obvious failure of Frémont's science came during a dramatic event on the first journey. Highlighted by the *Intelligencer* in 1845, in his 1856 biography, and in his 1887 *Memoir*, Frémont's depiction of the Corps' harrowing experience shooting the rapids on the Sweetwater River was the narrative climax of the first expedition. Fresh off their meeting with the bee, the group's elation quickly faded as they picked through three cataracts in their India-rubber boats. They eventually made it to smooth water, but this safety proved ephemeral as they entered another narrow canyon laced with jagged rocks. When a wave swept a pair of saddlebags and sextant overboard, Frémont managed to save the scientific instrument, although the bags became "prey of the whirlpools." Using all their "strength and skill to avoid staving the boat on the sharp points," the flotilla finally found flat water.

Their relief was again premature, however, as they found themselves in a passage "much worse than the previous one." This time, it was Frémont's favorite man, Basil Lajeunesse, who went overboard ("'Cre' Dieu' cried Basil!"). The narrative tension was finally broken when the group, "flush with success, and familiar with the danger[,] . . . yielded to the excitement" and "broke into a Canadian boat song."[71]

As with any good adventure story, however, it is just at this moment of relief when the biggest threat appears. They were "in the midst of a chorus" when the boat struck a rock and capsized. "Every record of the journey, our journals and registers of astronomical and barometric observations [were] lost in a moment."[72] Although Frémont claimed to have duplicates of the most important barometrical observations, the sextant, the compasses, the large telescope, the horizon, the books, and the journals full of original observations were—in the Preuss's words— "gone to the Devil."[73]

What should have spelled disaster for the Corps, however, was a mere aside for Frémont. He did not even mention the loss of the equipment in the excerpted forms of the *Report*.[74] In fact, the loss of both the scientific readings and the instruments that created them was so unimportant that by 1856, damaged scientific instruments became proof of Frémont's scientific mastery. Another scene from the *Report* featured Frémont saving a damaged barometer through an acrobatic leap. The narrator used this incident to show how great Frémont's scientific knowledge had become: "The care with which Mr. Frémont records the preservation of this barometer lends interest to his subsequent account of its destruction and the ingenuity with which he repaired the loss." The narrator was not bothered that the fix involved the less-than-precise components of buffalo horn and a piece of wood.[75] Nor did he seem concerned that Charles Preuss was highly skeptical of such fixes. (After a chronometer broke at nearly the same point in the journey, Preuss wrote: "Frémont was jubilant when he heard again the ticking and ticktocking [but] in comparing we found that every twenty-fours it went wrong by an hour. Oh you American blockheads!")[76] Simply mentioning scientific instruments was deemed sufficient to prove Frémont's acumen.

FIGURE 7. *Fremont's Dangerous Passage through a Cañon in the Platte River.* Woodcut from John Bigelow's *Memoir of the Life and Public Services of John Charles Frémont* (New York: Derby and Jackson, 1856).

Frémont used scientific instruments and the precise knowledge that these instruments provided as symbols of American expansion. His inability to use them properly—or even to bring them back in working condition—did little to diminish their symbolic weight. Science's symbolic weight grew even stronger as it helped flatten the messy reality of the expedition into a two-dimensional clash of cultures. Contemporary critics lauded Frémont's use of field instruments as the reason to elevate his scientific explorations above Romantic

travel writing, with its "voluminous emptiness and conceited rodomontade." Not one critic, however, commented on scientific data's
more important rhetorical task: distinguishing Frémont's knowledge
from that of Indians.

"To Be among Indians in Waste Places"

Frémont learned more than just the application of science and the love
of country from his first mentor, Joel Poinsett. Between 1838 and 1841,
Poinsett was Martin Van Buren's secretary of war. As such, Poinsett had
overseen the final implementation of Andrew Jackson's orders to move
Indians living in the southeastern United States to Indian Country. In
the 1840 report in which Poinsett suggested that the scientific method
Joseph Nicollet employed should be extended westward, he also proudly
reported that forty-one thousand Indians had been relocated westward
since 1836. Poinsett was careful to add that the removed Indians were
"prosperous and happy."[77]

In an 1838 report, Poinsett argued that the only way to maintain
peace between settlers and the newly resettled Indians—and between
those Indians and the nonemigrant Indians—was to create two lines
of posts that would run from Fort Snelling on the Upper Mississippi to
Fort Towson on the Red River of the South. These posts could serve as
mustering points for military patrols as well as places of refuge for settlers during periods of tension.[78] Twice in the report, the secretary highlighted the limited geographical knowledge of the region, intimating the
importance of a cartographic survey.

Not coincidentally, Poinsett oversaw J. J. Abert and the U.S. Army's
Bureau of Topographical Engineers. In fact, at the moment that Poinsett
was delivering his report to Congress, Capt. W. G. Williams, John C.
Frémont, and two other members of the Bureau of Topographical Engineers were conducting a military reconnaissance in Cherokee country
(parts of North Carolina, Tennessee, and Georgia), under the orders of
the secretary. Frémont later defined this time spent surveying the Cherokee country in anticipation of armed conflict as the most important
of his life. Here he found "the path he was destined to walk." Frémont
defined his path not by science, nor by military service, nor by his country's expansionist cause. Instead, he defined his path through his relationships with Indians. Frémont defined the prime of his life as the time
he spent "among Indians and in waste places." Other events were simply
"incidents in this and grew out of it."[79] For Frémont, Indians were not

incidental to the scientific expansion of the American state; instead, they were necessary components by which that process could be measured.

From August 7 to August 28, 1845, the *Daily National Intelligencer* published a four-part serial, reprinted around the country, which excerpted from and commented on Frémont's new reports. After quoting Frémont's declaration that his map will be "more valuable to science" since it was "wholly founded upon positive data and actual observations in the field," the rhetorical parameters of these observations were established in the first passage the editors chose to excerpt.[80]

A few days into the journey, the company found an empty Kansas village near the mouth of the Vermillion River. The location of this village, the *Report* stated, was chosen with the Indians' "customary fondness for beauty of scenery." Still, it was not the specifics of the village that captured the editors' attention but rather Frémont's ability to use scientific reasoning to process information about the Indians who lived there:

> We make this short extraction because we are glad to add the testimony of so good an authority as Capt. Fremont in proof of this pleasing trait of the Indian character . . . [proving him] fitted in a peculiar manner for this enterprise. He had to traverse an immense country where the foot of civilized man had as yet scarcely trod . . . [and had] never been looked upon by the eye of science. How necessary was it therefore, that he should possess not only the feeling and taste which prompted to continued observation of what was around him, but also the judgment which could estimate, and the science which could describe, the novelties which he met.[81]

In contrast to the Indians, who understood only aesthetics, Frémont could analyze both the setting and its inhabitants in a scientific manner. Repeatedly in his reports—and highlighted in the most accessible versions of them—Frémont became the embodiment of science, while Indians were cast as its foil. Frémont described their route home from the second expedition, for example, by noting that the "savages [were] hardly above the conditions of mere wild animals," and the route was "absolutely new to geographical, botanical, and geological science."[82] Building on the differences between scientific knowledge and Indian knowledge, Thomas Benton explained to Congress in 1847 that the map created from Frémont's journeys would be: "Luminous with science. Upon a breadth of some fifty miles, and a length of two thousand it is resplendent with science. The results not merely of geography and of topography, but of all the kindred natural sciences are there. Astronomy, geology, geometry, botany, meteorology, are all there, with the names and abodes of savage tribes and the range of the wild animals upon which they live."[83]

During his failed run for president, Frémont created a timeline of important events in his life, which was reprinted in newspapers around the country with the instructions that readers should "cut [it] out for reference." This timeline offers a telling summation of what, by 1856, had become his personal origin story. Readers learned that, after his birth (*January 21, 1813, in Savannah Georgia*), he had many obstacles to overcome (*In 1818, when Frémont was only five, his father died and left him with his mother, a brother, and a sister*), on his way to becoming a self-made man (*In 1831, he began laboring at private surveyor*). Although his intelligence was undeniable (*In 1827, Dr. Robertson, now a classical teacher in Philadelphia, took great interest in his genius; In 1835, he was commissioned as Professor of Mathematics in the Navy*), classroom work and philosophical musing meant little to him (*In 1836, he was made Master of Arts by Charleston College without his solicitation*). Instead, it was his love of the Union (*In 1833, he was the first public servant under the Jackson Administration in sloop-of-war Natchez and sent to Charleston to put down nullification*) and practical science that drove his intellectual pursuits (*In 1838, he surveyed Cherokee Country for a military map and he was commissioned as Second-Lieutenant Topographical Engineers by Mr. Poinsett, Secretary of War as an "assistant possession science, energy, courage and enterprise"*).[84]

The timeline then annotates the 1842 expedition—his most highly regarded from a scientific point of view—with two events. The second, unsurprisingly, was his unfurling of the Star-Spangled Banner on "the highest peak of the Rocky Mountains, 13,570 feet above the Gulf of Mexico." The first was the decidedly unscientific "celebrated speech to the Indian Council at Fort Laramie." This scene was not only highlighted in the *Daily National Intelligencer*'s serial version of the *Report* in 1845—and in the newspaper clipping viewers were instructed to cut out—but by the time of the publication of Frémont's biography in 1856, this event had become the essence of the expedition. The narrator (in actuality, some combination of Frémont, Jessie Benton, and the purported author, John Bigelow) informed the reader that they should see the reports themselves for the "geographical and scientific results, which have received repeated acknowledgement from the most distinguished sources." Here, they would be limited to passing on a few extracts to demonstrate the more striking aspects of the expedition.[85]

There is nothing particularly striking about Frémont's "celebrated" speech. On July 21, four Lakotas delivered a letter to Frémont from two traders they had recently left at Fort Platte. The letter—written in French—had been dictated to the traders by the chiefs, and it warned Frémont that the young men of their band would attack the Corps at the first opportunity. They should not leave the fort until their warriors returned. Frémont would do no such thing. He did not believe the chiefs, and even if the Corp were attacked, did the Indians think the great white chief would not respond? Their villages would be swept away as quickly "as fire does the prairie in the autumn." After this staunch declaration, the travelers were not disturbed by Indians for the rest of their journey.[86] The narrator declined to explain that the reason Frémont and his men were "not disturbed" was because of the security detail that the Oglala and Brulé chiefs sent with the Corp to discourage their own young men from attacking.[87]

To understand why this relatively insignificant moment of military posturing became such a central feature in Frémont's narrative, we must follow the trajectory that Frémont himself laid out. Only through this scene-setting can the reader—and the twenty-first-century historian— understand what was at stake. On their way to Fort Laramie on July 12, Frémont's Cheyenne guides were alarmed by the rapid approach of a group of Indians. Had they been "disencumbered by instruments," Frémont wrote, they would have fought the group. As it was, they sat and waited for what turned out to be a friendly group of Arapaho.[88] This false alarm did not stop Frémont's men from believing that the country around Fort Laramie was "swarming with scattered war parties." According to Frémont, there was a common understanding that the group "could not escape without some sharp encounters with the Indians." Understanding the inevitability of such an encounter, one of Frémont's most experienced men made out his will.[89]

After establishing the potential dangers of the Indians, the excerpt continues by contrasting the Indians' savagery with science. Although the recently feared Arapahos joined the expedition (Frémont thought it wise to recruit "an interpreter and two or three old men"), their primary role was inhibiting scientific endeavors: "So far as frequent interruptions from the Indians would allow, we occupied ourselves in making some astronomical calculations and bringing up the general map to this stage of the journey." Whether disturbing astronomical calculations or creating "incessant interruptions" while he was trying to fix a barometer, so many women and children came to Frémont's tent that the chiefs had to drive them away. Despite his annoyance, Frémont understood he needed to forgive the Indians for their excitement over these instruments and the knowledge they provided: "The numerous strange instruments, applied to still stranger uses, excited awe and admiration among them, and those which I used in talking with the sun and stars they looked upon with special reverence, as mysterious things of 'great medicine.'"[90]

The rhetorical and dramatic juxtaposition of science and Indians came to a head on July 21, 1856. In the narrative moment before Otter Hat, the Breaker of Arrows, the Black Night, and the Bull's Tails delivered their transcribed ultimatum to Frémont, the lieutenant described the instruments and the processes by which he established that "the longitude of Fort Laramie is 7 hours 01 minutes, 21 seconds, and from lunar distance 7 hours 01 minutes 29 seconds—giving for the adopted longitude 104 degrees 47 minutes 48 seconds." It did not matter that these readings were wrong. What mattered was that these measurements were taken just before "several . . . powerful [chiefs] . . . forced their way into the room in spite of all opposition."[91] For Frémont, Indians were the perfect foil to his scientific endeavors. Whether meeting the bee "13,570 feet above the Gulf of Mexico" or giving a speech at Fort Laramie, the scientific success of the expedition was not measured against any universal truths but rather against Indian savagery.

"As If Indians Did Not Rob and Kill Scientific Men"

Certainly part of the reason for juxtaposing Indians with scientific knowledge was to demonstrate the metaphysical superiority Americans had over their indigenous counterparts.[92] More subtly, focusing on the differences between Indian and Euro-American knowledge also turned what many contemporary Americans criticized as deliberate geopolitical expansion into an inevitable—if unfortunate—clash of cultures. Between 1845 and Frémont's presidential run in 1856, the complicated reality of the Corps' mission was transformed into a purely scientific endeavor.

In the preface to the original printing, Frémont acknowledged that, while his report would certainly "add something to science," it was "chiefly contemplated a military topographical survey."[93] One month after the *Report* was printed, the *Democratic Review* lauded the science produced by the expedition, but the newspaper's editor acknowledged that "the military examination was the first object." Understanding the nebulous nature of the Corps' objectives, the editor made no distinction between Frémont's scientific and military equipment: "sextants, refracting circles, chronometers, barometers, thermometers and telescopes, as well as rifles and the howitzer, formed a part of the young officer's equipment."[94] Considering Frémont's original appropriation for the expedition proposed a "military and geographical survey west of the Mississippi," it is easy to understand the editor's inability to classify the Corps' equipment.[95]

Although newspapers reported that Frémont had been furnished with the brass twelve-pound howitzer, he had decided on his own to bring the field artillery piece on the second journey, earning him a formal sanction from Joel Poinsett, the secretary of war, and J. J. Abert, head of the Topographical Corps.[96] Describing the rationale for the censure, Abert explained that the procurement of the field gun meant that Frémont "looked more to military than scientific result."[97] But whereas Abert and his boss, Poinsett, believed that applied science alone could elevate Euro-American expansion from Indian savagery, Frémont understood the dangers of Indians and their "waste places." In a letter to Abert—a few months before he acquired the gun to start his second expedition—Frémont explained what he perceived to be the true purpose of his trips. Describing his interaction with some headmen of an Arapahoe and Cheyenne village, Frémont wrote: "Our host asked a number of questions relative to the object of our journey, of which I made no concealment; telling him simply that I had made a visit to see the country, preparatory to the establishment of military posts on the way to the mountains. Although this was information of the highest interest to them, and by no means calculated to please them, it excited no expression or surprise, and in no way altered the grave courtesy of their demeanor."[98]

As late as 1846, military goals remained an important part of Frémont's expeditions. In the popular periodical *Living Age*, readers were offered glimpses of what would become the memes of Frémont's life, including topographical surveys in the Cherokee country of Georgia (all the while expecting that the "hostilities of the southern Indians" would require "military operations") and two years aiding the "eminent savan" Joseph Nicollet on his travels between the Mississippi and Missouri Rivers.[99] Despite acknowledging Frémont's technical training, however, the author was still unsure how to classify his two now-legendary trips to the West, writing, "his military reconnaissance in which he was engaged, became also scientific explanations."[100]

It was not until 1847—during his appeal to Congress to fund what became the famous seven-part map of the Oregon Trail—that Thomas Hart Benton hit on the rhetorical power of Alexander von Humboldt. By comparing Frémont to the celebrated explorer, Benton could prove Frémont's scientific bona fides simply by invoking the latter's name. In midcentury America, no scientist was as famous as the German explorer and naturalist. Due to the same practical exploration that would popularize Frémont, Humboldt's trips through South America had earned him the title of the "scientific discoverer of America." In 1869, hundreds of thousands of people throughout the United States celebrated the one-hundredth anniversary of Humboldt's birth, and he was deemed more famous than Columbus.[101] Once Benton struck on the rhetorical comparison between Frémont and Humboldt, the geopolitical import of Frémont's trips was obscured by the mere proximity to the latter's legacy: "The natural history of the country now may be studied, and even an almanac constructed, for nearly two thousand miles of prairies and mountains, on a view of this road map. It is a new thing, and an era in our conception of map-making, and belongs to a school of which originality and science are the characteristics, and of which the illustrious Humboldt is the great illustration."[102] Comments about methodological incompetence and geopolitical strategies were all drowned out by the cacophony of Humboldtian reverence.

The year after Benton declared Humboldt to be the true muse of the explorations, another senator declared that Frémont had reached the "most commanding position as a scientific explorer" and had earned the title of "the American Humboldt."[103] That same year, both a college professor and an American diplomat wrote Senator Benton, each breathlessly declaring Humboldt's interest in Frémont's work. (After explaining that Humboldt thought Frémont's work displayed talent, courage, and enterprise, the diplomat could hardly contain his excitement at the proximity to greatness, declaring "these are the worlds literally used by Mr. Von Humboldt.")[104] In 1850, *Living Age* explained that the "patriarch of modern science, the venerable Alexander von Humboldt" praised Frémont's contributions to geographical science, while newspapers around the country reprinted the sixth sketch in the *Gallery of Illustrious Americans*, listing John James Audubon, Humboldt, and Frémont as the greatest explorers of the American West. Whereas Audubon was the interpreter of nature, it was Frémont who followed in Humboldt's footsteps and "unfolded to science" the great map of the West.[105] By the time of his presidential run, Frémont's narrative of scientific journey had fully usurped his tale of military reconnaissance.

In 1856, opposition to the expansion of slavery had pushed Free-Soil Democrats to join with former Whigs to create the Republican Party.[106] Frémont became the party's first presidential candidate, and with the help of John Bigelow, he advertised his legitimacy by publishing his first biography. Rather than a military survey, the first expedition was described simply as a "geographical survey." The memoir was dedicated to Alexander von Humboldt, who was described as being among the first to discover Frémont's scientific genius.[107] The symbolic bee story even included a footnote from Humboldt himself: "To the surprise of adventurous travelers, the summit of Frémonts peak was visited by bees. It is probable that these insects, like the butterflies which I found at far higher elevations in the Andes . . . were drawn tither by ascending currents of air."[108] Lest anyone miss this connection to the famed explorer, in the 1856 newspaper featuring the "Chronicles of Frémont's Life," which readers were instructed to "cut out for reference," 1850 was defined by Frémont's receipt of medals from the Royal Geographical Society of London and the King of Prussia, both of which were "accompanied by a letter from Baron Humboldt."[109] As Frémont's backers knew, though Frémont's science may have been assailable, Alexander von Humboldt's was not.

By the time Thomas Hart Benton wrote his own memoirs, the purpose of Frémont's expeditions was no longer in question. Scientific knowledge alone had driven the Corps' goals, and any military activity was incidental. Commenting on the formal sanctions brought against Frémont for bringing the howitzer into the field, Benton scoffed, "As if Indians did not kill and rob scientific men [who are] not in a position to defend themselves."[110] Benton's assertion was based on the fact that his geopolitical goal of annexing Oregon had been met. Just as importantly, Frémont's backers had successfully transformed the nature of the first two expeditions into wholly scientific affairs. In so doing, however, the cartographic creation of the American West had been transformed into a clash of cultures.

"We Have Aided You to the Best of Our Abilities"

The American public did not need John Charles Frémont to draw a distinction between scientific and indigenous knowledge. However, the particular brand of science that Frémont and Benton articulated went beyond the simple elevation of the trans-Missouri West from the fantastical world of Indians. It defined science in violent opposition to the lifeways of Native people, creating a dichotomy that persists into the twenty-first century. It is helpful, therefore, to explore just how different that science might have looked.

Frémont was neither Thomas Hart Benton's nor Joel Poinsett's first choice to explore the Great Plains. Until he became too ill to travel, it was the French astronomer Joseph Nicollet who was supposed to lead explorations into the trans-Missouri West. As Indian agent John Talia-ferro wrote of Nicollet's abilities, "No man is better calculated than Mr. N. to answer . . . any object of a Scientific nature desired by the government."[111] Secretary of War Joel Poinsett and head of the Topographical Corps J. J. Abert agreed, and in 1838, they sent Nicollet, Frémont, and two other Corps members on two expeditions to map the watershed of Upper Mississippi.

Just like the funds for Frémont's first survey, the money that Abert gave to Nicollet for his Mississippi voyage came from appropriations to aid the "defense of the Atlantic and western frontier."[112] Unlike his protégé, however, Joseph Nicollet had little interest in either politics or military matters, once complaining that such talk left him "melancholy" and "distressed."[113] In describing how he would organize his first trip to the Mississippi region, Nicollet insisted that no military attachment be included. "This is the only way of succeeding according to the principles of good science," Nicollet wrote.[114] Nicollet might have been referring to the burden that the military equipment would add to his group's travels. Just as possible was Nicollet's understanding that the success of his scientific tour required the assistance—rather than the submission—of Indians.

Before he even had government approval for his explorations, Nicollet's first task when he reached St. Louis was to seek the help from the famous Chouteau family.[115] It was not funding or supplies that he hoped to secure from the fur-trading magnates but rather their connections with Native people in the region. As he would later write in his *Report*, the name Chouteau "commands safety and hospitality among all the Indian nations of the United States."[116] The ability to understand the existing social and cultural practices in the region would prove to be very important to Nicollet's science.

Unlike Frémont—who needed to be reminded to give Indian people presents for traveling through their country, Nicollet was aware that proper protocol required that powerful groups be notified when visitors were coming and that gift giving was a requirement for all interactions with Indians.[117] Nothing exemplified this better than Nicollet's interaction with Yankton, Yanktonai, and Sisseton Sioux on his way to Mini-wakan (Devil's Lake).

> Eight miles off there was an encampment of three hundred
> lodges. . . . It was deemed advisable before advancing to have some

previous conversations with the chiefs of the party. . . . [They] invited us to their camp where we had a most entertaining reception. I caused many presents to be distributed among them, which brought about talks, feasts, dances, songs, and the whole series of their usual ceremonies. This lasted twenty-four hours; after which we resumed our usual line march, parting on terms of perfect amity from our new acquaintances.[118]

Nicollet's activities with these Sioux could not have been any more different from Frémont's behavior two years later when he gave his "celebrated" speech. Although the Nakota and Dakota to whom Nicollet gave presents had different geopolitical agendas than their Lakota counterparts, the methods that each explorer took influenced the outcomes of these interactions. Where Nicollet recorded opportunities for gift giving and diplomacy, Frémont reported only danger and antagonism.

Although Nicollet had a deep interest in Native peoples, his gift giving came from more than just cultural respect. Nicollet understood that he needed Indian support for his scientific expedition to be successful. As he wrote to Poinsett, a few hundred dollars and a few kind words from the Great Father in Washington "did more to ensure our safety, and peace and friendship with the United States, than an expensive escort of 400 dragoons could have done."[119] And successful he was. With Frémont's help, Nicollet created what many scholars consider to be the first topographically accurate map of the trans-Mississippi West. Produced on the basis of nearly one hundred thousand instrument readings and astronomical observations from 326 locations, the map symbolized the next wave of scientific exploration.[120] It was during these explorations overseen by Nicollet that the Topographical Corps first used barometers to measure altitude in the field. Nicollet was also the first to use fossils to correlate various geological strata.[121]

When describing Nicollet's importance to the cartographic creation of the American West, William H. Emory wrote that it was not only his map—considered to be the most scientific compilation of the American West to date—based on the tables Nicollet computed, but the entire "idea of forming such a map was originated by the lamented Mr. Nicolet [sic]."[122] Yet, as Nicollet well understood, this scientific map relied on Native information.

Belying the rhetorical role that Indians would play in his later expeditions, Frémont explained how important the Sisseton Sioux were to the Corps' cartographic project: "We are occupied quietly among

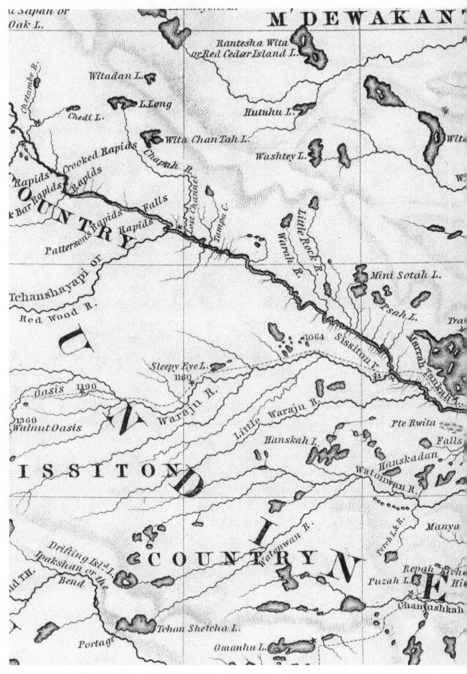

MAP 37. *Detail of Hydrographical Basin of the Upper Mississippi River* (1843).

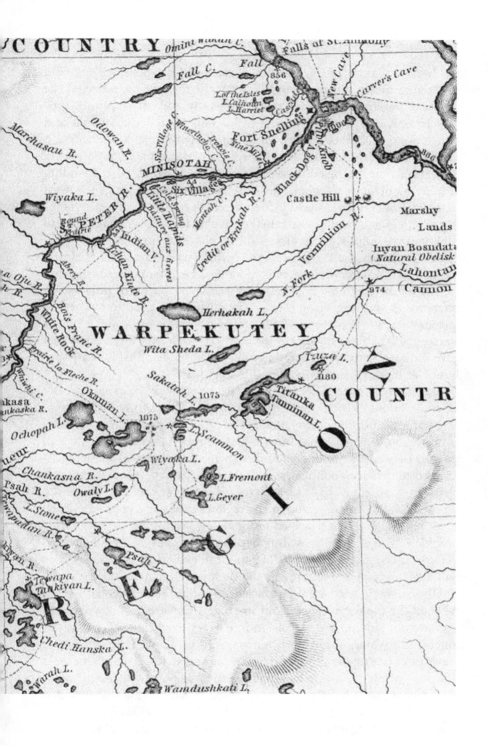

the Indians, Mr. Nicollet, as usual, surrounded by them, with the aid of the interpreter getting them to lay out the form of the lake and the course of the streams entering the river near by, and after repeating pronunciations, entering their names in his note-book." These forms and names were then fixed to latitudinal and longitudinal points through astronomical observations, which were later transcribed onto a master projection after the expedition returned to Washington. After spending "three friendly days together," the expedition continued on its way west to the Missouri.[123] The importance of Nicollet's recording of Native naming practices will be discussed further in chapter 6; it is enough here to highlight the impossibility of separating Native from non-Native processes in the way the West was drawn, which was a fact Nicollet clearly understood. A letter written in Dakota by a headman at Lac qui Parle to Nicollet attests to the importance of Native people in his process: "In reference to your exploring tour . . . [w]e have aided you to the best of our abilities. We hope you will remember us on this account."[124] For his part, Nicollet chastised the United States for ignoring the treaties that gave Indians "without exception, protection, friendship and the right to hunt," on lands promised to them in perpetuity.[125]

Nicollet recognized that Indians played important roles in virtually all explorations of the trans-Mississippi West. Although Native motivation was clearly different from that of their American counterparts, there is no reason to believe that Indians were duped into participating in a process they could not understand. As with any historical actors, Indians had complicated political, social, economic, and personal reasons for choosing the actions they did. Still, regardless of the impetus, we cannot discount Native participation in the region's exploration because of the eventual displacement it helped bring about. From giving direct cartographic information to providing necessary supplies, Indians helped to determine the success or failure of American exploring parties, and they had profound impacts on the way the West was drawn.

Ultimately, it was Frémont's science—rather than Nicollet's—that has had the more lasting cultural impact.[126] The strength of Frémont's rhetoric not only turned expansion into a sterilized clash of cultures in antebellum America, but it has encouraged contemporary scholars to view the cartographic process of the 1840s and 1850s as one that used a discrete system of knowledge—defined in large part by its exclusion of Native people—rather than understanding it as a process that included both Native knowledge and Native practice. Nicollet knew better. In his journal, the Frenchman described encountering a Dakota chief named

Wahanantan—along with a dozen of his warriors—on the Coteau des Prairies:

> We are happy to see them, and this pleasure appeared to be mutual. If there are still suspicious, egotistical, and quarrelsome persons who do not think mutual affection is possible between whites and Indians, I will say for the satisfaction of any with such an unfortunate temperament that I had a particular interest in seeing again these brave and intelligent Indians: They are going to give me information about the country, to clarify our route, and help us get off this plateau where our progress has been uncertain for the last twenty-four hours.

After an ample lunch, the combined group set out, "marching to the sound of Indian chants with the flag at the head of our procession." It is tempting to wonder how different the geopolitical landscape might have looked had it been Nicollet's scene with a flag, rather than Frémont's, that became the symbol of an expanding nation.[127]

PART 3

Reclaiming Indian Country

6 / The Metaphysics of Indian Naming

In 1855, Bvt. Brig. Gen. William Harney was sent on an expedition "against the Sioux Indians for the purpose of chastising them," for killing Lieutenant Grattan and 29 men of the Sixth infantry the previous year. According to historian Jeffrey Ostler, Grattan had taken "twenty-nine men, two howitzers and a drunk interpreter" to demand the arrest of a Brulé ox thief. Harney now faced Brulé chief Little Thunder, one of the perpetrators of what American papers were calling the "Grattan Massacre." Despite Little Thunder's declarations that he "did not want to fight" and had done "all he could for peace," the general showed little patience for negotiations. "[I] do not mind what you say more than a barking prairie dog," Harney spat. He had "not come out here for nothing" and the chief should "go and tell his young men they must fight."[1]

Harney was accompanied by Gouverneur Kemble Warren, a young lieutenant from the Corps of Topographical Engineers. It is through Warren that we know the horrors Harney and his men inflicted at Ash Creek. There is perhaps no better counterpoint to the narrative of objective, scientific conquest that John Frémont created in his *Memoirs* than the journal of his fellow topographer Gouverneur Warren in 1855: "The sight on top of the hill was heart-wrenching. Wounded women and children crying and moaning, horribly mangled by the bullets. . . . [One] cried so much and was continually turning her babe and singing the most distressing tones. . . . I had endeavored to take a topographical sketch of the scene but the calls of humanity prevented my doing much."[2] Intended to make the Lakotas submissive, the Ash Creek attack actually had the opposite effect, compelling many Lakotas to harden their stance against the Americans. Crazy Horse, who had been living with Little Thunder's people, returned from a hunt to find the destruction, and he quickly pledged to fight the United States for the rest of his life.[3]

The severity of the slaughter and the inhumane treatment of the Lakotas horrified Warren, who was "disgusted with the tales of valor in the field, for there were but few who killed anything but a flying foe." Over the next few years, he would repeatedly articulate his ambivalence about—and sometimes outright criticism of—his role in the dispossession of the region's inhabitants. After returning from an expedition in Dacotah Territory, Warren wrote, "I sympathize with them in their desperation and almost feel guilty of a crime in being a pioneer to the white men who will . . . drive the red man from their last patch of hunting ground." In another report, he explained that the present U.S. policy of pushing Indian groups farther west—where they would have no choice but to fight groups already living there—was "the best calculated that could be devised for exterminating the Indian."[4]

Warren's criticism of U.S. policy—and his ambivalence about being one of its agents—shows the emotions of one army officer at the heart of American colonialism. This also helps to explain Warren's most lasting legacy: the *Map of the Territory of the United States from the Mississippi to the Pacific Ocean*. Warren's *General Map* inscribed the contestation and negotiation that actually produced the states of South Dakota, Nebraska, and Kansas onto what one cartographic historian at the Library of Congress calls the "most important map of the American West prior to the Civil War."[5]

Although cartographic scholars refer to his masterwork as the *General Map*, Warren called it the "Indian map," for obvious reasons. In what he considered the authoritative printing, a colorful patchwork covers the western United States, indicating which tribe(s) controlled which territory. With the exception of a few relocated groups along the Missouri, these regions did not correspond with treaties or any formal claims. Instead, they depicted the current geopolitical situation by acknowledging Indian control of the trans-Missouri West.[6] While other versions of Warren's map were printed, both Warren and A. A. Humphreys, the head of the Topographical Bureau, believed that the two thousand four-color maps depicting the "Indian boundaries" were "much the best."[7]

In the historical records, Warren never explained why he so strongly inscribed Indian presence on a map created ostensibly to find the best transcontinental railroad route. Perhaps this map assuaged some of the guilt Warren felt after Ash Creek. Or perhaps he wanted to give a realistic assessment of the geopolitical landscape to those planning to push into the region. Regardless, when commercial mapmaker J. H. Colton, the cadets at West Point, the General Land Office, or the king of Bavaria received their copies, possible railroad routes were not what they would have noticed—they are not even marked on this version—but the overwhelming presence of Indians.[8]

In this chapter, I argue that the cartographic creation of the trans-Missouri West was dependent upon, and a result of, both Native and Euro-American practices. I explain how the northern and central Great Plains, as inscribed by the most important map of the time, were truly syncretic creations. An example of neither indigenous knowledge ripped from its epistemological moorings nor an "American" map drawn over authentic Indian places, Warren's 1857 map exemplified the complex nature of place making in the American West.[9] Focusing on place-names, I argue that this map helped codify some of the power imbalances on the ground, including those among different Indian groups, and was subject to the same local contingencies that created the region. "The most important map of the American West prior to the Civil War" neither revealed an objective reality nor obscured an authentic indigenous existence. Instead, Warren's map exemplified the contested nature of how the West was drawn.

The Science of Nation Building

Four years before Warren witnessed the atrocities at Ash Creek, Congress appropriated $150,000 to "ascertain the most practicable and economical route for a railroad from the Mississippi river to the Pacific Ocean." Proposed by a northern senator and championed by a southern sympathizer, the report tried to break the political logjam over the location of a transcontinental railroad. By sending survey parties along four proposed latitudes, Secretary of War Jefferson Davis hoped to subdue the fervent emotions embedded in sectionalism by scientifically determining the most appropriate route across the country. According to Davis, "preconceived opinion or prejudice, personal interest, and sectional rivalry, must be held subject to the developments of instrumental survey."[10] This route would be shown in a map compiled by a lieutenant in the new Office of Exploration and Surveys by the name of Gouverneur Kemble Warren.

Although the twelve-volume compilation was not even completed when Davis presented his preliminary findings to Congress two years

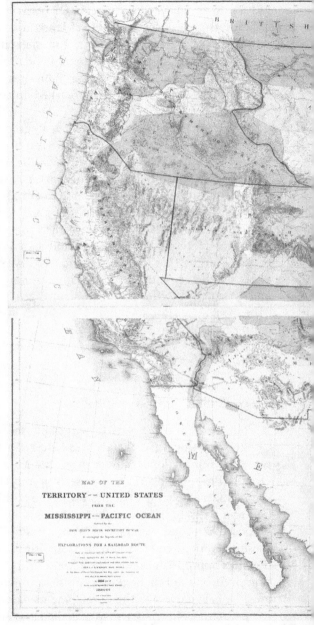

MAP 38. Warren's *Map of the Territory of the United States from the Mississippi to the Pacific Ocean* (1857). Courtesy of Library of Congress.

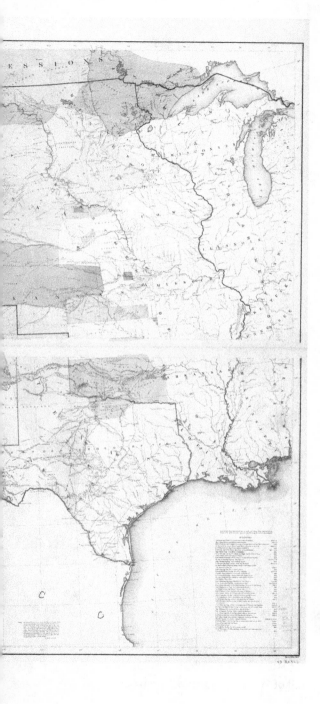

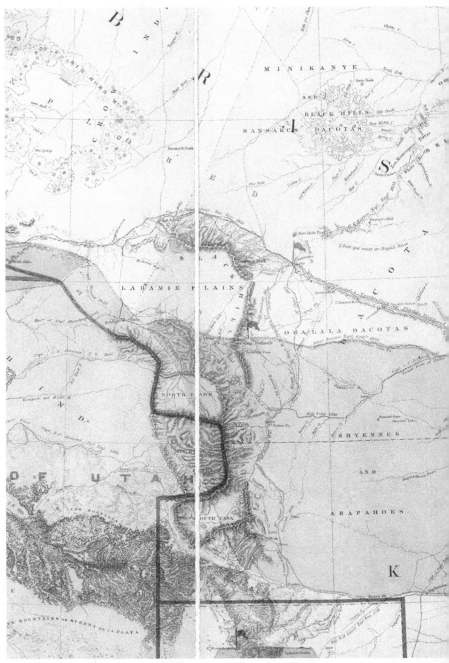

MAP 39. Study areas as detail of Warren's *General Map* (1857).

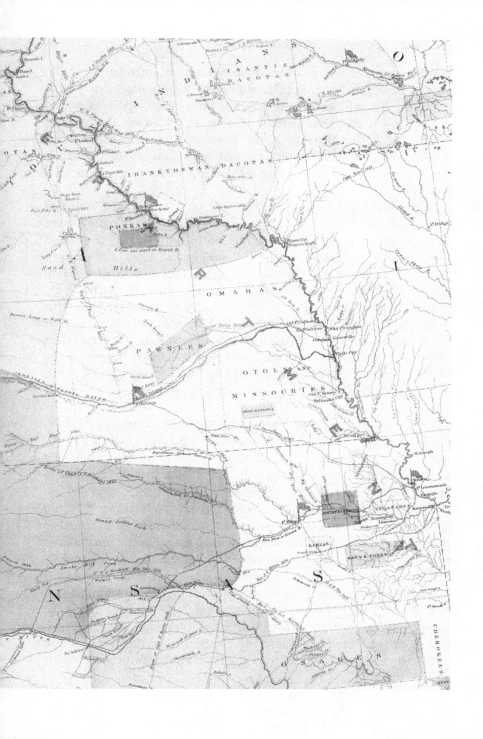

after the appropriation, Warren's map was clearly intended to be the crowning jewel of the project: "Based on the most reliable astronomical data . . . [i]t will present more minute information upon the region embraced by it than has heretofore been exhibited on any general map . . . [and] will be of great value in showing what further explorations are necessary and in determining their direction and intent."[11] Warren's map, in other words, was to serve as the blueprint for future American expansion.

The finished *Reports of Explorations and Surveys from the Mississippi River to the Pacific Ocean, 1853–54* did not disappoint. Costing more than $1.2 million to produce, the large quarto volumes cost more than two and a half times as much as the explorations did. Awed by his copy of the *Reports*, Senator James Harlan said, "Every unusual swell of the land, every unexpected or unanticipated gorge in the mountains has been displayed in a beautiful picture." As geographer John Kryger writes, for Harlan and many of his contemporaries, "the reports *were* the American West." And no single document embodied that sentiment better than Gouverneur Warrens's *Map of the Territory of the United States from the Mississippi to the Pacific Ocean, Ordered by the Hon. Jeffn Davis, Secretary of War to accompany the Reports of the Explorations for a Railroad Route.*[12]

William Goetzmann, the eminent historian on American exploration, has declared Warren's map "a monumental work which encompassed the whole West . . . the culminating achievement of the Great Reconnaissance period."[13] It is easy to see why. In a letter accompanying the finished map, Warren reminded his supervisor, Captain A. A. Humphreys, of his instructions to "read every report, and examine every map of survey, reconnaissance, and travel which could be obtained to ascertain their several values, and to embody the authentic information on the map."[14] Warren's work consolidated all the information currently available to the Topographical Corps, including information from the U.S. Land Office, the Coast Survey, the Mexican Boundary Commission, the adjutant general, the quartermaster general, the Indian Bureau, the Smithsonian Institution, and the Bureau of Topographical Engineers. Warren also gathered maps and information from the trappers and traders who had spent decades traveling through the Plains and into the Rocky Mountains.[15]

In addition to the information from other sources, the map was based on the celestial observations, provided by five separate surveying efforts—four of which were east-west routes and the fifth was a

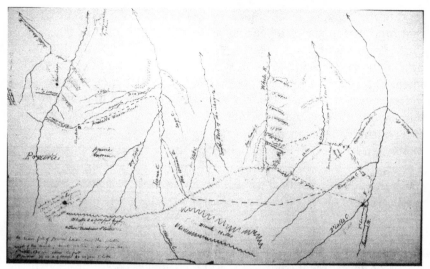

MAP 40. Warren gathered information from established traders, who often included maps in their descriptions of the region, like this one from James Bordeaux. Courtesy of Gouverneur Kemble Warren Papers, New York State Archives

north-south line on the West Coast—which Warren consolidated into a single map to accompany the survey reports.[16] The northernmost route was championed by the new governor of Washington Territory, Isaac I. Stevens, and it examined a line between the forty-seventh and forty-ninth parallels. The second, heralded by Lt. E. G. Beckwith, surveyed the forty-first parallel in the vicinity of Salt Lake City. A third route along the old Santa Fe Trail was investigated by Capt. J. W. Gunnison (until his death at the hands of a band of Ute Indians), while Capt. A. W. Whipple looked at a fourth route along the thirty-fifth parallel.[17]

Contemporary scholars have lauded the map for its scientific depiction of geographic knowledge in the mid-nineteenth century. As historian Susan Schulten writes, Warren's map is "one of the most important foundation maps" of the nineteenth century because it "brought *precision* to the West: it carefully represented relief and drainage features, and left spaces blank where definitive information was lacking."[18] As with Frémont's similarly scientific creation, however, the map's true power lay in its role as a symbol of an expanding nation. Its geopolitical importance lay in its iconography as much as its usefulness. As sectionalism and the possibility of secession grew in the 1850s, national maps offered a vision of a persistent union. The head of the Topographical Engineers declared as much when he claimed that funding for surveying parties must continue, since "the integrity of the Union" was at stake.[19] Martin Brückner explains a similarly anxious debate about the country's future in the early nineteenth century: "The image of the national map was one of the few visual artifacts demonstrating what many perceived to be either an abstract or even untenable fiction, namely that there could be a national union between disjointed regions and politically disparate people."[20]

Warren's map not only included the most recent territorial acquisitions, but it was the first map of the entire Union seemingly created through purely "scientific" means. An anonymous reviewer lauded "the publication of those scientific works," with which "the national honor is inseparably connected."[21] Warren's map became part of a system of knowledge in which an anxious nation could find hope. Unlike the troubling debate over slavery that seemed to be destroying the very mechanisms of government, the *Pacific Railroad Reports* were proof that the political system still worked. The creation of an American map using only scientific means proved what geopolitics could not: a unified country still existed.

Historian Raymond Craib describes a similar process in nineteenth-century Mexico. As he points out in his study of the Mexican *carta general*, a small-scale map like Warren's would have minimal instrumental value. Military forces would get little information about where to ford a river, for instance.[22] In the case of the *Pacific Railroad Reports*, engineers relied on topographical maps of exponentially larger scale to determine a route for the transcontinental railroad. In 1856, the problems with small-scale national maps was articulated by California senator John B. Weller. Weller questioned the role of engineer-explorers who take "instruments to ascertain the altitude of mountains." Providing Congress with a book of more than seventy-five thousand signatures supporting his cause, Weller asked that the road be completed by "practical men . . . [who] take their shovels and spades and go to work and they overcome the difficulties of the mountain while an engineer, perhaps, is surveying the altitude of a neighboring hill."[23] Even more modest development projects needed to use local maps of various forms.

The importance of a map such as Warren's or the Mexican *carta general* lay in what Craib calls the "metaphysics of nationalism." He describes this process in the nascent nation-state of Mexico: "A scale map of a nation-state, which furthered the ideological mirage of neutrality by applying objective mathematical principles to map construction, thus argued backward from the desired conclusion, serving as a model for, rather than of, what is purportedly represented."[24] The process of scientific exploration helped create the nation they were attempting to depict. Through the process of "knowledge assemblage," a naturalized space amenable to being mapped is created.[25]

Further, by situating the national map into the seemingly ahistorical system of longitude and latitude, Warren—and most nineteenth-century cartographers—proposed a nation discovered *in situ*; for them, the state was an objective reality waiting to be discovered. In effect, the map naturalized the nation.

In order to create his map, Warren needed to know both where something existed on the graticule and what that something was. This act of "fixing" gave a map its authority. As John Frémont explained in his *Memoirs*:

> And in going over waste regions which were but little known, or not at all, to other parts where people get their knowledge by reading only, I found that it would be necessary to give the relative position to those other parts, and to say also what means I have used to fix these positions. Then, the flower, and the rock, with the fixed locality, would together tell their own useful story about soil and climate, and give valuable indications to men who travel for scientific knowledge, or to emigrants searching for new homes.[26]

To fix points on large regional maps, the Corps of Topographical Engineers—which oversaw U.S. mapping in the mid-nineteenth century—relied on a process called traverse surveying.[27] Appropriated from nautical navigation, whose practitioners also tried to map trackless expanses, traverse surveys relied on astronomical observations to place their location on the graticule. If a place's longitude and latitude could be observed, it could be positioned on a map. During each day's travels, a surveyor would fix his geographic position through astronomical observations. Another team member would record the geographic features onto topographic sheets. Thus, a sketch drawn at a specific location could be transferred to a larger set of sketches, which were then consolidated to create the map of a region.

Determining geographical latitude was a relatively straightforward process. By measuring the angle of elevation of a celestial body from the horizon—usually Polaris, although other bodies, including the sun, were also used—and performing a set of calculations, explorers could fix latitude in relation to the celestial poles. Since there are no fixed poles on the equator, however, finding longitude was a complicated affair, which relied on the comparison of local time with that of a fixed meridian. Surveyors either had to rely on a sturdy chronometer or, more commonly, observe the occultation of given stars by the moon—whereby the moon passes between the star and the observer—and compare these with tables of the same phenomena in Greenwich time. Even at his most diligent, a surveyor could only produce a longitude calculation accurate to within about four geographical miles.[28]

For the region with which we are concerned—roughly between the Arkansas River on the south, the front range of the Rocky Mountains on the west, and the Missouri River watershed on the north and east—Warren relied most heavily on the reports of John Frémont and Joseph Nicollet, while also including the findings of William Franklin and William Emory in 1845 and 1846, Howard Stansbury in 1849, F. T. Bryan in 1856, and Warren's own expeditions to Nebraska and Dacotah Territories in 1855 and 1856.[29] As described in chapter 5, it does not take much digging in the reports to uncover the almost comic missteps taken on the way to "scientific accuracy," during Frémont's expeditions. He was not alone.

Lt. William Franklin—who took observations on Stephen Kearny's expedition in 1845—could not determine even the accuracy of his instruments. He had intended to take some observations at Fort Leavenworth to compare with documented observations to rate his chronometer, which he would use as a basis to compute longitudes obtained from the sun. Unfortunately, during their entire stay at the fort, "neither the sun nor stars were visible." Thus, Franklin could not even determine a baseline for his chronometer, and his observations were deemed useless.[30]

Warren had no better luck with his own instrumentation. He reported mishaps throughout his journeys into Nebraska and Dacotah: "Benson barometer was found on examination to have air in the tube"; "on reaching St. Louis, thermometer no. 1145 was found to be broken and the tube did not seem to have been well filled"; "found that Green had packed up a thermometer case by mistake without its thermometer"; and "found that the artificial horizon had not been sent with my instruments." Even with his instruments working properly, Warren could no better control the weather than William Franklin could. Warren's group could not take a reading on Polaris for more than one hundred miles after leaving St. Joseph. Sometimes it was not the clouds—but rather the insects—that made accurate readings impossible. On July 6, 1857, an officer under Warren wrote, "The messquitos [sic] were very bad all last night—interfering with our taking the meteorological observations." Finally, there is genuine humor in Warren's particularly bad string of days in August 1857:

> Aug. 24th—In the afternoon I had the outside box of the transit set in the ground and mounted the instrument prepatory [*sic*] to getting it in the meridian on the succeeding evening. Found one of the wires broken.
>
> Aug. 25th—In endeavoring to replace the broken wire of the transit with wax. In doing this I kept breaking others till I had only two remaining of the 15.
>
> Aug. 26th—Attempted to get the transit fixed in the meridian but failed on account of the clouds.
>
> Aug. 28th—I observed to night on the moon culminating stars with tolerable success but found that 4th and 8th wires had become broken.

Whether due to insects, weather, or simply a "want of experience," Warren's attempts to establish longitude were only "partially successful," according to his journal.[31]

The value of traverse surveys hung on the explorer's ability to fix precise points. Repeatedly, however, the men entrusted to achieve that accuracy explained the follies of the task. Warren himself acknowledges the deficiencies of this process multiple times in his *Memoir*: "The maps used in the compilation have been mostly made from reconnaissances, and but few possess very great accuracy. The geographical positions are therefore rarely determined absolutely, or even relatively, with certainty."[32] In his report following his 1855 explorations—on which he relied for the construction of his 1857 map—Warren wrote, "The longitude of no point on this map, distant from the boundary of the United States, can be considered certain within 5 to 10 miles."[33]

Warren's inability to find the exact longitude of any point on his map was not simply a case of broken chronometers and cloudy skies. The nature of a "scientific map" requires that all knowledge be universalized and removed of any subjectivity. Yet, at every point where information was collected, social relations and real-world experiences tempered the map's ostensible objectivity. The process of mapping a region was supposed to strip the area of subjective influences, but as Timothy Mitchell explains in his depiction of Egyptian mapping in the early twentieth century, "The surveyor's map presented itself as a picture of a reality on the ground . . . [but that reality] did not stay there, it entered into the making of the map."[34]

Surveying was not the only process by which reality became part of the map. At every part of its creation, human beings became part of the "knowledge assemblage." Warren complained, for example, that since one bureau in Washington was compiling a map, "all the others are [*sic*] one way or another strove to withhold their information." Even when he could gather all the necessary information, trying to reconcile all the projections caused a "good deal of contortion and discrepancies." Problems transferring sketches to the copper plates that would engrave the map also led to "serious errors, particularly in the meandering of rivers." Had these technical issues been resolved, Warren acknowledged that the map was still a human creation, and it would require "frequent additions and corrections."[35] If Warren's map was neither the appropriate size to help with nation building, nor free from the human subjectivities that affect all knowledge assemblages, we are left with the question, What cartographic elements created the semiotic consistency needed to facilitate either the metaphysics of nationalism or the mechanics of nation building?

"Names We Might Fix upon Them"

Warren's map, like Stephen Long's, John Frémont's, and Joseph Nicollet's, mostly represented rivers and mountains. Still, the forms themselves did not make a map useful but rather the labels attached to the forms. While it did not take explorers to affirm that a geographic reality existed at a giving point on the graticule, that reality without a corresponding name to signify it would have been almost useless for state-building purposes.[36] Stephen Long articulated this problem more than thirty years before Warren's expedition, while he was traveling through southern Dacotah country. After Long explained that his party made numerous astronomical observations for latitude and longitude, he said he was not convinced of their import, as "many of the observations were made at places which are not, and at present cannot be known by any names we might attempt to fix upon them."[37] For this reason, it has been nearly impossible for historians to delineate Long's precise route.

Of course, for the majority of the map's viewers, the need to accurately fix specific topographical features in the trans-Missouri West was moot. What mattered was not that the topographic elements were more accurately placed in relation to one another but that they *appeared* to be more accurately placed—because they were "scientific." Symbolically, names affirm the extension of control. The ability to associate a place with a name gives a map creator legitimacy by demonstrating his or her knowledge of that place.[38] Whether it was for administrative purposes or the suffusion of the "metaphysics of nationalism," inscribed names made maps useful tools of the state. And like the explorations, those names relied on both Native and non-Native participation.

Linguists frequently break down place-names—also called toponyms—into categories according to their derivation. *Descriptive names*, for example, describe something people encounter in a certain location; they cannot exist without the place to which the name is attached. Because of this intimate connection between name and place, many scholars associate descriptive names with indigenous naming practices. Geographer Margaret Pearce writes: "In the traditional indigenous relationship to mapping and landscape, toponyms are not arbitrarily assigned. Rather than make reference to a distant place or person, the place-name refers to *what is there*. . . . Toponyms based on use may refer to the kind of plants or animals that can be harvested, gathered, or hunted there. The stories that are associated with place-name provide a moral, as well as historical and spiritual character to a site."[39] Jared Farmer distinguishes Native from non-Native practices when he writes: "In the pre-contact period, Native Americans seem to have shared a common attitude toward toponymy. Their place names are preponderantly and richly descriptive, whereas Anglo-American place names are disproportionally commemorative and possessive."[40] As Pearce and Farmer indicate, it has become a scholarly truism that Native peoples chose place-names according to their lived experiences. Although little evidence may be found to categorize the naming practices of all Native peoples living in precontact North America, it seems fair to argue that descriptive naming was the standard for many indigenous peoples.[41]

If descriptive names were more closely associated with Indian naming practices, there should be a paucity of descriptive names in Warren's map. This, however, is not the case. His map is a veritable catalogue of the region's physical characteristics. Black Earth River, White Earth Creek, Blue Earth River, Cherry Creek, Cedar River, Sage Creek, Wakarusa (river of big weeds), Niobrara (spreading, or running, water), and Big and Little Tarkio (full of walnuts) are just a few of the dozens of examples in Warren's map. While the etymology of some names can be found in the historical record—for example, Lt. F. T. Bryan was informed by his Delaware guides that Parsnip Creek was named from the "quantities of vegetable growing wild on its banks"—the inspiration for Sage or Muddy Creeks, for example, can only be assumed.[42] Between the toponyms

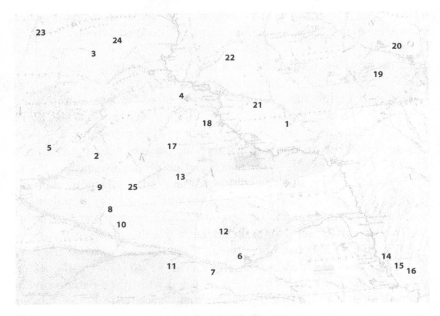

MAP 41. Study area with descriptive names highlighted: 1. Black Earth Creek. 2. White Earth Creek. 3. Cherry Creek. 4. Cedar River. 5. Sage Creek. 6. Wood River. 7. Plum Creek. 8. Cold Water Creek. 9. Niobrara (spreading, or running, water) River. 10. Blue Water River. 11. Cottonwood River. 12. Muddy Creek. 13. Long Pine Creek. 14. Nishnabotana (canoemaking) River. 15. Big Tarkio (full of walnuts). 16. Nadoway. 17. Keya Paha. 18. White River. 19. Waraju (cottonwood). 20. Minnesota. 21. Chaka Wakan or Fire Steel Creek. 22. Eyo Paha Wakan or East Medicine Knoll River. 23. Wah pa Chan Shoka or thick timbered River. 24. Moreau or Owl River. 25. Wamdushka W. or Snake River. Map created by author.

written in English and those that are phonetic transcriptions, descriptive names make up the vast majority of toponyms on Warren's map. This demonstrates not only the importance of specific Native geographies but also the difficulty of separating "Indian" from "Euro-American" naming practices.

Farmer uses the example of Muddy Creek to highlight another difference he sees in Euro-American and Indian naming practices: "When settlers did create descriptive names, their specifics tended to be general— Muddy Creek ad nauseam."[43] Considering that Warren fervidly collected

"Indian names as well as the French and English to objects and localities, and in writing Dacotah words I have adopted, as far as possible, the spelling used in the *Dacotah Grammar and Dictionary*, published by the Smithsonian Institution," the name likely came from one of his Indian informants.[44] More importantly, we must acknowledge that Indians, too, used generic descriptive names for landforms.

Joseph Nicollet clarified this point in his 1839 report on the hydrographical basin of the Upper Mississippi. "It is to be remarked," Nicollet wrote, "of the prairies of this region, that they present such low insulated hillocks, to which the Sioux apply the somewhat generic name of ré or *pahah*, as they are more or less elevated above the surrounding plain." Even sacred sites were noted with the generalized *Wakan*, indicating the site was remarkable, "or even sacred, a spot which they select in preference to some of their ceremonies." While Warren did not transfer the inscription of the aforementioned "Pahah-Wakan" from Nicollet's map, he did include the English translation of what the voyageurs called "Butte de Medicine" (Medicine Hill). This signifier does not appear to lose specificity, as both "Medicine Hill" and "Pahah-Wakan" indicate a hill that has spiritual connotations (see map 43).[45]

Sometimes Warren would include both a phonetic approximation of a Native word and an English translation: Chaka Wakan, or Fire Steel Creek; Eyo Paha Wakan, or East Medicine Knoll River; Moreau, or Owl River; and Wamduscka Wakan, or Snake River. More often, we are left with only translations. Our evidence for some inscriptions is limited to our knowledge of how Warren determined names; other times, it is clear from the historical record. During his 1857 travels, for example, Warren passed the Turtle Hill River, which was "green with pine" at its mouth. Warren reported that the river was named "Wazi-haska, which means in the Dacotah tongue 'the place where the pine extends far out.'" Whereas Nicollet had simply inscribed "Wazi Hanzkah" on his *Map of the Upper Missouri Basin*, Warren's map labels the river "Wazi Hanskiya," or Long Pine Creek. On the 1857 map, this label is further Anglicized to read simply "Long Pine Cr." Similar processes led to the transition from "Hopa Wajupi," or R. Petite Arc to Bow Creek, for example, or "Rantsha Wita" to First Cedar Island.

I am not arguing that the inscriptions Long Pine Creek and Wazi Hanzkah are interchangeable.[46] I am also not dismissing the cultural damage that the gradual alteration of this name surely perpetrated.[47] Instead, I propose that the processes of inscribing the trans-Mississippi West were the result of negotiation and contestation on the ground.

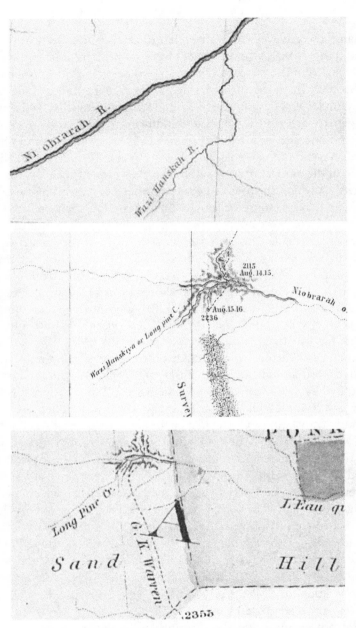

MAP 42. Details of Nicollet's map (1843), Warren's *Reconnoissances in the Dakota Country* (1857). and Indian map (1857) showing the transformation of Wazi Hanzkah to Long Pine Creek.

If we are to accept that Indians were more than passive victims in the nineteenth-century trans-Mississippi West, we must also accept that the cartographic creation of that region was an authentic—if culturally damaging—process that reflected the circumstances in which it was made. Wherever people with different cultures interact there will be hybridization and syncretism. The naming process was no different. Although these names do reflect the cultural violence inflicted upon Native peoples, these inscriptions were not entirely new creations. Neither purely Native nor Euro-American, these toponymic amalgamations typify the syncretic nature of how the West was drawn.

Despite Nicollet's and Warren's attentiveness to indigenous names, most scholars have focused only on the erasure of Native geographies in the nineteenth century. While scholars interested in nineteenth-century Mexican statecraft have highlighted that country's practice of using indigenous orthography to attest to the depth of national space, it is usually said that the United States officials left Indian names out "any consideration of national geography, thus rendering them invisible."[48] Yet, just as Mexican officials had hoped the inclusion of Aztec geography would prove historical legitimacy, American lawmakers also called for the preservation of Indian names. None other than Thomas Hart Benton made this desire clear in his discussion of his son-in-law's maps:

> This map of Oregon and California is not to be limited to the materials collected by Colonel Fremont but is to contain everything authentic on the subject. . . . It will be scrupulously so in the orthography of aboriginal or Indian names of places. Indians and all people in their primitive or early state, give significant names— names descriptive of the place, or commemorative of some event. As a mere matter of taste we would always prefer to have these names correctly spelled, and their meanings thus preserved and known, rather than have them metamorphosed into some strange vernacular of analogous sounds and senseless import. . . . All these names (and there are a great number of them) will lose their own identity, and be lost to historical observation unless accurately preserved by the first explorers. Colonel Fremont's attention was much turned in that direction. In his map and report already published, he has given the aboriginal names as he has caught them from the mouths of the resident Indians.[49]

Benton's desire to maintain indigenous names does not absolve him from his part in the violent dispossession of the Native people in the trans-Missouri West. It does, however, complicate the simple binary of Euro-American cartography displacing a more authentic Indian one.

Names, particularly those on a map of the nation-state, always reflect power imbalances on the ground. These changes in power, however, had been happening long before the arrival of Euro-Americans. For example, Joseph Nicollet wrote in his journal that the Sioux name Mankizitka River should be translated as Smoking-Earth River for the color of the sediment in its current. This recognition apparently did not stop him from including the simpler White Earth River on his map, along with the Lakota signifier.[50] This meaning was altered further when Warren inscribed the name as simply White River in his 1857 map.[51]

Following only Nicollet's and Warren's maps of this river, the following trajectory emerges: a highly descriptive Lakota oral signifier was transcribed, translated, and finally truncated, leaving an impotent Euro-American version of a culturally rich Sioux name. While at some level accurate, such an interpretation greatly simplifies a more complicated past. The Arapahos, Crows, Kiowas, and Cheyenne all claimed this region throughout the eighteenth century and into the nineteenth. The Oglala and Brulé did not gain control of the White River region until they made an 1820s alliance with the Cheyenne.[52] While these groups might have used similar descriptions of the sediment to name the river, they certainly did not use the Lakota term "Mankizitka."

Further, while this region was contested by the Arapahos, Crows, Kiowas, and Cheyenne, the term "White River" was just as likely a translation of a Mandan or Hidatsa word. Nicolas King first inscribed the words "White River" in his 1806 version of Meriwether Lewis and William Clark's manuscript map, which they had created during their five-month stay among the Mandan and Hidatsa in 1804. Clark wrote that the base for his map was "compiled from the Authorities of the best informed travelers." Still, much of the specific information he gleaned "principally from Indian information."[53] Consequently, it would seem that his information regarding the signifier for this waterway came either from Hidatsa or Mandan informants or one of the "band of Assinniboins," whose villages are inscribed directly on the river, but not a Lakota speaker. Thus the name "Mankizitka" is probably no closer to the Arapaho, Crow, Kiowa, Hidatsa, or Mandan signifier for the region than "White River" is to "Mankizitka." When Joseph Nicollet inscribed the Lakota word on his 1839 map, he was not uncovering an "authentic" Sioux landscape but helping to solidify Lakota control in a region that they had held for no more than two decades.

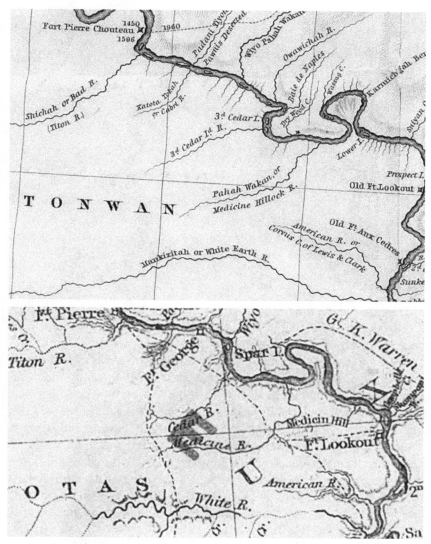

MAP 43. Details of Nicollet's *Hydrographical Basin of the Upper Mississippi River* (1843) and Warren's *General Map* (1857), showing the transformation of Paha Wakan to Medicine River, and Mankizitka to White River. 34th Cong, S. Ex. Doc 76–1.

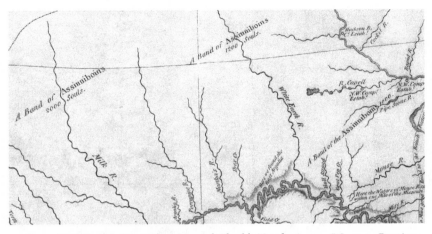

MAP 44. Detail of *A Map of Lewis and Clark's Track, Across Western Portions of North America from the Mississippi to the Pacific Ocean* (1814). Courtesy of David Rumsey Historical Map Collection.

Here we see the fundamental problem with viewing the cartographic creation of the West simply as a spurious Euro-American landscape being drawn over a more authentic Indian one. For one thing, this belief depends on the false assumption that a consistent Native landscape ever existed. This was certainly not the case for the region in question, particularly for the area between the Missouri and Platte Rivers. In 1858, when Warren visited, the Brulé controlled the area, but during previous fifty years, the Ponca, Cheyenne, Omaha, and Skidi Pawnee had all made claims to the region, with frequent incursions by the Sac, Meskwaki, Iowa, and other tribes of Lakota. Even John Frémont—who wished nothing more than to erase the Native presence from the region—acknowledged that names reflected a changing landscape: "Throughout this region, the rivers and lakes and other noticeable features of the country, bear French and Indians names, Sioux or Chippewa and sometimes Shayan [Cheyenne]."[54] The names inscribed on Warren's map reveal this dynamic history.

For example, no river played a greater part in mid-nineteenth-century overland migration than the Platte—or Nebraska—River. Platte is a derivation of the French name La Rivère Plate (flat river), given by the Mallet brothers in 1739. Similarly, "Nebraska" originated in either the Otoe "Ni brathka" (flat water) or the Omaha "Ni bthaska" (flat water), raising the question whether the brothers translated what an Indian informant told them or were struck by the same physical characteristics as their Native counterparts. Regardless, whether Platte or Nebraska, the meanings were essentially the same.[55]

The Dakota name (which has been approximated as either Pankseka Wakpa or Kanpeska Wakpa), however, is made up of a first signifier, meaning "shell" or "moonshell," and a second, meaning "river." According to anthropologist M. R. Gilmore, Dakota would meet at the river and trade pink iridescent shells. Such a conclusion could also be applied by examining the names of the waterway employed by other groups: the Gros Ventres' Abits wii ni tse (big moonshell river), the Kiowas' Kodaliaton Pa (necklace shell river), and the Cheyennnes' Minniohe (shell river).[56] In a unique twist for the region, the Sioux name was ignored in favor of another indigenous-based signifier. More often, the more powerful Lakotas' names took precedence over less powerful Siouan and Caddoan peoples.

Much like the descriptive names, Warren's application of *incident* names demonstrates the difficulty of separating Indian and Euro-American naming practices. Most scholars understand incident names to be indigenous phenomena. Keith Basso's description of Western Apache history is, in essence, a series of incident names: "The country of the past—and with it Apache history—is never more than a narrated place-world away. It is thus very near, as near as the working of their own imaginations, and can be easily brought to life at almost any time. . . . Answering the question 'What happened here?' it deals in the main with single events, and because these are tied to places within Apache territory, it is pointedly local and unfailingly episodic."[57] Scholars have applied this model of indigenous place-making to an idealized pan-Indian epistemology. Jared Farmer cites Basso, concluding "similar incident names (historical and mythological) abounded in North America in the pre-contact and early contact periods."[58]

Whether they existed in the early contact periods or not, Nicollet found evidence of incident naming practices among the Sioux. Among his examples of Lakota incident-naming practices were: Karanzi R., or river where the Kansas were killed; Okshidanom-witchaktepi, or the place where the two young men were killed (by the Sauks); Shamoni Hinyanka, or the lake where they ran the races; Toka Kiahe R., or river where the enemy appeared on the hill; and Padani Otapi R., or place where the Pawnee dies. Two other inscriptions on his 1837 map, Punished Woman Lake and Old Sioux Turkey Hunting Grounds, may or

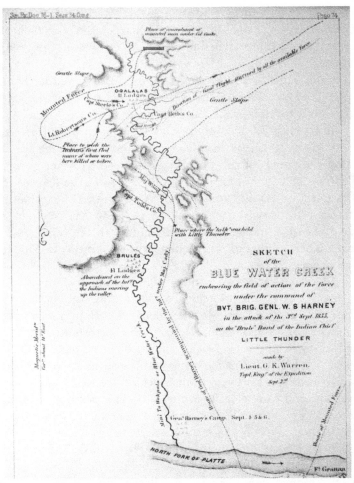

MAP 45. Warren's map of the Ash Creek Massacre. 34th Cong., S. Ex. Doc 76–1.

may not be incident specific, but they seem to satisfy Basso's primary question, "What happened here?"[59]

This definition raises the question, Were incident naming practices among the Sioux qualitatively different from those among their Euro-American counterparts? Was there an epistemological difference between the origins of Karanzi River, or river where the Kansas were killed, and Floyd's River—named after Sergeant Floyd of Lewis and Clark's expedition—who died there in 1804?[60] Does the etymology of Okshidanom-witchaktepi, or the place where the two young men were killed (by the Sauks), differ in any meaningful way from Pullman's Fork, named after a trapper who, according to John Frémont, was killed there by Gros Ventre Indians; from Soldiers Cliff, named by Warren in honor of Joseph M. Lake, a dragoon under Warren's command who died at the base of the cliff in 1855; from Clough Creek, named after Private Clough of Maj. Clifton Wharton's detachment, who "fell dead from his horse" in 1844?[61] The same questions can be asked of Scott's Bluff, Brady Island, or Dixon's Bluff, which along with Floyd's River are inscribed on Warren's 1858 map.[62] While their names may have reflected different aspects of the conflict, the Brulé would have had no difficulty understanding the significance of many names fixed on the Gouverneur Warren's map of Ash Creek. That map included the inscription: "Place to which the Indians first fled many of whom were here killed or taken."

Warren's use of incident names that Brulé or Oglala warriors would have recognized, for example, highlights the danger of categorizing the naming process into binary categories of "Indian" and "white." Further, this example shows the contested nature of the region and reminds us to be as critical of the origin of Native incident names as we are of Euro-American ones. While the Lakota may have memorialized incidents in their cultural and physical landscapes, for example, other groups were doing the same. In the 1880s, ethnologist James Dorsey collected place-names of the tributaries of the Niobrara and surrounding rivers from Omaha Joseph La Flesh and Ponca chief Buffalo Chips. Not only were some of the names Dorsey recorded likely unfamiliar to the Sioux (Where Tenuga Was Killed), others were openly hostile (Where They Danced over the Head of a Dakota).[63] As with descriptive names, incident names were employed by different Native groups to refer to the same geographic location in entirely different ways, again reminding us of the danger of viewing the mapping of the American West as the outcome of a binary clash of cultures.

Claiming Names

As with the case of "Where They Danced over the Head of a Dakota," incident names frequently reflected larger geopolitical struggles. Thus, the inclusion or exclusion of names on Warren's map indicated the presence (or lack of) military power. The translation of this Ponca name was

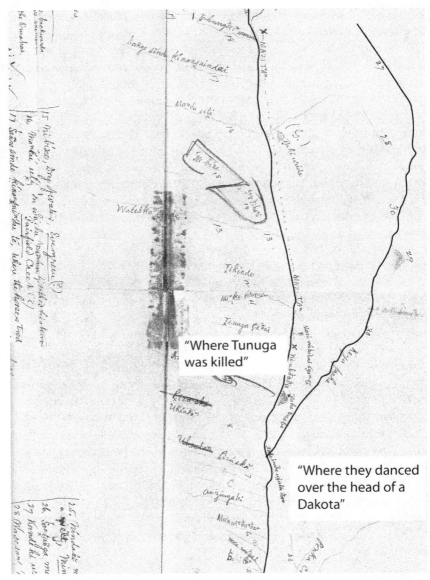

MAP 46. Detail of *Sketch Map of Country of Omahas and Poncas* (1882). Courtesy of National Anthropological Archives, Smithsonian Institution, Dorsey Papers, MS 4800 (130).

not inscribed on Warren's map because it was the Brulé and Oglala—not the Ponca—from whom Warren gathered his information. Similarly, the paucity of Euro-American incident names was due to the absence of American state power in Kansas, Nebraska, and Dacotah Territory.

There were two places in the region, however, where the United States exerted military control in the mid-nineteenth century: the Oregon and Santa Fe overland trails. Here, we find the largest concentration of English names that are neither transcriptions nor translations of Native words, like Chimney Rock, Court House Rock, Grand Island, and Council Grove. As highlighted throughout this book, Indians played integral roles in the American exploration of the region, but it is in these names that Indian participation is the most obscure. This is also where historians have pointed to blatant examples of Euro-American geographies writing over Native ones. Even in a name such as Council Grove, which commemorated a meeting between Americans and Osages, it can be argued that this inscription came to represent unequal colonialism rather than a geopolitical negotiation.

On August 5, 1824, George Champlin Sibley met with a number of Osage chiefs near the headwaters of the Neosho River, a few hundred miles west of the new Missouri state line, to negotiate a treaty to establish what would become the Santa Fe Trail. After a session during which the Osages were promised eight hundred dollars' worth of goods, Sibley suggested "the propriety of naming the place 'Council Grove' which was agreed to, & directed Capt. Cooper to select a suitable tree, & to record this name in strong and durable characters—which was done."[64] The acknowledgment of its origins demonstrates the syncretic nature of the name Council Grove and implies geopolitical compromise. The cultural history of the name, however, hints at the growing colonial inequities that the name reflected.

Despite its etymology, Council Grove quickly acquired a new history. The *Evansville Indian Journal* reported that Council Grove was "the ancient site of a once proud and mighty city. . . . Here the Pawnee, Arapahoe, Comanchee, Loups and Eutaw Indians, all of whom who are at war with each other, meet and smoke the pipe in peace. Every person and the things are sacred for many miles around this peaceful grove." Another traveler wrote that the spot was consecrated, "as the name indicates, to national councils, the wampum belt, the festive sports, and green corn dances. There is a beauty almost a sublimity in the thought, that while wars have raged around it . . . no cry of vengeance or shout of defiance, rising to Heaven, have quivered in *those* forest tops." It took a direct refutation by Josiah Gregg and Sibley himself to quash these misconceptions.[65]

Distortions around the origins of the name Council Grove put it in the category of the vanishing Indian trope described in chapter 4 of this book, exemplified by Lydia Sigourney's 1834 poem "Indian Names."

Ye say they all have passed away,
That noble race and brave,
That their light canoes have vanished
From off the crested wave;
That 'mid the forest where they roamed
There rings no hunter's shout,
But their name is on your waters,
Ye may not wash it out.[66]

Mary Louise Pratt has argued that such naming practices inscribed Indians as objects of historical study rather than people with political power. In this way, Pratt writes, "Indigenous history and culture has been revived as *dead*."[67] While the name Council Grove commemorated a geopolitical negotiation, the history of the name's use tells a more one-sided story of cultural imperialism.

Yet, we must not assume a universal understanding of the names on Warren's map. Otherwise, in the words of scholar Amy Kaplan, we risk "reproducing the teleological narrative that imperialism tells about itself; the inexorable westward march of empire."[68] Like Council Grove, the cultural history of Pawnee Rock's name can be understood as relegating the Pawnees to a distant past: Kit Carson took refuge there and killed his first Pawnee; a band of Pawnee horse thieves were killed there by a group of Comanches; trappers led by Old Bill Williams took shelter there from sixty marauding Pawnees; various tribes of Pawnees met in general council on top of the rock. From the perspective of a twenty-first-century scholar, any one of these interpretations could be understood as reviving the Pawnees "as dead."[69]

A similar interpretation from a Pawnee, however, changes what could have easily been interpreted as cultural imperialism to the epitome of an Indian incident name. According to Chaui Mary Faw-Faw's deposition during the 1950s Indian Claims Commission hearings, Pawnee Rock got its name from a harrowing battle sometime in the mid-nineteenth century. As the Pawnees tried to cross the swollen Arkansas River returning from a hunt, "a different tribe of Indians watching them, laying for them, and when these Indians saw that they could not get across on account of that river being up they attacked. . . . When they swam across they ran for that rock and these other Indians came along and quite a few, very many, out-numbered the Pawnees and these Indians went up on that rock and that is where they stayed. They had a battle there. . . . They was killed except four." When asked if she knew any of the four who escaped, Faw-Faw said one of them was her grandfather.[70] Like the creation of names in the process of mapping the trans-Mississippi West, the *use* of those names is best understood as negotiated and contested territory.

Conclusion

Of course, the process of mapping America did not stop with Gouverneur Warren's map. Despite the Pawnees' refusal to let Deputy Surveyor Manners continue his work in 1855, the General Land Office pressed on with its mission to divide the trans-Missouri West into multiples (and divisions) of the 640-acre section. Land grants to railroads and settlers and a federal policy that restricted Indians to reservations continued to undermine Indian land tenure, changing not only territorial control but also the region's names.

Yet, these changes, too, happened within a context of contestation and negotiation. Between 1864 and 1876, for example, hundreds of Pawnees (mostly Skidi) helped protect the survey crews of the Union Pacific Railroad. Their service was so valuable that, in 1870, the Nebraska State Legislature passed a joint resolution thanking them "for the heroic manner in which they have assisted in driving hostile Indians from our frontier settlements." As with previous alliances with the United States, however, the Pawnees had their own reasons for joining the Americans. This furthers my argument that people have multiple ways of making and remembering places. It is easy, for example, to imagine the cultural importance that Plum Creek, Nebraska, gained among the tribe after 35 Pawnee Scouts defeated Turkey Leg and 150 of his Cheyenne warriors there in 1867.[1] For those Pawnees who participated in this battle, fruits were no longer the primary ingredients in place making; warfare was. Places are never static but are constantly being reassessed, reimagined, and reformed.[2]

Herein lies the fundamental premise of this book. The story of how the West was drawn is not a singular narrative. Examined from the post-colonial viewpoint of a twenty-first-century academician, it is relatively easy to dismiss the mapping of the trans-Mississippi West as simply an "imperial construction of U.S. national space."[3] This model limits our understanding of the past. For example, the 1833 treaty between leaders from the four bands of Pawnees and U.S. government representatives resulted in the United States' appropriation of a large part of what became Kansas and Nebraska. We must remember, however, that for ten years following the treaty, such a negotiation appeared to be an astute political maneuver. In exchange for the ineffable claim of "ownership," Indian leaders received promises of protection from a growing power in the region and the continued sociopolitical esteem of controlling American gifts and payments. Had the United States lived up to its promises of protection, our stories of both Pawnees and the region might be quite different.

The importance of such an understanding goes beyond academic "what ifs." The Lakotas' struggle over the Black Hills exemplifies the importance of Indian participation in the cartographic construction of the trans-Mississippi West. The 1851 Treaty of Fort Laramie that inscribed Lakota control of the Black Hills and the surrounding region became the basis for the boundaries of the Great Sioux Reservation, established at the 1868 Treaty of Fort Laramie. Over the next twenty years, the United States illegally claimed portions of the reservation, disregarding the boundaries it had created with Lakota leaders. In 1980, after a century of legal wrangling, the United States Supreme Court upheld the Indian Claims Commission's award of $102 million for the Lakotas—the largest sum ever awarded to an Indian tribe—for the illegal taking of the Black Hills. The Lakotas rejected the settlement, arguing that only the return of the Black Hills would right the wrongs of the past. By 2007, interest on the award increased the total due the Lakotas to $750 million.[4]

Although much of the public debate surrounding the return of the land to the Lakotas has been about their spiritual connection to the Black Hills, the Supreme Court's decision was based solely on the federal government's violation of the 1868 treaty.[5] In fact, as a Supreme Court decision became more likely in the late 1970s, the Black Hills Alliance, a group of Lakota and rural white activists, highlighted this fact in their publicity materials.[6] A lapel button produced by the group shows the same state boundaries for which Aaron Carapella was so maligned in his map of Native people.

FIGURE 8. Lakota logo-map, by the Black Hills Alliance of South Dakota. This illustration and map come from a lapel button. The lapel button emphasizes the size and boundaries of the territory promised the Sioux in the 1868 Fort Laramie Treaty.

The political capital that the Lakotas have gained from the Supreme Court's decision has not precluded projects that focus on a Lakota-specific understanding of the Black Hills.[7] One could argue that the legal fight for the return of the Black Hills has been foundational for contemporary Lakota identity. As with the Ojibwes' struggle to maintain fishing rights, or the fight of the descendants of those murdered by Americans at Sand Creek to locate a proper memorial, some of the most potent formations of contemporary Native identity have grown out of the colonial process.[8]

For scholars interested in examining the discursive tools of nation building, the cartographic process *does* offer poignant evidence. By the end of the eighteenth century, maps and mapmaking became primary avenues for American intellectuals to distinguish the fledgling country from its colonial past. As historian Susan Schulten writes, cultural and academic leaders "wanted *American* knowledge that grew from *American* minds," and this desire influenced the nation's emerging cartographic industry.[9] Based in the cultural center of Philadelphia, the nascent community of map printers and publishers literally "represented the nation and the world to literate society," according to scholar John Rennie Short.[10] A great variety in the scales, styles, and contents of the maps permeated Euro-American material culture, and their similarities were enough to become shorthand for the nationalist project. This "map-as-logo," in Benedict Anderson's terms, made for a powerful cultural construction.[11]

Yet, nothing inherent in these maps distinguished them from their indigenous counterparts. As Matthew Edney writes, "The construction, normalization, and naturalization of 'states' and 'empires' depend neither on the content of the maps nor on cartographic technologies but rather how they are deployed within spatial discourses."[12] Scholars must be careful not to confuse the discourse historical actors used with actual epistemological difference. Such a view both simplifies our past and dehumanizes historical actors, reducing complex interactions to ahistorical clashes of culture.

When Frémont wrote about his interaction with a bumblebee on what he believed to be the highest point in the Rockies, he was using the rhetoric of science to draw false distinctions between the Indians—who proved to be so valuable to his explorations—and the "advance of civilization."[13] Acknowledging the inherent violence in Frémont's words is necessary to understanding nineteenth-century Euro-American political culture. The mapping process in the mid-nineteenth century proved to be a powerful affirmation of American expansion and the power of the state. Still, we should not believe that this distinction existed beyond the discourse in which it was deployed. As I have argued throughout this book, the distinction between "Indian" and "American" mapping in the middle of the nineteenth century existed—however powerfully— only discursively.[14] As historians, we must do more than simply take contemporary situations and determine how these circumstances came into being. Otherwise, we are left with only colonialism, dispossession, and "imperial constructions." We must try to re-create the world in which these actors lived to bring human decisions back into larger national narratives.

In the cartographic construction of the nineteenth-century American West, no single person had a greater impact on its expansionist flavor than John C. Frémont. Yet, that legacy would have been unknown if the Skidis had not protected him from South Band leaders intent on killing him. The Skidis did this not for the sake of American cartography. They did it because, in their estimation, a meaningful geopolitical alliance with the Americans was still feasible in 1843. Thus, what appears to be a side note in the tale of one man's expansionist fervor becomes, upon closer inspection, the center of a more complicated story of Pawnee geopolitics, revealing the contested nature of American expansion within a powerful Indian society. Moving beyond the categories and narratives employed by the colonizing people and more fully historicizing the practices of individual historical actors, we will not only enhance our understanding of the context in which those actors lived, but we may also even be able to find new, more inclusive national narratives.[15]

Notes

Introduction

1. Cindy Yurth, "Putting Them on the Map: Native Cartographer Offers a Different Picture of America," *Navajo Times*, January 7, 2013, http://navajotimes.com/news/2013/0113/011713map.php#.U6pVA164mlI.

2. http://Tribalnationsmaps.com/about.

3. Yurth, "Putting Them on the Map"; Alysa Landry, "Changing Perceptions and Making Connections—One Map at a Time," *Indian Country Today*, March 10, 2015, http://indiancountrytodaymedianetwork.com/2015/04/10/changing-perceptions-and-making-connections-one-map-time-159925; Hansi Lo Wang, "The Map of Native American Tribes You've Never Seen Before," NPR, "Codeswitch: Frontiers of Race, Culture and Ethnicity," June 24, 2014, www.npr.org/sections/codeswitch/2014/06/24/323665644/the-map-of-native-american-tribes-youve-never-seen-before.

4. Facebook Group, Native American and American Indian Issue, comments responding to Aaron Carapella's July 26, 2015, post of NPR article "The Map of Native American Tribes You Have Never Seen Before," www.facebook.com/groups/NAAIissues/search/?query=tribal%20nations%20map.

5. Debbie Reese, "American Indians in Children's Literature," June 25, 2014, http://americanindiansinchildrensliterature.blogspot.com/2014/06/aaron-carapellas-map-native-american.html.

6. http://nitanahkohe.tumblr.com/post/83460297016/aaron-carapellas-tribal-nations-maps-do-not-do.

7. Facebook Group, Native American and American Indian Issues, comments responding to Aaron Carapella, July 26, 2015, post of NPR article, "The Map of Native American Tribes You Have Never Seen Before," www.facebook.com/groups/NAAIissues/search/?query=tribal%20nations%20map. This belief that mapping is inherently "un-Indian" has academic adherents. Peter Nabokov has argued that the term "indigenous cartography" is a "problematic cover term for the often opposed vested interests

of cartography and cosmology ... [where] the real-world consequences of that opposition are clearly visible on any maps of the shrunken Indian land base today" (Nabokov, "Orientations from Their Side," 245, 249, 261).

8. Gena Pone's comment on American Indians in Children's Literature, June 25, 2014, http://americanindiansinchildrensliterature.blogspot.com/2014/06/aaron-carapellas-map-native-american.html.

9. Facebook Group, Native American and American Indian Issues, comments responding to Sparky Malarkey Schwakhofer-Coxon's untitled post from August 20, 2015, www.facebook.com/groups/NAAIissues/search/?query=tribal%20nations%20map.

10. Karl Jacoby succinctly articulates this dilemma: "To ignore ... Native epistemologies risks draining the project of recapturing Native history of much of its meaning. At the same time, however, this very same impulse also risks rendering Native American histories distinct from other forms of history, transforming each into a unique and isolated version of the past" (Jacoby, "Indigenous Empires and Native Nations: Beyond History and Ethnohistory in Pekka Hämäläinen's *The Comanche Empire*," *History and Theory* 52 [February 2013]: 64; see also Melissa L. Meyer and Kerwin Lee Klein, "Native American Studies and the End of Ethnohistory," in *Studying Native America*, ed. Thornton, 182–216; R. White, "Using the Past: History and Native American Studies," ibid., 217–43; Porter, "Imagining Indians: Differing Perspectives on Native American History"; Richter, "Whose Indian History?"; and Mihesuah, ed., *Natives and Academics*; and Martin, ed., *The American Indian and the Problem of History*).

11. Nietschmann, as qtd. in Wood, *Rethinking the Power of Maps*, 134. Numerous scholars have used these Nietschmann quotes as points of departure (see Joe Bryan, "Where Would We Be without Them? Knowledge, Space, and Power in Indigenous Politics," *Futures* 41 [2009]: 24–25).

12. Wheat, *Mapping the Trans-Mississippi West 1540–1804*, 2:43.

13. This is my answer to Jean M. O'Brien's call to "challenge national narratives that naturalize Indian conquest and erase Indian peoples from the landscape" (see O'Brien, "Colonialism," paper presented at "Keywords in Native American Studies" conference, University of Michigan, January 11–13, 2008, as taken from Barr, "Geographies of Power," 9n8).

14. Sparke, *In the Space of Theory*, 12.

15. In this way, I build on work from the history of science. As Neil Safier writes, "The manner by which indigenous peoples of the Americas and elsewhere actually contributed to processes of collection, codification, and dissemination of inquiries into the natural world has in turn become a core issue for those attempting to write more integrated and global histories of science" (Safier, "Global Knowledge on the Move: Itineraries, Amerindian Narratives, and Deep Histories of Science," *Isis* 101, no. 1 [March 2010]: 133–45 [quote on 136]).

16. Continental Congress, "The Northwest Ordinance," July 13, 1787, www.law.ou.edu/hist/ordinanc.html.

17. Matthew Edney was among the first to point out the importance of the rhetoric of enlightened cartographic science in the expansion of empires (Edney, *Mapping an Empire*). See also Burnett, *Masters of All They Surveyed*; Craib, "Cartography and Power in the Conquest and Creation of New Spain"; Safier, *Measuring the New World*; and Withers and Livingston, *Geography and Enlightenment*.

18. Jacoby, "Indigenous Empires and Native Nations," 66.

19. D. Scott, *Conscripts of Modernity*, 7–8.

20. Harley, "Deconstructing the Map," 1–20; Harley, "Maps, Knowledge, and Power," 301–3. A posthumously published collection of Harley's work contains versions of both articles mentioned: Harley, *The New Nature of Maps*. The most cited postmodern works include Foucault, *Discipline and Punish;* Giddens, *The Contemporary Critique of Historical Materialism*; Said, *Orientalism*; and Certeau, *The Practice of Everyday Life*.

21. For a description of the map as process rather than text, see Rundstrom, "Mapping, Postmodernism," 1–12; and Edney "Cartography without 'Progress,'" 54–68. Other critiques of Harley's approach include Belyea, "Images of Power"; and H. Scott, "Contested Territories," 166–88. A summary of this critique can be found in Edney, "The Origins and Development of J. B. Harley's Cartographic Theories," with further discussion in Cosgrove, "Epistemology, Geography, and Cartography," 202–9.

22. Nobles, "Straight Lines and Stability," 9–35; See also Boelhower, "Inventing America"; Hannah, "Space and Social Control in the Administration of the Oglala Lakota ('Sioux'), 1871–1879," 412–32; Hannah, *Governmentality and the Mastery of Territory in Nineteenth-Century America*; Francavaiglia, *Mapping and Imagination in the Great Basin*; and Witgen, "The Rituals of Possession," 639–68. For studies outside of the United States, see Lewis and Wigen, *The Myth of Continents*; Brealey, "Mapping Them 'Out,'" 140–56; Sparke, "A Map That Roared and an Original Atlas," 463–95; Byrnes, *Boundary Markers*; Piper, *Cartographic Fictions*; Orlove, "Mapping Reeds and Reading Maps," 3–38; and "Geographies at Work in Asian History," special issue of *Journal of Asian Studies* 59, no. 3 (2000). Many scholars at the forefront of this movement attended a conference at the Newberry Library in 2004. This conference was followed by a book of the same name: James R. Ackerman, ed., *The Imperial Map*.

23. Thongchai, *Siam Mapped*, 129–30.

24. Belyea, *Dark Storm Moving West*, 73. An entry point into this scholarship is G. Lewis, ed., *Cartographic Encounters*; and Woodward and Lewis, *The History of Cartography*, vol. 2, bk. 3, 51–181. See also Belyea "Amerindian Maps: the Explorer as Translator," 267–77; and Warhus, *Another America*. Belyea has been a vocal critic of the scholars whom she perceives as categorizing Indian maps as immature versions of western geographic knowledge, including G. Malcolm Lewis and Denis Wood (see Belyea, "Review Article of Denis Wood's *The Power of Maps* and the Author's Reply," 94–99. For a further discussion of this debate, see Edney, "Cartography without 'Progress,'" 54–68).

25. Parks, "Interpreting Pawnee Star Lore: Science or Myth," 63–64; Gartner, "An Image to Carry the World within It," in *Early American Cartographies*, ed. Brückner. See also Von Del Chamberlain, *When the Stars Came Down to Earth*.

26. This segregation is epitomized in the 131-page entry "Native North American Maps" in the seminal *The History of Cartography*, which considers only the cultural characteristics of Indian maps. The volume on Renaissance mapping, on the other hand, has separate sections for the political economic, military, and religious contexts of maps made in Italy, Portugal, Spain, German Lands, Low Countries, France, the British Isles, Scandinavia, East-Central Europe, and Russia. For a discussion of the literary constructions of "otherness," see Todorov, *The Conquest of America*.

27. Van der Woude, "Why Maps Matter," 1074.

28. Adam Jortner, "The Empty Continent, Cartography, Pedagogy, and Native American History," in *Why You Can't Teach United States History without American Indians*, ed. Susan Sleeper-Smith, Juliana Barr, Jean M. O'Brien, Nancy Shoemaker, and Scott Stevens (Chapel Hill: University of North Carolina Press, 2015), 74. His quote is from W. Dirk Raat, "Innovative Ways to Look at New World Geography," *History Teacher* 37 (May 2004): 289. On the rhetorical power of blank spaces, see J. B. Harley, "Silences and Secrecy: The Hidden Agenda of Cartography in Early Modern Europe," *Imago Mundi* 40 (1988): 57–76.

29. See, for example, Nabokov, "Orientations from Their Side"; Robert Rundstrom, "The Role of Ethics, Mapping, and the Meaning of Place in Relations between Indians and Whites in the United States," *Cartographica* 30 (1993): 21–28; and Belyea, *Dark Storm Moving West*.

30. J. T. Carson, "Ethnogeography and the Native Past," *Ethnohistory* 49, no. 4 (2002): 783. Although the original quote regarding "statements of territorial appropriation" is from Brian Harley's seminal "Rereading the Maps of the Columbian Encounter," 522. I am quoting here from Juliana Barr's synopsis of American mapping to demonstrate the persistence of this interpretation (Barr, "Geographies of Power," 7).

31. Barr, "Geographies of Power," 7. See also Witgen, "The Rituals of Possession," 639–68.

32. Susan Schulten, "The Civil War and the Origins of the Colorado Territory," *Western Historical Quarterly* 44, no. 1 (2013): 29.

33. Farmer, *On Zion's Mount*, 11.

34. Good entry points into this vast literature include Basso, *Wisdom Sits in Places*; Pearce and Louis, "Indigenous Depth of Place," 107–26; Paul Nadasdy, "The Politics of TEK: Power and the 'Integration' of Knowledge," *Arctic Anthropology* 36, no. 1–2, 1999, 1–18; Biolosi, "Imagined Geographies," 249–59; Cruikshank, "Getting the Words Right," 52–65; Rundstrom, "GIS, Indigenous Peoples, and Epistemological Diversity," 45–57; and Brody, *Maps & Dreams*.

35. For a discussion of the problems of "indigenous knowledge," see Agrawal, "Dismantling the Divide," 413–39; and Turnbull, *Masons, Tricksters and Cartographers*.

36. Gregg, *Commerce of the Prairies or the Journal of a Santa Fe Trader*, 19–23.

37. Barr, "Geographies of Power," 10.

38. Martin Brückner, for example, writes: "The Lewis and Clark map and, to a certain degree, also their journals are thus the product of authorial collaboration, the combined product of Jefferson's map and expedition orders, Native American testimonies and Lewis and Clark's geographical transcripts and observations. . . . As a consequence of their efforts in transcription and translation, the expedition leaders became spatially and textually disoriented. . . . Unable to reconcile the European mode of geographic representation with that of Native Americans, the discovered the limits of their geographical literacy" (*Geographic Revolution in Early America*, 208). For more on Amerindian contributions to North American mapping, see Galloway, "Debriefing Explorers," in *Cartographic Encounters,* ed. Lewis; G. Malcolm Lewis, "Indian Maps: Their Place in the History of Plains Cartography," *Great Plains Quarterly* 4 (1984): 91–108; Rhonda, "A Chart in His Way," 81–92; Belyea, "Amerindian Maps," 267–77; Belyea, "Mapping the Marias," 165–84; and Waselkov, "Indian Maps of the Colonial Southeast," 435–53.

39. This critique is largely aimed at cartography scholars who study the United States. A growing body of literature outside of the United States works to create

narratives that include both Native and imperial mapping practices within state formation (see Offen, "Creating Mosquitia," 254–82; Craib, *Cartographic Mexico*; and Safier, *Measuring the New World*). For an analysis of the state of the field, see Craib, "Relocating Cartography," 481–90.

40. One of the most astute critics of the racialized Indian/white binary is not part of this academic historiography. Roger Echo-Hawk writes that stories of particular Indian groups' assertions of social power—in his case, Pawnee—have come to matter less to members of these groups than the "tale of how American adherents to racial whiteness victimized and dispossessed Pawnee adherents to racial Indianhood. . . . Passing along racial identity, generations of Pawnees found it useful to hand down versions of history that helped to perpetuate the tenets and structures of American racialism" (Echo-Hawk, "Settling the Land between Two Rivers," 2009, www.roger-echo-hawk.com/resources/SettlingTheLandBetweenTwoRivers.html; see also Echo-Hawk, *The Magic Children*).

41. Blackhawk, "Look How Far We've Come," 13–17. For works that interrogate the Indian-white binary in the colonial and early national periods, see, for example, Merrell, *The Indians' New World*; Gallay, *The Indian Slave Trade*; Brooks, *Captives and Cousins*; Saunt, *A New Order of Things*; R. White, *The Middle Ground*; and Daniel K. Richter, *The Ordeal of the Longhouse: The Peoples of the Iroquois League in the Era of European Colonization* (Chapel Hill: University of North Carolina Press, 2011).

42. DuVal, *The Native Ground*; Hämäläinen, *The Comanche Empire*; DeLay, *War of a Thousand Deserts*; Bowes, *Exiles and Pioneers*.

1 / Constructing Indian Country

1. Sharitarish is the name shared by a long line of patrilineal chiefs who dominated Pawnee politics during the first half of the nineteenth century. This Chaui lineage is referred to in various documents as "Charaterish," "Sharitarish," "Shah-re-ta-riches," and "Saritsaris." For consistency, I will use Sharitarish throughout the book. Pawnee scholar James Riding In translates the name as Raging Horse, whereas George Hyde established the more common interpretation by arguing the name was an abbreviation of the Pawnee *lesharo* (chief) and *cherish* (angry or cross) (Riding In, "Keeper of Tirawahut's Covenant," 129: Hyde, *The Pawnee Indians*, 152).

2. Carleton, *The Prairie Logbooks*, 62–65.

3. Carleton, "The Expedition of Major Clifton Wharton in 1844," 272–305.

4. Enlightenment thought is increasingly examined outside of the narrow chronological period previously ascribed to it. As Charles W. J. Withers and David Livingstone write, "Enlightenment historians now consider it more helpful to look at the Enlightenment as a series of debates, which necessarily took different shapes and forms in particular national and cultural contexts" (Withers and Livingstone, eds., *Geography and Enlightenment*, 3). In the context of the United States, Mathew Edney has related this Enlightenment model to cartography in the nineteenth, rather than eighteenth, century (see Edney, "Reflection Essay").

5. Belyea, "Amerindian Maps," 267–77. Margaret Wickens Pearce also finds the narrative of mutual unintelligibility unsatisfactory: "Because conventional map history depends heavily on works that are products of colonial rhetoric, the assumption is made that the colonial cartography inevitably obliterated or overlaid any existing

native cartography in the same way that colonial settlement invariably obliterated and overlaid existing native settlement" (Pearce, "Native Mapping in Southern New England, 158). Pearce, however, focuses on the persistence of Native mapping in the face of American expansion, whereas this projects holds that Native practices cannot be delineated from the national cartographic project.

6. Brückner, *The Geographic Revolution in Early America*, 209, 224–25.

7. See the introduction of this volume for examples of such arguments.

8. This characteristic is most clearly defined by Peter Nabokov in "Orientations from Their Side," 243.

9. For two recent interpretations of Indian participation in the creation of the permanent Indian territory, see Bowes, *Exiles and Pioneers*; and Unrau, *The Rise and Fall of Indian Country*.

10. Descriptions of most extant Native maps created before the twentieth century can be found in Woodward and Lewis, eds., *Cartography in the Traditional African, American, Arctic, Australian, and Pacific Societies*.

11. Wishart, *An Unspeakable Sadness*, 16. For a starting point into the literature on Indian territoriality, see Imre Sutton, ed., *American Indian Territoriality: An Online Research Guide*, http://thorpe.ou.edu/treatises/aitchptr%20pdfs/index.htm.

12. Juliana Barr and Kathleen DuVal have come to the same conclusion concerning Native groups in the early American Southwest (Barr, "Geographies of Power," 5–46; DuVal, *The Native Ground*). Margaret Wickens Pearce also finds evidence of distinct Indian boundaries in colonial New England (see Pearce, "Native Mapping in Southern New England," 162).

13. Dunbar, "The Pawnee Indians," 250. There are some documents that contradict such an interpretation. Lewis and Clark reported that the Pawnee had "no idea of an exclusive possession of any country" (Thwaites, ed., *Original Journals of the Lewis and Clark Expedition, 1804–1806*, 6:85–87).

14. *A Map Exhibiting the Territorial Limits of Several Nations and Tribes of Indians agreeable to the notes of A. Chouteau . . . by A. Paul, February 1816*, National Archives Map and Cartography Division, Record Group 75, Central Map File, no. 884.

15. Henry Atkinson, "Expedition up the Missouri," as found in *News of the Plains and Rockies 1803–1865: Original narratives of Overland Travel and Adventure Selected from Wagner-Camp and Becker Bibliography of Western Americana*, vol. 1, *Early Explorers and Fur Hunters*, comp. David A. White (Spokane WA: Arthur A. Clark, 1996), 203.

16. Unrau, *The Kansa Indians*, 157.

17. Missouri Historical Society (hereafter MHS), George Sibley Papers, Miscellaneous File, B. H. Reeves to James Barbour, April 15, 1826.

18. MHS, Native American Collections, box 1, folder 6, A. P. Chouteau to Milicour Papin, December 11, 1823.

19. MHS, Native American Collections, box 2, Dougherty to Clark, July 5, 1830.

20. "Mr Benton . . . communicating the Memorial of the General Assembly of the State of Missouri, on the subject of Indians residing within that state," May 14, 1824, 18th Cong., 1st sess., 1824, S. Doc. 79, 1.

21. For more biographical details of McCoy's life, see Schultz, *An Indian Canaan*.

22. Wheat, *Mapping the Trans-Mississippi West*, 2:142–43. Henry Phelps's 1832 *Map of the United States*, for example, includes the following note: "The Publisher is

indebted to M. Isaac McCoy U.S. Surveyor for the use of his Surveys of the situation of the several tribes of Indians lying West of the Arkansas and Missouri." After he submitted one of his maps to Congress in 1838, McCoy wrote in his typical understated fashion of his project, "This map contributed somewhat to the fixing of the bounds of the Indian territory in the public mind" (McCoy, *History of Baptist Missions*, 541).

23. McCoy, *History of Baptist Missions*, 516–20.

24. National Archives (hereafter NA), Record Group (hereafter RG) 279 (Records of the *Indian Claims Commission Hearings)*, docket 35, box 579, claimants' ex. 121 and 122, Clark to Calhoun, June 25, 1820, and December 8, 1823.

25. NA, RG 75 (Records of the Bureau of Indian Affairs), T494 (*Documents Relating to the Ratified and Unratified Treaties)*, roll 1, June 8 and June 11, 1825, William Clark to James Barbour.

26. *Transactions of the Kansas State Historical Society* 4 (1886–88), 298–301. NA, RG 75, M234 (Letters Received by the Office of Indians Affairs), roll 753 (St. Louis Superintendency, 1842–45), Clark to Langham July 9, 1826, copy, included in letter from Supt. of Ind. Affairs D. D. Mitchell to Commissioner of Indian Affairs, April 18, 1842.

27. As Kathleen DuVal writes, "Contrary to assumptions that only Europeans drew borders, Indians across the continent defined, defended, and disputed geographic and metaphoric borders long before Europeans arrived" (DuVal, *The Native Ground*, 28).

28. Schubert, ed., *March to South Pass*, 30.

29. McDermott, ed., "Isaac McCoy's Second Exploring Trip in 1828," 441–45.

30. Joseph Nicollet, "A Report Intended to Illustrate a Map of the Hydrographical Basin of the Upper Mississippi River," 26th Cong., 2d sess., 1841, S. Doc. 237.

31. "Report of Mr. A. W. Tinkham . . . in Reports of Explorations and Surveys to ascertain the most practicable and economical route for a railroad from the Mississippi River to the Pacific Ocean, 1853–1854," 33rd Cong., 2d sess., 1856, S. Exec. Doc. 78, 228; William Emory, "Notes of a Military Reconnaissance from Fort Leavenworth in Missouri to San Diego California including part of the Arkansas, Del Norte, and Gila Rivers," 30th Cong., 1st sess., 1847, S. Ex. Doc. 41, 24.

32. While there are more than spellings of "Iowa"—the term used to designate the tribe—these variations were phonetic pronunciations of the name used by the Indians themselves, such as *"aj u wej"* (Mott, "A Synonym of Names for the Iowa Indians," 48–72). I will use the name Iowa, unless a different name is used in the original documents.

33. Skinner, "Ethnology of the Ioway Indians," 183–85. For further anthropological information, including creation stories, see "James Owen Dorsey Papers" group (4800), Anthropology Archives, Smithsonian Institution, Suitland, Maryland, esp. subgroups (294) and (296). For an ethnohistory of the Iowas, see Blaine, *The Iowa Indians*; Wedel, "The Iowa Indians," 432–46; Anderson, "Ioway Ethnohistory: A Review," pts. 1 and 2, 1228–41; and *Annals of Iowa* 42, no. 1 (1973): 41–59.

34. McKenney and Hall, *Biographical Sketches and Anecdotes,* 146.

35. McCarter & English Indian Claims Cases, Princeton Collections of Western Americana (hereafter PCWA), docket 135, exhibit 18.

36. These investigations have interrogated the primacy of tribal allegiance in regional social structures. A particularly concise account of the inquiry can be found in Patricia Albers and Jeanne Kay: "In order to understand American Indian territoriality it is necessary to look at land-use from a regional rather than tribally-based perspective, and to distinguish between ideological claim to and the actual use of a

specific territory. . . . In areas which have a history of multiple tribal use, the conditions of 'sharing' must be analyzed to determine what kinds of land-claims members of different tribes hold and on what basis these rights are being asserted. What are the sociopolitical bodies which hold land in common and are these groups always organized along single tribal lines? Can relationships, then, such as those based on kinship, manage land-rights independent of tribal allegiances?" (Albers and Kay, "Sharing the Land," 53; see also Albers, "Changing Patterns of Ethnicity in the Northeastern Plains, 1780–1870").

37. Albers and Kay, "Sharing the Land."

38. See R. White, *The Middle Ground*; for the ravages of smallpox, see Fenn, *Pox Americana*.

39. PCWA, box 39, folder 11, Anthony F. C. Wallace, "The Iowa and Sac-and-Fox Indians in Iowa and Missouri," unpublished findings as expert witness before U.S. Claims Commission, October 1954, 17–21.

40. Auguste Chouteau, original unknown. Defendant's exhibit 12, docket 153, Indian Claims Commission, *Sac, Fox, and Iowa Indians III: Commission Findings on the Sac, Fox, and Iowa Indians* (New York, 1974), 16.

41. R. White, "The Winning of the West," 319–32.

42. Blaine, *The Iowa Indians*, 115.

43. PCWA, docket 135, exhibit 46, William Clark to Secretary of War, St. Louis, October 18, 1815, original location unknown.

44. In addition to America's protection, the Iowas may have understood the 1815 treaty as an alliance of reciprocity. In an effort to maintain control of the valuable Mississippi and Missouri watersheds during the War of 1812, Americans provided various tribes with twenty thousand dollars' worth of goods; they also selected a few chiefs, including Hard Heart of the Iowas, to receive peace medals that professed their status as leaders and their ability to negotiate with others of the same rank. Perhaps not coincidentally, Hard Heart's is one of the fifteen signatures on the 1815 treaty. It is not hard to imagine that Hard Heart's personal bonds of reciprocity with the Americans—established during the War of 1812—influenced his decision to seek protection from the Americans in 1815 (see Lowrie, Franklin, and Clark, eds., *American State Papers*, 2:7).

45. Wilhelm, *Travels in North America 1822–1824*, 302.

46. Lewis, *Original Journals*, 44–47; PCWA, box 39, folder 11, Wallace, "The Iowa and Sac- and Fox Indians in Iowa and Missouri."

47. Carter, comp. and ed., *The Territorial Papers of the United States*, 15:562–64.

48. Wilhelm, *Travels in North America 1822–1824*, 316.

49. In 1955, the United States Indian Claims Commission finally decided on the annuities due to each tribe. Most of the proceedings centered on the question of historic territorial control, with the 1825 treaty playing an important role.

50. Schoolcraft, *Thirty Years with the Indian Tribes*, 215–16.

51. Kappler, *Indian Affairs* 2, "Treaty with the Sioux, Etc., 1825," articles 2 and 3.

52. NA, RG 75, T494, roll 2, Minutes of Council held at Prairie du Chien, July 7–16, 1830. Native participation in market economies is historiographically contested. For economic discussions that mirror the universalist versus dualist divide in other aspects of Indian history, see Trigger, "Early Native North American Responses to European Contact," 1195–215; Ray and Freeman, *Give Us Good Measure*; and Martin,

Keepers of the Game. This debate has been particularly acute surrounding discussions of the buffalo (see, for example, Hämäläinen, "The Western Comanche Trade Center," 485–513; Flores, "Bison Ecology and Bison Diplomacy," 465–87; Ostler, "They Regard Their Passing as Wakan," 475–97; Krech, *Ecological Indian*; Dobak, "Killing the Canadian Buffalo"; and Isenberg, *The Destruction of the Bison*).

53. For other studies that complicate this view of the region, see, for example, Murphy, *A Gathering of Rivers*, in which Murphy describes the Fox Indians' successful mining operations; and Hoxie, *Parading through History*. See also Anderson, *Kinsmen of Another Kind*; and Thorne, *The Many Hands of My Relations*. For a discussion of American expansionism in the early republic, see Horsman, *Expansion and American Indian Policy*.

54. NA, RG 75, T494, roll 2, Minutes of Council held at Prairie du Chien, July 7–16, 1830.

55. NA, RG 75, M21 (Letters Sent by Office of the Bureau of Indian Affairs) roll 12, Hughes to Secretary of War Cass, April 12, 1834.

56. Kappler, *Indian Affairs* 2, Treaty with the Iowa, etc., 1836.

57. PCWA, docket 153, exhibit 162. Original, NA, RG 75, Letters Received, Great Nemaha, Hughes to Clark, August 26, 1837.

58. NA, RG 46, Records of the U.S. Senate; 25th Cong., Committee Reports and Papers, Committee on Indian Affairs, box 20, John Dougherty to Thomas Benton, December 10, 1838; 22nd Cong., Committee Reports and Papers, Committee on Indian Affairs, box 16, Wm. Clark to Benton, January 14, 1832; MHS, Native American Collections, box 2, folder 3.

59. PCWA, docket 138, exhibit 155. Original NA, RG 75, Letters Received, Great Nemaha, H-62 Document B, 1837.

60. NA, RG 75, T494, roll 3, Journal of Proceedings at Council, October 7, 1837. See Mott, "The Relation of Historic Indian Tribes," 227–314; and Wedel, "Indian Villages," 561–92.

61. For a further analysis of the sites on the map, see "Maps, Material Culture, and Memory: On the Trail of the Ioway," a digital project by the Iowa State Archeologist, http://archaeology.uiowa.edu/1837-ioway-map.

62. Belyea, "Inland Journeys, Native Maps," 141.

63. An example of a map in which the scale is dependent upon the viewer's point of view is the famous 1976 Saul Steinburg illustration *The New Yorkers' View of the World,* published on the cover of the issue dated March 29, 1976. For a discussion of the importance of the "God's-eye view" in the political appropriation of space, see Pickles, *A History of Spaces*, 80; and Haraway, *Simians, Cyborgs and Women*.

64. Turnbull, *Maps Are Territories*, 23.

65. William Green, "Untitled Article on Iowa Map of 1837," in *An Atlas of Early Maps of the American Midwest: Part II, Illinois State Museum Scientific Papers 29,* comp. W. Raymond Wood (Springfield: Illinois State Museum, 2001).

66. Blaine, *The Iowa Indians*, 169.

67. PCWA, docket 153, exhibit 175. Original, NA, BIA, RG 75, Letters Received, Great Nemaha 1837, Dougherty to Clark, May 30, 1838.

68. Kansas State Historical Society, Isaac McCoy Papers (hereafter IMP), Isaac McCoy to John McCoy, Aug. 2 1837; Instructions to Surveyor of Sac and Fox Lands, March 16, 1838; Field Notes of the Survey of Sac and Iowa Lands, 1838.

69. Kappler, *Indian Affairs* 2, Treaty with the Iowa, 1838.

2 / Sharitarish and the Possibility of Treaties

1. Kappler, *Indian Affairs: Laws and Treaties,* vol. 2, digital version from Oklahoma State University library; Wishart, "The Pawnee Claims Case."

2. Cronon, Miles, and Gitlin, eds., *Under an Open Sky,* 15.

3. Riding In, "Keeper of Tirawahut's Covenant," 149; Unrau, *The Rise and Fall of Indian Country,* 88.

4. United States, "Commission Findings," in *Pawnee and Kansa (Kaw) Indians: Report of the Indian Claims Commission* (New York: Garland, 1974), 297.

5. See the introduction of this volume for a discussion of the meaning of "ideological arrows."

6. For more information on the Comanches, see Hämäläinen, *The Comanche Empire*; and DeLay, *War of a Thousand Deserts.* For more on the Osages, see DuVal, *The Native Ground.* As Colin Calloway writes: "People like the Osages and Comanches were hardly people caught between powerful empires. They dominated the worlds they inhabited, exploited foreigners who tentatively impinged on their domains, and preserved their independence and their lands" (Calloway, *One Vast Winter Count,* 313).

7. Between 1819 and 1827, Pawnee agent Benjamin O'Fallon visited a Pawnee village only once (MHS, John Dougherty Papers, Dougherty to Lewis Cass, March 9, 1832).

8. Holder, *The Hoe and Horse,* 42–47. Holder writes that, while no community member was barred from access to the sacred knowledge of the bundles, the lengthy apprenticeship normally limited participation to leader's families, who had the necessary resources. Thus, as Richard White writes: "A strict distinction between Pawnee chiefs and Pawnee priests is artificial. Although all priests did not rule as chiefs, a chief could often be a priest, or he might only possess a bundle and leave its care and ceremonies in the hands of a priest" (R. White, *The Roots of Dependency,* 173). James Murie narrates a long-ago fight between the chiefs and the priests that almost destroyed them both. The damage was so great that "after this occurrence, the chiefs and medicine men never quarreled" (Murie, "Pawnee Indian Societies," 639; see also Weltfish, *The Lost Universe,* 19, 272).

9. Weltfish, *The Lost Universe,* 131.

10. For another introduction to Pawnee history, see Wishart, *Encyclopedia of the Plains.*

11. Dunbar, "The Pawnee Indians," 244, 251–53; Grinnell, *Pawnee Hero Stories and Folk-Tales,* 218–33; Dorsey, *The Pawnee Mythology,* 8, 19; Murie, *Pawnee Indian Societies,* 549; Dunbar, "Missionary Life among the Pawnee," 276; Weltfish, *The Lost Universe,* 4; James, Long, and Say, *James's Account of S. H. Long's Expedition,* 15:16. For a good (if sometimes conflicting) secondary synthesis, see Riding In, "Keepers of Tirawahut's Covenant," 7–9, 74–75; R. White, *Roots of Dependency,* 148–50; and Wishart, *Unspeakable Sadness,* 4–5. The relationships among the South Bands and smaller Siouan groups—such as the Omaha and Otoes—were more stable than their relationship with the Kansa, but they still had their fair share of bloodshed.

12. For a description of how this colonial violence spread from the Spanish Southwest, see Blackhawk, *Violence over the Land.* For a more specific discussion of the horse's role in this violence, see Hämäläinen, "The Rise and Fall of Plains

Indian Horse Cultures." The seminal works on the consequences of the horse and the gun trade are Secoy, *Changing Military Patterns of the Great Plains Indians*; and Holder, *The Hoe and Horse on the Plains*. For a broader discussion of trade on the Plains, see Fowler, "The Great Plains from the Arrival of the Horse to 1885," 1–55; Swagerty, "Indian Trade in the Trans-Mississippi West to 1870," 351–74; Calloway, *One Vast Winter Count*, 264–301; Ewers, "The Indian Trade of the Upper Missouri before Lewis and Clark," 14–33; and John, *Storms Brewed in Other Men's Worlds*. For a description of how this violence spread from the East, see Neal Salisbury, *Native Peoples and European Settlers in Eastern North America, 1600–1783*, in *The Cambridge History of the Native Peoples of the Americas* 1, pt. 1, ed. Trigger and Washburn, 399–460; R. White, *The Middle Ground*; and Calloway, *One Vast Winter Count*, 313–56.

13. Hämäläinen, "The Rise and Fall of Plains Indian Horse Cultures"; Hämäläinen, *Comanche Empire*, 19–55; R. White, *Roots of Dependency*, 151–53, 179; Blackhawk, *Violence over the Land*, 16–54; Fowler, "Great Plains until 1870," 5–15; Calloway, *One Vast Winter Count*, 276. For a discussion of grass as energy, see West, *The Contested Plains*, 67.

14. For the most extensive discussion of the impacts of the horse on Pawnee life, see R. White, *Roots of Dependency*, 178–88; and R. White, "Cultural Landscape of the Pawnees," 67–69; see also Riding In, "Keepers of Tirawahut's Covenant," 81–84; and Weltfish, *Lost Universe*, 168–72. For primary references to trade, see Dunbar, *Magazine of American History* 4, no. 4, 255; James, Long, and Say, *James's Account of S. H. Long's Expedition*, 1:302; C. Murray, *Travels in North America*, 301, accessed through *American Memory*, http://memory.loc.gov/ammem/lhtnhtml/lhtnhome.html.

15. While an overall benefit to Pawnee life, the horse was not without its drawbacks. In addition to having to care for the animals, the increased productivity of the hunts burdened the women, who had to clean and tan the hides. Horses required the Pawnees to increase their seasonal burnings to provide forage, and they also repeatedly required the Pawnees to find environmentally suitable locations for their villages, a job that also fell primarily to women. When a new village site was found, the women had to not only move the dwellings and their contents but also to establish new horticultural zones around the new village. For other discussions of how socioeconomic changes affected gender relations and women on the Plains, see Patricia Albers and Beatrice Medicine, "The Role of Sioux Women in the Production of Ceremonial Objects: The Case of the Star Quilt," and Albers, "Sioux Women in Transition: A Study of their Changing Status in a Domestic and Capitalist Sector of Production," in *The Hidden Half: Studies of Plains Indian Women*, ed. Albers and Medicine (Lanham MD: University Press of America, 1983).

16. Riding In, "Keepers of Tirawahut's Covenant," 83. Richard White is one of the few dissenting voices to a broad consensus about the impact of horses on horticultural villages on the eastern Plains. Most scholars—largely archaeologists and anthropologists—view the arrival of the horse as the time when viable village societies came to an end on the Plains. This interpretation asserts that horticulturalists were cultural reactionaries who refused to embrace equestrianism and thus were at the mercy of the nomadic tribes (Ewers, *Indian Life on the Upper Missouri*; Wedel "Introductions to Pawnee Archeology," 97–98; Holder, *Hoe and Horse*, 111). In contrast, Richard White writes: "[The horse] did not overwhelm culture and force drastic

new adaptations to the plains and prairies. It did not demand nomadism" (R. White, *Roots of Dependency*, 89).

17. Calloway, *One Vast Winter Count*, 387.

18. Dunbar, "The Pawnee Indians: Their History and Ethnology," 255; James, Long, and Say, *James's Account of S. H. Long's Expedition*, 2:207–8. For more information on seventeenth- and eighteenth-century Plains Indian trade networks, see Hämäläinen, "The Western Comanche Trade Center," 485–513; and Wishart, *Unspeakable Sadness*, 30–31.

19. In a story told to ethnologist George Dorsey, Roaming-Chief (Chaui) recounts how a powerful chief's favorite son was deemed unworthy of succeeding his father and not allowed to join the war path. It was only after proving that he could hunt buffalo, capture horses, and defend his village that he regained his stature ("The Buffalo and the Wild Horse Dance," as told by Roaming-Chief [Chaui], in Dorsey, *The Pawnee Mythology*, 355).

20. Murie, *Ceremonies of the Pawnee*, 7–21; Dunbar, "The Pawnee Indians: Their History and Ethnology," 261; Dunbar, "The Pawnee Indians: Their Habits and Customs," 341; James, Long, and Say, *James's Account of S. H. Long's Expedition*, 4:166; see also Weltfish, *Lost Universe*, 5–7, 14–19; and R. White, *Roots of Dependency*, 176–77.

21. James, Long, and Say, *James's Account of S. H. Long's Expedition*, 4:166. For more examples of the chiefs' gift giving, see ibid., 2:148; Dunbar, "Missionary Life among the Pawnee'" 272. For more on the importance of gift giving, see Weltfish, *Lost Universe*, 14–19; Dorsey and Murie, "Notes of Skidi Pawnee Society," 112; and Holder, *Hoe and Horse*, 37, 44.

22. R. White, *Roots of Dependency*, 180, 187; Fowler, "Great Plains until 1870," 9. For examples of hierarchical gift giving in Pawnee society, see James, Long, and Say, *James's Account of S. H. Long's Expedition*, 2:157.

23. R. White, *Roots of Dependency*, 174; Dunbar, "The Pawnee Indians: Their History and Ethnology," 260.

24. Dorsey and Murie, "Notes on Skidi Pawnee Society," 113; Murie, *Pawnee Indian Societies*, 557. For a description of the *raripakusus*, see Ralph Linton, "The Thunder Ceremony of the Pawnee," *Field Museum Leaflet 5* (Chicago, 1922), 4.

25. Irving, *Indian Sketches Taken during an Expedition to the Pawnee Tribe*, 123–26. Wild Horse may have been *Ah-sah-ron-kah-re* (Wild Stud Horse), one of the signers of the 1833 treaty.

26. Irving, *Indian Sketches*, 85.

27. Dunbar, "Letters Concerning the Presbyterian Mission in the Pawnee Country, near Bellvue, Neb., 1831–1849," 652.

28. R. White, *Roots of Dependency*, 190–93. For Pawnee solicitations, see Pierre Chouteau to Secretary of War, December 14, 1809, in *Territorial Papers of the United States*, vol. 14, *Louisiana and Missouri*, comp. and ed. C. Carter, 344.

29. Colin Calloway explains this process in *Pen and Ink Witchcraft*, esp. chap. 1.

30. Calumet ceremonies evolved in the thirteenth century on the Plains as way of ensuring bonds between groups. They frequently lasted several days and involved smoking a calumet pipe, later known to Euro-Americans as a "peace pipe." For more on the Hako ceremony, see Fletcher and Murie, *The Hako*; and Weltfish, *Lost Universe*, 175–77.

31. Dunbar, "The Pawnee Indians: Their History and Ethnology," 261; Wedel, ed., *The Dunbar-Allis Letters on the Pawnee*, 641; Holder, *Hoe and Horse*, 123.

32. In 1776, by royal order, the provinces of Nueva Vizcaya, Coahuila, Texas, New Mexico, Sinaloa, Sonora, and California were placed under the military and political government of a commandant general, who was directly responsible to the king of Spain. From 1800 to 1813, Nemesio Salcedo was commandant general of the Interior Provinces (Bolton, *Guide to Materials*, 75–77).

33. Nemesio Salcedo to Joaquin del Real Alencaster [governor of New Mexico], Chihuagua, September 9, 1805, in Pike and Jackson, *The Journals of Zebulon Montgomery Pike*, 2:104–6. See also Salcedo to Alencaster October 2, 1805, and Salcedo to the Marques de Casa Calvo October 8, 1805, ibid., 110–11.

34. C. Carter, comp. and ed., *Territorial Papers of the United States*, 13:243; Jackson, ed., *Letters of the Lewis and Clark Expedition*, 265–66, 282–83; George Sibley to Samuel Sibley, Fort Osage, January 18, 1809, in Sibley Papers, Missouri Historical Society; White, comp., *From News of the Plains and Rockies 1803–1865*, 1:109 (originally in *Louisiana Gazette* 4, no. 195, May 16, 1812). For analysis of imperial struggles on the middle border, see Aron, *American Confluence*; and DuVal, *Native Ground*.

35. For full descriptions of Pike's role in American expansion, see Mathew L. Harris and Jay H. Buckley, eds., *Zebulon Pike, Thomas Jefferson and the Opening of the American West* (Norman: University of Oklahoma Press, 2012); and Jared Orsi, *Citizen Explorer: The Life of Zebulon Pike* (New York: Oxford University Press, 2014).

36. Pike and Jackson, *The Journals of Zebulon Montgomery Pike*, 2:5–9. For another description of this entrance, see ibid., 1:328–29.

37. For a discussion of the legal foundations of the Louisiana Purchase as part of the "Doctrine of Discovery," see Miller, *Native America, Discovered and Conquered*. For the role of military explorations in the colonization of the American West, see Goetzmann, *Exploration and Empire*; Goetzmann, *Army Exploration in the American West*; and Garver, "The Role of the United States Army in the Colonization of the Trans-Missouri West."

38. When Pike first met Sharitarish, he was wearing both American and Spanish medals (Pike and Jackson, *The Journals of Zebulon Montgomery Pike*, 1:329).

39. In 1819, the chronicler of Stephen Long's expedition explained that the Pawnees still preferred European goods to American: "They prefer the Mackinaw guns, blankets, &c., and will give a higher price for them, knowing that they are greatly superior to those furnished by American traders" (James, Long, and Say, *James's Account of S. H. Long's Expedition*, 4:154).

40. Pike and Jackson, *The Journals of Zebulon Montgomery Pike*, 2:2, 5–9, 12–13, 34–37, 104–6, 148–49, 181–82, 276–77, 104n. In Pike's version, he suggested that the Pawnees raise the Spanish flag once they had left, so as not to cause friction between the Indians and the Spanish. The sequence described here—one that Donald Jackson also surmised to be true—was taken from an interview of a soldier in Pike's party after he was captured and taken to Santa Fe immediately following their visit.

41. Hämäläinen, *Comanche Empire*, 202–9.

42. Sibley, "Notes of an Official Excursion," 18–25; White, comp., *News of the Plains and Rockies 1803–1865*, 1:109 (originally in *Louisiana Gazette*, vol. 4, May 16, 1812).

43. Ibid.

44. MHS, Native American Collections, box 1, folder 6, Vizcarra, Joseph Anthony to Gov. Alexander McNair of Missouri, September 8, 1823 [two letters with this date on same subject]. Also in the Native American Collections, see O'Fallon to Clark, box 2, folder 2; O'Fallon to His Excellency the G. of Santa Fee Province of New Mexico, August 1, 1823, box 1 folder 6; William Clark to Calhoun February 11, 1824, box 2, folder 1; O'Fallon to Gov. of the Province of New Mexico, September 9, 1824, box 2, folder 1; and O'Fallon to Clark, May 7, 1824, box 2, folder 1. The latter can also be found in NA, RG 75, M234, roll 747. See also Sibley, *Road to Santa Fe*, 155.

45. Sibley, "Notes of an Official Excursion," 18–25; White, comp., *News of the Plains and Rockies 1803–1865*, 1:109 (originally in *Louisiana Gazette* 4 [May 16, 1812]); Pike and Jackson, *The Journals of Zebulon Montgomery Pike*, 1:278.

46. MHS, John Dougherty Papers, Dougherty to Lewis Cass, March 9, 1832.

47. Paul Wilhelm, Duke of Württemberg, "First Journey to North America in the Years 1822 to 1824," trans. William G. Bek, *South Dakota Historical Collections* 19 (1938): 439.

48. As discussed in the opening to this chapter, the standard historical interpretation of this period depicts a self-contained Pawnee people who were not interested in a political alliance, especially not with the Americans (see Riding In, "Keepers of Tirawahut's Covenant," 33–63; and Wishart, *An Unspeakable Sadness*, 71–100).

49. MHS, folder 4, William Ashley Papers, Ashley to William C. Lane, October 29, 1824. Kathleen Duval describes a similar rhetorical tactic that was used by the Osages, who increasingly differentiated between "legitimate" Osages and "outlaws," as a way to deflect Spanish ire at continued offenses (Duval, *The Native Ground*, 170).

50. MHS, Native American Collections, box 2, folder 1, O'Fallon to Clark, December 13, 1824.

51. James, Long, and Say, *James's Account of S. H. Long's Expedition*, 4:347–56; appendix C, "Indian Speeches"; and 4:152–54.

52. This nomenclature is my own.

53. Pita-risaru is frequently referred to as Petalesharo in other accounts.

54. James, Long, and Say, *James's Account of S. H. Long's Expedition*, 4:153; 1:247; 2:157; Weltfish, *The Lost Universe*, 115.

55. Chapter 3 explicitly addresses the validity of words attributed to Sharitarish II that contradict this interpretation.

56. MHS, Native American Collections, box 1, folder 2, Dougherty to Clark, November 4, 1828; Dunbar, "Pawnee Indians: Their History and Ethnology," 242. For other reports of violence against American traders, see "Letter of Dr. James S. Craig," *Arkansas Gazette* (Little Rock), January 18, 1832, as cited in White, ed. and comp., *News of the Plains and Rockies 1803–1865*.

57. Hämäläinen, *The Comanches*, 170.

58. William Thomas, "Journal of a Voyage from St. Louis, Louisiana, to the Mandan Village," in White, ed., *News of the Plains and Rockies 1803–1865*, 96; Pike and Jackson, *The Journals of Zebulon Montgomery Pike*, 407, accessed through www.americanjourneys.org; De Voe, *Legends of the Kaw*, 91; Unrau, *The Kansa Indians*, 88–89.

59. Linguistically, the tribes living directly north and east of the Pawnees can be broken down into three subgroups of central-Siouan speakers and one group of central-Algonquian speakers: The Dakotans, primarily Yankton, Yanktonai, and Teton; the Chiwere-Winnebago, which includes the Iowa, Otoe, Missouri, and Winnebago; and

the Dhegia, which includes the Poncas to the west of the Pawnees, the Omaha to the east, and the Kansa and Osage to the southeast. The central-Algonquian-speaking people included here are the Sauk and Meskwaki.

60. There are limited regional histories that deal systematically with Indian groups living immediately west of the better-documented Ohio River valley groups like the Shawnees and Delawares. Two notable exceptions are Thorne, *The Many Hands of My Relations*; and Murphy, *A Gathering of Rivers*. The following tribal histories are also useful: Blaine, *The Ioway Indians*; William T. Hagan, *The Sac and Fox Indians* (Norman: University of Oklahoma Press, 1958); R. David Edmunds, *The Potawatomis, Keepers of the Fire* (Norman: University of Oklahoma Press, 1978); Arrell Morgan Gibson, *Kickapoos: Lords of the Middle Border* (Norman: University of Oklahoma Press, 1963); Unrau, *The Kansa Indians*. David Wishart gives a good description of the dispossession of the Omahas, Otoes, and Missouris in *An Unspeakable Sadness*. For additional tribal histories, see Boughter, *Betraying the Omaha Nation*; and Chapman, *The Otoes and Missourias*. For further discussion of the Iowa Indians, see Bernstein, "We Are Not Now as We Once Were," 605–37.

61. Maxwell, "Notes on the Missouri River and Some of the Native Tribes in Its Neighborhood," 354, 359.

62. As qtd. in Jackson, ed., *The Letters of the Lewis and Clark Expedition*, 200. For more on Osage hegemony, see Williard Rollings, *The Osage: An Ethnohistorical Study of Hegemony on the Prairie-Plains* (Columbia: University of Missouri Press, 1992); DuVal, *The Native Ground*; and Calloway, *One Vast Winter Count*, 379–82.

63. DuVal, *The Native Ground*, 197; LaVere: *Contrary Neighbors*, 63–72. Calloway, *One Vast Winter Count*, 380–84. For other examples of Indians as the first wave of Euro-American expansion, see R. David Edmunds, "Indians as Pioneers: Potawatomis on the Frontier," *Chronicles of Oklahoma* 65 (1987–88): 340–53; Bowes, *Exiles and Pioneers*; and Aron, *American Confluence*.

64. As with the Pawnees, the Osages were not a unified political body, and many of their geopolitical machinations had as much to do with intertribal rivalries as with external pressures. Like the Pawnees, the Osages saw an alliance with the United States as an important strategy (DuVal, *The Native Ground*, 197–226).

65. Rollings, *The Osage*, 270–72.

66. MHS, Native American Collections, box 2, folder 3, Dougherty to Clark, March 15, 1831; Foreman, *Indians & Pioneers*, 246–47; MHS, Native American Collections, box 2, folder 4, Sam Houston, June 24, 1829.

67. For a more detailed description of the ethnogenesis that was occurring, see Albers and Kay, "Sharing the Land," 53l; Albers, "Changing Patterns of Ethnicity in the Northeastern Plains, 1780–1870"; and Binnema, *Common and Contested Ground*.

68. James Wilkinson to Henry Dearborn, May 27, 1806, in Pike and Jackson, *The Journals of Zebulon Montgomery Pike*, 2:104–6.

69. C. Carter, comp. and ed., *The Territorial Papers of the United States*, 13:243–44; William Connelly, ed., "Indian Treaties and Councils Affecting Kansas: Dates and Places, Where Held, Names of Tribes, Commissioners and Indians Concluding Same," *Kansas State Historical Collections* 16 (1925): 746–47; James, Long, and Say, *James's Account of S. H. Long's Expedition*, 1:272; Elliott Coues, ed., *The Expeditions of Zebulon Montgomery Pike*, 2:562, 576, 585 (digital version through *Early Encounters in North America*).

70. "Extracts from the Diary of Major Sibley," *Chronicles of Oklahoma* 5 (1927): 199; James, Long, and Say, *James's Account of S. H. Long's Expedition*, 1:195.

71. James, Long, and Say, *James's Account of Long's Expedition*, 1:91; Francois Marie Perrin Du Lac, *Travels through the Two Louisianas among the Savage Nations of the Missouri* (London, 1807), 56.

72. Barry, *Beginning of the West*, 183; Lowrie, Franklin, and Clark, eds., *American State Papers* 4:709, as qtd. in Champe and Fenenga, "Notes on the Pawnee," 96; Missouri History Museum, Library and Research Center, Pilcher Papers, folder 1, subfolder 1820–1829, Dougherty to Clark, April 15, 1827; MHS, Native American Collections, box 2, folder 3, Beauchamp to Dougherty, October 26, 1829; White, comp., *News of the Plains and Rockies 1803–1865*, 203; MHS, Native American Collections, , box 2, folder 3, Dougherty to Clark, April 7, 1831; MHS, Native American Collections, box 2, folder 3, Dougherty to Clark., September 14, 1829.

73. *Missionary Herald*, 29:134, as qtd. in Barry, *Beginning of the West*, 215.

74. Kappler, *Indian Affairs*, vol. 2 (*Treaties*), digital version from Oklahoma State University Library; Bowes, *Exiles and Pioneers*, 132–35; Unrau, *Kansa Indians*, 104–9 (see chapter 3 for a further discussion of these boundaries).

75. 23rd Cong., S. Doc. 512, "The Correspondence on the Subject of the Emigration of Indians 1831–33," vol. 2, serial 245, p. 431; *St. Louis (MO) Beacon*, October 7, 1830; McDermott, ed., "Isaac McCoy's Second Exploring Trip," 357–58.

76. McCoy, *History of Baptist Missions*, 407–12; 23rd Cong., S. Doc. 512, "The Correspondence on the Subject of the Emigration of Indians 1831–33," 2:430–38.

77. For McCoy's use of Langham's map, see Barnes, ed., "Journal of Isaac McCoy for the Exploring Expedition of 1830," 339–41; 23rd Cong., S. Doc. 512, "The Correspondence on the Subject of the Emigration of Indians 1831–33," 2:436.

78. 23rd Cong., S. Doc. 512, "The Correspondence on the Subject of the Emigration of Indians 1831–33," 2:436.

79. Ibid., 3:306–10.

80. 23rd Cong., 1st sess., serial 263, H. Rep. 474, 78, appendix T. Agent at Fort Gibson February 10, 1834, to Sec. of War.

81. James, Long, and Say, *James's Account of S. H. Long's Expedition*, 2:204–10. For a history of Cheyenne migrations and politics, see West, *Contested Plains*, esp. 63–94; and Donald J. Berthrong, *The Southern Cheyenne* (Norman: University of Oklahoma Press 1963), 3–26.

82. MHS, John Dougherty Papers, "Copy of Report Made by John Dougherty When Indian Agent," 31; Hyde, *The Pawnee Indians*, 181. For more accounts of Pawnee conflicts in the Southwest, see Steven Watts Kearny letter of May 1, 1831, in MHS–Army Collection taken from National Archives, RG 94, M567, roll 62; Sibley, *The Road to Santa Fe*, 155.

83. Hyde, *The Pawnee Indians*, 181

84. The Tetons, Yanktons, and Yanktonais are three of seven Dakota or Sioux groups that comprise the Oceti Sakowin (Seven Council Fires). The other four groups—together known as the Santees—are the Mdewakanton, Wahpeton, Sisseton, and Wahpekute. The Tetons are further divided into seven groups: the Oglala, Sicangu (Brulé), Hunkpapa, Miniconjou, Sihasapa (Blackfoot), Oohenunpa (Two Kettle), and Itazipco (Sans Arcs). Geographically, these groups are broken into Dakota (Santee), Nakota (Yankton-Yanktonai), and Lakota (Teton). For more on Sioux ethnology, see

John C. Ewers, *Teton Dakota, Ethnology and History* (Berkeley: University of California Press, 1937); James Howard, "Yanktonai Ethnohistory and the John K. Bear Winter Count," *Plains Anthropologist*, Memoirs 11, 21 (1976). For an analysis of the importance of Yanktonai diplomacy to the Western Sioux Confederacy, see Galler, "Sustaining the Sioux Confederation," 467–90.

85. R. White, "The Winning of the West," 319–32; Hämäläinen, "The Rise and Fall of Plains Indian Horse Cultures," 857; Fowler, "The Great Plains to 1885," 15–17.

86. R. White, "Winning of the West," 328–34; Wishart, *The Fur Trade of the American West*, 64; Dougherty to Clark, October 29, 1831, as qtd. in Champe and Fenenga, "Notes on the Pawnee," 66.

87. Irving, *Indian Sketches*, 123. For information on the death of Sharitarish II, see Thomas L. McKenny and James Hall, *History of the Indian Tribes of North America with Biographical Sketches and Anecdotes of the Principal Chiefs*, vol. 2 (Philadelphia, 1836–44), 163 (digital version accessed through University of Washington Libraries Digital Collection). The Chaui chief's name on the treaty is written "Shah-re-ta rich-Ill Natured Man." Hyde calls him the "second chief or principal war chief" (Hyde, *The Pawnee Indians*, 136). John Irving Treat not only describes Sharitarish as head chief, but he also names Long Hair as the second chief of the Chaui. In addition, as we shall see, Colonel Dodge recognized Angry-Man, another translation of Sharitarish, as the principal chief of the Grand Pawnees (see "Journal of the March of a Detachment of Dragoons under Dodge," in *American State Papers*, ed. Lowrie, Franklin, and Clark, 6:133–34). A concurring interpretation can be found in Irving, *Indian Sketches*, 123n5.

88. NA, RG 75, T494, roll 3 "Council with the Pawnee Nation (of the Platte River) Oct. 9th 1833 at Republican Village on South of Platte"; 23rd Cong., S. Doc. 512, no. 247, vol. 4, 601. The addition of the suffix to Sharitarish's name to describe his lineage is my terminology. He was never referred to as such in any document.

89. Kappler, *Indian Treaties*.

90. The figure of twenty thousand dollars can be found in MHS, John Dougherty Papers, "Copy of Report made by John Dougherty When Indian Agent," Dougherty to Lewis Cass, March 9, 1832.

91. Kappler, *Indian Treaties*. After supplying the Pawnees with medals following the 1825 treaty, Clark wrote, "Medals and flags are the greatest boast of a chief among those distant tribes who considers himself supported by the Gov't bestowing on him those marks of distinction in addition to the influence he has with his own tribe and is so considered by other tribes" (NA, RG 75, M234, roll 749 [St. Louis Superintendency, 1829–31]).

92. MHS, Native American Collections, box 2, folder 2, Beauchamp to Dougherty, October 26, 1829. For more on the concept of the Great Father, see R. White, "The Fictions of Patriarchy," 110–11.

93. Dunbar, "The Pawnee Indians: Their History and Ethnology," 255. In vol. 4, no. 5, of this series, Dunbar makes a similar conclusion: "To be sure, in obedience to the supposed restrictions of the treaty of 1833, for several years thereafter they refrained from any aggressive hostilities, and to a considerable degree even remitted defensive measures; still this was an obvious divergence from the ordinary tenor of their life."

94. "Report on the Expedition of the Dragoons, Under Colonel Henry Dodge, to the Rocky Mountains in 1835," in *American State Papers*, ed. Lowrie, Franklin, and Clark, Military Affairs, 134.

95. Ibid., 142, 146.

96. "Journal of Colonel Dodge's Expedition from Fort Gibson to the Pawnee Pict Village," Senate Documents, 23rd Cong., 2d sess., August 27, 1834 (serial 266), 73–93; and House Documents, 23rd Cong., 2d sess., August 26, 1834 (serial 271), 70–91. For a new interpretation of the importance of the Comanche empire, see Hämäläinen, *The Comanches*.

97. A. G. Harrison to C. A. Harris, July 1837; Major Dougherty to Wm Clark, June 28, 1837; Dougherty to William Clark, May 31, 1838, all found in NA, LR OIA, Council Bluffs Agency, 1836–43, M234, R215.

98. "Report on the Expedition of the Dragoons, Under Colonel Henry Dodge, to the Rocky Mountains in 1835," in *American State Papers*, ed. Lowrie, Franklin, and Clark, Military Affairs, 137–44; C. Murray, *Travels in North America*, 290.

99. When the missionary John Dunbar came to live with the Chaui in 1835, he lived with the second chief of the Pawnee, since a trader lived with the first chief, and the Pawnees felt Dunbar would be annoyed by the constant comings-and-goings (Wedel, ed., *The Dunbar-Allis Letters*, 623).

100. "Report on the Expedition of the Dragoons, Under Colonel Henry Dodge, to the Rocky Mountains in 1835," in *American State Papers*, ed. Lowrie, Franklin, and Clark, Military Affairs, 135; S. Doc 654, 24th Cong., 1st sess., 134–37.

101. NA, RG 75, T494, roll 3.

102. MHS, Native American Collections, box 2, folder 2, Beauchamp to Dougherty October, 26, 1829.

103. For a similar interpretation of Osage requests for Spanish representatives to live with them, see DuVal, *The Native Ground*, 170. DuVal describes how the Osage leadership developed a "rhetorical dissociation" with the so-called "outlaw bands" of Osage to "deflect Spanish ire and to obviate the sort of coalition against them that might have driven them from the Arkansas River entirely."

104. Wedel, ed., *Dunbar-Allis Letters*, 596; Hyde, *The Pawnee Indians*, 191. It is unclear exactly with whom Dunbar lived during his residency with the Chaui. During the winter of 1835, which was his first tour with the Pawnees, Dunbar lived with "second chief of the Grand Pawnees." Unfortunately, Dunbar never refers to the rank or name of his host again. In 1908, Dunbar's son wrote that his father lived with "Sarecherish [or] Angry Chief . . . a second chief" ("Centennial Celebration at Pike's Pawnee Village—The Biography of John Brown Dunbar," *Kansas State Historical Collections* 10, no. 3 [1908]: 100). Considering that Sharitarish was clearly the lead diplomat in 1833, 1835, and 1839, the younger Dunbar's recollection seems incorrect. In fact, this contradicts what Dunbar recalled nearly thirty years earlier in his series in the *Magazine of American History*, when he wrote that Sarecherish was among a short list of chiefs whose "will . . . was law" (Dunbar, "The Pawnee Indians: Their History and Ethnology," 261). Hyde gets around this problem by claiming the existence of two men named Sharitarish (Hyde, *The Pawnee Indians*, 190). While this may be possible, it seems more likely that Reverend Dunbar only briefly lived with the second chief in 1835 before living with Sharitarish. Another possibility is that Reverend Dunbar mistook Sharitarish's standing. Sharitarish was not a war chief, and Dunbar might not have grasped the complicated hierarchical system so early in his stay.

105. Dunbar, "The Presbyterian Mission among the Pawnee Indians in Nebraska, 1834–1836," 323–32.

106. Dunbar, "Missionary Life among the Pawnee," 272.

107. Dunbar, "Letters Concerning the Presbyterian Mission in the Pawnee Country," 608; Wedel, ed., *Dunbar-Allis Letters*, 630.

108. Kappler, *Indian Treaties*. For more on the Plains Indians' concepts of land ownership, see Binnema, *Common and Contested Ground*. On Indians' views more generally, see Cronon, *Changes in the Land*, 62–68.

109. Carleton, "The Expedition of Major Clifton Wharton in 1844," 284–85; Treat, *Indian Sketches*, 171–72; C. Murray, *Travels in North America*, 179.

110. United States, "Commission Findings," in *Pawnee and Kansa (Kaw) Indians: Report of the Indian Claims Commission* (New York: Garland, 1974), 297.

3 / Nonparticipatory Mapping

1. Rather than relying on astronomical observations to place oneself on an imaginary grid, as did the members of the Topographical Corps of Engineers, surveyors from the General Land Office measured physical distances using a Gunther's Chain to create the (in)famous patchwork pattern in the western United States. For a history of the Topographical Corps of Engineers, see Schubert, *Vanguard of Expansion*. For a history of the rectangular survey, see C. A. White, *A History of the Rectangular Survey System*; Linklater, *Measuring America*; and Hubbard, *American Boundaries*. For a more critical view of this process, see Berkhofer, "Americans versus Indians," 91–108.

2. "Report of the Commissioner of the General Land Office," in *Report of the Secretary of the Interior for 1855* (Washington DC, 1856), 319–20.

3. West, *Contested Plain*.

4. "Report of the Commissioner of the General Land Office," *Report of the Secretary of the Interior for 1855* (Washington DC, 1856), 319–20, italics in original.

5. See the introduction to this volume for a discussion of whether these interactions should be understood as conflicting knowledge systems.

6. I use the critical cartography term "participatory mapping" very purposefully here. Contemporary debates over participatory cartography often center around the question of whether participating in state-sponsored mapping projects helps or hurts indigenous land-claims. As Bjørn Sletto writes, "By fixing and making visible the boundaries of indigenous land based on hegemonic, specifically instrumental-legal notions of indigeneity, these cases validated state territoriality and thus, paradoxically, deepened state hegemony in these very same indigenous lands" (Sletto, introduction to "Indigenous Cartographies," special issue, *Cultural Geographies* 16 [2009]: 147–52). Yet as Sletto concedes, such concerns are premised on the notion of a binary between indigenous concepts of space—a "contingent product of subjectivities and lived experiences"—and state spatial constructs—"normatively determined by power." As I argue in this chapter, that is a false dichotomy.

7. NA, RG 75, M234, roll 883 (Upper Missouri Agency, 1824–74), Dougherty to James Barbour, June 28, 1827, and Dougherty to Clark, November 4, 1828; "First Journey to North America in the Years 1822 to 1824 by Paul Wilhelm, Duke of Württemberg," *South Dakota Historical Collections* 19 (1938): 389.

8. Wedel, ed., *The Dunbar-Allis Letters on the Pawnee*, 639.

9. For a graphic depiction of the location of Pawnee villages, see Wishart, *An Unspeakable Sadness*, 40.

10. Wedel, ed., *Dunbar-Allis Letters on the Pawnee*, 637, 639.

11. NA, RG 75 , M234, roll 215 (Council Bluffs Agency, 1836–43), Mitchell to Crawford, December 17, 1842; Timothy Ranney, "Letters Concerning the Presbyterian Mission in Pawnee Country near Bellvue, Nebraska, 1831–1849," *Kansas State Historical Collections* 14 (1915–18): 577; Wedel, ed. *Dunbar-Allis Letters on the Pawnee*, 648–49.

12. Allis, "Forty Years among the Indians on the Eastern Border of Kanas," 155; Ranney, "Letters Concerning the Presbyterian Mission in Pawnee Country near Bellvue, Nebraska, 1831–1849," 656–59, 750–51; Wedel, ed., *Dunbar-Allis Letters on the Pawnee*, 657, 662.

13. Carleton, *The Prairie Logbooks*, 63; Allis, "Forty Years among the Indians on the Eastern Border of Kansas," 156. For information on the construction of Pawnee lodges, see George Sibley, "Notes of an Official Excursion form Fort Osage to the Konzes-Pawnees-Osages-the Grand Saline and Rock Saline in May June and July 1811," Missouri State Historical Society, Sibley Papers; and Weltfish, *The Lost Universe*, 88.

14. Dorsey, *The Pawnee Mythology*, 15–16; Weltfish: *The Lost Universe*, 44–47; Riding In, "Keeper of Tirawahut's Covenant."

15. Dorsey, *The Pawnee Mythology*, 15–16. See also Murie, *Pawnee Indian Societies*, pt. 7 (1914); and Murie, *Ceremonies of the Pawnee*, pt. 1: "The Skiri."

16. R. White, *The Roots of Dependency*, 173–77. For more on gender roles in Native society, see Nancy Shoemaker, ed., *Negotiators of Change: Historical Perspectives on Native American Women* (New York: Routledge, 1995); and Lisa Frink, Rita Shepard, and Gregory Reinhardt, eds., *Many Faces of Gender: Roles and Relationships through Time in Indigenous Northern Communities* (Boulder: University Press of Colorado, 2002).

17. Riding In, "Keepers of Tirawahut's Covenant," 179. See also Weltfish, *Lost Universe*, 103; and Murie, "Pawnee Indian Societies," 555–56.

18. NA, RG 75, M234, roll 215 (Council Bluffs Agency, 1836–43), Mitchell to Crawford, July 13, 1843. For more on the "Great Peace" of 1840, see West, *Contested Plains*, 77.

19. Samuel Allis, "Forty Years among the Indians on the Eastern Border of Nebraska," 145.

20. NA, RG 75, M234, roll 753 (St. Louis Superintendency, 1824–45), Mitchell to Crawford, September 29, 1843.

21. NA, RG 75, M234, roll 216 (Council Bluffs Agency, 1844–46), Miller to Mitchell, December 23, 1843.

22. NA, RG 75, M234, roll 216 (Council Bluffs Agency, 1844–46), Miller to Mitchell, December 23, 1843.

23. Wedel, ed., *Dunbar-Allis Letters on the Pawnee*, 656.

24. Ibid., 730; NA, RG 75, M234, roll 215 (Council Bluffs Agency, 1836–43), Mitchell to Crawford, July 13, 1843.

25. Wedel, ed., *Dunbar-Allis Letters on the Pawnee*, 664, 730–32. Allis claimed it was the coldest he had ever seen, and the Indians "lost most of their horses and many Indians froze to death" (ibid., 663–65; Allis, "Forty Years among the Indians on the Eastern Border of Nebraska," 152).

26. Ranney, "Letters Concerning the Presbyterian Mission in Pawnee Country near Bellvue, Nebraska, 1831–1849," 785; NA, RG 75, M234, roll 216 (Council Bluffs Agency, 1844–46), Harvey to Crawford.

27. Carleton described the fields as "generally upon the rich little patches of land that stretch across the bottom and are irrigated by small springs in the bluffs. These fields were literally fenced in by sunflowers curiously woven together. Here and there a few slight stakes and withes served to support them, but the body and bulk of the fences were composed of the stout stalks of the plant" (Carleton, *Prairie Logbooks*, 75).

28. NA, RG 75, M234, roll 216 (Council Bluffs Agency, 1844–46), Allis and Cleghorn to Superintendent; Ranney "Letters Concerning the Presbyterian Mission in Pawnee Country near Bellvue, Nebraska, 1831–1849," 762–68.

29. Ranney, "Letters Concerning the Presbyterian Mission in Pawnee Country near Bellvue, Nebraska, 1831–1849," 762–68. For a discussion of the cultural meaning of having no ears, see DeMallie, "These Have No Ears," 515–38.

30. DeMallie, "These Have No Ears," 515–38.

31. Ibid.; Wedel, ed., *Dunbar-Allis Letters on the Pawnee*, 668–71, 783.

32. Ranney, "Letters Concerning the Presbyterian Mission in Pawnee Country near Bellvue, Nebraska, 1831–1849," 762–68; Wedel, ed., *Dunbar-Allis Letters on the Pawnee*, 668–71, 783.

33. Ranney, "Letters Concerning the Presbyterian Mission in Pawnee Country near Bellvue, Nebraska, 1831–1849," 762–68; Wedel, ed., *Dunbar-Allis Letters on the Pawnee*, 668–71, 783.

34. It is unclear whether chief was Us-sa-ru-ra-kur-ek, a rather impotent Chaui chief, or the Skidi chief, who seemed to have more authority in the mission villages

35. Ranney, "Letters Concerning the Presbyterian Mission in Pawnee Country near Bellvue, Nebraska, 1831–1849," 762–68.

36. Ibid.

37. Ibid.

38. Marcy to Medill, June 15, 1847, Office of Indian Affairs Report Book 5, as qtd. in Trennert, *Alternative to Extinction*, 143.

39. *Nebraska State Historical Society Publications* 20 (1922): 122; *New York Weekly Tribune*, July 8, 1843.

40. NA, RG 75, M234, roll 216 (Council Bluffs Agency, 1844–46), Miller to Mitchell, February 5, 1844.

41. NA, RG 75, M234, roll 753 (St Louis Superintendency 1842–45), Harvey to Crawford, October 8, 1844.

42. NA, RG 75, M234, roll 754 (St Louis Superintendency 1846–47), Harvey to Medill, September 5, 1846.

43. NA, RG 75, M234, roll 217 (Council Bluffs Agency, 1847–51), Miller to Marcy, January 30, 1848.

44. NA, RG 75, M234, roll 216 (Council Bluffs Agency, 1844–46), May 2, 1844, Miller to Mitchell, caps in original.

45. NA, RG 75, M234, roll 216 (Council Bluffs Agency, 1844–46), May 2, 1844, Statements for Bent St. Vrain and Co., for claim against Pawnees.

46. MHS, Oregon-California Collection, "Fort Childs, Nebraska Territory Oct. 6 1846," *Daily Missouri Republican*.

47. While this Sharitarish may or may not have been the same person who spoke for the nation in 1833 and 1839, he nonetheless held the same impressive authority.

48. Carleton, "Expedition of Major Clifton Wharton," 273–83.

49. Carleton, *Prairie Logbooks*, 83.

50. Carleton, "Expedition of Major Clifton Wharton," 284.

51. Carleton, *Prairie Logbooks*, 87–91

52. Ibid.; Carleton, "Expedition of Major Clifton Wharton," 285–86.

53. Carleton, *Prairie Logbooks*, 87–91; Carleton, "Expedition of Major Clifton Wharton," 285–86.

54. Carleton, "Expedition of Major Clifton Wharton," 298–99.

55. John Charles Frémont, *Report of the Exploring Expedition to the Rocky Mountains in the Year 1842, and to Oregon and North California in the Years 1843–'44* (Washington DC, 1845), 287–90, 293; 28th Cong., 2d sess. S. Doc. 1, serial 449, 440–44.

56. John Charles Frémont, *A Report on an Exploration of the Country Lying between the Missouri River and the Rocky Mountains on the Line of the Kansas and Great Platte River* [1843], in *The Expeditions of John Charles Frémont*, ed. Jackson and Spence, 1:282–83.

57. Carleton, *Prairie Logbooks*, 89–92; Carleton, "Expedition of Major Clifton Wharton," 296.

58. Barry, *The Beginnings of the West*, 565.

59. *Saint Joseph (MO) Gazette*, November 20, 1846; *Weekly Tribune* (Liberty MO), December 5, 1846.

60. NA, RG 75, M234, roll 217 (Council Bluffs Agency, 1847–51), McElroy to Miller, May 17, 1847, underlining in original.

61. For an analysis of the impact of newspaper circulation on racial issues, see Saxton, "Problems of Class and Race in the Origins of the Mass Circulation Press," 211–34.

62. NA, RG 75, M234, roll 749 (St. Louis Superintendency, 1829–31), "A Tabular statement showing the number of places American Citizens who have been killed or robbed while engaged in the Fur Trade or Inland trade to Mexico since the Late war with Great Britain." Of the 234 William Clark listed as killed or robbed, only three were listed as "Panis."

63. Wedel, ed., *Dunbar-Allis Letters on the Pawnees*, 685. Elliott West describes a similar rise in militancy in a group of young Cheyenne warriors known as the Dog Soldiers (West, *Contested Plains*, 196–200, 284–87).

64. *St. Louis Daily Union*, September 21, 1846; *St. Louis Reveille* (daily), June 20, 1847; *Weekly Tribune* (Liberty MO), December 5, 1846; *Saint Joseph (MO) Gazette*, November 20, 1846.

65. *Saint Joseph (MO) Gazette*, November 20, 1846; *New York Weekly Tribune*, December 12, 1846; *St. Louis Daily Union*, November 23, 1846; "John D. Lee's 'Diar,'" *New Mexico Historical Review* 42 (1967): 313.

66. NA, RG 75, M234, roll 217 (Council Bluffs Agency, 1847–51), Miller to Harvey, March 20, 1848.

67. *New York Weekly Tribune*, December 8, 1849; *New York Daily Tribune Supplement*, December 10, 1849; *Missouri Republican* (St. Louis), November 1 and 24, 1849.

68. NA, RG 75, M234, roll 217 (Council Bluffs Agency, 1847–51), Harvey to Medill, regarding letter written June 5, 1847, and McElroy to Harvey.

69. Carleton, *Prairie Logbooks*, 91.

70. Holder, *The Hoe and Horse*, 46–47.

71. R. White, *Roots of Dependency*, 174; Dunbar, "Missionary Life among the Pawnee," *Collections of the Nebraska State Historical Society* 16 (1911): 277.

72. NA, RG 75, M234, roll 216 (Council Bluffs Agency, 1844–46), "Notes of Council held with Pawnees at their village June 11th 1845 with Maj. Harvey."

73. NA, RG 75, M234, roll 217 (Council Bluffs Agency 1847–51), McElroy to Miller, May 17, 1847.

74. Ranney, "Letters Concerning the Presbyterian Mission in Pawnee Country near Bellvue, Nebraska, 1831–1849," 762–68.

75. Dunbar, "The Pawnee Indians," 328.

76. Grinnell, *Pawnee Hero Stories and Folk-Tales*, 129–31.

77. Dunbar, "The Pawnee Indians," 742.

78. Ibid.

79. Grinnell, *Pawnee Hero Stories and Folk-Tales*, 47.

80. Ibid., 49.

81. For a concurring opinion, see Mark Van de Logt, *War Party in Blue: Pawnee Scouts and in the U.S. Army* (Norman: University of Oklahoma Press, 2010), chap. 1.

82. NA, RG 75, M234, roll 218 (Council Bluffs Agency, 1852–57), Wheeling to Warren, January 19, 1852. For more on the importance of warfare in Pawnee society, see Riding In, "Keepers of Tirawahut's Covenant," 195–99.

83. Wishart, *An Unspeakable Sadness*, 92–94, 192; NA, RG 75, LR Otoe Agency, M234, Dennison to Robinson, July 16, 1859.

84. "Fort Childs, Nebraska Territory, October 6 1846," *Daily Missouri Republican*, Oregon-California Collection, MHS.

85. "Report of the Commissioner of Indian Affairs," in *Annual Report of the Commissioner of Indian Affairs* [1848], 389–90, accessed through the University of Wisconsin Digital Collections (hereafter UWDC): http://digital.library.wisc.edu/1711.dl/ History.AnnRep4650.

86. "Report of the Commissioner of Indian Affairs," 389–90. In addition to works already cited on the end of the permanent Indian territory, two of the most frequently cited are Unrau and Miner, *The End of Indian Kansas*; and Gates, *Fifty Thousand Acres*.

87. "Report of the Department of the Interior, Office of Indian Affairs, November 30, 1849," in *Annual Report of the Commissioner of Indian affairs [1849], Transmitted with the Message of the President at the Opening of the First session of the Thirty-First Congress, 1849–1850*, 131–33, UWDC: http://digital.library.wisc.edu/1711.dl/History. AnnRep4650. For more calls to initiate a grand meeting on the Plains, see *Annual Report of the Commissioner of Indian Affairs [1846]*, 286–87; *Annual Report of the Commissioner of Indian Affairs [1847]*, 835; NA, RG 75, M234, roll 889 (Upper Platte Agency, 1846–56), Fitzpatrick to Harvey, December 18, 1847. For continued calls for Pawnee protection, see "Report of the Office of the Superintendent of Indian Affairs, St. Louis, Oct. 4, 1848"; and "Report of Council Bluffs Agency, Sept. 15, 1848," in *Annual Report of the Commissioner of Indian Affairs [1848]*, 437, 464.

88. "Report of the Department of the Interior, Office of Indian Affairs, November 30, 1849," in *Annual Report of the Commissioner of Indian Affairs [1849]*, 131–33, UWDC: http://digital.library.wisc.edu/1711.dl/History.AnnRep4650.

89. Trennert, for example, makes a distinction between the actions of the War Department and those of the Indian Office (Trennert, *Alternative to Extinction*, 145). We must not see this as part of a grand plan but as another step in a negotiation that ended in Indian dispossession. As in the Treaty of Prairie du Chien, Indian groups had reasons for participating in the treaty, and we must understand this as a negotiated

process, not one simply imposed by the United States. Yet, the strongest push for the first treaty session to include such diverse Indian groups came from the United States. For various interpretations of the 1851 Fort Laramie treaty, see Ostler, *The Lakotas and the Black Hills*, esp. chap. 2; Richmond L. Clow, "A New Look at Indian Land Suits: The Sioux Nation's Black Hills Claim as a Case for Tribal Symbolism," *Plains Anthropologist* 28, no. 102, pt. 1 (1982): 315–24; Lazarus, *Black Hills/White Justice*; Sundstrom, "The Sacred Black Hills," 185–212; and Worster, *Under Western Skies*, chapter titled "The Black Hills: Sacred or Profane."

90. Circular recently discovered in the De Smet Papers (Jesuit Missouri Province Archives). Initial publication can be found in Killoren, *"Come Blackrobe,"* 107.

91. Ibid.

92. "Treaty with the Pawnee, 1857," in Kappler, comp., *Indian Affairs Laws and Treaties*, http://digital.library.okstate.edu/kappler/Vol2/treaties/paw0571.htm. In 1950, the Indian Claims Commission ruled that the Pawnees had no compensable interest for the land north of the Platte River that they had ceded in 1857. Three years later, however, the Court of Claims used a letter written by Commissioner of Indian Affairs J. W. Denver (*Senate Confidential Documents*, vol. 50, 35th Cong., 1857–53–54) to overturn this decision and send it back to the commission for further review. In his letter, Denver (who negotiated the treaty) described in detail the Pawnees' boundaries and the lands they ceded during the treaty. For a history of the Pawnees' land claims case, see Wishart, "The Pawnee Claims Case."

93. "D. D. Mitchell, Treaty Comr., to Comr. of Indian Affairs, November 11, 1851, Reporting the Conclusion of the Treaty and Details of the Negotiations," *Documents Relating to the Negotiation of the Treaty of September 17, 1851, with the Sioux Indians*, UWDC: http://digital.library.wisc.edu/1711.dl/History.IT1851unnumbered.

94. "Report of Sub-Agent J. E. Barrow-Council Bluffs Agency," *Annual Report of the Commissioner of Indian Affairs [1850], Transmitted with the Message of the President at the Opening of the Second Session of the Thirty-Second Congress, 1850*, 41, UWDC: 41; Oehler and Smith, *Description of a Journey and Visit to the Pawnee Indians*, 20; NA, RG 75, M234, roll 889 (Upper Platte Agency, 1846-56), Fitzpatrick to Harvey, Oct. 19, 1847; Carleton, *Prairie Logbooks*, 68–77.

95. "Report of the Commissioner of Indian Affairs," in *Annual Report of the Commissioner of Indian Affairs [1848]*, 389–90, UWDC: http://digital.library.wisc.edu/1711.dl/History.AnnRep4650; MHS, Oregon-California Collection, *Daily Missouri Republican*, "Fort Childs, Nebraska Territory Oct. 6 1846."

96. NA, RG 75, M234, roll 884 (Upper Missouri Agency, 1836–51), Harvey to Medill, May 6, 1846; Pierre-Jean de Smet, *Life, Letters, and Travels of Father de Smet*, vol. 3, ed. Hiram Martin Chittenden and Alfred Talbot Richardson (New York: Arno, 1969), 1188.

97. Report of D. D. Mitchell, superintendent, *Papers accompanying the Annual Report of the Commissioner of Indian Affairs for the year 1851* (Washington DC: U.S. General Printing Office, 1851).

98. Ibid.

99. Trennert, *Alternative to Extinction*, 163; *St. Louis Reveille*, September 14, 1846. For more on the life of Fitzpatrick, see LeRoy R. Hafen, *Broken Hand: The Life Story of Thomas Fitzpatrick, Chief of the Mountain Men* (Denver CO: Old West, 1931).

100. NA, RG 75, LR St. Louis Superintendency, Fitzpatrick to Harvey, January 3, 1847; *Annual Report of the Commissioner of Indian Affairs [1848]*, 437, 464, 470. For

more on Fitzpatrick's unfavorable view of Indians, see: NA, RG 75, M234, roll 889 (Upper Platte Agency, 1846–56), Fitzpatrick to Harvey October 19 and December 18, 1847, and October 6, 1848.

101. NA, RG 75, M234, roll 218 (Council Bluffs Agency, 1852–57), Wheeling to Warren, January 19, 1852.

102. NA, RG 75, M234, roll 218 (Council Bluffs Agency, 1852–57), Wharton to McDowell, June 6, 1852.

103. "Letter from the Mayor, Fort Laramie, Sept. 1," *Daily Missouri Republican*, no. 230, September 26, 1851, 2. Unknown to Captain Duncan, the Shoshones had sent most of the tribe back, while a few delegates continued on, coming within a day of Fort Laramie before the escort met them. For a further description, see Trennert, *Alternative to Extinction*, 186–87.

104. "Report Regarding the Treaty with Prairie Tribes at Fort Laramie Office of Superintendent of Indian Affairs, St. Louis, Nov 11, 1851," in *Annual Report of the Commissioner of Indian Affairs [1851]*, 27–29, accessed through The History Collection, University of Wisconsin–Madison, http://digital.library.wisc.edu/1711.dl/History.AnnRep4650.

105. "Treaty of Fort Laramie with Sioux, etc., 1851," Kappler, *Indian Affairs Laws and Treaties* vol. 2, http://digital.library.okstate.edu/kappler/Vol2/treaties/sio0594.htm, *Daily Missouri Republican*, no. 267, November 10, 1851. For the final ratified version, see Charles D. Bernholz and Brian Pytlik Zilligy, *In the Most Friendly & Conciliatory Manner: A Proposed Final Version of the Treaty of Fort Laramie with Sioux, etc., 1851* (Lincoln: Faculty Publications, UNL Libraries, University of Nebraska–Lincoln, 2010), accessed through http://digitalcommons.unl.edu/libraryscience/206. For the importance of the 1851 treaty on Sioux sovereignty, see James V. Fenelon, *Culturicide, Resistance, and Survival of the Lakota ("Sioux Nation")* (New York: Routledge, 1998); New Holy, "The Heart of Everything That Is," 317–54; and Charles Wilkinson, *Blood Struggle: The Rise of Modern Indian Nations* (New York: Norton, 2005). There are indications from the Fort Laramie treaty that the Platte had been considered a dividing line between the Cheyenne, Arapahoe, and Crow, on the south, and the Lakota, on the north.

106. "Explorations in the Dacota Country in the 1855 by Lieut. G. K. Warren," 34th Cong. 1st sess., S. Ex. Doc. 76, 8–9.

107. NA, RG 279 (Records of the Indian Claims Commission), Closed Docketed Case Files, 1947–82, docket 10, box 16, "Oral Testimony of Tom Roberts."

108. The Poncas' description of their territory is also noteworthy for its definitive boundaries.

109. NA, RG 75, T494 (*Documents Relating to the Negotiation of Ratified and Unratified Treaties with Various Indian Tribes*), roll 6, "Description of Delegation in Indian Office Waiting to Sign Treaty on March 12, 1858."

110. "Letter to the Editor, Treaty Ground, near Fort Laramie, Sept. 11, 1851," *Daily Missouri Republican*, no. 267, November 10, 1851, 1.

111. Ibid.; R. White, *Winning of the West*; Ostler, *The Plains Sioux and U.S. Colonialism*. For further descriptions of Lakota political economy, see DeMallie, "Sioux until 1850," in *Handbook of North American Indians*, vol. 13, *Plains*, ed. Sturtevant.

112. *Daily Missouri Republican*, published as *Sunday Morning Republican* (St. Louis), no. 260, November 2, 1851, 2.

113. Ibid., "Letter to the Editor, Treaty Ground, near Fort Laramie, Sept. 11, 1851," *Daily Missouri Republican*, no. 267, November 10, 1851, 1.

114. Ibid.; "Treaty Ground near Fort Laramie, Sept. 15, 1851," *Daily Missouri Republican*, no. 279, November 24, 1851, 1. Mah- toe-wah-ye-whey or Matoiya was killed by Lieutenant Grattan in 1854 ("Explorations in the Dacota Country in the 1855 by Lieut. G. K. Warren," 34th Cong., 1st sess., S. Ex. Doc. 76, 17).

115. "Treaty Ground near Fort Laramie, Sept. 15, 1851, *Daily Missouri Republican*, no. 279, November 24, 1851, 1.

116. "Report Regarding the Treaty with Prairie Tribes at Fort Laramie," in *Annual Report of the Commissioner of Indian Affairs [1851] with The Message of the President at the Opening of the First Session of the Thirty-Second Congress*, 27–29.

117. The map is generally referred to as *De Smet's Map*.

118. "Report of the Office of Indian Affairs," in *Annual Report of the Commissioner of Indian Affairs [1849]*, 130–31, accessed through UWDC: http://digital.library.wisc.edu/1711.dl/History.AnnRep4650; "Report Regarding the Treaty with Prairie Tribes at Fort Laramie," in *Annual Report of the Commissioner of Indian Affairs [1851]*, 27–29; Killoren, *"Come Blackrobe,"* 133.

119. In addition to other works mentioned regarding the Black Hills case, see New Holy, "The Heart of Everything That Is," 317–59. See also Jill St. Germain, *Broken Treaties: United States and Canadian Relations with the Lakotas and the Plains Cree, 1868–1885* (Lincoln: University of Nebraska Press, 2009).

4 / The Cultural Construction of "Indian Country"

1. Carl, *Mapping the Trans-Mississippi West*, 2:56–59.

2. Calloway, *Pen and Ink Witchcraft*, esp. chaps. 5 and 6.

3. Whereas the formal proposals for the region usually called it "Indian Territory," for this chapter concerned with its cultural rather than political meaning, I use "Indian Territory" and "Indian Country" interchangeably.

4. "Our Indian Policy (with a map)," *Democratic Review* 14, no. 68 (February 1844).

5. For more information on the impact of Woodbridge's methods, see Schulten, *The Geographical Imagination in America*, 95; and Schulten, *Mapping the Nation*, chap. 3.

6. Annie Heloise Abel, "The History of Events Resulting in Indian Consolidation West of the Mississippi," in *Annual Report of the American Historical Association for the Year 1906* (Washington DC: U.S. Government Printing Office, 1908), 1:233–439.

7. Report of the Committee on Public Lands, January 9, 1817, in *American State Papers: Indian Affairs*, ed. Lowrie, Franklin, and Clark, 2:123–24.

8. James Monroe, "Eighth Annual Message," December 7, 1824, online by Gerhard Peters and John T. Woolley, American Presidency Project, www.presidency.ucsb.edu/ws/?pid=29466.

9. James Barbour to John Cocke, February 3, 1826, in *American State Papers: Indian Affairs*, ed. Lowrie, Franklin, and Clark, 2:647–48. See also Rhonda, "We Have Country," 744–45.

10. Andrew Jackson, First and Second Annual Message, December 8, 1829 and December 6, 1830, Andrew Jackson: "First Annual Message," December 8, 1829, online by Gerhard Peters and John T. Woolley, American Presidency Project, www.presidency.ucsb.edu/ws/?pid=29471.

11. For the legal importance of the decisions, see David E. Wilkins and K. Tsianina Lomawaima, eds., *Uneven Ground: American Indian Sovereignty and Federal Law* (Norman: University of Oklahoma Press, 2002); and Jill Norgren, *The Cherokee Cases: Two Landmark Federal Decisions in the Fight for Sovereignty* (Norman: University of Oklahoma Press, 2004).

12. Daniel Walker Howe, *What Hath God Wrought: The Transformation of America, 1815–1848* (New York: Oxford University Press, 2007), esp. chap. 11.

13. "Regulating the Indian Department," *Report from the Committee on Indian Affairs*, 23rd Cong., 1st sess., H. Rep. 474, 17.

14. Deloria, *Playing Indian*, 2. See also Conn *History's Shadow*; Berkhofer, *The White Man's Indian*; Krech, *Ecological Indian*; Bataille, ed., *Native American Representations*; Paige Raibmon, *Authentic Indians: Episodes of Encounter from the Late-Nineteenth-Century Northwest Coast* (Durham NC: Duke University Press 2005). For a discussion of the literary constructions of "otherness," see Todorov, *The Conquest of America*.

15. Dippie, *The Vanishing American*, 16.

16. Henry R. Schoolcraft, *An Address, Delivered before the Was-ah Ho-de-no-son ne, or New Confederacy of the Iroquois, August 14, 1846* (Rochester NY: 1846), 5–6, as taken from Dippie, *The Vanishing American*, 17.

17. Dippie, *The Vanishing American*, 16.

18. Deloria, *Playing Indian*, 5.

19. Catlin, *Letters and Notes*, 1:20–21.

20. Quotes from Dippie, *The Vanishing American*, 13.

21. Jared Sparks to Lewis Cass, October 28, 1829, in *The Life and Writings of Jared Sparks, Comprising Selections from His Journal and Correspondence*, ed. Herbert B. Adams (Boston: Houghton, Mifflin, 1893), 1:282.

22. NA, RG 107 (Records of the Office of the Secretary of War), M271 (Letters Received by the Office of the Secretary of War), roll 3, Benjamin O'Fallon to John C Calhoun, April 5, 1821; "General Atkinsons and Major O'Fallon (Indian agent) arrived in this place on Sunday last from Council Bluffs," *Daily National Intelligencer* (Washington DC), November 14, 1821: n.p., *19th Century U.S. Newspapers*.

23. Thomas McKenney, *History of the Indian Tribes of North America* (Philadelphia: D. Rice and Co., 1972), 1:33–34.

24. "Aboriginal Eloquence," *Daily National Intelligencer* (Washington DC), February 16, 1822: n.p., *19th Century U.S. Newspapers*.

25. Ibid.

26. See, for example, Albert L. Hurtado and Peter Iverson, eds., *Major Problems in American Indian History: Documents and Essays*, 2nd ed. (Boston: Cengage, 2000); Calloway, *Our Hearts Fell to the Ground*; Herman Viola, *Diplomats in Buckskin: A History of Indian Delegations in Washington City* (Norman: University of Oklahoma Press, 1995); Virginia Irving Armstrong, *I Have Spoken: American History through the Eyes of Indians* (Chicago: Swallow Press, 1971); and Peter Nabokov, *Native American Testimony: Chronicle Indian White Relations from Prophecy Present* (New York: Penguin, 1993), 71, although Nabokov attributes this speech to Skidi chief Petalesharo. Despite the editorial comments in his reader listed above, Calloway's *One Vast Winter Count* is one of the few monographs that views American expansion as an opportunity for the Pawnees. Calloway writes: "Nations like the Blackfeet, Lakotas, Osages, and

Comanches had established, were in the process of establishing, or were trying to hold onto impressive regional and interregional hegemonies. Other less powerful or less fortunately situated peoples like the Shoshones, Crows, and Pawnees saw the coming of Americans as an opportunity rather than a harbinger of disaster" (Calloway, *One Vast Winter Count*, 430).

27. For more on the power of commemorative depictions of Indians, see Brian Dippie, "Photographic Allegories and Indian Destiny," *Montana: The Magazine of Western History* 42, no. 3 (1992): 40–57.

28. MHS, George Sibley Papers, "Notes of an Official Excursion from Fort Osage to the Konzes-Pawnees-Osages-the Grand Saline and Rock Saline in May June and July 1811," 18–25; see also Dunbar, "The Pawnee Indians: Their History and Ethnology," 277; R. White, *The Roots of Dependency*, 147–211; J. E. Weaver, *Native Vegetation of Nebraska* (Lincoln: Univeristy of Nebraska Press, 1956), 33–35; Waldo Wedel, "Contributions to the Archaeology of the Upper Republican Valley," *Nebraska History* 15 (1934); and Waldo Wedel, "Introduction to Pawnee Archeology," *Bulletin of the American Bureau of Ethnology* 112 (1936).

29. "The Cannibal Witch and the Boy Who Conquered the Buffalo," as told by Chief Curly Hair (Kitkahahki) in Dorsey, *The Pawnee Mythology*, 72; Grinnell, *Pawnee Hero Stories and Folk-Tales*, 254.

30. For more on the importance of Mother Corn, see Murie, *Ceremonies of the Pawnee*, pt. 1:37, 61, and pt. 2:13, 404; Murie, *Pawnee Indian Societies*, pt. 7 (1914); Fletcher and Murie, *The Hako*; Grinnell, *Pawnee Hero Stories and Folk-Tales*, 253–54; Weltfish, *The Lost Universe*, 124–26, 153, 236, 254–57, 364.

31. For examples of the control of trade, see James, Long, and Say, *James's Account of S. H. Long's Expedition*, 2:149, 157, and 4:166, http://memory.loc.gov/gc/lhbtn/06902/ThwaitesOutline.html.

32. Dorsey and Murie, "Notes on Skidi Pawnee Society," 113; Murie, *Pawnee Indian Societies*, 557. For a description of the *raripakusus*, see Linton, "The Thunder Ceremony of the Pawnee," 4.

33. Weltfish, *Lost Universe*, 210; Dunbar, "The Pawnee Indians: Their History and Ethnology," 261.

34. For a discussion of the highly controlled aspect of Pawnee trade on which my interpretation is based, see R. White, *Roots of Dependency*, 189–93. See also Riding In, "Keepers of Tirawahut's Covenant," 47.

35. Dunbar, "Letters Concerning the Presbyterian Mission in the Pawnee Country, near Bellvue, Neb., 1831–1849," 608; Flores, "Bison Ecology and Bison Diplomacy," 475; West, *Contested Plains*, 77, 192; West, *The Way to the West*, 60–67. More generally, see Isenberg, *The Destruction of the Bison*. For a further discussion of buffer zones east of the Missouri, see Harold Hickerson, "The Virginia Deer and Intertribal Buffer Zones in the Upper Mississippi Valley," in *Man, Culture, and Animals*, ed. Anthony Leeds and Andrew Vayda (Washington DC: American Association for the Advancement of Science, 1965), 43–65; and Helen Hornbeck Tanner, ed., *Atlas of Great Lakes Indian History* (Norman: University of Oklahoma Press, 1987), 14–15, 20–21.

36. Riding In, "Keepers of Tirawahut's Covenant," 11; see also Grinnell, *Pawnee Hero Stories and Folk-Tales*, 252–54.

37. Paul Wilhelm (Duke of Württemberg), "First Journey to North America in the Years 1822 to 1824," *South Dakota Historical Collections* 19 (1938): 432.

38. For information on other Indians' understanding of buffalo populations, see Krech, *Ecological Indian*; Flores, "Bison Ecology and Bison Diplomacy"; Dobak, "Killing the Canadian Buffalo"; and Ostler, "They Regard Their Passing as Wakan," 475–97.

39. Thomas Guthrie, "Good Words: Chief Joseph and the Production of Indian Speech(es), Texts and Subjects," *Ethnohistory* 54, no. 3 (2007): 536. On approaches to uncovering Native voices in mediated texts, see the following works by Arnold Krupat, "An Approach to Native American Texts," *Critical Inquiry* 9, no. 2 (1983): 323–38; "Post-Structuralism and Oral Literature," in *Recovering the Work: Essays on Native American Literature* (Berkeley: University of California Press, 1987); and *The Voice in the Margin: Native American Literature and the Canon* (Berkeley: University of California Press, 1989).

40. "To the Editors," *Daily National Intelligencer* (Washington DC), February 11, 1822, n.p., *19th Century U.S. Newspapers*.

41. Conn, *History's Shadow*, 93.

42. Brückner, *The Geographic Revolution in Early America*, 239.

43. Joseph Story, "The Indians," in *The Library of Choice Literature and Encyclopedia of Universal Authors*, vol. 9, ed. Answroth R. Spofford and Charles Gibbon (Philadelphia: Gebbie & Co., 1893), Google Books.

44. On Morse, see John Rennie Short, *Representing the Republic: Mapping the United States, 1600–1900* (London: Reaktion, 2001), 107–26; Richard J. Moss, *The Life of Jedidiah Morse* (Knoxville: University of Tennessee Press, 1995), 38–51; and Brückner, *The Geographic Revolution in Early America*, 113–16. For cartography as a tool for learning in classrooms, see Schulten, *Mapping the Nation*, chap. 3.

45. Morse, *A Report to the Secretary of War of the United States on Indian Affairs*, 11.

46. See chapter 1 for this description.

47. "Anecdote of a Pawnee Chief," *Daily National Intelligencer* (Washington DC) January 29, 1822, n.p., *19th Century U.S. Newspapers*.

48. Morse, *Report to the Secretary of War*, 248.

49. Moss, *The Life of Jedidiah Morse*, 148.

50. Morse, *Report to the Secretary of War*, 313. For more on Morse's attitudes about a permanent Indian territory," see Annie Heloise Abel, "The History of Events Resulting in Indian Consolidation West of the Mississippi," *Annual Report of the American Historical Association for the Year 1906* (Washington DC: U.S. Government Printing Office, 1908), 1:299–305.

51. "Multiple Classified Advertisements," *Daily National Intelligencer* (Washington DC), March 13, 20, 26, 27, 1822, n.p., *19th Century U.S. Newspapers*.

52. Ibid., March 13, 20, 26, 27, 1822, n.p., *19th Century U.S. Newspapers*.

53. Mark van de Logt, "Brides of Morning Star: The Petalesharo Legend and the Skiri Pawnee Rite of Human Sacrifice in American Popular Fiction," in *The Challenges of Native American Studies*, ed. Barbara Saunders and Lea Zuyderhoudt (Leuven, Belgium: Leuven University Press, 2004), 207–20.

54. Catlin, *Letters and Notes*, 1:2–6, Internet Archive; James Buss, *Catlin's Lament: Indians, Manifest Destiny, and the Ethics of Nature* (Lawrence: University Press of Kansas, 2009); Dippie, *Catlin and His Contemporaries*, chap. 1; Gareth E. John, "Benevolent Imperialism: George Catlin and the Practice of Jeffersonian Geography," *Journal of Historical Geography* 30 (2004): 597–617. John argues that Catlin was explicitly geographical in his construction of national teleological principles.

55. Dippie, *Catlin and His Contemporaries*, 14. For an analysis of the art produced by Long's expedition, see Kenneth Haltman, *Looking Close and Seeing Far: Samuel Seymour, Titian Ramsay, and the Art of the Long Expedition, 1818–1823* (University Park: University of Pennsylvania Press, 2008).

56. Hiram Martin Chittenden, *The American Fur Trade of the Far West*, vol. 2 (New York: Press of the Pioneers, 1935), 578.

57. James, Long, and Say, *James's Account of S. H. Long's Expedition*, 2:201.

58. Historians and geographers have written voluminously on the concept of the Great American Desert and continue to debate its cultural importance. For a sample, see Walter Prescott Webb, *The Great Plains* (Boston: Ginn, 1931); Henry Nash Smith, *Virgin Land: The American West as Symbol and Myth* (Cambridge: Harvard University Press, 1950); G. Malcolm Lewis, "William Gilpin and the Concept of the Great Plains Region," *Annals of the Association of American Geographers* 56 (March 1966): 33–51; Martyn J. Bowden, "The Great American Desert and the American Frontier, 1800–1882: Popular Images of the Plains," in *Anonymous Americans: Exploration in Nineteenth-Century Social History*, ed. Tamara K. Haravan (Englewood Cliffs NJ: Prentice Hall, 1971); and Bowden, "The Great American Desert in the American Mind: The Historiography of a Geographical Notion," *Geographies of the Mind*, ed. David Lowenthal and Martyn J. Bowden (New York: Oxford University Press, 1976), 119–57; Allen, "Patterns of Promise," 41–62; and Allen, "The Garden Desert Continuum," 207–20.

59. James, Long, and Say, *James's Account of S. H. Long's Expedition*, 1:37–38.

60. Ibid., 1:35–36.

61. There are surprisingly few monographs devoted to Long's expedition. Those that exist usually focus on the noncartographic scientific contributions of his journey. For example, see Howard Evans Ensign, *Natural History of the Long Expedition to the Rocky Mountains* (New York: Oxford University Press, 1997); Roger L. Nichols, *Stephen Long and American Frontier Exploration* (Norman: University of Oklahoma Press, 1980); and George J. Goodman, *Retracing Major Stephen H. Long's 1820 Expedition: The Itinerary and Botany* (Norman: University of Oklahoma Press, 1995).

62. James, Long, and Say, *James's Account of S. H. Long's Expedition*, 1:40–42.

63. Ibid., 4:94–99.

64. Ibid., 1:191.

65. As taken from Kris Fresonke, *West of Emerson: The Design of Manifest Destiny* (Berkeley: University of California Press, 2003), 72.

66. Joel R. Poinsett, "Discourse on the Objectives and Importance of the Science" (Washington DC: P. Force, 1841), 16.·

67. Richard H. Dillon, "Stephen Long's Great American Desert," *Proceedings of the American Philosophical Society* 111 (1967): 93–108. Tanner and Carey incorporated this concept from the map that Long included in his report. The printed version was not available until 1823. Information on Woodbridge's map can be found in Francis P. Prucha, "Indian Removal and the Great American Desert," *Indian Magazine of History* 59 (1963); and Garver, "The Role of the United States Army," 101.

68. The manuscript map included in the expedition reports was at a larger scale than the more famous map published in 1823 in James, Long, and Say, *James's Account of S. H. Long's Expedition*, titled *Country Drained by the Mississippi Western Section*. For more on Long's map, see Wheat, *Mapping the Trans-Mississippi West*, 2:79–81. Wheat's five-volume masterpiece is a necessary first stop for any scholar interested in American mapping.

69. Further reinforcing the idea that the entire Great Plains was a desert, the summary's appendix groups the entire region "lying between 96 and 105 degrees west of longitude, and between 35 and 42 degrees of north latitude" as one geological region (this despite the obvious differences that James himself notes between the verdant eastern section and the dry western Plains). Similarly, it lists Council Grove as the eastern terminus of this vast expanse (James, Long, and Say, *James's Account of S. H. Long's Expedition*, 4:133–34).

70. Menard, *Sight Unseen*, 11, 14.

71. William C Woodbridge and Emma Willard, *Universal Geography* (Hartford, 1824), 266, 503–4; Henry Phelps, *Map of the United States* (1832); Eleazer Huntington, *Map of the United States*, in Carey and Lea's *Atlas* of 1822. For other contemporary uses of Long's map, see Tanner, *Geographical Memoir,* 7; and Wheat, *Mapping the Transmississippi West*, 2:79–83, 140–42.

72. James, Long, and Say, *James's Account of S. H. Long's Expedition*, 1:199–206.

73. Ibid., 3:56–62

74. Ibid., 3:139, 180, 181; and 4:94–99.

75. Ibid., 3:122, 164, ed. note on 106.

76. Ibid., 3:180.

77. Ibid., 3:174.

78. Ibid., 3:225–27. For more on the guides, see 2:190–93 and 220 and note 134. For more on the importance of French traders, see Gitlin, *The Bourgeois Frontier.*

79. James, Long, and Say, *James's Account of S. H. Long's Expedition*, 2:204–10. For a history of Cheyenne migrations and politics, see West, *Contested Plains*, esp. 63–94; and Berthrong, *The Southern Cheyenne*, 3–26.

80. James, Long, and Say, *James's Account of S. H. Long's Expedition*, 3:56.

81. Thomas Farnham, *Travels in the Great Western Prairies, the Anahuac and Rocky Mountains, and in the Oregon Territory,* in *Early Western Travels, 1748–1846,* ed. Thwaites, 28–29:12.

82. Amelia Hadley, "Journal of Travails to Oregon," in *Covered Wagon Women: Diaries and Letters from the Western Trails, 1840–1890,* ed. and comp. Kenneth L. Holmes, vol. 3 (Lincoln NE: Bison, 1995), 57. Karen Piper comments: "Western identity is formulated by pushing something off the map, then safely embracing the map as the self; but knowledge of the margins is always waiting to return as the uncanny. . . . Th[e] sentimentalization of being lost signals a desire to evade the effects of "overcivilization" and so to jump off the official map and into the margins or blank spaces" (Piper, *Cartographic Fictions*, 17).

83. J. Butler Chapman, *History of Kansas and Emigrant's Guide* (Akron OH: Teesdale, Elkins & Co., 1855), 12–14.

5 / Science and the Destruction of "Indian Country"

1. John Charles Frémont, *A Report on an Exploration of the Country Lying between the Missouri River and the Rocky Mountains on the Line of the Kansas and Great Platte River* (1843), in *The Expeditions of John Charles Frémont,* ed. Jackson and Spence, 1:269–71. For consistency, all citations of Frémont's reports will be taken from Jackson and Spence, unless otherwise noted. In fact, Frémont only reported one of the two sets of readings taken at the peak. Charles Preuss—the cartographer who often took such

observations—hastily made attempts at determining the altitude, neither taken with sufficient care, according to Preuss: "When the time comes for me to make my map in Washington, he will more than regret this unwise haste" (Preuss, *Exploring with Frémont*, 44).

2. Frémont climbed what is now Woodrow Wilson Peak (elev. 13,502 feet). Gannet's Peak to the north is 13,785 feet, and Mount Elbert in central Colorado is 14,431 feet.

3. Both Frémont's actions—and the act of inscribing them in a memoir—were all part of a public performance necessary for Enlightenment thought. As Neil Safier writes: "European empirical practices and instrumental observations were socially embedded performances comprising repetitive and theatric gestures; that the recording of data in material form was a crucial stage through which instrumently based observations were transformed into codified measurements; and, finally, that public display was an inherent and essential element in the collection, analysis, and communication of those measurements to a broader audience" (Safier, *Measuring the New World*, 5).

4. For the publication history of these reports, see Jackson and Spence, eds., *The Expeditions of John Charles Frémont*, 1:168–69.

5. *U.S. Magazine and Democratic Review* 17, no. 85 (July–August 1845): 77.

6. Not all were so taken with Frémont's writing. Ironically, it was one of the fathers of the American Romantic tradition, Ralph Waldo Emerson, who criticized Frémont for his constant references to the self and the "eternal vanity of how we must look" (Ralph Waldo Emerson, *Journals and Miscellaneous Notebooks*, 16 vols., ed. Ralph H. Orth and Alfred Gerguson [Cambridge: Harvard University Press, 1960–82], 9:431). For the importance of romantic rhetoric in the expansion of empire, see Greenfield, *Narrating Discovery*; Pratt, *Imperial Eyes*; Sachs, *The Humboldt Current*; Alex Hunt "Mapping the Terrain, Marking the Earth," in *American Literary Geographies*, ed. Brückner and Hsu; and John Hausdoerffer, *Catlin's Lament: Indians, Manifest Destiny, and the Ethics of Nature* (Lawrence: University Press of Kansas, 2009).

7. Miller, *Overland in a Covered Wagon*, 42–43. Despite Joaquin Miller's recollection that Frémont paused to let the bee "go at its will," the episode described in the explorer's journal—imaginary or not—did not end so bucolically. Instead, Frémont "carried out the law of this country, where all animated nature seems at war," and he squashed the bee between the pages of his specimen book ("Letter to Colonel J. J. Abert, Chief of the Corps of Topographic Engineers," in Jackson and Spence, *The Expeditions of John Charles Frémont*, 1:270).

8. Others who have made this claim include Goetzmann, *Exploration and Empire*, 242–44; Chaffin, *Pathfinder*, 144–45; Menard, *Sight Unseen*, 147–58; and Hume, "The Romantic and the Technical in Early Nineteenth-Century Exploration."

9. John Bigelow, *Memoir of the Life and Public Service of John Charles Fremont* (New York: Derby and Jackson, 1856), 54. See also Samuel M. Smucker, *The Life of Col. John Charles Fremont, and His Narrative of Explorations and Adventures in Kansas, Nebraska, Oregon, and California* (New York: Miller, Orton & Mulligan, 1856).

10. J. Hector St. John de Crèvecoeur, *Letters from an American Farmer* (New York: Fox, Duffield, 1904), 176.

11. John Bradbury, *Travels in the Interior of America* (Cleveland OH: Arthur H. Clark, 1904), 34.

12. Irving, *A Tour of the Prairies* (1835), chap. 9.

13. Wheat, *Mapping the Trans-Mississippi West*, 2:194, 199.

14. Bernard DeVoto, *The Year of Decision* (Boston: Little Brown, 1943), 38–39.

15. Goetzmann, *Exploration and Empire*, 250.

16. Robert M. Utley, *A Life Wild and Perilous: Mountain Men and the Paths to the Pacific* (New York: Henry Holt, 1997), 202–3.

17. Michael P. Conzen and Diane Dillon, eds., *Mapping Manifest Destiny: Chicago and the American West* (Chicago: Newberry Library, 2008), 56.

18. Chaffin, *Pathfinder*, 241, xxix. For other assessments highlighting the science in Frémont and Preuss's map, see Cohen, ed., *Mapping the West*, 130.

19. Chaffin, *Pathfinder*, 141.

20. See the introduction of this book for a general discussion of Native erasure.

21. Menard, *Sight Unseen*, xxix.

22. "Map Portfolio," in *The Expeditions of John Charles Frémont*, ed. Jackson and Spence, 1:14.

23. Gouverneur Kemble Warren, unpublished journal, Warren Papers, New York State Archives, box 9, folder 10; G. K. Warren, "Memoir to Accompany the Map of the Territory of the United States from the Mississippi River to the Pacific Ocean," in *Reports of Explorations and Surveys to Ascertain the Most Practicable and Economical Route for a Railroad form the Mississippi River to the Pacific Ocean* (hereafter PRR), 33rd Cong., 2d. sess., S. Ex. Doc. 91, 47.

24. "Letter to Colonel J. J. Abert, Chief of the Corps of Topographic Engineers," in *The Expeditions of John Charles Frémont*, ed. Jackson and Spence, 1:225–29.

25. Carleton, *Prairie Logbooks*, 89–92; Carleton, "Expedition of Major Clifton Wharton," 296.

26. For other examples of Indian assistance, see Jackson and Spence, eds., *The Expeditions of John Charles Frémont*, 1:14–16, 170, 184, 282–83; Frémont and Frémont, *Memoirs of My Life* (1887), 39.

27. "Letter from Frémont to John Torrey," September 15, 1844, in *The Expeditions of John Charles Frémont*, ed. Jackson and Spence, 1:366.

28. Jackson and Spence, eds., *The Expeditions of John Charles Frémont*, 1:426–29.

29. Ibid., 1:184.

30. For a good start on this vast literature on science and nationalism, see Carol E. Harrison and Ann Johnson, eds., introduction to "Science and National Identity" special issue, *Osiris* 24, no. 1; (2009): 1–14; Roy MacLeod, *Nature and Empire: Science and the Colonial Enterprise* (Chicago: University of Chicago Press, 2000); Richard Drayton, *Nature's Government: Science, Imperial Britain, and the Improvement of the World* (New Haven: Yale University Press, 2000). On cartographic science being used in the name of the state, see the introduction to this book.

31. Deepak Kumar, *Science and the Raj: A Study of British Indian,* 2nd ed. (New York: Oxford University Press, 1995).

32. Jackson and Spence, eds., *The Expeditions of John Charles Frémont*, 1:184.

33. David Turnbull, "Travelling Knowledge: Narratives, Assemblage, and Encounters," in *Instruments, Travel, and Science: Itineraries of Precision from the Seventeenth to the Twentieth Century*, ed. Marie-Noëlle Bourguet, Christian Licoppe, and H. Otto Sibum (London: Routledge, 2002), 273–94; Helen Watson-Verran and David Turnbull, "Science and Other Indigenous Knowledge Systems," in *Handbook of Science and Technology Studies,* ed. Sheila Jasanoff, Gerald E Markle, James C Petersen, and Trevor Pinch (Thousand Oaks CA: Sage, 1995), 115–39.

34. For "centers of calculation," see Bruno Latour, *Science in Action: How to Follow Scientists and Engineers through Society* (Cambridge: Harvard University Press, 1987), chap. 6. For other works that confound the distinction between science and indigeneity, see Agrawal, "Dismantling the Divide between Indigenous and Scientific Knowledge," 413–39; and Fa-ti Fan, "Science in Cultural Borderlands: Methodological Reflections on the Study of Science, European Imperialism, and Cultural Encounter," *East Asian Science, Technology and Society: An International Journal* 1, no. 2 (December 2007): 213–31.

35. This dynamic was far from unidirectional. For Native stories that shaped knowledge for both indigenous peoples and Europeans during encounters in colonial spaces, see Cameron Strang, "Indian Storytelling, Scientific Knowledge, and Power in the Florida Borderlands," *William and Mary Quarterly* 70, no. 4 (October 2013): 671–700; Julie Cruikshank, *Do Glaciers Listen? Local Knowledge, Colonial Encounters, and Social Imagination* (Vancouver: University of British Colombia Press 2005); and Neil Safier, "Global Knowledge on the Move: Itineraries, Amerindian Narratives, and Deep Histories of Science," *Isis* 101, no. 1 (March 2010): 133–45. Kapil Raj has suggested approaching "circulation itself as a 'site' of knowledge formation" in colonial contact zones (Raj, *Relocating Modern Science*, 20).

36. Sibley, *The Road to Santa Fe*, 6; Goetzmann, *Exploration and Empire*, 240.

37. Thomas Hart Benton, *Thirty Years' View* (New York: Appleton, 1883), 1:14.

38. *Register of Debates in Congress, 1824–25* (Washington DC: Gales and Seaton), 109–10.

39. For a history of the corps, see Goetzmann, *Army Exploration in the American West*; Shubert, *Vanguard of Expansion, Army Engineers in the Trans-Mississippi-West, 1819–1879* (Washington DC: U.S. Government Printing Office, 1980); and U.S. Corps of Topographical Engineers Living History Group, www.topogs.org.

40. Benton, *Thirty Years' View*, 1:178.

41. Frémont and Frémont, *Memoirs of My Life* (1887), chap. 2.

42. Chaffin, *Pathfinder*, 99; Vernon L. Volpe, "The Origins of the Fremont Expeditions: John J. Abert and the Scientific Exploration of the Trans-Mississippi West," *Historian* 62, no. 2 (December 2000): 246–48.

43. NA, M66, "Letters Sent by the Topographical Bureau of the War Department and by the Successor Divisions in the Office of the Chief Engineers, 1829–1870," roll 7, November 2, 1843–October 17, 1844.

44. Benton, *Thirty Years' View*, 2:478.

45. Benton to Abert, n.d; Abert to Benton, April 28, 1842; Abert to Frémont, April 28, 1842, all in the Frémont Collection, Southwest Museum, Los Angeles. As taken from Vernon L. Volpe, "The Origins of the Frémont Expeditions: John J. Abert and Scientific Exploration of the Trans-Mississippi West," *Historian* 62, no. 2 (2000): 254–57.

46. Frémont and Frémont, *Memoirs of My Life* (1887), 70.

47. Volpe, "The Origins of the Fremont Expeditions," 258; Chaffin, *Pathfinder*, 99.

48. Cannon, *Science in Culture*; Sachs, *Humboldt Current*.

49. The most comprehensive biography of Poinsett was written by James Fred Rippy, *Joel R. Poinsett, Versatile American* (1935; repr., St. Clair Shores MI: Scholarly Press, 1970).

50. For more on the influence of Poinsett on Frémont, see Chaffin, *Pathfinder*, 26–27; and Anne Hyde, *Frémont's First Impressions: The Original Report of his Exploring Expeditions of 1842–1844* (Lincoln: University of Nebraska Press, 2012), ix.

51. Charles Janeway Stillé, *The Life and Services of Joel R. Poinsett* (Philadelphia, 1888), 57; *Charleston Courier*, March 19, 1833. For Poinsett's roll in nullification, see Richard E. Ellis, *The Union at Risk* (New York: Oxford University Press, 1987); William W. Freehling, *Prelude to Civil War* (New York: Harper and Row, 1965); and Joshua Matthew Cain, "Jacksonian Nationalist: Joel R. Poinsett's Role in the Nullification Crisis" (master's thesis, Georgia Southern University, 2008).

52. In an advertisement for his presidential candidacy that highlighted the important dates in his life, Frémont claimed that he was sent aboard the *Natchez* in 1833 to "put down nullification" (*Milwaukee [WI] Daily Sentinel*, July 26, 1856).

53. Sally Kohlstedt, "A Step toward Scientific Self-Identity in the United States: The Failure of the National Institute," *Isis* 62 no. 3 (Autumn 1971): 339–42. For more on the relationship between the Smithsonian and cartography, see Schulten, *Mapping the Nation*, esp. chap. 3.

54. Joel R. Poinsett, "Discourse on the Objectives and Importance of Science" (Washington DC: P. Force, 1841), 10.

55. Ibid., 7.

56. Harrison and Johnson, eds., introduction to "Science and National Identity," 3–4.

57. Cong. Globe, *Report of the Secretary of War*, 26th Cong., 1st sess., December 5, 1840, appendix 11–12.

58. Poinsett, "Discourse on the Objectives and Importance of Science," 15–18.

59. Alexis de Tocqueville, *Democracy in America* (1840), vol. 2, chap. 10. See also Ann Johnson, "Material Experiments: Environment and Engineering in the Early American Republic," *Osiris* 24 (2009): 53–74; and Carol Sheriff, *The Artificial River: The Erie Canal and the Paradox of Progress, 1817–1862* (New York: Hill and Wang, 1996), esp. chap. 2.

60. Frémont and Frémont, *Memoirs of My Life* (1887), 64–65.

61. *U.S. Magazine and Democratic Review* 17, no. 85 (July–August 1845): 70, 72.

62. *Daily National Intelligencer* (Washington DC), October 16, 1845, 189.

63. Bigelow, *Memoir of the Life and Public Services of John Charles Frémont* (1856), 67–68.

64. For a history of the rhetoric of precision, see Norton Wise, ed., *The Value of Precision* (Princeton NJ: Princeton University Press, 1995).

65. Poinsett "Discourse on the Objectives and Importance of Science," 36.

66. Nicollet to Englemann, June 7, 1841, as qtd. in Bray, *Nicollet and His Map*, 265.

67. Preuss, *Exploring with Frémont*, 8.

68. Jackson and Spence, eds., *The Expeditions of John Charles Frémont*, 1:312.

69. Ibid., 1:176.

70. Preuss, *Exploring with Frémont*, 21.

71. *Daily National Intelligencer* (Washington DC), August 9, 1845, 131.

72. Frémont admitted that "much of what we had collected was lost" (*Daily National Intelligencer* [Washington DC], August 9, 1845, 131).

73. Preuss, *Exploring with Frémont*, 54.

74. For more on Frémont's seeming indifference regarding the care of his instruments, see Tom Rea, "The Pathfinder's Lost Instruments; John C. Frémont's Cavalier Attitude Toward his Scientific Apparatus," *Common Place* 4, no. 4 (July 2004), www.common-place-archives.org/vol-04/no-04/rea/4.shtml.

75. Bigelow, *Memoir of the Life and Public Service of John Charles Fremont* (1856), 48–50.

76. Preuss, *Exploring with Frémont*, 30.

77. Cong. Globe, *Report of the Secretary of War*, 26th Cong., 1st sess., December 5, 1840, appendix pages 11–12.

78. Joel R. Poinsett, *Protection of the Western Frontier: Letter from the Secretary of War Transmitting Various Reports in Relation to the Protection of the Western Frontier*, 25th Cong., 2d sess., H. Doc. 59, January 3, 1838.

79. Frémont and Fremont, *Memoirs of My Life* (1887), 24.

80. *Daily National Intelligencer* (Washington DC), August 7, 1845, 129.

81. Ibid.

82. *U.S. Magazine and Democratic Review* 17, no. 85 (July–August 1845), 75, quoting from page 196 of the *Report*.

83. *Daily National Intelligencer* (Washington DC), May 14, 1847, 677.

84. *Milwaukee [WI] Daily Sentinel*, July 26, 1856.

85. Bigelow, *Memoir of the Life and Public Services of John Charles Frémont* (1856), 38.

86. Ibid., 44–46. For description of the scene from the original report, see Jackson and Spence, eds., *The Expeditions of John Charles Frémont*, 1:225–29.

87. "Letter to Colonel J. J. Abert, Chief of the Corps of Topographic Engineers," in *The Expeditions of John Charles Frémont*, ed. Jackson and Spence, 1:225–29.

88. Frémont and Frémont, *Memoirs of My Life* (1887), 97.

89. Bigelow, *Memoir of the Life and Public Services of John Charles Frémont* (1856), 39; *Daily National Intelligencer* (Washington DC), August 7, 1845, 129.

90. Bigelow, *Memoir of the Life and Public Services of John Charles Frémont* (1856), 39.

91. Ibid., 43.

92. For a similar narrative juxtaposition, see Barry Alan Joyce, "Elisha Kent Kane and the Eskimo of Etah: 1853, 54, 55," in *Surveying the Record*, ed. E. Carter, 103–17.

93. *Daily National Intelligencer* (Washington DC), August 7, 1845.

94. *U.S. Magazine and Democratic Review* 17, no. 85 (July–August 1845): 68.

95. NA, RG 77 (Records of the Office of the Chief of Engineers), letters sent, Abert to Secretary of War, January 5, 1843, as qtd. in Volpe, "The Origins of the Fremont Expeditions," 259.

96. Donald Jackson, "The Myth of the Frémont Howitzer," *Bulletin of the Missouri Historical Society* 23 (April 1967): 205–14; Frémont and Frémont, *Memoirs of My Life* (1887), 168; and Jackson and Spence, eds., *The Expeditions of John Charles Frémont*, 1:358.

97. NA, RG 77, M66 ("Letters Sent by the Topo Bureau of War Departments and by the Successor Division in the Office of Chief Engineers, 1829–1870"), roll 6, Abert to Jesse Fremont, June, 3, 1843.

98. Jackson and Spence, eds., *The Expeditions of John Charles Frémont*, 1:200.

99. *Living Age* 8, no. 87 (January 10, 1846): 76–77.

100. Ibid.

101. Sandra Nichols, "Why Was Humboldt Forgotten in the United States?" *Geographical Review* 96, no. 2 (July 2009): 399.

102. *Daily National Intelligencer* (Washington DC), May 14, 1847, 677.

103. Ibid., August 5, 1848, 59.

104. Ibid., appendices B and C.

105. *Gallery of Illustrious Americans*, no. 6, "Fremont." Brady & Co. Broadway 1850. Excerpts from the book were regularly printed in periodicals as a form of advertising (see *Emancipator and Republican* [Boston] Thursday, June 27, 1850, no. 9; and *Living Age* 26, no. 324 [August 3, 1850]).

106. For a description of the party, see Eric Foner, *Free Soil, Free Labor, Free Men: The Ideology of the Republican Party before the Civil War* (Oxford: Oxford University Press, 1995).

107. Bigelow, *Memoir of the Life and Public Services of John Charles Fremont* (1856), 34.

108. Ibid., 56. Footnote is taken from Humboldt, *Aspects of Nature*, 32–34.

109. *Milwaukee [WI] Daily Sentinel*, July 26, 1856.

110. Benton, *Thirty Years' View*, 2:134.

111. Taliaferro to Harris, June 19, 1837, as qtd. in Nicollet, *Nicollet on the Plains and Prairies*, 212.

112. Abert to Poinsett, January 17, 1838, Office of Chief of Engineers, letters sent M50, 6 RG 77, as qtd. in Bray, *On the Plains*, 215–16

113. Chaffin, *Pathfinder*, 52–53.

114. Nicollet to Sibley Bray, in Nicollet, *Nicollet on the Plains and Prairies*, 218.

115. Bray, *Nicollet and His Map*, 134.

116. Joseph Nicollet, "Report Intended to Illustrate a Map of the Hydrographical Basin of the Upper Mississippi River," 26th Cong, 2d sess., S. Doc. 237.

117. Benton to Fremont, Washington City, March 20, 1843, as qtd. in Jackson and Spence, eds., *The Expeditions of John Charles Frémont*, 1:164. For other examples of Nicollet's understanding, see Fremont to Poinsett, September 5, 1838, as qtd. ibid., 1:22.

118. 26th Cong., 2d sess., S. Doc. 237, 48.

119. Nicollet to Poinsett, St Louis, December 28, 1838, in Bray, *On the Plains and Prairies*, 233.

120. Allen, "Patterns of Promise," 51.

121. Bray, *On the Plains and Prairies*, 2; Goetzmann, *Exploration and Empire*, 242.

122. Emory to Wheeler, May 21, 1874, in Bray, *Nicollet and His Map*, 270. In the report of his expedition, Emory stated that all of his readings were based on Nicollet's longitude at Fort Leavenworth (30th Cong., 1st sess. S. Ex. Doc. 41).

123. Frémont and Frémont, *Memoirs of My Life* (1887), 14–17.

124. As qtd. in Bray, *On the Plains and Prairies*, 278.

125. Ibid., 150.

126. By 1858, Nicollet's achievements had been so overshadowed that a Minnesota newspaper editor incorrectly claimed that Nicollet County was named after a traveler from Quebec in 1639. The article, copied first from the *Glencoe Register*, then to the *St.*

Paul Pioneer, was later found in the *Daily Missouri Republican* (St. Louis), December 23, 1858.

127. Bray, *On the Plains and Prairies*, 209.

6 / The Metaphysics of Indian Naming

1. New York State Archives, Warren Papers (hereafter WP), "Draft of Journal while on Sioux Expedition of 1855," box 19, folder 5; "Explorations in the Dacota Country in the 1855 by Lieut. G. K. Warren," U.S. Cong., 1st sess., S. Ex. Doc. 76, 34. For more on the "Grattan massacre" and Ash Hollow, see Ostler, *The Plains Sioux and U.S. Colonialism*, 40–43; and Utley, *Frontiersmen in Blue*, 115.

2. WP, "Draft of Journal while on Sioux Expedition of 1855," box 19, folder 5. Highlighting his unconscionable actions, Harney was called "Woman Killer." For more on Lakota views of the attack, see Clow, "Mad Bear"; and Susan Bordeaux Bettelyoun and Josephine Waggoner, *With My Own Eyes: A Lakota Woman Tells Her People's History*, ed. Emily Levine (Lincoln NE: Bison, 1998). In 2016, South Dakota lawmakers voted to restrict the power of the state board it had created in 2009 after the South Dakota Board on Geographic Names recommended that the state should rename Harney Peak (James Nord, "Panel Moves to Restrict Renaming Places Such as Harney Peak," *New Canaan News*, January 22, 2016, www.newcanaannewsonline.com/news/article/House-committee-approves-changes-to-geographic-6776974.php).

3. Ostler, *The Plains Sioux and U.S. Colonialism*, 43.

4. WP, "Drafts of Niobrara and Nebraska Reports," box 9, folder 15; Warren and Schubert, *Preliminary Report of the Explorations in Nebraska and Dakota in the Years 1855–1856–1857*, 57. For more on Warren, see Frank Shubert's introduction to Engineer Historical Studies no. 2 (Warren and Schubert, *Explorer on the Northern Plains*); and Emerson Gifford Taylor, *Gouverneur Kemble Warren: The Life and Letters of an American Soldier, 1830–1882* (New York: Houghton Mifflin, 1932).

5. Patricia Molen van Ee, "The Coming of the Transcontinental Railroad," in Cohen, *Mapping the West*, 172–75.

6. NA, RG 49, Records of the Office of Exploration and Surveys (hereafter ROES), "Reports, Field Notes and Related Records Miscellaneous Records, 1854–1861," box 1, binder 2, "Request for Copies of the Report and Maps Relating to the Pacific Railroad Route, and Letters Acknowledging the Receipt of Reports and Maps, etc, Already Received, 1854–1861."

7. NA, RG 49, ROES, Correspondence, 1852–1861, "Letters Received Relating to the Publication of the Pacific Railroad Survey Report," box 4, binder 1.

8. NA, RG 49, ROES, "Letters Received Acknowledging Receipt of Various Published Reports, 1854–1861," boxes 7 and 8.

9. See the introduction of this volume for a discussion of Indian authenticity. Also, it is important to reiterate that I acknowledge the existence of indigenous places, both sacred and nonsacred, that lay outside the purview of Euro-Americans.

10. *Report of the Secretary of War*, 33rd Cong., 1st sess., S. Ex. Doc. 1, 17–35.

11. Ibid., 33rd Cong., 1st sess., S. Ex. Doc. 129, serials 736–39, 3. The final edition was not finished before Davis's report in 1855, but he followed through on his promise to Congress that the map would be ready before the final volumes of the report were printed. The final map can be found volume 11 of 33rd Cong., 2d sess.,

S. Ex. Doc. 78, in 13 vols., serials 758–68. For more on the Pacific Railroad debate, see Goetzmann, *Army Exploration in the American West*, 264. For a discussion of the various editions of the *Pacific Railroad Reports,* see Wheat, *Mapping the Trans-Mississippi West,* 4:67–71.

12. Harlan, as qtd. in R. Taft, *Artists and Illustrators of the Old West, 1850–1900* (New York: Scribner's Sons, 1953), 7; Krygier "Envisioning the West," 27–50. See also Ron Tyler, "Illustrated Government Publications Related to the American West, 1843–1863," in *Surveying the Record,* ed. E. Carter.

13. Goetzmann, *Exploration and Empire,* 316.

14. Warren, "Memoir to Accompany the Map of the Territory of the United States," 2.

15. The best information on the sources of Warren's map is Warren himself, as he writes extensively of his sources in "Memoir to Accompany the Map of the Territory of the United States." For further information on Warren's Pacific Railroad maps, see Schulten "Mapping American History"; van Ee, "The Coming of the Transcontinental Railroad, in Cohen, *Mapping the West,* 172–75; and Wheat, *Mapping the Trans-Mississippi West,* 4:58, 84–91.

16. Warren's papers also include maps from Jim Baker, Michael Desomet, Joseph Jewitt, Alexander Culbertson, Colin Campbell, and Joe Merrivale (WP, manuscript sketch maps of West, box 5, folder 18).

17. For more on the maps in the PRR, see Wheat, *Mapping the Trans-Mississippi West,* 4:67–91.

18. Schulten, "Mapping American History," 184–85.

19. NA, RG 77, M66, "Letters Sent by the Topographical Bureau of the War Department and by Successor Divisions in the Office of the Chief of Engineers," roll 3, Abert to Stephen Markoe, Washington, May 18, 1849.

20. Brückner, *The Geographic Revolution in Early America,* 120.

21. Anonymous, "The Colorado of the West," *Debow's Review* 1, no. 8 (1859): 282–86.

22. Craib, *Cartographic Mexico,* 20–34.

23. Cong. Globe, 34th Cong. 1st and 2d sess. (1855–56), vol. 25, 1297–98.

24. Craib, *Cartographic Mexico,* 24.

25. David Turnbull, "Travelling Knowledge: Narratives, Assemblage, and Encounters," in *Instruments, Travel, and Science: Itineraries of Precision from the Seventeenth to the Twentieth Century,* ed. Marie-Noëlle Bourguet, Christian Licoppe, and H. Otto Sibum (London: Routledge, 2002), 273–94.

26. Frémont and Frémont, *Memoirs of My Life,* (1887), 603.

27. For a history of the Corps of Topographical Engineers, see Schubert, *Vanguard of Expansion*; and Garver, "The Role of the United States Army."

28. For a discussion of the difficulty of traverse surveying, see Edney, *Mapping an Empire,* 85–91; and Burnett, *Masters of All They Surveyed,* 84–99.

29. Warren, "Memoir to Accompany the Map of the Territory of the United States."

30. William B. Franklin, "Journal of the Kearny Expedition of 1845," in *March to the South Pass,* ed. Schubert, 1. For another account of Kearny's expedition, see Philip St. George Cook, *Scenes and Adventures in the Army* (Philadelphia: Lindsay and Blakston, 1859).

31. WP, box 19, folder 7, "Journal in 1857"; ibid., box 19, folder 5, "Journal while on Sioux Expedition in 1855"; ibid., box 19, folder 6, "Journal in 1856"; ibid., box 9, folder 10; ibid., box 9, folders 6–7, "Snowden's Journals."

32. *Memoir*, 2. He repeats these problems on page 92.

33. *Explorations in the Dacota Country in the Year 1855, by Lieut. G. K. Warren*, 34th Cong., 1st sess., S. Ex. Doc. 76, 20.

34. Timothy Mitchell, *Rule of Experts: Egypt, Techno-Politics, Modernity* (Berkeley: University of California Press, 2002).

35. NA, RG 49, ROES, "Correspondence, 1852–1861, Letters Received Relating to the Publication of the Pacific Railroad Survey Report," box 4, binder 1.

36. As Raymond Craib describes in his analysis of Mexico: "Place-names tethered the grid to the ground by providing a unique and differentiated named place to each abstract coordinate. A map with no names would be worthless for administrative purposes" (Craib, *Cartographic Mexico*, 151).

37. James, Long, and Say, *James's Account of S. H. Long's Expedition*, 3:136. For the same reason, it has been virtually impossible to delineate the precise route of Long's party.

38. The literature on colonialism, naming, and possession is extensive. For a sample, see Boelhower, "Inventing America," 475–97; Patricia See, *Ceremonies of Possession in Europe's Conquest of the New World, 1492–1640* (Cambridge: Cambridge University Press, 1995); Mark Monmonier, *From Squaw Tit to Whorehouse Meadow: How Maps Name, Claim, and Inflame* (Chicago: University of Chicago Press, 2006); Witgen, "The Rituals of Possession," 639–68; and Winona LaDuke, *Recovering the Sacred: The Power of Naming and Claiming* (Cambridge MA: South End Press 2005). For an analysis of naming practices that goes beyond the commonplace assertion that naming only constituted cultural possession, see P. Carter, *The Road to Botany Bay*.

39. Pearce, "Native Mapping in Southern New England," 159.

40. Farmer, *On Zion's Mount*, 242, 246. Farmer's use of the present tense "are" for both Native Americans and Anglo-Americans hints at his reluctance to periodize Indian names. It seems unlikely that Farmer would have used the present tense to describe only Anglo naming practices from five centuries earlier.

41. See Basso, *Wisdom Sits in Places*; Pearce and Louis, "Indigenous Depth of Place," 107–26; Biolosi, "Imagined Geographies," 249–59; Cruikshank, "Getting the Words Right," 52–65; Rundstrom, "GIS, Indigenous Peoples, and Epistemological Diversity," 45–57; Brody, *Maps & Dreams*; Peter Nabokov, *Where Lightning Strikes: The Lives of American Indian Sacred Places* (New York: Penguin, 2006); and LaDuke, *Recovering the Sacred*.

42. "Report of Secretary of War," 35th Cong., 1st sess. H. Exec. Doc 2, appendix H, 475.

43. Farmer, *On Zion's Mount*, 242.

44. *Explorations in the Dacota Country in the Year 1855, by Lieut. G. K. Warren*, 5.

45. *Report Intended to Illustrate a Map of the Hydrographical Basin of the Upper Mississippi River, made by I. N. Nicollet*, 26th Cong., 2d sess., S Rep. 237, 12, 44–45. For sites that had celestial—but not necessarily spiritual—connotations, the signifier *wi* is added; as Nicollet points out, *wi* is the equivalent of the French word *austre*.

46. For more on the importance of language in human relations, see Lera Boroditsky, "How Does Language Shape the Way We Think?" in *What's Next: Dispatches on*

the Future of Science, ed. Max Brockman (New York: Vintage, 2009); Lera Boroditsky, "Linguistic Relativity," in *Encyclopedia of Cognitive Science*, ed. L. Nadel (London: Macmillan, 2003), 917–21; D. Casasanto et al., "How Deep Are Effects of Language on Thought? Time Estimation in Speakers of English, Indonesian Greek, and Spanish," *Proceedings of the 26th Annual Conference of the Cognitive Science Society* (2004): 575–80; and Lera Boroditsky, "Do English and Mandarin Speakers Think Differently about Time?" *Proceedings of the 48th Annual Meeting of the Psychonomic Society* (2007): 34.

47. There is an entire subfield of anthropology dedicated to understanding how language shapes social life, and I do not diminish the importance of such studies. Instead, by highlighting instances of common understanding and negotiation, I historicize why such work became important. It is only because of colonial processes that understanding differences in language and power has become necessary.

48. Barbara Mundy, "National Cartographies and Indigenous Space in Mexico," in *Early American Cartographies*, ed. Martin Brückner (Chapel Hill: University of North Carolina Press, 2011), 269. For more on Mexico's "indigemania" in the nineteenth century, see Craib, *Cartographic Mexico*, 45, 152–53. Edward Said classifies "indigemania" as a postcolonial "search for authenticity" (Said, *Culture and Imperialism*, 226).

49. Thomas Hart Benton, "Fremont's Scientific and Topographical Maps," *Daily National Intelligencer* (Washington DC), May 14, 1847, 677.

50. *Report Intended to Illustrate a Map of the Hydrographical Basin of the Upper Mississippi River, made by I. N. Nicollet*, 26th Cong., 2d sess., S. Doc. 237, 13, 36.

51. WP, "Draft of Niobrara River and Nebraska Report," box 9, folder 15. Hudson Snowden transcribed the river as *Mca Sca Wakpa* (WP, "Snowden's Journal," box 9, folder 6–7).

52. R. White, "The Winning of the West," 319–32.

53. Allen, "The Maps of the Lewis and Clark Expedition," 86.

54. Jackson and Spence, eds., *The Expeditions of John Charles Frémont*, 1:14–16.

55. Fitzpatrick, *Nebraska Place-Names*, 178–80. In the transcription of an Omaha speech, James gives the name Platte and parenthetically writes "Ne-bras-kuh or Flat Water," so it appears that all the three were in use in 1819 (James, Long, and Say, *James's Account of S. H. Long's Expedition*, 1:291).

56. Fitzpatrick, *Nebraska Place-Names*, 179.

57. Basso, *Wisdom Sits in Places*, 32.

58. Farmer, *On Zion's Mount*, 247.

59. Nicollet, *Report Intended to Illustrate a Map of the Hydrographical Basin of the Upper Mississippi River*, 14. There are many ongoing projects to re-create Lakota landscapes, including James Sanovia's *Black Hills Visualization Project*: www.slideshare.net/Makowapi/gis-portfolio-for-linked-in/

60. James, Long, and Say, *James's Account of S. H. Long's Expedition*, 2:91n22.

61. Jackson and Spence, eds., *The Expeditions of John Charles Frémont*, 1:710. For information on Joseph Lake, see James Hanson, "A Forgotten Fur Trade Trail," *Nebraska History* 68, no. 1 (1987): 2–9. For Clough, see Schubert, ed., *March to South Pass*, 1. For Dixon's Bluff, see Nicollet, *Report Intended to Illustrate a Map of the Hydrographical Basin of the Upper Mississippi River*, 35.

62. Scott's Bluffs was named after trader Hiram Scott, who died near this bluff in 1828 (Mattes, *The Great Platte River Road*, 434). Brady Island was named after a man killed near this landform on the Platte in either 1827 or 1833 (Jackson and Spence, eds.,

The Expeditions of John Charles Frémont, 1:188). See also William Marshall Anderson, *The Rocky Mountain Journals of William Marshall Anderson: The West in 1834*, ed. Dale Morgan and Eleanor T. Harris (San Marino CA: Huntington Library, 1967), 190.

63. National Anthropological Archives, Smithsonian Institution, Dorsey Papers, MS 4800, "Notes Accumulated in Preparing a Map of the Omahas and Poncas."

64. Sibley, *The Road to Santa Fe*, 33.

65. *Niles National Register*, December 4, 1841, quoting the *Evansville Indian Journal*; Plains and Rockies 1803–1865: David A. White, comp., *Original Narratives of Overland Travel and Adventure Selected from Wagner-Camp and Becker Bibliography of Western Americana*, vol. 2. (Spokane WA: Arthur A. Clark, 1996), 140–41.

66. L. H. Sigourney, *Poems* (Philadelphia, 1834), 164–66.

67. Pratt, *Imperial Eyes*, 134. In his study of Mexican cartography, Craib makes a distinction between the colonial and nationalist projects: "Unlike the colonial project, in which naming (or more correctly, renaming) functioned as a routing mechanism for possession, in which a new cultural presence was imprinted onto the land to both confirm and create a space upon which colonization could occur, the nationalist project resurrected or actively perpetuated names that alluded to a history prior to the colonial origin" (Craib, *Cartographic Mexico*, 176).

68. Kaplan, *The Anarchy of Empire in the Making of U.S. Culture*, 18.

69. NA, RG 279, *Records of the Indian Claims Commission*, Docket 10, claimants' exhibit 153, deposition of Gus Hadwiger, 20; claimants' exhibit 59, *Cyclopedia of Kansas History* 2:455; Hyde, *The Pawnee Indians*, 93, 200; Stanley Vestal, *The Old Santa Fe Trail* (Lincoln: University of Nebraska Press, 1996), 115; William G. Cutler, *History of the State of Kansas* (Chicago, 1883), 763; Sandy Nestor, *Indian Placenames in America*, vol. 1 (Jefferson NC: McFarland, 2001), 141–44.

70. NA, RG 279, *Records of the Indian Claims Commission*, docket 10, claimants' exhibit 153, deposition of Mary Faw Faw, 45–47.

Conclusion

1. Robert Bruce, *The Fighting Norths and Pawnee Scouts* (Lincoln: Nebraska State Historical Society, 1932), 2, 29. For more on the Pawnee Scouts, see George Bird Grinnell, *Two Great Scouts and Their Pawnee Battalion: The Experiences of Frank J. North and Luther H. North, Pioneers in the Great West, 1856–1882, and Their Defense of the Building of the Union Pacific Railroad* (Cleveland, 1928); and Mark van de Logt, *War Party in Blue: Pawnee Scouts in the U.S. Army* (Norman: University of Oklahoma Press, 2010).

2. For example, neither the family history of the millions of immigrants who came through the city of New York—nor any national narrative—needs to include the fact that Samuel Ellis was a landowner who, after an unsuccessful bid to sell, ceded his island to the United States in 1808.

3. Mark Rifkin, *Manifesting America: The Imperial Construction of U.S. National Space* (New York: Oxford University Press, 2009).

4. Ostler, *The Lakotas and the Black Hills*; Lazarus, *Black Hills/White Justice*; press release, Monday August 24, 2009, *Lakota Country Times*, www.lakotacountrytimes.com/news/2009-09-01/local_news/008.html.

5. Worster, "The Black Hills: Sacred or Profane," in *Under Western Skies: Nature and History in the American West*, by Worster; Sundstrom, "The Sacred Black Hills," 185–212.

6. Zoltan Grossman, "Unlikely Alliances: Treaty Conflicts and Environmental Cooperation between Native American and Rural White Communities" (University of Wisconsin–Madison, PhD diss., 2002).

7. There are numerous projects aimed at mapping Lakota landscapes, including James Sanovia's *Black Hills Visualization Project:* www.slideshare.net/Makowapi/gis-portfolio-for-linked-in.

8. David Truer, *Rez Life: An Indian's Journey through Reservation Life* (New York: Grove, 2012); Ari Kelman, *A Misplaced Massacre: Struggling over the Memory of Sand Creek* (Cambridge: Harvard University Press, 2013).

9. Susan Schulten, "Mapping American History," in *Maps,* ed. Ackerman and Karrow Jr., 174.

10. John Rennie Short, *Representing the Republic: Mapping the United States, 1600–1900* (London: Reaktion, 2001), 145.

11. Benedict Anderson, *Imagined Communities: Reflections on the Origins and Spread of Nationalism* (London: Verso, 1983).

12. Matthew Edney, "The Irony of Imperial Mapping," in *The Imperial Map*, ed. Ackerman, 13.

13. John Charles Frémont, *A Report on an Exploration of the Country Lying between the Missouri River and the Rocky Mountains on the Line of the Kansas and Great Platte River* [1843], in *The Expeditions of John Charles Frémont,* ed. Jackson and Spence, 1:269–71.

14. The most succinct critique of cartography as a uniquely "Western" discourse is in Craib, "Relocating Cartography," 481–90. For other empirical studies that help make the point, see Laura Hostetler, "Contending Cartographic Claims? The Qing Empire in Manchu, Chinese and European Maps," in *The Imperial Map*, ed. Akerman, 93–132; Neil Safier, "The Confines of the Colony: Boundaries, Ethnographic Landscapes, and Imperial Cartography in Iberoamerica," ibid., 133–84; Michael A. Osborne, "Science and the French Empire," *Isis* 96, no. 1 (March 2005): 80–87; and, most recently, Helen Tilley, *Africa as a Living Laboratory: Empire, Development and the Problem of Scientific Knowledge, 1870–1950* (Chicago: University of Chicago Press, 2011).

15. See the introduction of this volume for a description of Scott's "problem spaces."

Select Bibliography

Archives

Kansas State Historical Society, Topeka
    Indian Files
    Diaries of Reverend Samuel M. Irvin
    Johnston Lykins Collection
    Isaac McCoy Papers
    Jotham Meeker Papers
    John G. Pratt Papers
Missouri History Museum, Library and Research Center, Saint Louis
    William Ashley Papers
    John Dougherty Papers
    Native American Collections
    Oregon-California Collection
    Joshua Pilcher Papers
    George Sibley Papers
    National Anthropological Archives, Smithsonian Institution, Washington DC
    James Owen Dorsey Papers
National Archives, Washington DC
    Record Group 49–Records of the General Land Office
    Record Group 75–Records of the Bureau of Indian Affairs
    Record Group 275–Records of the Indian Claims Commission
National Archives, Map and Cartography Division, College Park, Maryland
    Record Group 75–Records of the Bureau of Indian Affairs
Newberry Library, Chicago
    Edward Ayers Collection

Everett D. Graff Collection
New York State Archives, Albany
  Gouverneur Kemble Warren Papers
Princeton Collections of Western Americana, Princeton, New Jersey
  McCarter and English Indian Claims Cases
Wisconsin State Historical Society, Madison
  Draper Manuscripts
  Wisconsin Historical Society Collections, vol. 1.

Published Works

Abel, Annie H. "Proposal for an Indian State, 1778–1878." *Annual Report of the American Historical Association* (1907): 87–104.

Ackerman, James R., ed. *The Imperial Map: Cartography and the Mastery of Empire*. Chicago: University of Chicago Press, 2009.

Adams, Franklin G. "Reminiscences of Frederick Chouteau." *Transactions of the Kansas State Historical Society* 8 (1903–4): 423–34.

Adelman, Jeremy, and Stephen Aron. "From Borderlands to Borders: Empires, Nations-States, and the Peoples in between in North American History." *American Historical Review* 104, no. 3 (1999): 814–41.

Agrawal, Arun. "Dismantling the Divide between Indigenous and Scientific Knowledge." *Development and Change* 26 (1995): 413–39.

Albers, Patricia C. "Changing Patterns of Ethnicity in the Northeastern Plains, 1780–1870." In *History, Power, and Identity: Ethnogenesis in the Americas, 1492–1992*, edited by Johnathan D. Hill, 90–118. Iowa City: University of Iowa Press, 1996.

Albers, Patricia C., and Jeanne Kay, "Sharing the Land: A Study in American Indian Territoriality." In *A Cultural Geography of North American Indians*, edited by Thomas E. Ross and Tyrel G. Moore. Boulder: University of Colorado Press, 1987.

Allen, John L. "The Garden Desert Continuum: Competing Views of the Great Plains in the Nineteenth Century." *Great Plains Quarterly* 5, no. 4 (1985): 207–20.

———. "Patterns of Promise: Mapping the Plains and Prairies, 1800–1860." In *Mapping the North American Plains: Essays in the History of Cartography*, edited by Frederick C. Luebke, Frances W. Kaye, and Gary E. Moulton. Norman: University of Oklahoma Press, 1983.

Allis, Rev. Samuel. "Forty Years among the Indians on the Eastern Border of Kansas." *Transactions and Reports of the Nebraska State Historical Society* 2 (1887): 133–66.

Anderson, Duane. "Ioway Ethnohistory: A Review." *Annals of Iowa* 41, no. 8 (1973): 1228–41; *Annals of Iowa* 42, no. 1 (1973): 41–59.

Anderson, Gary Clayton. *Kinsmen of Another Kind: Dakota-White Relations in the Upper Mississippi Valley, 1650–1862.* Lincoln: University of Nebraska Press, 1984.

Annual Reports of the Commissioner of Indian Affairs. Washington DC: U.S. Government Printing Office, 1840–81.

Aron, Stephen. *American Confluence: The Missouri Frontier from Borderland to Border State.* Bloomington: University of Indiana Press, 2006.

Baker, Emerson W., Edwin A. Churchill, Richard S. D'Abate, Kristine L. Jones, Victor A. Konrad, and Harald E. L. Prins, eds. *American Beginnings: Exploration, Culture, and Cartography in the Land of Norumbega.* Lincoln: University of Nebraska Press, 1994.

Barnes, Lela, ed. "Journal of Isaac McCoy for the Exploring Expedition of 1828." *Kansas Historical Quarterly* 5 (1936): 227–77.

———. "Journal of Isaac McCoy for the Exploring Expedition of 1830." *Kansas Historical Quarterly* 5 (1936): 339–77.

Barr, Juliana. "Geographies of Power: Mapping Indian Borders in the 'Borderlands' of the Early Southwest." *William and Mary Quarterly* 3rd. ser., 60, no. 1 (2011): 5–46.

Barry, Louis. *Beginning of the West: Annals of the Kansas Gateway to the American West, 1540–1854.* Topeka: Kansas State Historical Society, 1972.

Basso, Keith. *Wisdom Sits in Places; Landscape and Language among the Western Apache.* Albuquerque: University of New Mexico Press, 1996.

Belyea, Barbara. "Amerindian Maps: The Explorer as Translator." *Journal of Historical Geography* 18, no. 3 (1992): 267–77.

———. *Dark Storm Moving West.* Calgary: University of Calgary Press, 2007.

———. "Images of Power: Derrida, Foucault, Harley." *Cartographica* 29, no. 2 (1992): 1–9.

———. "Mapping the Marias: The Interface of Native and Scientific Cartographies." *Great Plains Quarterly* 17 (1997): 165–84.

———. "Review Article of Denis Wood's *The Power of Maps* and the Author's Reply." *Cartographica* 29, no. 3/4 (1992): 94-99.

Berkhofer, Robert F., Jr. "Americans versus Indians: The Northwest Ordinance, Territory Making, and Native Americans." *Indiana Magazine of History* 84 (1988): 91–108.

Binnema, Theodore. "Allegiances and Interests: Niitsitapi (Blackfoot) Trade, Diplomacy, and Warfare, 1806–1831." *Western Historical Quarterly* 37, no. 3 (2006): 327–50.

———. *Common and Contested Ground: A Human and Environmental History of the Northwestern Plains.* Norman: University of Oklahoma Press, 2001.

Biolosi, Thomas. "Imagined Geographies: Sovereignty, Indigenous Space, and American Indian Struggle." *American Ethnologist* 32, no. 2 (2005): 249–59.

Blackhawk, Ned. "Look How Far We've Come: How American Indian History Changed the Study of American History in the 1990s." *OAH Magazine of History* 19, no. 6 (2005): 13–17.

———. *Violence over the Land: Indians and Empires in the Early American West.* Cambridge: Harvard University Press, 2006.

Blaine, Martha R. *The Iowa Indians.* Norman: University of Oklahoma Press, 1979.

———. *The Pawnee: A Critical Bibliography.* Bloomington: Indiana University Press, 1980.

———. *Some Things Are Not Forgotten: A Pawnee Family Remembers.* Lincoln: University of Nebraska Press, 1997.

Boelhower, William. "Inventing America: A Model of Cartographic Semiosis." *Word and Image* 4, no. 2 (1989): 475–96.

Boughter, Judith. *Betraying the Omaha Nation, 1790–1916.* Norman: University of Oklahoma, 1998.

Bowes, John. *Exiles and Pioneers: Eastern Indians in the Trans-Mississippi West.* New York: Cambridge University Press, 2007.

———. "Opportunity and Adversity: Indians and American Expansion in the Nineteenth-Century Trans-Mississippi West." PhD dissertation, UCLA, 2003.

Brealey, Kenneth G. "Mapping Them 'Out': Euro-Canadian Cartography and the Appropriation of the Nuxalk and Ts'ilhqot'in First Nations' Territories, 1793–1916." *Canadian Geographer* 39, no. 2 (1995).

———. "Networks of Power: Cartography as Ideology." *Western Geography* 3 (1993): 15–50.

Brody, Hugh. *Maps & Dreams; Indians and the British Columbia Frontier.* Prospect Heights IL: Waveland, 1981.

Brooks, James F. *Captives and Cousins: Slavery, Kinship, and Community in the Southwest Borderlands.* Chapel Hill: University of North Carolina Press, 2002.

Brückner, Martin. *The Geographic Revolution in Early America: Maps, Literacy, and National Identity.* Chapel Hill: University of North Carolina Press for the Omohundro Institute of Early American History and Culture, 2006.

Brückner, Martin, and Hsuan L. Hsu. *American Literary Geographies: Spatial Practice and Cultural Production, 1500–1900.* Newark: University of Delaware Press, 2007.

Buisseret, David, ed. *From Sea Charts to Satellite Images: Interpreting North American History through Maps.* Chicago: University of Chicago Press, 1990.

Burnett, D. Graham. *Masters of All They Surveyed: Exploration, Geography, and a British El Dorado.* Chicago: University of Chicago Press, 2000.

Byrnes, Giselle. *Boundary Markers: Land Surveying and the Colonization of New Zealand.* Wellington NZ: Bridget Williams Books, 2001.

Calloway, Colin. *One Vast Winter Count: The Native American West before Lewis and Clark.* Lincoln: University of Nebraska Press, 2009.

———. *Pen and Ink Witchcraft: Treaties and Treaty Making in American Indian History.* New York: Oxford University Press, 2013.

Cannon, Susan F. *Science in Culture: The Early Victorian Period.* New York: Science History Publications, 1978.

Carleton, Henry J. "The Expedition of Major Clifton Wharton in 1844." *Collections of the Kansas State Historical Society* 16 (1923–25): 272–305.

———. *The Prairie Logbooks: Dragoon Campaigns to the Pawnee in 1844.* Edited by Louis Peltzer. Lincoln: University of Nebraska Press, 1993.

Carter, Clarence E., comp. and ed. *The Territorial Papers of the United States.* 26 vols. Washington DC: U.S. Government Printing Office, 1934–62.

Carter, Edward C., II, ed. *Surveying the Record: North American Scientific Exploration to 1930.* Philadelphia: American Philosophical Society, 1999.

Carter, Paul. *The Road to Botany Bay: An Exploration of Landscape and History.* New York: Knopf, 1988.

Catlin, George. *Letters and Notes on the Manners, Customs, and Conditions of the North American Indians.* 2 vols. New York: Dover, 1973.

"Centennial Celebration at Pike's Pawnee Village—The Biography of John Brown Dunbar." *Kansas State Historical Collections* 10 (1908): 99–119.

Certeau, Michel de. *The Practice of Everyday Life.* Translated by Steven Rendall. Berkeley: University of California Press, 1984.

Chaffin, Tom. *Pathfinder: John Charles Frémont and the Course of American Empire.* New York: Hill and Wang, 2002.

Champe, John L., and Franklin Fenenga. "Notes on the Pawnee." In *Pawnee and Kansa (Kaw) Indians.* New York: Garland, 1974.

Chapman, Berlin Basil. *The Otoes and Missourias: A Study of Indian Removal and the Legal Aftermath.* Oklahoma City: Times Journal Publishing, 1965.

Clow, Richmond L. "Mad Bear: William S. Harney and the Sioux Expedition of 1855–1856." *Nebraska History* 61 (1980): 132–51.

Cohen, Paul E. *Mapping the West: America's Westward Movement 1524–1890.* New York: Rizzoli, 2002.

Conn, Steve. *History's Shadow: Native Americans and Historical Consciousness in the Nineteenth Century.* Chicago: University of Chicago Press, 2004.

Cosgrove, Denis. "Epistemology, Geography, and Cartography: Matthew Edney on Brian Harley's Cartographic Theories." *Annals of the Association of American Geographers* 97, no. 1 (2007): 202–9.

Craib, Raymond B. *Cartographic Mexico: A History of State Fixations and Fugitive Landscapes.* Durham NC: Duke University Press, 2004.

———. "Cartography and Power in the Conquest and Creation of New Spain." *Latin American Research Review* 35, no. 1 (2000): 7–37.

———. "Relocating Cartography." *Postcolonial Studies* 12, no. 4 (2009): 481–90.

Cronon, William. *Changes in the Land Indians, Colonists, and the Ecology of New England.* New York: Hill and Wang, 1983.

Cronon, William, George Miles, and Jay Gitlin, eds. *Under an Open Sky: Rethinking America's Western Past.* New York: Norton, 1992.

Cruikshank, Julie. "Getting the Words Right: Perspectives on Naming and

Places in Athapaskan Oral History." *Arctic Anthropology* 27, no. 1 (1990): 52–65.

DeLay, Brian. *War of a Thousand Deserts: Indian Raids and the U.S.–Mexican War.* New Haven: Yale University Press, 2008.

Del Chamberlain, Von. *When the Stars Came down to Earth: Cosmology of the Skidi Pawnee Indians of North America.* Los Altos CA: Ballena, 1982.

Deloria, Philip. *Playing Indian.* New Haven: Yale University Press: 1998.

De Vorsey, Louis, Jr. "American Indians and the Early Mapping of the Southeast." In *The Southeast in Early Maps,* edited by William P. Cumming, 65–98. 3rd ed. Chapel Hill: University of North Carolina Press, 1998.

Dippie, Brian. *Catlin and His Contemporaries: The Politics of Patronage.* Lincoln: University of Nebraska Press, 1990.

———. *The Vanishing American: White Attitudes and U.S. Indian Policy.* Lawrence: University of Kansas Press, 1982.

Dobak, William A. "Killing the Canadian Buffalo, 1821–1881." *Western Historical Quarterly* 27 (1996).

Dorsey, George. *The Pawnee Mythology.* Washington DC: Carnegie Institute, 1906.

Dorsey, George, and James Murie. "Notes on Skidi Pawnee Society." *Anthropological Series of the Field Museum of Natural History* 27, no. 2 (1940): 67–119.

Draper, Lyman C., ed. "Recollections of Prairie du Chien." *Wisconsin Historical Collections* 9 (1882): 282–302.

Dunbar, Rev. John. "Letters Concerning the Presbyterian Mission in the Pawnee Country, near Bellvue, Neb., 1831–1849." *Kansas Historical Collections* 14 (1918): 570–784.

———. "Missionary Life among the Pawnee." *Nebraska State Historical Society Collections* 16 (1911): 268–87.

———. "The Presbyterian Mission among the Pawnee Indians in Nebraska, 1834–1836." *Kansas Historical Collections* 11 (1909–10): 323–32.

Dunbar, John B. "The Pawnee Indians." *Magazine of American History* 8 (November 1881): 738–41.

———. "The Pawnee Indians: Their Habits and Customs." *Magazine of American History* 5 (November 1880): 321–42.

———. "The Pawnee Indians: Their History and Ethnology." *Magazine of American History* 4 (April 1880): 241–79.

DuVal, Kathleen. *The Native Ground: Indians and Colonists in the Heart of the Continent.* Philadelphia: University of Pennsylvania Press, 2006.

Echo-Hawk, Roger. *The Magic Children: Racial Identity at the End of the Age of Race.* Walnut Creek CA: Left Coast Press, 2010.

Edmunds, R. David. "Blazing New Trails or Burning Bridges: Native American History Comes of Age." *Western Historical Quarterly* 39, no. 1 (2008): 5–15.

Edney, Mathew H. "Cartography without 'Progress': Reinterpreting the Nature and Historical Development of Mapmaking." *Cartographica* 30, nos. 2 and 3 (1993): 54–68.

———. *Mapping an Empire: The Geographical Construction of British India, 1765–1843*. Chicago: University of Chicago Press, 1990.

———. *The Origins and Development of J. B. Harley's Cartographic Theories*. Cartographica Monograph 54. *Cartographica* 40, nos. 1, 2. Toronto: University of Toronto Press, 2005.

———. "Putting 'Cartography' into the History of Cartography: Arthur H. Robinson, David Woodward, and the Creation of a Discipline." *Cartographic Perspectives* no. 51 (2005): 14–29.

———. "Reflection Essay: Progress and the Nature of 'Cartogography.'" In *Classics in Cartography: Reflections on Influential Articles from Cartographica*, edited by Martin Dodge (Hoboken NJ: Wiley-Blackwell, 2011): 305–29.

Ewers, John C. "The Indian Trade of the Upper Missouri before Lewis and Clark." In *Indian Life on the Upper Missouri*, edited by Ewers. Norman: University of Oklahoma Press, 1968.

Farmer, Jared. *On Zion's Mount: Mormons, Indians, and the American Landscape*. Cambridge: Harvard University Press, 2008.

Fenn, Elizabeth. *Pox Americana: The Great Smallpox Epidemic of 1775–82*. New York: Hill and Wang, 2001.

Fitzpatrick, Lilian L., and John T. Link. *Nebraska Place-Names: Including Selections from the Origin of the Place-Names of Nebraska*. Lincoln: University of Nebraska Press, 1960.

Fletcher, Alice, and James Murie. *The Hako: Song, Pipe and Unity in a Pawnee Calumet Ceremony*. Lincoln: University of Nebraska Press, 1996.

Flores, Dan. "Bison Ecology and Bison Diplomacy: The Southern Plains from 1800 to 1850." *Journal of American History* 78, no. 2 (1991): 465–87.

Foreman, Grant. *Advancing the Frontier, 1830–1860*. Norman: Oklahoma University Press, 1933.

———. *Indians & Pioneers: The Story of the American Southwest before 1830*. Norman: University of Oklahoma Press, 1936.

Foucault, Michel. *Discipline and Punish: The Birth of Prisons*. Translated by Alan Sheridan. New York: Pantheon, 1977.

Fowler, Loretta. "The Great Plains from the Arrival of the Horse to 1885." In *The Cambridge History of the Native Peoples of the Americas*, vol. 1, pt. 2, edited by Bruce C. Trigger and Wilcomb E. Washburn, 1–55. New York: Cambridge University Press, 1996.

Francaviaglia, Richard V. *Mapping and Imagination in the Great Basin: A Cartographic History*. Reno: University of Nevada Press, 2003.

Frémont, John C., and Jessie B. Frémont. *Memoirs of My Life*. Chicago: Belford, Clarke & Co, 1887.

Galler, Robert W., Jr. "Sustaining the Sioux Confederation: Yanktonai Initiatives and Influence on the Northern Plains, 1680–1880." *Western Historical Quarterly* 39, no. 4 (2008): 467–90.

Garver, John Baltzly, Jr. "The Role of the United States Army in the Colonization of the Trans-Missouri West: Kansas, 1804–1861." PhD dissertation, Syracuse University, 1981.

Giddens, Anthony. *The Contemporary Critique of Historical Materialism: Power, Property and the State.* Berkeley: University of California Press, 1981.

Gitlin, Jay. *The Bourgeois Frontier: French Towns, French Traders, and American Expansion.* New Haven: Yale University Press, 2010.

Gittenger, Roy. "The Separation of Nebraska and Kansas from the Indian Territory." *Mississippi Valley Historical Review* 3 (1917): 442–61.

Goetzmann, William. *Army Exploration in the American West, 1803–1863.* New Haven: Yale University Press, 1965.

———. *Exploration and Empire: The Explorer and the Scientist in the Winning of the American West.* New York: History Book Club, 1966.

Goodman, Ronald. *Lakota Star Knowledge in Lakota Stellar Theology.* Rosebud SD: Sinte Gleshka University Press, 1990.

Green, Michael D. "'We Dance in Opposite Directions': Mesquakie (Fox) Separatism from the Sac and Fox Tribe." *Ethnohistory* 30 (1983): 129–40.

Green, William. Untitled article on Iowa map of 1837. In *An Atlas of Early Maps of the American Midwest: Part II, Illinois State Museum Scientific Papers* 29, compiled by W. Raymond Wood. Springfield: Illinois State Museum, 2001.

Greenfield, Bruce. *Narrating Discovery: The Romantic Explorer in American Literature, 1790–1855.* New York: Columbia University Press, 1992.

Gregg, Josiah. *Commerce of the Prairies or the Journal of a Santa Fe Trader during eight expeditions across The Great Western Prairies and residence of nearly nine years in Northern Mexico.* Vol. 2, 5th ed. New York: H. G. Langley, 1844.

Grinnell, George Bird. *Pawnee Hero Stories and Folk-Tales.* 1925. Reprint, Lincoln: University of Nebraska Press, 1990.

Hahn, Steven C. *The Invention of the Creek Nation, 1670–1763.* Lincoln: University of Nebraska Press, 2004.

Hämäläinen, Pekka. *The Comanche Empire.* New Haven: Yale University Press, 2008.

———. "The Rise and Fall of Plains Indian Horse Cultures." *Journal of American History* 90, no. 3 (2003): 833–62.

———. "The Western Comanche Trade Center: Rethinking the Plains Indian Trade System." *Western Historical Quarterly* 29 (1998): 485–513.

Hammond, George P., and Agapito Reys, eds. and trans. *Don Juan de Onate, Coloniser of New Mexico 1595–1628.* Pt. 2, vol. 4. Albuquerque: University of New Mexico Press, 1953.

Hannah, Matthew G. *Governmentality and the Mastery of Territory in Nineteenth-Century America.* Cambridge Studies in Historical Geography 32. Cambridge: Cambridge University Press, 2000.

——. "Space and Social Control in the Administration of the Oglala Lakota ("Sioux"), 1871–1879." *Journal of Historical Geography* 19, no. 4 (1993): 412–32.

Harley, J. B. "Deconstructing the Map." *Cartographica* 26, no. 2 (1989): 1–20.

——. "Maps, Knowledge, and Power." In *The Iconography of Landscape: Essays on the Symbolic Representation, Design and Use of Past Environments*, edited by Denis Cosgrove and Stephen Daniels, 277–312. Cambridge Studies in Historical Geography 9. Cambridge: Cambridge University Press, 1988.

——. *The New Nature of Maps: Essays in the History of Cartography*, edited by Paul Laxton. Baltimore: Johns Hopkins University Press, 2001).

——. "Rereading the Maps of the Columbian Encounter." Edited by Karl W. Butzer and William M. Denevan. *Annals of the Association of American Geographers* 82 (1992): 522–36.

Harmon, Alexandra. "American Indians and Land Monopolies in the Gilded Age." *Journal of American History* 90, no. 1 (2003): 106–33.

Holder, Preston. *The Hoe and Horse on the Plains: A Study of Cultural Development among North American Indians*. Lincoln: University of Nebraska Press, 1970.

Horsman, Reginald. *Expansion and American Indian Policy, 1783–1812*. Norman: University of Oklahoma Press, 1992.

Hoxie, Frederick. *Parading Through History: Making of the Crow Nation in American 1805–1935*. New York: Cambridge University Press, 1995.

Hubbard, Bill. *American Boundaries: The Nation, the States, the Rectangular Survey*. Chicago: University of Chicago Press, 2009.

Huggan, Graham. "Decolonizing the Map: Post-Colonialism, Post-Structuralism and the Cartographic Connection." *Ariel* 20, no. 4 (1989): 115–31.

Hume, Brad. "The Romantic and the Technical in Early Nineteenth-Century Exploration." In *Surveying the Record: North American Scientific Exploration to 1930*, edited by Edward Carter II. Philadelphia: American Philosophical Society, 1999.

Hyde, George. *The Pawnee Indians*. Norman: University of Oklahoma Press, 1951.

Irving, John Treat. *Indian Sketches Taken during an Expedition to the Pawnee Tribe*. Edited by John Francis McDermott. Norman: University of Oklahoma Press, 1955.

Isenberg, Drew. *The Destruction of the Bison: An Environmental History, 1750–1920*. New York: Cambridge University Press, 2000.

Jacob, Christian. *The Sovereign Map: Theoretical Approaches in Cartography throughout History*. Translated by Tom Conley. Edited by Edward H. Dahl. Chicago: University of Chicago Press, 2006. Originally published as *L'Empire des cartes: Approche théorique de la cartographie à travers l'histoire*. Paris: Bibliothèque Albin Michel, 1992.

Jackson, Donald, and Mary Lee Spence, eds. *The Expeditions of John Charles Frémont*. 2 vols. Urbana: University of Illinois Press, 1970

Jackson, Donald, ed. *Letters of the Lewis and Clark Expedition, with Related Documents, 1783–1854*. Urbana: University of Illinois Press, 1962.

James, Edwin. *An Account of an Expedition from Pittsburg to the Rocky Mountains, Performed in the Years 1819, 1820*. 2 vols. Philadelphia: H. C. Carey and I. Lea, 1822–23.

James, Edwin, Stephen H. Long, and Thomas Say. *James's Account of S. H. Long's Expedition, 1819–1820*. In *Early Western Travels*, vols. 14–17, edited by Reuben G. Thwaites. Cleveland OH: A. H. Clark, 1905.

Kain, Roger J. P., and Elizabeth Baigent. *The Cadastral Map in the Service of the State: A History of Property Mapping*. Chicago: University of Chicago Press, 1992.

Kaplan, Amy. *The Anarchy of Empire in the Making of U.S. Culture*. Cambridge: Harvard University Press. 2005

Kappler, Charles J., comp. *Indian Affairs: Laws and Treaties*. 5 vols. Washington DC: U.S. Government Printing Office, 1904

Killoren, John J. *"Come, Blackrobe": De Smet and the Indian Tragedy*. Norman: University of Oklahoma Press, 1994.

Klein, Kerwin Lee. *Frontiers of the Historical Imagination: Narrating the Conquest of Native America, 1890–1990*. Berkeley: University of California Press, 1997.

Krech, Shephard. *The Ecological Indian: Myth and History*. New York: Norton, 1999.

Krupat, Arnold. *Ethnocentrism: Ethnography, History, Literature*. Berkeley: University of California Press, 1992.

Krygier, John B. "Cartography as an Art and a Science?" *Cartographic Journal* 32 (1995): 3–10.

——."Envisioning the West: Maps, the Representational Barrage of 19th Century Expedition Reports, and the Production of Scientific Knowledge." *Cartography and Geographic Information Systems* 24, no. 1 (1997): 27–50.

La Vere, David. *Contrary Neighbors: Southern Plains and Removed Indians in Indian Territory*. Norman: University of Oklahoma Press, 2000.

Lazarus, Edward. *Black Hills/White Justice: The Sioux Nation versus the United States: 1775 to the Present*. New York: HarperCollins, 1991.

Lefebvre, Henri. *The Production of Space*. Translated by Donald Nicholson-Smith. Oxford: Blackwell, 1991.

"Letters Concerning the Presbyterian Mission in Pawnee Country near Bellvue, Nebraska, 1831–1849." *Kansas Historical Collections* 14 (1915–18): 570–784.

"Letters from the Indian Missions in Kansas." *Kansas Historical Collections* 16 (1923–25): 227–71.

Lewis, G. Malcolm, ed. *Cartographic Encounters: Perspectives on Native American Mapmaking and Map Use*. Chicago: University of Chicago Press, 1998.

———. "Indicators of Unacknowledged Assimilations from Amerindian Maps on Euroamerican Maps of North America: Some General Principles Arising from a Study of La Verendrye's Composite Map, 1728–29." *Imago Mundi* 38 (1986): 9–34.

Lewis, Martin, and Kären Wigen. *The Myth of Continents: A Critique of Meta-geography.* Berkeley: University of California Press, 1997.

Lewis, Meriwether. *Original Journals of Lewis and Clark Expedition.* Edited by Reuben Gold Thwaites. Scituate MA: Digital Scanning, 2001.

Linklater, Andro. *Measuring America: How an Untamed Wilderness Shaped the United States and Fulfilled the Promise of Democracy.* New York: Walker, 2002.

Linton, Ralph. "The Thunder Ceremony of the Pawnee." *Field Museum Leaflet* 5. Chicago: Field Museum, 1922.

Louis, Renee Pualani. "Indigenous Hawaiian Cartographer: In Search of Common Ground." *Cartographic Perspectives* 48 (2004): 7–23.

Lowrie, Walter, Walter S. Franklin, and Matthew St. Clair Clark, eds. *American State Papers: Indian Affairs.* 2 vols. Washington DC: Gales and Seaton, 1832–34.

Luebke, Frederick C, Frances W. Kaye, and Gary E. Moulton, eds. *Mapping the North American Plains: Essays in the History of Cartography.* Norman: University of Oklahoma Press, 1987.

Malin, James C. "Indian Policy and Westward Expansion." *Bulletin of the University of Kansas Humanistic Studies* 2 (1921): 5–108.

———. "The Nebraska Question." *Nebraska History* 35 (1954):1–15.

Martin, Calvin, ed. *The American Indian and the Problem of History.* New York: Oxford University Press, 1987.

———. *Keepers of the Game: Indian-Animal Relationships and the Fur Trade.* Berkeley: University of California Press, 1978.

Mattes, Merrill J. *The Great Platte River Road: The Covered Wagon Mainline via Fort Kearny to Fort Laramie.* Lincoln: Nebraska State Historical Society, 1969.

McCoy, Rev. Isaac. *The Annual Register of Indian Affairs within the Indian (or Western) Territory.* Shawnee Baptist Mission, Ind. Ter.: Isaac McCoy, 1835

———. *History of Baptist Missions.* Washington DC: William H. Morrison, 1840.

McDermott, John Francis, ed. "Isaac McCoy's Second Exploring Trip in 1828." *Kansas Historical Quarterly* 8, no. 7 (1945): 441–15.

McKenney, Thomas L., and James Hall. *Biographical Sketches and Anecdotes of Ninety-Five of 120 Principal Chiefs from the Indian Tribes of North America.* Philadelphia, 1838.

Meinig, D. W. *The Shaping of America: A Geographical Perspective on 500 Years of History.* Vol. 2 of *Continental America, 1800–1867.* New Haven: Yale University Press, 1993.

Merrifield, Andy. *Henri Lefebvre: A Critical Introduction*. New York: Routledge, 2006.

Meyer, Melissa, and Kerwin Lee Klein. "Native American Studies and the End of Ethnohistory." In *Studying Native America: Problems and Prospects*, edited by Russell Thornton. Madison: University of Wisconsin Press, 1998.

Mihesuah, Devon, ed. *Natives and Academics: Researching and Writing about Native Americans*. Lincoln: University of Nebraska Press, 1998.

Miller, Joaquin, and Sidney G. Firman. *Overland in a Covered Wagon: An Autobiography*. New York: Appleton, 1930.

Monmonier, Mark. *How to Lie with Maps*. 1991. 2nd ed. Chicago: University of Chicago Press, 1996.

Moore, John H., ed. *The Political Economy of the North American Indians*. Norman: University of Oklahoma Press, 1993.

Morse, Rev. Jedidiah. *A Report to the Secretary of War of the United States on Indian Affairs*. New Haven CT: S. Converse, 1822. https://archive.org.

Mundy, Barbara E. *The Mapping of New Spain: Indigenous Cartography and the Maps of the Relaciones Geográficas*. Chicago: University of Chicago Press, 1996.

Murie, James R. *Ceremonies of the Pawnee*. Edited by Douglas R. Parks. 2 vols. Smithsonian Contributions to Anthropology 27. Washington DC: Smithsonian Institution Press, 1981.

———. *Pawnee Indian Societies*. Anthropological Papers of the American Museum of Natural History 11, pt. 7. New York, 1914.

Murphy, Lucy Eldersveld. *A Gathering of Rivers: Indians, Metis, and Mining in the Western Great Lakes, 1737–1832*. Lincoln: University of Nebraska Press, 2000.

Murray, Charles A. *Travels in North America during the Years 1834, 1835 & 1836: Including a Summer Residence with the Pawnee Tribe of Indians and a Visit to Cuba and the Azore Islands*. New York: Da Capo, 1974.

Murray, David. *Forked Tongues: Speech, Writing, and Representation in North American Indian Texts*. Bloomington: Indiana University Press, 1998.

Nabokov, Peter. "Orientations from Their Side: Dimensions of Native American Cartographic Discourse." In *Cartographic Encounters: Perspectives on Native American Mapmaking and Map Use*, edited by G. Malcolm Lewis. Chicago: University of Chicago Press, 1998.

Nasatir, Abraham, ed. *Before Lewis and Clark: Documents Illustrating the History of the Missouri, 1785–1804*. 2 vols. St. Louis: St. Louis Historical Documents Foundation, 1952.

New Holy, Alexandra. "The Heart of Everything That Is: Paha Sapa, Treaties, and Lakota Identity." *Oklahoma City University Law Review* 23 (1998): 317–59.

Nicollet, J. N. *Joseph N. Nicollet on the Plains and Prairies: The Expeditions of*

1838–39, with Journals, Letters, and Notes on the Dakota Indians. St. Paul: Minnesota Historical Society Press, 1976.

Nietschmann, B. Q. "Defending the Miskito Reefs with Maps and GPS: Mapping with Sail, Scuba, and Satellite." *Cultural Survival Quarterly* 18, no. 4 (1995): 34–37.

Nobles, Gregory H. "Straight Lines and Stability: Mapping the Political Order of the Anglo-American Frontier." *Journal of American History* 80, no. 1 (June 1993): 9–35.

Oehler, Gottlieb F., and David Z. Smith. *Description of a Journey and a Visit to the Pawnee Indians.* 1914. Reprint, Fairfield WA: Ye Galleon, 1974.

Offen, Karl H. "Creating Mosquitia: Mapping Amerindian Spatial Practices in Eastern Central America, 1629–1779." *Journal of Historical Geography* 33, no. 2 (2007): 254–82.

Orlove, Benjamin. "Mapping Reeds and Reading Maps: The Politics of Representation in Lake Titicaca." *American Ethnologist* 18, no. 1 (1991): 3–38.

Ostler, Jeffrey. *The Lakotas and the Black Hills: The Struggle for Sacred Ground.* New York: Viking, 2010.

———. *The Plains Sioux and U.S. Colonialism from Lewis and Clark to Wounded Knee.* Cambridge: Cambridge University Press, 2004.

———. "'They Regard Their Passing as Wakan': Interpreting Western Sioux Explanations for the Bison's Decline." *Western Historical Quarterly* 30, no. 4 (1999): 475–97.

Padrón, Ricardo. *The Spacious Word: Cartography, Literature, and Empire in Early Modern Spain.* Chicago: University of Chicago Press, 2004.

Parks, Douglas R. "Interpreting Pawnee Star Lore: Science or Myth." *American Indian Culture and Research Journal* 9, no. 1 (1985): 53–65.

Pearce, Margaret Wickens. "Native Mapping in Southern New England." In *Cartographic Encounters: Perspectives on Native American Mapmaking and Map Use,* edited by G. Malcolm Lewis. Chicago: University of Chicago Press, 1998.

Pearce, Margaret Wickens, and Renee Paulani Louis. "Indigenous Depth of Place." *American Indian Culture and Research Journal* 32, no. 3 (2008): 107–26.

Pickles, John. *A History of Spaces: Cartographic Reason, Mapping and the Geo-Coded World.* London: Routledge, 2004.

Pike, Zebulon Montgomery. *An Account of expeditions to the sources of the Mississippi, and through the western parts of Louisiana, to the sources of the Arkansas, Kansas, La Platte, and Pierre Juan, Rivers; performed by order of the Government of the United States during the years 1805, 1806, and 1807; and a tour through the interior parts of New Spain, when conducted through these provinces, by order of the Captain-General, in the year 1807.* Philadelphia: C. & A. Conrad, 1810.

Pike, Zebulon Montgomery, and Elliott Coues. *The Expeditions of Zebulon Montgomery Pike*. New York: Dover, 1987.

Pike, Zebulon Montgomery, and Donald Jackson. *The Journals of Zebulon Montgomery Pike: With Letters and Related Documents*. Norman: University of Oklahoma Press, 1966.

Piper, Karen. *Cartographic Fictions: Maps, Race, and Identity*. New Brunswick NJ: Rutgers University Press, 2002.

Porter, Joy. "Imagining Indians: Differing Perspectives on Native American History." In *The State of U.S. History*, edited by Melvyn Stokes. New York: Oxford, 2003.

Pratt, Mary Louise. *Imperial Eyes: Travel Writing and Transculturation*. New York: Routledge, 1992.

Preuss, Charles. *Exploring with Frémont: The Private Diaries of Charles Preuss, Cartographer for John C. Frémont on His First, Second, and Fourth Expeditions to the Far West*. Edited and translated by Erwin G. Gudde and Elisabeth K. Gudde. Norman: University of Oklahoma Press, 1958.

Raj, Kapil. *Relocating Modern Science: Circulation and the Construction of Knowledge in South Asia and Europe 1650–1900*. New York: Palgrave Macmillan, 2007.

Report of the Secretary of the Interior for 1855. Washington DC: Gales and Seaton, 1856.

Rhonda, James F. "'A Chart in His Way': Indian Cartography and the Lewis and Clark Expedition." In *Mapping the North American Plains*, edited by Frederick C. Luebke, Frances W. Kaye, and Gary E. Moulton. Norman: University of Oklahoma Press, 1987.

Richter, Daniel K. *Facing East from Indian Country: A Native History of Early America*. Cambridge: Harvard University Press, 2001.

———. "Whose Indian History?" *William and Mary Quarterly*, 3rd ser., 50, no. 2 (1993): 379–93.

Rice, Julie. "Cartographic Heritage of the Lakota Sioux." Master's thesis, Kent State University, 2000.

Riding In, James. "Keeper of Tirawahut's Covenant: The Development and Destruction of Pawnee Culture." Ph.D. dissertation, UCLA, 1991.

Robinson, Arthur H., and Barbara Bartz Petchenik. *The Nature of Maps: Essays toward Understanding Maps and Mapping*. Chicago: University of Chicago Press, 1976.

Royce, Charles C. *Indian Land Cessions in the United States*. Eighteenth Annual Report of the Bureau of American Ethnology, 1896–1897, part 2. Washington DC: U.S. Government Printing Office, 1899.

Rundstrom, Robert A. "GIS, Indigenous Peoples, and Epistemological Diversity." *Cartography and Geographic Information Systems* 22, no. 1 (1995): 45–57.

———. "Mapping, Postmodernism, Indigenous People and the Changing Direction of North American Cartography." *Cartographica* 28, no. 2 (1991): 1–12.

Sachs, Aaron. *The Humboldt Current: Nineteenth-Century Exploration and the Roots of American Environmentalism.* New York: Viking, 2006.

Safier, Neil. *Measuring the New World: Enlightenment Science and South America.* Chicago: University of Chicago Press, 2008.

Said, Edward. *Culture and Imperialism.* New York: Vintage, 1994.

———. *Orientalism.* New York: Vintage, 1979.Satz, Ronald N. *American Indian Policy in the Jacksonian Era.* Lincoln: University of Nebraska Press, 1975.

Saunt, Claudio. *A New Order of Things: Property, Power, and the Transformation of the Creek Indians, 1733–1816.* New York: Cambridge University Press, 1999.

Schubert, Frank N., ed. *March to South Pass: Lieutenant W. B. Franklin's Journal of the Kearny Expedition.* Engineer Historical Studies no. 1. Washington DC: Historical Division Office of Administrative Services Office of the Chief of Engineers, 1978.

———. *Vanguard of Expansion: Army Engineers in the Trans-Mississippi West, 1819–1879.* Washington DC: U.S. Government Printing Office, 1980.

Schulten, Susan. *The Geographical Imagination in America, 1880–1950.* Chicago: University of Chicago Press, 2001.

———. "Mapping American History." In *Maps: Finding Our Place in the World,* edited by James Akerman and Robert Karrow Jr. Chicago: University of Chicago Press, 2007.

———. *Mapping the Nation: History and Cartography in Nineteenth-Century America.* Chicago: University of Chicago Press, 2013.

Schultz, George A. *An Indian Canaan: Isaac McCoy and the Vision of an Indian State.* Norman: University of Oklahoma Press, 1972.

Scott, David. *Conscripts of Modernity: The Tragedy of Colonial Enlightenment.* Durham NC: Duke University Press, 2004.

Scott, Heidi. "Contested Territories: Arenas of Geographical Knowledge in Early Colonial Peru." *Journal of Historical Geography* 29 (2003): 166–88.

Scott, James C. *Seeing Like a State: How Certain Schemes to Improve the Human Condition Have Failed.* New Haven: Yale University Press, 1998.

Secoy, Frank. *Changing Military Patterns of the Great Plains Indians.* 1953. Reprint, Lincoln: University of Nebraska Press, 1993.

Sibley, George Champlin. *Road to Santa Fe: The Journal and Diaries of George Champlin Sibley.* Edited by Kate L. Gregg. Albuquerque: University of New Mexico Press, 1952.

Sillitoe, Paul, ed. *Local Science vs Global Science: Approaches to Indigenous Knowledge in International Development.* New York: Berghahn, 2007.

Skinner, Alanson. "Ethnology of the Ioway Indians." *Bulletin of the Public Museum of the City of Milwaukee* 5, no. 4 (1926): 183–85.

Sparke, Matthew. *In the Space of Theory: Postfoundational Geographies of the Nation-State.* Minneapolis: University of Minnesota Press, 2005.

———. "A Map That Roared and an Original Atlas: Canada, Cartography, and the Narration of Nation." *Annals of the Association of American Geographers* 88 (1998): 463–95.

Spivak, Gayatri Chakravorty. "Can the Subaltern Speak?" In *Marxism and the Interpretation of Culture*, edited by Cary Nelson and Lawrence Grossberg. Urbana: University of Illinois Press, 1988.

Stansbury, Howard. *A Reconnaissance of a New Route through the Rocky Mountains*. Philadelphia: Lippincott, Grambo, 1855.

Sundstrom, Linea. "Mirror of Heaven: Cross-Cultural Transferences of the Sacred Geography of the Black Hills." *World Archaeology* 28, no. 2 (1996): 177–89.

———. "The Sacred Black Hills: An Ethnohistorical Review." *Great Plains Quarterly* 17 (1997): 185–212.

Swagerty, William R. "Indian Trade in the Trans-Mississippi West to 1870." In *History of Indian-White Relations*. vol. 4 of *Handbook of the North American Indians*, edited by Wilcomb E. Washburn, 351–74. Washington DC: Smithsonian Institution Press, 1988.

Tanner, Henry S. *Geographical Memoir*. Philadelphia, 1823.

Thongchai Winichakul. *Siam Mapped: A History of the Geo-Body of a Nation*. Honolulu: University of Hawai'i Press, 1994.

Thorne, Tanis. *The Many Hands of My Relations: French and Indians on the Lower Missouri*. Columbia: University of Missouri Press, 1996.

Thrower, Norman J. W. *Maps and Civilization: Cartography in Culture and Society*. Chicago: University of Chicago Press, 1996.

Todorov, Tzvetan. *The Conquest of America: The Question of the Other*. Norman: University of Oklahoma Press, 1984.

Trennert, Robert A. *Alternative to Extinction: Federal Indian Policy and the Beginnings of the Reservation System, 1846–51*. Philadelphia: Temple University Press, 1975.

Trigger, Bruce. "Early Native North American Responses to European Contact: Romantic versus Rationalistic Interpretations." *Journal of American History* 77 (1991): 1195–215.

Turnbull, David. *Maps Are Territories: Science Is an Atlas: A Portfolio of Exhibits*. 1989. Reprint, Chicago: University of Chicago Press, 1993.

———. *Mason's Tricksters and Cartographers: Comparative Studies in the Sociology of Scientific and Indigenous Knowledge*. New York: Routledge, 2000.

Turner, Frederick Jackson. *The Frontier in American History*. New York: Holt, Rinehart, and Winston, 1920.

Unrau, William. *The Kansa Indians: A History of the Wind People, 1673–1873*. Norman: University of Oklahoma Press, 1971.

———. *The Rise and Fall of Indian Country, 1825–1855*. Lawrence: University of Kansas Press, 2007.

Unrau, William, and H. Craig Miner. *The End of Indian Kansas: A Study of Cultural Revolution, 1857–1871*. Lawrence: University of Kansas Press, 1978.

U.S. Congress. House. 23rd Cong., 1st sess., 1834. H. Rep. 474. Serial 263.
———. Senate. 23rd Cong. S. Doc. 512. Serial 244–48. *Correspondence on the Emigration of Indians, 1831–33.* 5 vols.
———. Senate. 26th Cong, 2d sess., 1841 S. Doc. 237. Serial 449.
———. Senate. 27th Cong., 3rd sess., 1842. S. Doc. 243. Serial 416.
———. Senate. 29th Cong., 1st sess., 1846. S. Doc. 438.
———. Senate. 33rd Cong., 2d sess., 1856. S. Exec. Doc. 78.
———. Senate. 30th Cong., 1st sess., 1847. S. Exec. Doc. 41.
———. Senate. 33rd Cong., 2d sess., 1856. S. Exec. Doc. 91.
———. Senate. 33th Cong., 2d sess., 1856. S. Exec. Doc. 78.
———. Senate. 34th Cong., 1st sess., 1856. S. Exec. Doc. 76.
Utley, Robert M. *Frontiersmen in Blue: The United States Army and the Indian, 1848–1865.* New York: Macmillan, 1967.
van der Woude, Joanne. "Why Maps Matter: New Geographies of Early American Culture." *American Quarterly* 6, no. 4 (2010): 1073–87.
Viola, Herman. "Invitation to Washington." *American West* 9, no. 1 (1972): 1931.
Warren, G. K., and Frank N. Schubert. *Explorer on the Northern Plains: Lieutenant Gouverneur K. Warren's Preliminary Report of Explorations in Nebraska and Dakota, in the Years 1855–1856–1857.* Engineer Studies 2. Washington DC: Historical Division, Office of Administrative Services, Office of the Chief of Engineers, 1981.
Waselkov, Gregory. "Indian Maps of the Colonial Southeast." In *Powhatan's Mantle: Indians in the Colonial Southeast,* edited by Waselkov, Peter H. Wood, and Tom Hatley. Lincoln: University of Nebraska Press, 2006.
Wedel, Mildred Mott. "Indian Villages on the Upper Iowa River." *Palimpsest* 47, no. 12 (1961): 561–92.
———. "The Iowa Indians." In *Handbook of North American Indians,* vol. 13, bk. 1. Washington: Smithsonian Institution, 2001.
———. "The Relation of Historic Indian Tribes to Archaeological Manifestations in Iowa." *Iowa Journal of History and Politics* 36, no. 1 (1962): 227–314.
———. "A Synonym of Names for the Iowa Indians." *Journal of the Iowa Archeological Society* 29 (1978): 48–72.
Wedel, Waldo R., ed. *The Dunbar-Allis Letters on the Pawnee.* New York: Garland, 1985.
Weisiger, Marsha. *Dreaming of Sheep in Navajo Country.* Seattle: University of Washington Press, 2010.
Weltfish, Gene. *The Lost Universe: The Way of Life of the Pawnee.* 1965. Reprint, New York: Ballantine, 1971.
West, Elliot. *The Contested Plains; Indians, Goldseekers, and the Rush to Colorado.* Topeka: University of Kansas Press, 1998.
———. *The Way to the West: Essays on the Central Plains.* Albuquerque: University of New Mexico Press, 1995.

Wheat, Carl. *Mapping the Trans-Mississippi West.* 6 vols. San Francisco: Institute of Historical Cartography, 1957.

White, David Archer, ed. *News of the Plains and Rockies, 1803–1865.* Spokane WA: Arthur H. Clark Company, 1996–2001.

White, C. A. *A History of the Rectangular Survey System.* Washington DC: U.S. Department of the Interior, Bureau of Land Management, 1983.

White, Richard. "The Cultural Landscape of the Pawnees." *Great Plains Quarterly* 2, no. 1 (1982): 31–40.

———. "The Fictions of Patriarchy." In *Native Americans and the Early Republic*, edited by Frederick Hoxie, Ronald Hoffman, and Peter J. Alberts. Charlottesville: Published for the United States Capitol Historical Society by the University Press of Virginia, 1999.

———. *The Middle Ground: Indians, Empires, and Republics in the Great Lakes Region, 1650–1815.* New York: Cambridge University Press, 1991.

———. *The Roots of Dependency: Subsistence, Environment, and Social Change among the Choctaws, Pawnees and Navajos.* Lincoln: University of Nebraska Press, 1983.

———. "Using the Past: History and Native American Studies." In *Studying Native America: Problems and Prospects*, edited by Russell Thornton. Madison: University of Wisconsin Press, 1998.

———. "The Winning of the West: The Expansion of the Western Sioux in the Eighteenth and Nineteenth Centuries." *Journal of American History* 65, no. 2 (1978): 319–32.

Wilhelm, Paul (Duke of Württemberg). *Travels in North America 1822–1824.* Edited by Savoie Lottinville. Translated by W. Robert Nitske. Norman: University of Oklahoma Press, 1973.

Wishart, David. *The Fur Trade of the American West: A Geographical Synthesis.* Lincoln: University of Nebraska Press, 1992.

———. "The Pawnee Claims Case." In *Irredeemable America: The Indians' Estate and Land Claims*, edited by Imre Sutton. Albuquerque: University of New Mexico Press, 1985.

———. *An Unspeakable Sadness: The Dispossession of the Nebraska Indians.* Lincoln: University of Nebraska Press, 1994.

Witgen, Michael. "The Rituals of Possession: Native Identity and the Invention of Empire in the Seventeenth-Century Western North America." *Ethnohistory* 54, no. 4 (2007): 639–68.

Withers, Charles W. J., and David Livingston. *Geography and Enlightenment.* Chicago: University of Chicago Press, 1999.

Wood, Denis. "The Fine Line between Mapping and Mapmaking." *Cartographica* 30, no. 4 (1993): 50–60.

———. *Rethinking the Power of Maps.* New York: Guilford, 2010.

Wood, Denis. *The Power of Maps.* With John Fels. New York: Guilford, 1992.

Woodward, David, and G. Malcolm Lewis. *Cartography in the Traditional Afri-*

can, American, Arctic, Australian, and Pacific Societies. Vol. 2, bk. 3 of *The History of Cartography*. Chicago: University of Chicago Press, 1998.

Worster, Donald. *Under Western Skies: Nature and History in the American West*. New York: Oxford University Press, 1992.

INDEX

Shades of Gray: Writing the New American Multiracialism
by Molly Littlewood McKibbin

The Limits of Liberty: Mobility and the Making of the Eastern U.S.-Mexico Border
by James David Nichols

Native Diasporas: Indigenous Identities and Settler Colonialism in the Americas
edited by Gregory D. Smithers and Brooke N. Newman

Shape Shifters: Journeys across Terrains of Race and Identity
edited by Lily Anne Y. Welty Tamai, Ingrid Dineen-Wimberly, and Paul Spickard

The Southern Exodus to Mexico: Migration across the Borderlands after the American Civil War
by Todd W. Wahlstrom

To order or obtain more information on these or other University of Nebraska Press titles, visit nebraskapress.unl.edu.